CONCISE BIBLE PROPHETS

AMG Publishers

CONCISE BIBLE PROPHETS

DAVID BOERSMA

CONCISE BIBLE PROPHETS

Published by AMG Publishers
6815 Shallowford Rd.
Chattanooga, Tennessee 37421

Previously self-published under the title, *Prophets of the Bible.*

The illustrations in Chapter 2 are reproduced from watercolors painted especially for this book by Judy Nakari. Her work is shown in galleries in Tucson and Tubac, Arizona, as well as on her website, www.nakari.com.

ISBN 978-0-89957-589-6

First printing, April/May 2016

Cover designed by Bright Boy Design, Chattanooga, Tennessee
Interior designed by Pro Production Graphic Services, Chestnut Ridge, New York
Edited and proofread by Rick Steele and David Boersma

Printed in the United States of America
21 20 19 18 17 16 –R– 8 7 6 5 4 3 2 1

CONTENTS

Part II
Listings of Biblical Prophets

Part III
Special Topics

Illustrations

Figures

Tables

Insets

Author's Preface

"I was no prophet, nor was I the son of a prophet," wrote Amos, a prophet indeed. He made these denials to stress that his own call and prophetic messages came directly from God and not from formal education or long experience, nor were they a family trade or tradition. I can appropriate and apply these disclaimers to myself, but without Amos's inference of a higher calling. I attended no Bible college or seminary. None of my known relatives living or dead is an ordained minister of the word of God. I would not deny the prophecy of Joel, quoted by Peter in his famous Pentecost-day sermon (Acts 2), that "'in the last days,' says God, . . . 'I will pour out My Spirit on all flesh; your sons and your daughters shall prophesy, your young men shall see visions, your old men shall dream dreams, and on My menservants and on My maidservants I will pour out My Spirit in those days; and they shall prophesy." However, I do not claim to have received either vision or prophetic gifts that are superior or uncommon to most Christians. The Holy Spirit may have endowed me with a measure of the gift of prophecy, but it is neither outstanding nor developed. In short, I have no particular credentials for writing this book, which you may decide to close at this point.

If you are still with me, and if, like me, you were taught to eat the less tasty things on your plate first, you will understand that I must continue in this negative vein 'til all is gone. This is not a book of prophecy. No new visions. No predictions. No apocalypse. No particular message from God for our time, unless it is a call to hearken to the prophets and prophecies of the Bible, plus an occasional implication or observation based on the biblical record, which may or may not be an original thought. I do not seek, nor am I qualified, to interpret or explain biblical prophecy for modern (or is it postmodern?) man. Many good theologians and other divines have done that and are doing it still and well. This book is not a commentary; it is just a compendium, which I hope nevertheless will be interesting, useful, and at times even entertaining and enlightening.

One final vegetable on my plate, a brussels sprout. I am not even a scholar, in that I have almost no knowledge of the original Bible languages or primary source documents (manuscripts and texts). And although I have made some attempts to read what others have written on the subjects of prophecy and prophets, it has not been thorough research. My principal resources are English-language Bibles, concordances, and other books readily available to almost any English-speaking/reading Christian.

If you are still with me, long-suffering reader, you may be wondering if there is *any* tasty morsel on my plate. Perhaps there is. I have been blessed with Christian parents, a more or less "standard" Christian upbringing in the 1940s and 1950s in mid-America, a Christian wife, Christian brothers and sisters—both blood and spiritual, a number of godly ministers and teachers, some outstanding conference speakers (at the Pensacola Theological Institute and elsewhere), membership in four loving churches, books, and the ability to read them, especially the Bible, and most of all my patient, gracious Lord.

I have been given the opportunity to teach adult-level classes on Ezekiel (still my favorite), Daniel, 2 Kings 1–13 (life and times of Elisha), Acts, 1 and 2 Samuel (lives of Samuel, Saul, and David), and twice on the gifts of the Holy Spirit, during which study, the last time, came my final impetus to write this book. My wife, Wyolene, once taught a class on Isaiah which I did not attend but from which I learned by osmosis. Teaching, or rather studying to teach, has always been to me the best way of learning. I do not feel comfortable telling others facts and ideas, especially from Scripture, that I have not researched for myself and am satisfied of their truth and accuracy.

I love to discover and tell about little-known, ignored, overlooked, or misunderstood Scripture—not as trivia but for the hidden treasure. For example, despite the many illustrations of a handsome young man in children's storybooks and adult Bibles, Daniel was an old man of about ninety years when he was cast into a den of lions. Perhaps this sort of interest is one of the driving forces behind this book. I have a notion that prophets in the Bible are far more numerous, fascinating, human, and often surprising than is commonly known by Christians or Jews, including many clergy; and I want to tell their stories, however briefly.

I love the word of God: first of all, the word which was in the beginning and was once made flesh and now lives—our Lord Jesus Christ; and second, the written word, Holy Scripture, also made alive by His Holy Spirit. I love not only the Bible's main themes such as God's sovereignty, love, and salvation, but also its thrilling adventure, human interest, ironic wit, soaring poetry, biography, prophecy, humor, history, and even genealogy. I believe down to my toes that "all Scripture is given by inspiration of God, and is profitable for doctrine, for reproof, for correction, for instruction in righteousness, that the man of God may be complete, thoroughly equipped for every good work (2 Timothy 3:16–17)." *All* Scripture—even the more arcane prophets and their prophecies. And I perceive (or fancy) that some of these are commonly neglected in many classrooms and pulpits to the detriment and poverty of the people. Who knows, for example, the name of the first prophet? Jesus knew and cared. Who remembers a prophet named Ahijah, who turned the very steering wheel of history? Who knows that prophetesses go back in history at least as far as Moses and were important in Jesus's time on earth and in the apostolic church? Who realizes that at least one "canonical" prophet, and about a third of all the prophets named in the Bible, prophesied primarily with music? This, then, is my passion: to list all of the prophets in Scripture, whether named or anonymous, and to tell what is known about each of them, to compile and organize what Scripture itself says about prophecy and the office of prophet, and to trace the historical development of prophecy in the Bible.

I hope that this record of Bible prophets and the Bible's instruction about prophecy may be of use to church schoolteachers and rabbis, to Bible study leaders, to educators of all kinds, and even to preachers of the true word of God, who are our prophets. I pray that it may be of use to many students of the Bible.

April 10, 1999
Campsite 30, Petersburg Campground,
US Corps of Engineers,
Clarks Hill Reservoir,
Georgia

Author's Preface to the AMG Edition

I am honored and pleased that AMG Publishers is issuing this new edition of my book about biblical prophets, *Concise Bible Prophets*, which was formerly titled *Prophets of the Bible* (Xlibris, 2008). Several minor corrections have been made; the format has been changed to facilitate E-book publication by placing Scripture references and dates in the body of the text instead of in the margins and by changing footnotes to endnotes; and one prophet (Zadok) and one anonymous group of prophets have been added. The largest change is the addition of a topical index.

Having a publisher, AMG, that is well established in the field of Biblical reference books is a great advantage that was not enjoyed by *Prophets of the Bible.* So my hope expressed in the preface to that earlier edition is renewed and redoubled: that this compilation of Bible prophets and Bible teachings about prophets and prophecy will be found useful to Bible students and teachers, and to preachers—who may justly be called our prophets when they faithfully deliver His word.

August, 2014

Introduction

This is a handbook of the prophets of the Bible. As such, it is not designed to be read through from first to last. Each chapter stands alone. The first-time user is invited to turn to chapter 3 and browse through a few prophets, some well-known and some less known to the reader. This will quickly give the "flavor" of the book.

When the subject of biblical prophets comes up, many of us will think first of the sixteen men who wrote the last seventeen books of the Old Testament. Then we might add Samuel, Elijah, John the baptizer, and a few others. Actually the Bible identifies about two hundred individual prophets, most of them by name—men, women, and yes, even children—spread throughout the Old and New Testaments. It alludes to hundreds more. The primary task of this handbook is to list them all in an orderly way, with a biographical sketch of each prophet who is individually identified, based strictly on the Bible. Some of these biographical profiles include a characterization or synopsis of that prophet's prophecies or style, in order to better distinguish him or her, but they are never intended to be commentaries or exegeses of Scripture. In other words, this is a manual or reference book about biblical prophets, not a theological work about biblical prophecy.

However, in order to identify all the Bible's prophets, we must first know exactly what a prophet is. The Bible does not label all its prophets with a clear title such as "prophet," "prophetess," or "seer." Only about one-third of them are so labeled. If all who received special revelation (prophecy) from God, and then communicated God's word to other people in any way, were prophets; then in order to identify them, we must first learn exactly what *prophecy* is according to the Bible. Therefore a secondary task of this handbook—but a task that must be done first—is to gather and organize the Bible's direct, explicit teachings about prophecy itself and about prophets in general.

A third task of this book is to present two subjects that unexpectedly "fell out" of the first two tasks: musical prophecy and the biblical history of prophecy.

Chapter 1, "On Prophecy," is a compilation of the Bible's direct teachings about prophecy. This topic is placed first in order to better understand the principal subject, biblical prophets. There is at this time a widespread lack of understanding about the nature of prophecy, according to God's word. To read about biblical prophets without a biblical understanding of prophecy would be like reading about coal miners without knowing what coal is, where it is found, and why it should be mined. Care is taken in chapter 1 to extract from the Bible only what it plainly says about prophecy, not to elaborate or develop a doctrine. However, even in organizing biblical truth into nonbiblical categories, some interpretation creeps in.

Chapter 2, "The Biblical Prophet," attempts to extract and present what the Bible expressly teaches about prophets in general. It is less pedantic and more descriptive than chapter 1 and perhaps easier to read.

Chapters 3, 4, and 5 are the heart of this book. All of the prophets of the Bible are listed and characterized.

Chapter 3 presents 177 named prophets and prophesiers of God's word, as found in Scripture. It is believed that a listing this exhaustive is not elsewhere in print, and may not have been compiled before. For chapter 3, the definition of "prophet" includes not only those persons expressly called prophets, prophetesses, seers, and men of God but also any named person who prophesied, spoke by the Holy Spirit, or was a member of a prophesying group—including certain musical groups that proclaimed God's word in God's name. Even otherwise-false prophets and evil-hearted men such as Balaam and Caiaphas are included if they prophesied God's true revelation one or more times. A biographical and/or character sketch is given for each prophet, its content and length depending on the biblical information available. Unlike chapters 1 and 2, some "inferencing" from the Bible is made in this and the succeeding chapters. It is hoped that this is never taken too far, as Heschel wittily warns, concerning Hosea:

> From his use of certain striking figures of speech it has been suggested that he was a baker, lived as a farmer on the land, was associated with the priesthood and the sanctuaries, had a strongly developed sex instinct which he vigorously repressed. With the same right we could suggest that he was a lover of the desert and an expert on lions, panthers, and bears.[1]

Also, in chapter 3 especially, a position may be taken on a matter of ongoing scholarly debate such as the authorship of certain books of prophecy in the Bible. This is never done unless it is deemed important to an understanding of the prophet himself. For example, no position is necessary on whether there were one, two, or several authors of Isaiah, for only one has a name and a biblical persona. On the other hand, whether or not Jonah wrote Jonah is crucial to how we understand this prophet's character and prophecy.

Chapter 4 lists and sketches the Bible's anonymous individual prophets and groups of prophets excepting musical groups that are listed in chapter 6. Some of these unnamed prophets are quite important, especially in the history of Israel.

Chapter 5 catalogs false prophets mentioned in the Bible, either by name or by league. One of these, Balaam, is also listed in chapter 3 because of his true, if unwilling, prophecies in Numbers. One anonymous prophet is listed in both chapters 4 and 5.

The final two chapters deal with subjects that may not have been developed before, at least to this extent. When the work of listing the prophets was started, musical prophecy was not even contemplated by the author. As the fact of it became inescapable, and after it was found that the Bible contains about seventy-five named musical prophets, the subject demanded special treatment: chapter 6. There is a certain redundancy between the list of musical prophets in chapter 6 and the list of all named prophets in chapter 3, but they are presented differently.

The other realization that grew out of the process of listing prophets was that there is a definite history, or progression, of prophecy itself in the Bible. God revealed Himself and His will in different ways at different times, as stated in Hebrews 1:1. Chapter 7 is a first attempt to chronicle prophecy in terms of style or mode, abundance, the position of prophets in human society, and other parameters.

There are a few technical details that belong in the introduction. Scripture quotations are almost entirely from the New King James Version (NKJV), 1982, by Thomas Nelson, Inc. Other versions consulted and sometimes quoted are the New International Version (NIV), 1901 American Standard Version (ASV), New American Standard Bible (NASB), King James Version (KJV), Revised Standard Version (RSV), and a translation of the Septuagint (Greek) into English by Charles Thompson. The NKJV, like several others of the translations, uses the capitalized *LORD* for the holy, personal name of God as first revealed to Moses. A primary resource used to construct this handbook and to ensure its completeness, and occasionally for word sources and meanings, is Robert Young's *Analytical Concordance to the Bible* published by Associated Authors and Publishers.

Reference

1. Abraham J. Heschel, *The Prophets* (New York: HarperCollins, 1962; Prince Press Edition, 2000), page 39.

Part I

The Bible's Teachings on Prophets and Prophecy

This is a handbook of biblical prophets. The lists and descriptions of prophets begin at chapter 3. But to compile these lists, we must know who is a prophet and who is not. The Bible does not give every one of its prophets a clear label or title such as prophet or seer. Jesus said, "By their fruits you will know them" (Matthew 7:20). One fruit of prophets is true prophecy. Therefore, in order to thoroughly identify all the prophets in the Bible, we must know what prophecy is. In addition, we must know all the biblical titles, marks, equipments, and duties of prophets. Thus, the first part of this book consists of chapter 1, "On Prophecy," and chapter 2, "The Biblical Prophet."

Although developing these two chapters was necessary groundwork for preparing the lists and descriptions of prophets in chapters 3, 4, and 5 and to some extent the special topics of chapters 6 and 7, reading them is not necessary before *using* the rest of the book.

Endnotes and references are given at the end of each chapter. In chapters 1 and 2, references are numbered and endnotes are designated with capital letters.

Chapter 1

On Prophecy

The Holy Bible not only contains a great deal of prophecy, it also says a great deal *about* prophecy. Before we review these direct teachings, however, it is important to examine some popular notions about prophecy that may or may not be in agreement with Scripture.

What Others Say

Roget's Thesaurus lists the following synonyms for *prophecy* (noun): augury, presage, forecast, and prognosis.[1] The word *prophecy* is then cross-referenced to the major entry, *prediction*, for which the following synonyms are given: anticipation, divination, forecasting, fortune-telling, palmistry, crystal gazing, hariolation, mantic, manticism, prognostication, pythonism, soothsaying, vaticination, omen, augury, auspice, foreboding, forecast, presage, prognosis, prognostic, *prophecy*, horoscope, zodiac. (You have a magnificent vocabulary if it includes "hariolation"!)

There are two obvious and important differences between *Roget's* concept of prophecy and that which is taught in the Bible. First, several of the words given by Roget as synonyms for prophecy are absolutely opposed to biblical prophecy—for example, divination and soothsaying (see Deuteronomy 18: 14). Second, Roget reduces prophecy to the single dimension of prediction whereas the Bible has a much fuller view of prophecy as we shall presently see.

Webster's Dictionary gives two senses for the word *prophecy*: (1) a prediction, (2) a. the inspired utterance of a prophet, held to be a declaration of divine will; b. such a revelation revealed orally or in writing."[2] The second sense of this dictionary definition is much closer to biblical prophecy than *Roget's* narrow view as we shall see, but it still falls short.

A dictionary and a thesaurus are entirely secular sources. How is the term *prophecy* being used in popular *Christian* literature and sermons today? John Walvoord, one prominent author in this field, writes,

> Prophecy is that part of Scripture dealing with predictions of events that will occur in the future. Theologians call this doctrine *eschatology*, a word derived from the Greek *eschatos*, meaning "last" or "last things." It refers to the events that will

> climax human history. Included in Biblical eschatology are all predictions that were future at the time they were written, whether they have been fulfilled now or are still unfilled.[3]

Ouch! This not only goes back to Roget, it narrows prophecy even further. It says prophecy is only prediction, *and* only of "last things"! But, to give credit where due, this author's definition has captured and promulgated a prevailing popular notion of prophecy among Christians. Lest there be any doubt of this fact, consider that a random visit to a typical Christian bookstore on November 1, 2000,[A] discovered the following, *and only the following*, titles and subtitles on the shelves labeled Prophecy:

The Road to Armageddon: A Biblical Understanding of Prophecy and End Time Events[4]

From Daniel to Doomsday: The Countdown Has Begun[5]

Day of Deception: Separating the Truth from Falsehood in These Last Days[6]

Beginning of the End[7]

Final Dawn Over Jerusalem[7]

The Millennium Meltdown[8]

Quick and Easy Guide to Bible Prophecy,[9] Simple-to-understand answers to your questions about the end of the world, Armageddon, Judgment Day, Heaven, and much more

The Last Millenium,[10] A Revealing Look at the Remarkable Days Ahead and How You Can Live Them to the Fullest

Forewarning: Approaching the Final Battle between Heaven and Hell[11]

The Mysterious Bible Codes,[12] How events of today were encrypted in ancient codes

End Time Events: Journey to the End of the Age[13]

Jesus' Final Warning: Hearing the Savior's Voice in the Midst of Chaos[14]

Foreshocks of Antichrist[15]

Millenium: The 1000-Year Reign of King Jesus[16]

The Last Days According to Jesus,[17] When did Jesus say He would return?

Millennium:Beginning or End?[18] Unraveling the mystery of Christ's thousand-year reign on earth

Raptured: A Novel[19]

Final Mysteries Unsealed: Opening the Door to Your Destiny[20]

Messiah's Coming Temple: Ezekiel's Prophetic Vision of the Future Temple[21]

Some of the above titles were undoubtedly rushed into print for the end-of-millennium year 2000. We have not read these books. Nevertheless, there appears to be a near consensus in the *titles* of this sampling of popular Christian literature that prophecy equals eschatology, just as defined by Walvoord.[3] Nothing was in the prophecy section of that bookstore about prophecy as preaching,[B] nor on the spiritual gift of prophecy.[C] None of these bookstore titles or subtitles suggests the second dictionary definition of prophecy, "a declaration of divine will," except concerning end-time events.

Most Christian and Jewish scholars and theologians do, of course, understand the true nature of biblical prophecy. For example, Heschel writes,

> The prominent theme (of prophecy) is exhortation, not prediction. While it is true that foretelling is an important ingredient and may serve as a sign of the prophet's authority, . . . his essential task is to declare the word of God to the here and now.[22]

Such scholarly opinion does not seem to be getting into the popular Christian literature of our day, where the Walvoord opinion prevails.

But now let us turn to the Bible and see what it says, plainly and explicitly, about its own prophecy.

What Scripture Says

We do not need to rely on secular sources or even on theologians for a correct and thorough understanding of the nature of prophecy. This is one subject that God evidently wants us to know about, though many Christians and Jews do not. The Bible clearly gives the "what, why, and how" of prophecy. The following sections collect the Bible's direct teachings about what prophecy is, what the principal subject of prophecy is, secondary subjects, why God gives prophecy, and how God gives prophecy.

1. What Is Prophecy?

General Statements and Definition

Ten leading experts: ten canonical prophets,[D] no less—call their own prophecies, "The word of the LORD." (See Jeremiah 1:4; Ezekiel 1:3; Hosea 1:1; Joel 1:1; Amos 3:1 and 5:16; Jonah 3:1; Micah 1:1; Zephaniah 1:1; Haggai 1:1, 3 and 2:1; Zechariah 1:1, 7:1,4,8, and 8:1.)

Furthermore, a phrase used countless times by Bible prophets is "thus says the LORD," signifying that prophecy is God's word, pure and simple.

Other Scriptures that confirm and amplify this truth include

> I will raise up for them a Prophet like you from among their brethren, and will put My words in his mouth. (Deuteronomy 18:18)

> God, Who at various times and in various ways spoke in time past to the fathers by the prophets. (Hebrews 1:1)

> I [God] have also spoken by the prophets. (Hosea 12:10)

> The LORD God has spoken! Who can but prophesy? (Amos 3:8b)

> Prophecy never came by the will of man, but holy men of God spoke as they were moved by the Holy Spirit. (2 Peter 1:21)

> Now his father Zacharias was filled with the Holy Spirit and prophesied, saying, (Luke 1:67)

* * *

Prophecy is sometimes called a "burden," signifying the weightiness of God's word and its pressure upon the prophet to deliver it rightly. (See Nahum 1:1; Habakkuk 1:1; Zechariah 9:1, 12:1; Malachi 1:1.)

Another Scripture word for prophecy is *oracle*, which in Acts 7:38 refers to the Law as prophecy, and in 1 Peter 4:10–11, it means the utterances of Christians exercising the spiritual gift of prophecy. In the Old Testament the word *oracle* refers to a place: the Most Holy Place in the temple, the "speaking place" where God spoke to the high priest. (See 1 Kings 6: 5, 16, 19–23, 31 (KJV); cf. Leviticus 16:2; Exodus 25:21–22.)

Prophecy is a gift of the Holy Spirit given to certain Christians in and for the Church. (See Romans 12:6 and 1 Corinthians 12:7–10.)

Prophecy is revelation (αποκάλυψις, unveiling) from God. (See Revelation 1:1–3 with 22:7, 10, 18, 19.)

A short definition of prophecy derived from the above Scriptures is submitted:

Prophecy is God's word, message, or revelation, given by His Holy Spirit to individuals He selects, for dissemination in His name to other people.

This definition says nothing about the tense, subject matter, purpose, or means of prophecy. These topics are also elucidated by the Bible as summarized in sections that follow in this chapter. However, some other questions will be addressed first: Is the whole Bible prophecy? What is the difference between prophecy, revelation, and apocalypse? What about false prophecy?

The Whole Bible as Prophecy

According to the Scriptures cited just above, and the derived definition of prophecy, biblical prophecy includes whatever God communicates to people directly through His prophets. Does this mean that all Scripture is prophecy? Are all of the human authors of Scripture, prophets?

In addition to the books of the Bible known as "The Prophets" (Isaiah through Malachi), most of the rest of Scripture is clearly labeled as prophecy or as being written by prophet

- The Law, or Pentateuch—Genesis through Deuteronomy—was given through a prophet, Moses. (Hosea 12:13; Acts 7:37–38)
- The histories were written by Moses, Samuel, Ezra, and other prophets.
- The Psalms were written by the prophets David (Acts 2:25–30), Asaph (2 Chronicles 29:30), and others. Solomon, a prophet (q.v. chapter 3), wrote Ecclesiastes, Song of Solomon, and most of Proverbs.
- The book of Revelation is all prophecy by its own definition. (22:7, 18–19)
- The rest of the New Testament was written by apostles, all prophets. (q.v. each apostle in chapter 3)

To be sure, the Bible divides itself into categories: "Law and Prophets" (Matthew 7:12, 22:40; Luke 16:16), "law and testimony" (Isaiah 8:20), "Moses and the Prophets" (Luke 24:27), and "the Law of Moses and the Prophets and the Psalms" (Luke 24:44). The question is, were these phrases meant to differentiate, or were they meant to be sure that the hearers and readers knew that *all* of Scripture was meant? If these divisions mean that prophecy is found only in the seventeen books at the end of the Old Testament, then, obviously, the Law and the Psalms are not prophecy. But we have already seen that the Law and Psalms were written by Moses, David, and other prophets; and much of this Scripture (e.g., almost the entire book of Leviticus) is expressly identified as God's direct revelation. Furthermore, a parallel passage to Luke 16:16 actually says that both the prophets and the *Law* prophesied (Matthew 11:13). Even the elaborate descriptions of the tabernacle and of tabernacle worship found in Exodus and Leviticus were prophecy about heaven and about Jesus Christ (Hebrews 8, 9, 10). And Scripture clearly says that Psalms are prophecy (1 Chronicles 25:1–7; Acts 2:25–30). Luke 16:16 adds the gospel to the prophets and the Law that "prophesied" (Matthew 11:13).

Considering all of the above, the use of the term *prophecy* to include all of Scripture is justified. It follows that all human authors of Scripture, God's word, are prophets.

Revelation and Apocalypse

The word *revelation* as used in English-language Bibles is almost the same as, if not identical with, the word *prophecy* (see Revelation 1:1–3 with 22:7, 10, 18, 19; 1 Corinthians 14:6, 26). Revelation suggests the source of the message (God) and the unveiling of previously hidden truth. Prophecy suggests the human deliverer of the message (a prophet) and often connotes a public exposition, a proclamation.[23,24] In this latter sense prophecy is God's word preached. However, not all prophecy is preached; it can be conveyed through music, writing, and symbolic acts.

The English word *apocalypse* is technically identical with revelation; that is, the Greek word αποκάλυψις is usually translated *revelation* in English-language Bibles. Therefore "apocalypse" should also mean "prophecy." However, "apocalypse" has become so closely associated with eschatology, especially its more dramatic world and cosmic events, and even with imaginary catastrophes in books and movies, that it is no longer, in current culture, an advisable synonym for "prophecy" in the true biblical sense. The English translation of αποκάλυψις, "revelation," has thus far escaped being so radicalized as its English transliteration, "apocalypse."

False Prophecy

This chapter deals with real, true prophecy: God's word. Chapter 5 deals with false prophets and prophecy. It should be noted here, however, that the Bible once uses the word *prophecy* for the evil pronouncements of a false prophet (see

Nehemiah 6:12), and often uses the verb form, prophesy, for the babbling and lying of false prophets (e.g., Jeremiah 14:14; Ezekiel 13:2, 17; Zechariah 13:4). Since false prophets *claim* to receive and speak prophecy, they are sometimes met on their own terms—and refuted—in the Bible. But make no mistake: their "prophecy" is not prophecy.

Predictive and Nonpredictive Prophecy

A sharp distinction has so far been drawn between biblical prophecy and two popular concepts of prophecy (prophecy equals prediction only, and prophecy equals eschatology only). Now it must be said that most biblical prophecy, at least in the Old Testament, does indeed have a predictive element. Jesus Himself said that the Scriptures, the Law, and the Prophets, testified (in the future tense, when written) about Him (John 5:39; Luke 24:27; 44). Peter said and wrote that the Old Testament prophets "foretold" and "testified beforehand" (Acts 4:24 and 1 Peter 1:10–12). One biblical test of a false or presumptuous prophet is that his *predictions* do not come to pass (Deuteronomy 18:21–22).[E] Even the Law contains explicit or implicit predictions of future blessings or curses depending upon its observance or nonobservance. "Repent, and be saved" has a future sense.

But not *all* prophecy is predictive. Some just reveals who God *is* (like Psalm 8 and others). Or consider Micah 6:8:

> He has shown you, O man, what is good;
> And what does the LORD require of you
> But to do justly,
> To love mercy,
> And to walk humbly with your God?

There is no predictive element in this passage from a book of prophecy. And in the common vernacular of Jesus's day, prophecy was not necessarily prediction either. The soldiers who beat and mocked the blindfolded Jesus said, "Prophesy! Who is the one who struck You?" (Luke 22:64). "Struck" is in the past tense. They did not ask Jesus to prophesy the name of the one who would strike Him next. These soldiers, even in their depravity, intuitively used *prophesy* in a true sense, i.e., to speak what could only be known by divine revelation.

It is a serious error to reduce all or most prophecy to eschatology, for that misses the main focus of it: Jesus Christ, not just His return to earth although that is part of it. Biblical prophecy is not some kind of mysterious code to be cracked so that we can navigate through end-time calamities. It is plain, clear, revelation from God about Himself (especially Christ) and what He expects of His people.

2. The Principal Subject of Prophecy

Philip found Nathanael and said to him, "We have found Him of Whom Moses in the Law, and also the prophets, wrote—Jesus of Nazareth, the son of Joseph." (John 1:45)

You search the Scriptures, for in them you think you have eternal life; and these are they which testify of Me. (Jesus, in John 5:39)

All things must be fulfilled which were written in the Law of Moses and the Prophets and the Psalms concerning Me. (Jesus, in Luke 24:44)

And beginning at Moses and all the Prophets, He [Jesus] expounded to them in all the Scriptures the things concerning Himself. (Luke 24:27)

This man [John, the baptizer] came for a witness, to bear witness of the Light [Jesus]. (John 1:7)

Of this salvation the prophets have inquired and searched carefully, who prophesied of the grace that would come to you, searching what, or what manner of time, the Spirit of Christ Who was in them was indicating when He testified beforehand the sufferings of Christ and the glories that would follow. (1 Peter 1:10–11)

Then He said to them, "O foolish ones and slow of heart to believe in all that the prophets have spoken! Ought not the Christ to have suffered these things and to enter into His glory?" (Jesus, in Luke 24:25–26)

But those things which God foretold by the mouth of all His prophets, that the Christ would suffer, He has thus fulfilled. (Peter, in Acts 3:18)

Then Paul, as his custom was, went in to them (a synagogue in Thessalonica), and for three Sabbaths reasoned with them from the Scriptures, explaining and demonstrating that the Christ had to suffer and rise again from the dead, and saying, "This Jesus whom I preach to you is the Christ." (Acts 17:2–3)

Therefore, having obtained help from God, to this day I stand, witnessing both to small and great, saying no other things than those which the prophets and Moses said would come—that the Christ would suffer, that He would be the first to rise from the dead, and would proclaim light to the Jewish people and to the Gentiles. (Paul, in Acts 26:22–23)

> To Him (Jesus) all the prophets witness that, through His name, whoever believes in Him will receive remission of sins. (Peter, in Acts 10:43)
>
> But we preach (prophesy, if you will) Christ crucified . . . For I determined not to know anything among you except Jesus Christ and Him crucified. (Paul, in 1 Corinthians 1:23 and 2:2)
>
> For the testimony of Jesus is the spirit of prophecy (Revelation 19:10). The context shows that this refers to the testimony *about* Jesus that was held and preached by John and his brethren—not to the words (testimony) of Jesus Himself.
>
> But all this was done that the Scriptures of the prophets might be fulfilled (Jesus, in Matthew 26:56, referring to the events immediately preceding His arrest and crucifixion.)

There can be no question. According to the Bible itself,

> **Jesus Christ is the principal subject of biblical prophecy,**

whether that prophecy was issued before or after His incarnation. Furthermore, as seen from several of the passages quoted above,

> **Prophecy about Jesus Focuses on His Sufferings and His Glory.**

This is not to say that all prophecy in the Old Testament is *clearly* about Jesus Christ. Indeed, passages such as John 5:39, Luke 24:27, 1 Peter 1:10–11, and Acts 17:2–3 indicate that much prophecy about Jesus is hidden from view until revealed by the Holy Spirit, in these cases through a spirit-filled teacher such as Jesus, Paul, or Peter. Some prophecy is about historical events such as battle outcomes, persons such as kings, and places such as Nineveh—that existed and expired long before Jesus came in the flesh. Still, they are related to Him; for example, the story of Jonah (see Matthew 12:39–41). Even the priests' rituals spoke of Jesus (Hebrews 10:11–12). And the Old Testament is replete with types and forerunners of Christ (see Romans 5:14; Hebrews 7; Acts 3:22). This typology is a form of prophecy about Jesus.

And some Old Testament prophecy *is* clearly about Jesus Christ. Anointed One, Messiah, Branch, King of Glory, the Lord our Righteousness, Prophet like Moses, Suffering Servant, Son of God, Redeemer, Holy One, Prince of Peace, and Savior—all of these are Old Testament words and concepts. Of course virtually all New Testament prophecy is plainly, openly about Jesus Christ—come to earth, ministering, suffering, crucified, glorified, reigning, and coming again.

3. Other Prominent Subjects of Prophecy (Indirectly Related to Christ)

In the following Scriptures, the topic of prophecy is indicated in *italics*:

> *The day of the LORD* is coming. (Joel 2:1; see also Joel 1:15, 2:11, 2:31; Obadiah 15; Ezekiel 30:3; Amos 5:18, 5:20; Zephaniah 1:7, 1:14–15; Jeremiah 30:7; Isaiah 2:11–12; 2 Peter 3:10)
>
> Beware of *false prophets.* (Matthew 7:15; see also Jeremiah 23:9–40; Ezekiel 13; Revelation 16:3, 19:20, 20:10; 1 John 4:1; Matthew 24:5; Titus 1:10–14; Micah 2:6–11, 3:5–7)
>
> The prophets who have been before me and before you of old prophesied against *many countries and great kingdoms—of war and disaster and pestilence.* (Jeremiah 26:8; see also Jeremiah 26–41; Ezekiel 25–32; Daniel 8; Amos 1–2; Obadiah; Nahum; Isaiah 14:3–24:23; Matthew 24:7; Revelation 16:17–21)
>
> *The remnant* will return, the remnant of Jacob, to the Mighty God. (Isaiah 10:21; see also Zephaniah 3:13; Isaiah 1:9, 6:12–13, 10:20, 10:22, 11:11–16; Micah 2:12, 4:6–7; 1 Kings 19:18; cf. Romans 11:3–5; Jeremiah 15:11, 23:3)
>
> *The times of restoration of all things,* which God has spoken of by the mouth of all His holy prophets since the world began. (Acts 3:21; see also Isaiah 1:26, 2:2–4, 27:2–13, 44:28; Jeremiah 16:14–15, 27:22, 30:1–3, 30:10, 30:18–22; Ezekiel 40–48; Hosea 1:10–2:1; Amos 9:11–15; Obadiah 19–21; Micah 4:1–8; Zephaniah 3:20; Haggai 2:6–9; Zechariah 8:9–12; Acts 1:6)

4. Why God Gives Prophecy

In general, we cannot discern God's purposes, or why He does anything (Isaiah 55:8–9). However, He has told us quite explicitly some of the reasons that He gives prophecy. Eight of these reasons are listed below and enlarged upon in the sections that follow. This is an obvious, not an exhaustive list of God's reasons for giving prophecy. He gives prophecy:

1. To reveal to man something about Himself and His decrees
2. To set forth and reinforce His laws for mankind
3. To warn
4. To bring about repentance and restoration
5. To judge men and their institutions
6. To plant and to build

7. To comfort and bless
8. To help people praise and worship Him

These reasons are not inferences or deductions from Scripture. They are direct statements in God's word, collected but not interpreted below. Examples of prophecy that was given for each reason are included.

1. *God gives prophecy to make Himself known and to reveal something about Himself and His decrees.*

> Surely the Lord GOD does nothing,
> Unless He reveals His secret to His servants the prophets. (Amos 3:7)
>
> Now I [God, as a "man clothed in linen"] have come to make you [Daniel] understand what will happen to your people in the latter days, for the vision refers to many days to come. (Daniel 10:14; see also Daniel 7, 8, and 9:20–12:13 for the content of the vision, which by being published became prophecy)
>
> "You are My witnesses," says the LORD,
> "And My servant whom I have chosen,
> That you may know and believe Me,
> And understand that I am He." (Isaiah 43:10)
>
> But when it pleased God, Who separated me from my mother's womb and called me through His grace, to reveal His Son in me, that I might preach Him among the Gentiles. (Paul, in Galatians 1:15–16)
>
> The Revelation of Jesus Christ, which God gave Him to show His servants—things which must shortly take place. And He sent and signified it by His angel to His servant John, who bore witness to the word of God, and to the testimony of Jesus Christ, to all things that he saw. (Revelation 1:1–2)
>
> Now as He sat on the Mount of Olives, the disciples came to Him privately, saying, "Tell us, when will these things be? And what will be the sign of Your coming, and of the end of the age?" And Jesus answered and said to them: . . ." [what follows is the "Little Apocalypse," in which Jesus reveals some of God's decrees for the future.] (Matthew 24:3–4)
>
> Have you not known? Have you not heard? Has it not been told you from the beginning? Have you not understood from the foundations of the earth? It is He Who . . . [Various attributes and works of God are then given.] (Isaiah 40:21–29)

Examples of this type of prophecy are as follows:

> Thus says the LORD:
> "Let not the wise man glory in his wisdom,
> Let not the mighty man glory in his might,
> Nor let the rich man glory in his riches;
> But let him who glories glory in this,
> That he understands and knows Me,
> That I am the LORD, exercising lovingkindness, judgment, and righteousness in the earth,
> For in these I delight," says the LORD. (Jeremiah 9:23–24)
>
> And God said to Moses, "I AM WHO I AM." And He said,
> "Thus you shall say to the children of Israel, 'I AM has sent me to you.'" (Exodus 3:14)
>
> Hear, O Israel: The LORD our God, the LORD is One!" (Deuteronomy 6:4)
>
> He who does not love does not know God, for God is love. (1 John 4:8)
>
> For the LORD revealed Himself to Samuel in Shiloh by the word of the LORD. (1 Samuel 3:27)
>
> Know that the LORD, He is God;
> It is He who has made us, and not we ourselves;
> We are His people and the sheep of His pasture. (Psalm 100:3)

2. *God gives prophecy to set forth and to reinforce His commandments and expectations for people.*

> We have not obeyed the voice of the LORD our God, to walk in His laws, which He set before us by His servants the prophets. (Daniel 9:10)
>
> Yet surely My words and My statutes, which I commanded My servants the prophets, . . . (Zechariah 1:6)
>
> The law and the words which the LORD of hosts sent by His Spirit through the former prophets. (Zechariah 7:12)
>
> This is that Moses who said to the children of Israel, "The LORD your God will raise up a Prophet like me from your brethren. Him you shall hear." This is he who was in the congregation in the wilderness with the angel who spoke to him

> on Mount Sinai, and with our fathers, the one who received the living oracles to give to us. (Stephen, in Acts 7:37–38)

From the above four Scripture quotations, it is clear that the Mosaic Law was given and received as prophecy. Moses, the greatest Old Testament prophet, "set before us" (Daniel 9:10) the Law of God in Exodus, Leviticus, Numbers, and Deuteronomy. Almost the entire book of Leviticus, for example, comes in the form of prophecy:

> Now the LORD called to Moses, and spoke to him from the tabernacle of meeting, saying, "Speak to the children of Israel, and say to them: . . ." (Leviticus 1:1–2)

The fact that this Law is direct revelation from God, to be communicated to the people by the prophet, is reinforced throughout the book.[F] Leviticus contains more direct words of God, quoted verbatim by a prophet, than any other book of the Bible! It is almost pure "labeled" prophecy.

One other prophet, Ezekiel, received and gave detailed instructions from God concerning worship, government, and land allotments (Ezek. 40–48; cf. 43:10–12, 18; 45:9–12; 46:16–18; 47:13).

God reinforced and expanded upon His Law through many other prophets. A few examples follow.

> So Ezra the priest (and a prophet) brought the Law before the assembly of men and women and all who could hear with understanding on the first day of the seventh month. Then he read from it in the open square . . . from morning until midday . . . and the ears of all the people were attentive to the Book of the Law. (Nehemiah 8:2–3)

> Do not think that I came to destroy the Law or the Prophets. I did not come to destroy but to fulfill. For assuredly, I say to you, till heaven and earth pass away, one jot or one tittle will by no means pass from the law till all is fulfilled. Whoever therefore breaks one of the least of these commandments, and teaches men so, shall be called least in the kingdom of heaven; but whoever does and teaches them, he shall be called great in the kingdom of heaven. (Jesus, in Matthew 5:17–19)

> Bind up the testimony,
> Seal the law among my disciples. (Isaiah 8:16)

> He has shown you, O man, what is good;
> And what does the LORD require of you
> But to do justly,
> To love mercy,
> And to walk humbly with your God? (Micah 6:8)

> Thus says the LORD of hosts: "Execute true justice, show mercy and compassion everyone to his brother. Do not oppress the widow or the fatherless, the alien or the poor. Let none of you plan evil in his heart against his brother." (Zechariah 7:9–10)

> "Teacher, which is the greatest commandment in the Law?" Jesus said to him, "You shall love the LORD your God with all your heart, with all your soul, and with all your mind." This is the first and great commandment. And the second is like it: "You shall love your neighbor as yourself." On these two commandments hang all the Law and the Prophets. (Matthew 22:36–40)

> Therefore, whatever you want men to do to you, do also to them, for this is the Law and the Prophets. (Jesus, in Matthew 7:12)

> For thus says the LORD to the men of Judah and Jerusalem:
> "Break up your fallow ground,
> And do not sow among thorns.
> Circumcise yourselves to the LORD,
> And take away the foreskins of your hearts." (Jeremiah 4:3–4)

> And this is His commandment, that we should believe on the name of His Son Jesus Christ and love one another, as He gave us commandment. (1 John 3:23; cf. John 13:24)

3. *God gives prophecy to warn people.*

> Son of man, I have made you a watchman for the house of Israel; therefore hear a word from My mouth, and give them a warning from Me. (Ezekiel 3:17)

> Blessed is he who reads and those who hear the words of this prophecy, and keep those things which are written in it; for the time is near. (Revelation 1:3)

> Write the vision, and make it plain on tablets, that he may run who reads it. (Habakkuk 2:2)

Examples of specific warnings follow:

> Blow the trumpet in Zion,
> And sound an alarm in My holy mountain!
> Let all the inhabitants of the land tremble;
> For the day of the LORD is coming,
> For it is at hand:

> A day of darkness and gloominess,
> A day of clouds and thick darkness,
> Like the morning clouds spread over the mountains.
> A people come, great and strong,
> the like of whom has never been;
> Nor will there ever be any such after them,
> Even for many successive generations. (Joel 2:1–2)

> Therefore you also be ready, for the Son of Man is coming at an hour you do not expect. (Jesus, in Matthew 24:44; see also all of Matt. 24 and 25)

> And in those days prophets came from Jerusalem to Antioch. And one of them, named Agabus, stood up and showed by the Spirit that there was going to be a great famine. (Acts 11:27–28; see also Acts 21:10–11)

4. *God gives prophecy to bring about repentance and to restore people's hearts to Him.*

> Yet He sent prophets to them, to bring them back to the LORD. (2 Chronicles 24:19)

> The Lord is not slack concerning His promise, as some count slackness, but is longsuffering toward us, not willing that any should perish but that all should come to repentance" (through His word of prophecy). (2 Peter 3:9; cf. v. 2)

> And the LORD has sent to you all His servants the prophets, . . . They said, "Repent now everyone of his evil way and his evil doings, and dwell in the land that the LORD has given to you and your fathers for ever and ever." (Jeremiah 25:4–5)

> Therefore say to them, "Thus says the LORD of hosts: 'Return to Me,' says the LORD of hosts, 'and I will return to you,' says the LORD of hosts. 'Do not be like your fathers, to whom the former prophets preached, saying, "Thus says the LORD of hosts: 'Turn now from your evil ways and your evil deeds.'"'" (Zechariah 1:3–4)

> John came baptizing in the wilderness and preaching a baptism of repentance for the remission of sins. (Mark 1:4)

Following are examples of specific calls to repent:

> Let the wicked forsake his way,
> And the unrighteous man his thoughts;
> Let him return to the LORD,
> And He will have mercy on him;

And to our God,
For He will abundantly pardon." (Isaiah 55:7)

It may be that the house of Judah will hear all the adversities which I propose to bring upon them, that everyone may turn from his evil way, that I may forgive their iniquity and their sins. (Jeremiah 36:3)

Say to them: "As I live," says the Lord GOD, "I have no pleasure in the death of the wicked, but that the wicked turn from his way and live. Turn, turn from your evil ways! For why should you die, O house of Israel?" (Ezekiel 33:11)

"Now, therefore," says the LORD,
"Turn to Me with all your heart,
With fasting, and weeping, and with mourning."
So rend your heart and not your garments;
Return to the LORD your God,
For He is gracious and merciful,
Slow to anger, and of great kindness;
And He relents from doing harm. (Joel 2:12–13)

5. *God gives prophecy to indict, arraign, prosecute, convict, and pronounce sentence on impenitent evildoers and covenant-breakers.*

Hear the word of the LORD, you children of Israel,
For the LORD brings a charge against the inhabitants of the land. (Hosea 4:1)

Hear, all you peoples! Listen, O earth, and all that is in it! Let the LORD be a witness against you, . . . Hear, all you mountains, the LORD's complaint, and you strong foundations of the earth; for the LORD has a complaint against His people, and He will contend with Israel. (Micah 1:2, 6:2)

"Therefore I will yet bring charges against you," says the LORD. (Jeremiah 2:9)

The LORD stands up to plead,
And stands to judge the people.
The LORD will enter into judgment
With the elders of His people
And His princes. (Isaiah 3:13–14a)

Yet for many years You [God] had patience with them [Israel] and testified against them by Your Spirit in the prophets. (Nehemiah 9:30)

The following are specific examples of "courtroom" or "judgment" prophecy:

> For three transgressions of Damascus, and for four, I [God] will not turn away its punishment, because they . . ." (Amos 1:3; see also Amos 1:6, 9, 11, 13; 2:1, 4, 6 for other places being arraigned)

> The word of the LORD which came to Jeremiah the prophet against the nations. Against [y] . . ." (Jeremiah 46:1–2, 47:1, 48:1, 49:1, 7, 23, 28, 34, 50:1; see also Ezek. 25–32; Isaiah 13–24; Obad.; Nah.; Zeph. 2:4–15)
> (y = Egypt, the Philistines, Moab, the Ammonites, Edom, Damascus, Kedar, the kingdoms of Hazor, Elam, Babylon, and the land of the Chaldeans)

> MENE, MENE, TEKEL, UPHARSIN. (Daniel 5:25; see verses 26–28 for interpretation as judgment)

> Thus says the LORD: "Because you have let slip out of your hand a man whom I appointed to utter destruction, therefore your life shall go for his life, and your people for his people." (1 Kings 20:42; see also 1 Kings 21:17–26)

> Woe to you, Chorazin! Woe to you, Bethsaida! For if the mighty works which were done in you had been done in Tyre and Sidon, they would have repented long ago, sitting in sackcloth and ashes. But it will be more tolerable for Tyre and Sidon at the judgment than for you. And you, Capernaum, who are exalted to heaven, will be brought down to Hades. (Jesus, in Luke 10:13–15)

6. *God gives prophecy to plant and build—sometimes after tearing down.*

> So the elders of the Jews built [the temple], and they prospered through the prophesying of Haggai the prophet and Zechariah the son of Iddo. (Ezra 6:14)

> Behold, I [God] have put my words in your mouth. See, I have this day set you over the nations and over the kingdoms, to root out and to pull down, to destroy and to throw down, to build and to plant. (Jeremiah 1:9–10)

> I planted, Apollos watered, but God gave the increase. (Paul, in 1 Corinthians 3:6)

> Now, therefore, you are no longer strangers and foreigners, but fellow citizens with the saints and members of the household of God, having been built on the foundation of the apostles and prophets, Jesus Christ Himself being the chief cornerstone, in Whom the whole building, being fitted together, grows into a holy

temple in the Lord, in Whom you also are being built together for a dwelling place of God in the Spirit. (Ephesians 2:19–22)

And He Himself [Jesus] gave . . . some prophets . . . for the equipping of the saints for the work of ministry, for the edifying [building up] of the body of Christ. (Ephesians 4:11–12)

But he who prophesies speaks edification . . . to men. (1 Corinthians 14:3)

7. *God gives prophecy to heal, console, comfort, encourage, free, bless, instill hope, and promise good to men.*

The Spirit of the Lord GOD is upon Me,
Because the LORD has anointed Me
To preach good tidings to the poor;
He has sent Me to heal the brokenhearted,
To proclaim liberty to the captives,
And the opening of the prison to those who are bound;
To proclaim the acceptable year of the LORD,
And the day of vengeance of our God;
To comfort all who mourn,
To console those who mourn in Zion,
To give them beauty for ashes,
The oil of joy for mourning,
The garment of praise for the spirit of heaviness;
That they may be called trees of righteousness,
The planting of the LORD, that He may be glorified. (Isaiah 61:1–3; cf. Luke 4: 18–19)

Blessed is he who reads and those who hear the words of this prophecy, and keeps those things which are written in it. (Revelation 1:3)

But he who prophesies speaks . . . comfort to men. (1 Corinthians 14:3)

"Comfort, yes, comfort My people," says your God. (Isaiah 40:1)

He [God] sent His word and healed them,
And delivered them from their destructions. (Psalm 107:20)

Then Jesus said to those Jews who believed in Him, "If you abide in My word, . . . you shall know the truth, and the truth shall make you free." (John 8:31–32)

> For whatever things were written before [i.e., Scripture prophecy, in this case, specifically Psalm 69:9] were written for our learning, that we through the patience and comfort of the Scriptures might have hope. (Romans 15:4)

> But He [Jesus] said, "More than that, blessed are those who hear the word of God and keep it!" (Luke 11:28)

> Behold, I am coming quickly. Blessed is he who keeps the words of the prophecy of this book. (Jesus, in John's vision, Revelation 22:7)

These Scriptures clearly state that God gives prophecy to heal, comfort, and bless people. There is a large body of such prophecy in the Bible. For this reason specific examples will not be cited: There are too many of them! *Every* Old Testament writing prophet conveys, at some point in his prophecy (usually at the end), a message from God of encouragement, deliverance, and hope. Even Nahum, whose entire burden was against Nineveh (Nahum 1:1), includes promises of peace and restoration (1:15; 2:2). The prophecy of Isaiah contains wave after wave of God's comfort, assurance, and promises of victory, peace, and well-being. We have already touched on the promises in written prophecy of a righteous Messiah (see "The Principal Subject of Prophecy"). And New Testament prophecy is almost entirely about God's grace and blessing—even in the death of His Son.

8. *God gives prophecy to assist people to praise, thank, and worship Him.*

This may seem to be a paradox. After all, prophecy comes from God to man whereas praise, thanks, and worship go from people to God. So how can prophecy be praise? When can revelation be worship? The short answer is when God wants it to be. Much praise, worship, and thanksgiving come first from God as prophecy, and then people return it—as prophecy! This can be even more complicated: a prophet, such as David or Asaph, moved by the Holy Spirit (2 Peter 1:21), writes a psalm prophecy. Singers and other musicians are then trained to prophesy with the words of that psalm, which, more likely than not, praises and thanks God. This process is clearly outlined in Scripture:

> Moreover David and the captains of the army separated for the service some of the sons of Asaph, of Heman, and of Jeduthun, who should prophesy with harps, stringed instruments, and cymbals . . . the sons of Asaph were under the direction of Asaph, who prophesied according to the order of the king. Of Jeduthun, . . . six, under the direction of their father Jeduthun, who prophesied with a harp to give thanks and to praise the LORD. Of Heman, the sons of Heman: . . . All these were the sons of Heman the king's seer in the words of God, . . . All these were

> under the direction of their father(s) for the music in the house of the LORD, . . . for the service of the house of God. Asaph, Jeduthun, and Heman were under the authority of the king. So the number of them, with their brethren who were instructed in the songs of the LORD, all who were skillful, was two hundred and eighty-eight." (1 Chronicles 25:1–7)

Note especially the phrase about Jeduthun and his sons . . . who prophesied with a harp to give thanks and to praise the LORD. Also note that all of these musicians were "instructed in the songs of the LORD."

The book of Psalms contains most of this kind of prophecy found in the Bible. However, it is not absent elsewhere. Habakkuk, chapter 3, is prayer-song-praise-prophecy. The only recorded prophecy of the first prophetess is all praise and thanksgiving:

> Then Miriam the prophetess, the sister of Aaron, took the timbrel in her hand; and all the women went out after her with timbrels and with dances. And Miriam answered them:
>
> Sing to the LORD,
> For He has triumphed gloriously!
> The horse and its rider
> He has thrown into the sea! (Exodus 15:20–21)

Paul's God-inspired (prophecy) letter to Rome contains this outburst of praise and worship:

> Oh, the depth and the riches both of the wisdom and knowledge of God! How unsearchable are His judgments and His ways past finding out!
> "For who has known the mind of the LORD?
> Or who has become His counselor?"
> "Or who has first given to Him
> And it shall be repaid to him?"
> For of Him and through Him and to Him are all things, to Whom be glory forever. Amen. (Romans 11:33–36)

John also heard, and wrote in the Revelation (prophecy) of Jesus Christ as given to him, much praise and worship, e.g.,

> Holy, holy, holy,
> Lord God Almighty,
> Who was and is and is to come. (Revelation 4:8)

> You are worthy, O Lord,
> To receive glory and honor and power;
> For You created all things,
> And by Your hand they exist and were created. (Revelation 4:11; see also Rev. 5:9–10, 12–13; 7:11; 11:17–18; 15:3–4; 16:5)

All of this praise and worship—much of it still sung in His church—is in a book that God has clearly labeled as being entirely prophecy (Revelation 1:3; 22:7, 10, 18, 19).

5. How God Gives Prophecy

We have summarized the Bible's direct teachings on the *what* and *why* of prophecy. Now we consider what the Bible says about *how* God gives His messages to prophets. This will not be a treatise on divine inspiration; it is limited to what the Bible expressly teaches about how God dispenses prophecy to prophets. As will be seen, that is quite simple: ever since the time of Moses, ca. 1450 BC, God has almost always given prophecy in *dreams* and *visions.* No tarot cards, no horoscope, no divination, and no more (with one exception) face-to-face communications. Only Jesus and Moses, and perhaps some of the very ancient prophets before Moses, have received prophecy from God during vis-à-vis, wide-awake conversations. That *was* the exception, and *is* no more. There were also, historically, a few very unusual transmissions of prophecy from God, such as from a cloud at the door of the tabernacle or between the wings of the cherubim, and writing on a pair of stone tablets. After Moses, such dispatches also gave way to dreams and visions.

The Holy Spirit is at work in all dreams and visions in which prophecy is given by God, as well as in all actual prophesying by the people who had the dreams and/or visions. The question of whether or not prophecy can be totally spontaneous—under the influence of the Holy Spirit, yet without a dream or vision—will also be examined in this section.

The subject of how prophecy is communicated from the receiving prophet to other people will be deferred to chapter 2, "The Biblical Prophet," and to the sketches of prophets in succeeding chapters.

1. *Dreams and Visions*

> Then He [God] said, "Hear now My words: if there is a prophet among you, I, the LORD, make Myself known to him in a vision; I speak to him in a dream." (Numbers 12:6)

> I [God] have also spoken by the prophets,
> And have multiplied visions. (Hosea 12:10)

> Then You [God] spoke in a vision to Your holy one (or ones). (Psalm 89:19)

There are many examples in Scripture of God speaking to His prophets in dreams and visions. A few are

> Now Joseph had a dream, and he told it to his brothers . . . "Please hear this dream which I have dreamed: There we were, binding sheaves in the field. Then behold, my sheaf arose and stood upright; and indeed your sheaves stood all around and bowed down to my sheaf." (Genesis 37:5–7)

> According to all these words and according to all this vision, so Nathan [the prophet] spoke to David. (2 Samuel 7:17)

> The vision of Isaiah the son of Amoz, which he saw concerning Judah and Jerusalem. (Isaiah 1:1; see also Isaiah 6)

> Now it came to pass . . . that the heavens were opened and I saw visions of God. (Ezekiel 1:1)

> So when I saw it [the visions in Ezekiel 1:1, above] I fell on my face, and I heard a voice of One speaking. And He said to me, "Son of man, stand on your feet, and I will speak to you." Then the Spirit entered me when He spoke to me, and set me on my feet; and I heard Him who spoke to me. (Ezekiel 1:28c–2:2)

> In the first year of Belshazzar king of Babylon, Daniel had a dream and visions of his head while on his bed. Then he wrote down the dream, telling the main facts. Daniel spoke, saying, "I saw in my vision by night, and behold, . . ." (Daniel 7:1–2)

> The vision of Obadiah. (Obadiah 1)

> The book of the vision of Nahum the Elkoshite. (Nahum 1:1)

> The burden which the prophet Habakkuk saw. . . . Then the LORD answered me and said: "Write the vision and make it plain on tablets." (Habakkuk 1:1 and 2:2)

> On the twenty-fourth day . . . the word of the LORD came to Zechariah . . . the prophet: I saw by night, and behold. (Zechariah 1:7–8)

Prophetic visions and dreams did not cease with the coming of Jesus, nor with His resurrection. Far from it! For these were the days when, as Joel had prophesied,

> Your sons and your daughters shall prophesy,
> Your young men shall see visions,
> Your old men shall dream dreams . . .
> And they shall prophesy. (Acts 2:17–18)

Specific examples of prophetic dreams and visions in the New Testament include

> But he [Stephen], being full of the Holy Spirit, gazed into heaven and saw the glory of God, and Jesus standing at the right hand of God, and said, "Look! I see the heavens opened and the Son of Man standing at the right hand of God!" (Acts 7:55–56)

> Now there was a certain disciple at Damascus named Ananias; and to him the Lord said in a vision: "Ananias . . . Arise and go . . . and inquire for one called Saul of Tarsus, for behold, he is praying. And in a vision he has seen a man named Ananias coming." (Acts 9:10–12) [Prophecy is then given to Ananias during the vision (verses 15–16). Paul, recalling his encounter with Jesus on the Damascus road, called it a vision and added the fact that he received direct orders to prophesy (Acts 26:12–19).]

> Peter went up on the housetop to pray, . . . he fell into a trance and saw heaven opened and . . . a voice came to him . . . While Peter thought about the vision, the Spirit said to him. "Behold, . . ." (Acts 10:9, 10, 13, 19) [This is followed by Peter's prophesying in Cornelius's house about the inclusiveness of the gospel, verses 34–43.]

The book of Revelation is almost entirely a vision, or series of visions, but John does not use that word; he merely says, "I saw," numerous times.

- Circumstances of visions.

Quite often, visions came to prophets while they were praying (e.g. Daniel 9:20–21, Acts 10:9–13, Revelation 1:10ff). But sometimes they came when the prophet, or prophet-to-be, was doing anything but praying, like Paul (Saul), "still breathing threats and murder" on the Damascus road (Acts 9:1ff and 26:11–19). One of Daniel's visions came when he was standing on the bank of the Tigris River with some other men, who did not see the vision but felt a terror (Daniel 10:4–7). Ezekiel also had a vision by a riverside (Ezekiel 1:1). Ezekiel had other visions while he was sitting in his house with some elders (8:1–2; 14:1–2) and while he was standing on a plain (3:22). The boy Samuel had his first vision from God while he "lay down in his place" (1 Samuel 3:9)—not necessarily asleep. Stephen had a vision while he was already prophesying, defending himself and indicting Christ's enemies before the Jewish governing council (Acts 7:55–56). From these examples we conclude that prophets have visions from God under all kinds of circumstances and at sundry times, although being in deep prayer is somewhat conducive to having a vision.

Dreams, of course, come during sleep. Abraham had a "deep sleep" (Genesis 15:12) in the midst of, or mingled with, a vision (15:1) *and* real-world events (15:9–11).

- Third parties in dreams and visions.

Sometimes prophecy came through the dream of a nonprophet, but only if it was told to a prophet, who had his own dream or vision from God to interpret the other's dream. The butler and the baker in Pharoah's prison were not prophets but had dreams which they told to Joseph (Genesis 40). Joseph received the interpretations of their dreams (prophecy) in his own dream (Genesis 41:12). In another instance, Pharaoh told his dreams to Joseph (Genesis 41). Joseph insisted that the interpretations of Pharaoh's dreams came from God, not from Joseph's wisdom (Genesis 41:16). Similarly, Daniel interpreted Nebuchadnezzar's dreams (Daniel 2 and 4). God even told Daniel "in a night vision" (Daniel 2:19) what Nebuchadnezzar's first dream was. Daniel, like Joseph, was careful not to take credit for the interpretation (Daniel 2:28–30).

Although God often spoke directly to the prophet in a vision (Genesis 15:1; Isaiah 6:8–9; Jeremiah 1; Ezekiel 2:1; Hosea 1:2; Amos 7:15; Jonah 3:1–2; Habakkuk 2:2; 1 Samuel 3:11; 1 Kings 3:5, 19:9), sometimes, within the context of a dream or vision, He used third parties, angels, to convey or interpret His message. Thus Daniel was helped to understand one of his visions by "one of those who stood by" in his vision (Daniel 7:15–16); another time by "two holy ones" (8:13–14); twice by the angel Gabriel (8:16, 9:21–22); and again by "one having the likeness of a man," who may have been Gabriel or another angel or Christ Himself (10:11, 16, 18, 21). John received the Revelation through Christ's angel (Revelation 1:1). He also received a book of prophecy (or encouragement to prophesy) from "another mighty angel" (10:1–2, 8–11) in his vision—as did Ezekiel, from "a hand stretched out to me" (Ezekiel 2:9–3:4). God used an angel to speak to Zechariah (Zechariah 1:9, 14, and many other places). He used Gabriel to announce Jesus's birth and glory to Mary, who later prophesied it (Luke 1:26–33, 46–55). Another angel spoke, presumably in a vision of the night, to some shepherds, who then prophesied (Luke 2:8–12, 17–18). God used angels in a vision (Luke 24:22–23) to tell some women at Jesus's empty tomb that He was alive, and they told (prophesied) this message to others.

2. *Vis-à-vis*

After Sinai (ca. 1450 BC), there are only two prophets in Scripture who are known exceptions to the "dreams and visions" mode of receiving prophecy: Moses and Jesus. When God announced His policy of using dreams and visions, almost exclusively, to transmit prophecy to men, He added,

> Not so with My servant Moses;
> He is faithful in all My house.
> I speak with him face to face,
> even plainly, and not in dark sayings;
> and he sees the form of the LORD." (Numbers 12:7–8)

Actually, it was in deference to the Israelites' fear of hearing directly from God, and getting too near Him, that God agreed to restrict His face-to-face communications to Moses alone (Exodus 20:18–19, Deuteronomy 5:25–27). Even then, after Moses talked vis-à-vis with God, his face shone and people were afraid of him (Exodus 35:30, 35).

God promised another prophet like Moses (Deuteronomy 18:15–18). Although it seemed logical to assume that this was Joshua, Moses's immediate successor and truly a great prophet, such was not the case (Deuteronomy 34:10–12). The prophet like Moses was Jesus (John 6:14, 7:40; Acts 3:20–23), and of course Jesus spoke face-to-face with His own Father.

3. *The Holy Spirit*

The Holy Spirit motivates all true prophets.

> Prophecy never came by the will of man, but holy men of God spoke as they were moved by the Holy Spirit. (2 Peter 1:21)

> Then the Spirit entered me when He [God, in a vision] spoke to me. (Ezekiel 2:2; cf. 1:1)

> Your young men shall see visions,
> Your old men shall dream dreams.
> And on My menservants and on My maidservants
> I will pour out My Spirit in those days;
> And they shall prophesy. (Acts 2:17–18; cf. Joel 2:28–29)

In the latter two passages, both the Holy Spirit and visions are mentioned. In the definitive (first) passage from 2 Peter, the Holy Spirit is connected with the will of man, not the message itself. It seems that *normally* the message of prophecy comes in a vision or dream; and the motivation, ability, and will to prophesy it comes by the Holy Spirit. Not that they are completely separable, or that the Holy Spirit might not be in the prophet first, and then comes the vision, as it was with John (Revelation 1:10).

The question remains, however: Can a message of prophecy come without a dream or vision, but only by the immediate impulse of the Holy Spirit? Of course God can do anything, and this would be but a small thing for Him; but *would* He, in light of Numbers 12:6? (See *Dreams and Visions* as described above.) Consider the case of Saul:

> Then the Spirit of God came upon him, and he prophesied. (1 Samuel 10:10)

And a second time,

> Then the Spirit of God was upon him also, and he went on and prophesied. (1 Samuel 19:23)

There is no record of Saul having had a vision, dream, or even any particularly heavenly thoughts. In both instances he seems to have been simply "caught up" in the Spirit with a group of prophets prophesying, possibly with music. There are other similar occurrences in Scripture:

- Moses took seventy elders out to the tent of meeting in the wilderness

  > And it happened, when the Spirit rested upon them, that they prophesied. (Numbers 11:25)

- When Mary greeted her cousin Elizabeth

  > Elizabeth was filled with the Holy Spirit. Then she spoke out with a loud voice and said, "Blessed . . ." (prophecy follows). (Luke 1:41–42)

- When a certain king of Judah became corrupt

  > Then the Spirit of God came upon Zechariah the son of Jehoiada the priest, who stood above the people, and said to them, "Thus says God . . ." (2 Chronicles 24:20)

- When baby John (the future baptizer) was being circumcised and named

  > Now his father Zecharias was filled with the Holy Spirit, and prophesied, saying: . . . (Luke 1:67)
  > [It should be noted that Zecharias had had a vision, vv. 11, 22]

At the end of his life, David, who had written and sung a great deal of prophecy, said,

> The Spirit of the LORD spoke by me,
> And His word was on my tongue. (2 Samuel 23:2)

We do not know whether these people had previously been given the prophecy in dreams or visions, or if they simply opened their mouths and out came prophecy by the Holy Spirit.[G] We do know that the Holy Spirit bestows the ability to prophesy—the gift of prophecy (1 Corinthians 12:4, 7, 10).

4. *Unusual ways*

Before God told Moses, Aaron, and Miriam about His new policy of using only dreams and visions to speak to prophets, with two exceptions (Numbers 12:6–8, Deuteronomy 18:18), He gave revelation in other ways. Scripture simply says that "Enoch walked with God . . ." and that "God said to Noah, . . ." (Genesis 5:22, 6:13). The encounter of Abraham with angels who brought prophecy (Genesis 18) is not called a vision; indeed, it could hardly have been entirely a vision or dream, for two of the angels continued on to Sodom and performed deeds in the real, physical world (18:16; chapter 19).

During Israel's wilderness decades, God spoke to His prophets from a pillar of cloud at the door of the tent of meeting (Exodus 29:42, Numbers 12:5, and Deuteronomy 31:14–16). In Moses's case this was vis-à-vis (Exodus 33:9–11). God also spoke to Moses and/or Aaron from a cloud between the wings of the cherubim, the mercy seat, over the ark of the covenant of God in the holiest part of the tabernacle (Exodus 25:22, Leviticus 16:2). Indeed, the Most Holy Place in the temple built much later by Solomon was called God's oracle, which means "speaking place" (1 Kings 6, KJV). There is no record, however, of prophecy originating in the mercy seat after Moses/Aaron, unless it was to Samuel (Psalm 99:6–7).

God also spoke, in a sense, through the Thummim and/or the Urim on the breastplate of the ephod of the High Priest (Exodus 28:15–30). This was used more as a decision-making process (Numbers 27:21, Nehemiah 7:65) than as a source of verbal prophecy, although King Saul put it on a par with prophets and dreams (1 Samuel 28:6), and David inquired of it as the very voice of God (1 Samuel 23: 9–12 and 30:7–8). No other record of prophecy from the Urim and the Thummim is found in Scripture, although a proposal was made to use this method to determine whether or not certain people were legitimate Jews, or priests, in the rebuilt nation after the exile (Ezra 2:63; Nehemiah 7:65).

Finally, and most singular, was God's transmission of prophecy in His own handwriting on stone tablets given to Moses on Mount Sinai. He even made a second set after the first got broken (Exodus 31:8; 34:1).

6. How God Does *Not* Give Prophecy

1. *False visions*

False prophets are quick to claim divine visions. In some cases they may even have deluded themselves into thinking that their ordinary dreams were revelation from God. Actually, their prophecy was conceived in their own heart for base motives such as greed, power, or court favor; then they came up with interpretations of ordinary dreams, or complete fabrications of visions, to support their messages.

> And the LORD said to me [Jeremiah] "The prophets prophesy lies in My name. I have not sent them, nor spoken to them; they prophesy to you a false vision, divination, a worthless thing, and the deceit of their heart." (Jeremiah 14:14)
>
> Thus says the LORD of hosts:
> "Do not listen to the words of the prophets who prophesy to you.
> They make you worthless;
> They speak a vision of their own heart,
> Not from the mouth of the LORD." (Jeremiah 23:16)
>
> Thus says the Lord GOD: . . .
> "For no more shall there be any false vision or flattering divination within the house of Israel." (Ezekiel 12:23–24)
>
> [The above three passages all refer to the false prophecies of "peace, peace" just before Jerusalem's demise in 586 BC.]
>
> But the prophet who presumes to speak a word in My name, which I have not commanded him to speak, or who speaks in the name of other gods, that prophet shall die. (Deuteronomy 18:20)
>
> If there arises among you a prophet or a dreamer of dreams, . . . saying, "Let us go after other gods"—which you have not known—"and let us serve them," you shall not listen to the words of that prophet or that dreamer of dreams.
> (Deuteronomy 13:1–3)

2. *Proscribed sources*

Not only did God tell us how He *would* give prophecy, He also forbade other sources or methods of getting prophecy, many of them expressly:

> There shall not be found among you anyone who makes his son or daughter pass through the fire, or one who practices witchcraft, or a soothsayer, or one who interprets omens, or a sorcerer, or one who conjures spells, or a medium, or a spiritist, or one who calls up the dead. For all who do these things are an abomination to the LORD, . . . For these nations which you will dispossess listened to soothsayers and diviners; but as for you, the LORD your God has not appointed such for you. (Deuteronomy 18:10–14)

Other translations use the words "enchanter," "charmer," "observer of times," "consulter with familiar spirits," "wizard," "necromancer," "one that practiseth augury," "trance speaker," "astrologer," and "one who maketh use of drugs to practice incantation"[H] in the above passage.

Sad to say, no less than five of these abominations are given in *Roget's Thesaurus*[1] as being THE SAME AS prophecy! Sadder yet, these practices are still with us. The names may change from time to time, and other names are invented, such as "fortune-teller," "horoscope," "crystal gazer," "palm reader," and "psychic."

Endnotes for Chapter 1

A. A recheck in 2004 and again in 2006 showed many new titles but no substantive change. A cursory Internet search of "biblical prophecy" and "books on biblical prophecy" in 2015 yielded similar results, except for some shifting toward current events such as terrorism and a few books on the canonical prophets. A Wikipedia article starts fairly well with an acceptable definition of prophecy, and it does not focus entirely on eschatology; however, it devolves into a few arbitrarily selected prophecies such as "Ezekiel prophesied the permanent destruction of Tyre."

B. In contrast, for example, to the Puritan father William Perkins's book, *The Art of Prophesying*,[23] in which he states, "There are two parts to prophecy: preaching the word and public prayer."

C. cf. 1 Corinthians 12:8-10.

D. Prophets who wrote the books of the Bible from Isaiah through Malachi.

E. This is not a definitive test. False prophets can sometimes predict signs and wonders that come to pass (Deuteronomy 13:1–5).

F. See Leviticus 4:1; 6:8, 24; 7:22, 28; 11:1; 12:1; 15:1; 16:2; 17:1; 18:1; 19:1; 20:1; 21:1,16; 22:1,17; 23:1, 9, 23, 33; 24:1, 15; 25:1; 27:1, 34.

G. In all of the cases cited above, except that of David, the prophesiers were "temporary" prophets.

H. From the Septuagint Bible translated into English by Charles Thompson.[25] In the New Testament the words 'sorcerer,' 'sorcery,' and 'witchcraft' are sometimes English translations of the Greek 'pharmakos,' 'pharmakeia,' and 'pharmakeus,' enchanter or enchantment with drugs (Gal. 5:20; Rev. 9:21; 18:23; 21:8, 22:15).

References for Chapter 1

1. Peter Roget, *The New Roget's* Thesaurus, ed. Norman Lewis, based on C. O. Sylvester Mawson's alphabetical arrangement of the Roget system of word classification (New York: Garden City Books, 1961).

2. *Webster's II New College Dictionary* (Boston: Houghton Mifflin Co., 1999).

3. John F. Walvoord, *The Final Drama* (Grand Rapids, MI: Kregel Publications, 1997), 6.

4. Charles R. Swindoll, John F. Walvoord, J.D. Pentecost, et al., *The Road to Armageddon* (Word Publishing, 1999).

5. John Hagee, *From Daniel to Doomsday* (Thomas Nelson Pub., 1999).

6. John Hagee, *Day of Deception* (Thomas Nelson Pub., 1997).

7. John Hagee, *Beginning of the End, Final Dawn Over Jerusalem, Day of Deception,* Three books in one volume (Thomas Nelson Pub., 2000).

8. Grant R. Jeffrey, *The Millennium Meltdown* (Frontier Research Publications, 1998).

9. Brian R. Coffey, *Quick and Easy Guide: Bible Prophecy* (Tyndale House, 1999).

10. Mac Hammond, *The Last Millennium* (Harrison House, 1999).

11. W. T. James, ed., *Fore Warning* (Harvest House, 1998).

12. Grant R. Jeffrey, *The Mysterious Bible Codes* (Word Publishing, 1998).

13. Charles Capps, *End Time Events* (Tulsa OK: Harrison House, 1997).

14. David Jeremiah, *Jesus's Final Warning* (Word Publishing, 1999).

15. W. T. James, ed., *Foreshocks of Antichrist* (Harvest House, 1997).

16. G. Otis, Sr., *Millennium* (Albury Publishing, 2000).

17. R. C. Sproul, *The Last Days According to Jesus* (Baker Book House, 1998).

18. Jack Van Impe, *Millennium: Beginning or End?* (Word Publishing, 1999).

19. Ernest Angley, *Raptured* (Winston Press, 1950).

20. Jack Van Impe, *Final Mysteries Unsealed* (Word Publishing, 1998).

21. John W. Schmitt and J. Carl Laney, *Messiah's Coming Temple: Ezekiel's Prophetic Vision of the Future Temple* (Kregel Publications, 1997).

22. Abraham J. Heschel, *The Prophets* (HarperCollins Publishers, 1962; Prince Press Edition, 2000), 12.

23. William Perkins, *The Art of Prophesying* (first published in Latin, 1592 and in English, 1606; Banner of Truth Trust, Edinburgh, 1996).

24. Robert Young, *Analytical Concordance* (19th century; repr., Grand Rapids, MI: Associated Publishers and Authors, n.d.), see entry under PROPHECY, 4.

25. Charles Thompson, trans. (ca. 1808) and ed. C. A. Muses, *The Septuagint Bible* (Indian Hills, Co: The Falcon's Wing Press, 1954).

Chapter 2

The Biblical Prophet

Introduction

Each of us probably carries a mental picture of the typical biblical prophet. Perhaps it is a shaggy-bearded man wearing rough clothing who suddenly emerges out of a wilderness and challenges the establishment. Or perhaps it is a wise, skillful writer whose poetry sears the conscience and quickens the spirit. However, just a glance through the lists of prophets in chapters 3 and 4 shows that there is no stereotype. Prophets in the Bible are men and women, married and unmarried, as old as Enoch (365 years) and as young as the boy Samuel, rich as Solomon and unworldly as Jesus, honored by their nation (like Samuel) and persecuted or martyred (like many), writers, speakers, musicians, and demonstrators; famous and anonymous, Old Testament and apostolic, as false hearted as Balaam and as pure hearted as John, the baptizer. The only characteristic all prophets have in common is the obvious one: they prophesied.

A biblical prophet is a person who receives revelation from God and communicates His message to other persons, cities, nations, or peoples.

The illustrations on the next four pages depict a wide variety of prophet embodiments and, to a lesser extent, of means of prophesying.

Figure 1

Prophet

cf. Daniel 9:2; Mark 1:2; 2 Kings 22:8–13; Luke 4:17

Figure 2

Prophet

cf. Matthew 3:4; 1 Kings 17:3–4; Amos 7:14–18

Figure 3

Prophets

cf. Exodus 15:20–21; 1 Chronicles 25:1–7; Acts 21:9; 1 Samuel 10:5

Figure 4

Prophet

cf. 1 Samuel 3; Daniel 1:3–4; Genesis 37:1–10; Luke 2:41–50

As diverse as its prophets are, the Bible nevertheless contains a number of generalizations about them and about the office of prophet. However, even the Bible's own general statements about prophets do not apply to all those it names prophets or reports to have prophesied. There are prophets and there are Prophets. Of the lesser kind are false prophets, faithless prophets, spurious prophets, inadvertent prophets, and doubtless some Levites who prophesied as singers in a chorus, yet perfunctorily. None of these kinds of prophets was in view when James wrote, "My brethren, take the prophets, who spoke in the name of the Lord, as an example of suffering and patience" (James 5:10). When Scripture speaks of prophets in general, it is speaking about men and women of God who are deeply invested in their message and its giver. Peter called them "holy men of God" (2 Peter 1:21). Jesus said that real prophets are those He knows, and who do the will of His Father (Matthew 7:21–23). In this book they will be called fiducial prophets, this adjective signifying the element of faith. But this is not to say that any fiducial prophet, except Jesus, was perfect or attained some spiritual status unavailable to other people. "Elijah was a man with a nature like ours" (James 5:17).

About sixty-five fiducial prophets are actually called "prophet," or an equivalent title, in the Bible. There are also some well-known fiducial prophets who are never expressly called "prophet," or an equivalent title. These include several of the canonical prophets as well as Joshua, Paul, and most of the apostles including John, the author of Revelation, a book of prophecy.

Many other persons and groups, not expressly called prophets, are said in Scripture to have prophesied or to have spoken in or under the influence of the Holy Spirit. A good example is Zacharias (Luke 1:67). These are included in the lists of God's prophets, chapters 3, 4, and 6. Some may have prophesied rarely or just once—for example, the seventy elders in Numbers 11:24–25. Many were members of musical groups that prophesied, as clearly defined in 1 Chronicles 25. Biblical generalizations about prophets—fiducial prophets—may or may not apply to them.

On the other hand, some persons who are merely noted in passing as prophets or are said to have prophesied—such as the four daughters of Philip (Acts 21:9)—can be considered fiducial prophet(esse)s. In all, there are about one hundred known[A] fiducial prophets in the Bible. These are the prophets meant in the following Scripture appellations, descriptions, and other generalizations.

Scriptures about Prophets in General

1. *Bible Titles, Synonyms, and Metaphors for Prophet (in italics)*

> (Formerly in Israel, when a man went to inquire of God, he spoke thus: "Come, let us go to see the *seer*;" for he who is now called a *prophet* was formerly called a *seer.*) (1 Samuel 9:9)

> Now Deborah, a *prophetess,* . . . (Judges 4:4; see also 2 Chronicles 34:22; Luke 2:36)

> And he spoke to him [Elijah]: "*Man of God,* . . . " (2 Kings 1:9; see also 1 Kings 13; 2 Kings 5:8; 2 Peter 1:21)

> His [God's] *servants* the prophets. (Amos 3:7 ; see also Isaiah 44:26; Jeremiah 7:25; 25:4; 26:5; 29:19; 35:15; and 44:4; Ezekiel 38:17; Daniel 9:6, 10; Zechariah 1:6; Revelation 10:7; 11:8; and 22:6)
>
> "*God's servants*" is both a title and a characteristic (next section).

> *Your eyes,* namely, the prophets; and *your heads,* namely, the seers. (Isaiah 29:10)

> Behold, I send . . . [God's] *messenger,* . . . (Malachi 3:1; see also 2 Chronicles 36:16; Isaiah 42:19; 44:26; Matthew 11:9–10; Haggai 1:13)

> I have made you a *watchman* for the house of Israel; therefore you shall hear a word from My mouth and warn them for me. (Ezekiel 33:7; see also Isaiah 21:11–12; Jeremiah 6:17; Habakkuk 2:1)

> Noah, . . . a *preacher* of righteousness, . . . (2 Peter 2:5; see also Nehemiah 6:7; Ecclesiastes 1:1–2; Jonah 3:2; Zechariah 1:4; Luke 16:16; Romans 10:14; 15:19–20; 1 Timothy 2:7; Hebrews 4:2)

> Now a certain man of *the sons of the prophets* said . . . Then the prophet [the same man] departed, . . . and the king of Israel recognized him as one of the prophets. (1 Kings 20:35, 38, 41; see also Amos 7:14; 2 Kings 9:1–3)

Sometimes a metaphor is applied to just one prophet in the Bible, but outside the Bible it has been applied to prophets in general. Thus, only Aaron was named God's (and Moses's) *spokesman* (Exodus 4:16); but modern writers and preachers freely use this term for other prophets. Other titles and metaphors are applied to just one prophet in the Bible. Jeremiah was *a fortified city, an iron pillar, and bronze walls* (Jeremiah 1:18). John, the baptizer, was *a voice of one crying in the wilderness* (John 1:23; cf. Isaiah 40:3). Isaiah and, ultimately, Jesus, were called *polished shafts (arrows)* with *mouths like a sharp sword* (Isaiah 49:2). God called Ezekiel "*son of man*" (Ezekiel 33:7 and many other places); He once called Daniel this same thing (Daniel 8:17).

In summary, those faithful people in the Bible who received revelation from God and communicated it to other people are called *prophets, prophetesses, seers, men of God, God's servants, the eyes and heads of the people, preachers, and God's messengers, watchmen, spokesmen, and voices.* Some are likened to *penetrating weapons* and *impenetrable fortresses.* In the ninth and eighth centuries BC, some were called *sons of the prophets.* Ezekiel was often, and Daniel once, called *son of man.*

Jesus on Prophets

During His few years of ministry on earth, Jesus made a remarkably large number of general statements and observations about prophets. Some of them are rather enigmatic. Below are the collected sayings of Jesus about prophets in general. (He also spoke about many particular prophets, which remarks are not included below.)

> A prophet is not without honor except in his own country, among his own relatives, and in his own house. (Mark 6:4; see also Matt. 13:57; Luke 4:24; and John 4:44)
>
> You will know them [false prophets and, by inference, true prophets] by their fruits. Do men gather grapes from thornbushes or figs from thistles? Even so, every good tree bears good fruit, but a bad tree bears bad fruit. (Matthew 7:16–17)
>
> Blessed are the eyes which see the things you see; for I tell you that many prophets and kings have desired to see what you see, and have not seen it, and to hear what you hear, and have not heard it. (Luke 10:23–24)
>
> He who receives a prophet in the name of a prophet shall receive a prophet's reward. (Matthew 10:41)
>
> The law and the prophets were until John. Since that time the kingdom of God has been preached, and everyone is pressing into it. (Luke 16:16; see also Matthew 11:12–13)
>
> Woe to you also, lawyers! . . . For you build the tombs of the prophets, and your fathers killed them. In fact, you bear witness that you approve the deeds of your fathers; for they indeed killed them, and you build their tombs. Therefore the wisdom of God also said, "I will send them prophets and apostles, and some of them they will kill and persecute," so that the blood of all the prophets which was shed from the foundation of the world may be required of this generation, from the blood of Abel to the blood of Zechariah who perished between the altar and the temple. Yes, I say to you, it shall be required of this generation." (Luke 11:46–51; see also Matthew 23:29–36)

> Nevertheless I must journey today, tomorrow, and the day following; for it cannot be that a prophet should perish outside of Jerusalem. (Luke 13:33)
>
> O foolish ones, and slow of heart to believe in all that the prophets have spoken! Ought not the Christ to have suffered these things and to enter into His glory? [And beginning at Moses and all the Prophets, He expounded to them in all the Scriptures the things concerning Himself.] (Luke 24:25–27)
>
> These are the words which I spoke to you while I was still with you, that all things must be fulfilled which were written in the Law of Moses and the Prophets and the Psalms concerning Me. (Luke 24:44)

2. *Some Biblical Marks, Tests, and Characteristics of a Prophet (italicized)*

My brethren, take the prophets, who spoke in the name of the Lord, as *an example of suffering and patience.* (James 5:10)

And the LORD has sent you all *His servants* the prophets. (Jeremiah 25:4; see also Isaiah 44:26; Jeremiah 7:25; 26:5; 29:19; 35:15; and 44:4; Ezekiel 38:17; Daniel 9:6, 10; Amos 3:7; Zechariah 1:6; Revelation 10:7; 11:18; and 22:6)

He is a prophet, and *he will pray for you.* (Genesis 20:7)

[The characteristic and act of being an intercessor is exhibited in the lives of most fiducial prophets; see *Duties and Tasks of Prophets* below.]

Elijah [as a representative prophet] was a man with a nature like ours, and *he prayed earnestly.* (James 5:17)

[Earnest prayer, intercessory or not, was the business of most prophets; see *Duties and Tasks of Prophets*, below.]

A prophet is *not without honor except in his own country and in his own house.* (Matthew 13:57; see also Mark 6:4; Luke 4:24; John 4:44)

You will know them by *their fruits.* (Matthew 7:16)

[This statement was made about false prophets. Indirectly, it applies to fiducial prophets.]

One mark of a true or fiducial prophet is that his or her *predictions*, if any, actually *come to pass.* In the Bible, this test is stated in the negative with regard to false prophets:

> When a prophet speaks in the name of the LORD, if the thing does not happen or come to pass, that is the thing which the LORD has not spoken; the prophet has spoken it presumptuously; you shall not be afraid of him. (Deuteronomy 18:22)

Elsewhere in Scripture this test is stated sarcastically, again about false prophets:

> As for the prophet who prophesies of peace, when the word of the prophet comes to pass, the prophet will be known as one whom the LORD has truly sent. (Jeremiah 28:9)

CAUTION must be used in applying this test. It is not sufficient evidence of a true prophet. Moses specifically warns, "If there arises among you a prophet or a dreamer of dreams, and he gives you a sign or a wonder, and the sign or the wonder comes to pass, of which he spoke to you, saying, 'Let us go after other gods'—which you have not known—'and let us serve them,' you shall not listen to the words of that prophet or that dreamer of dreams, for the LORD your God is testing you to know whether you love the LORD your God with all your heart and with all your soul. But that prophet or that dreamer of dreams shall be put to death, because he has spoken in order to turn you away from the LORD your God, who brought you out of the land of Egypt and redeemed you." (Deuteronomy 13:1–3, 5).

Miracles are usually a mark of a true prophet; these are used by God to validate His message and His messenger. But miracles can also be faked or imitated: witness Pharaoh's wise men and sorcerers (Exodus 7:11), and Simon the sorcerer (Acts 8:9–11). We must weigh the prophet's message and, usually, his life along with his miracles.

> To the law and to the testimony! If they [mediums, wizards, and other false prophets] do not *speak according to this word*, it is because there is no light in them. (Isaiah 8:20)

> "The prophet who has a dream, let him tell a dream; and he who has My word, let him *speak My word faithfully*; what is the chaff to the wheat?" says the LORD. "Is not My word like a fire?" says the LORD, "And like a hammer that breaks the rock in pieces?" (Jeremiah 23:28–29)

If we use as a mark or test of a prophet, that his message be like "fire" and like a "hammer," we must do so with great discretion. This passage was specifically given to contrast Jeremiah's true prophecy with the oily lies of soothsayers who were saying what people liked to hear: "Peace, peace." Jeremiah's message at that time was a hard one, burning the soul like fire, breaking traditions and institutions. But at other times, other prophets were told, like Isaiah, "Comfort, yes, comfort My people!" (Isaiah 40:1). So, we must remember that "fire and brimstone" in his message is not necessarily the mark of a true prophet—except when it is necessary.

3. *The Calling, Commissioning, and Anointing of Prophets*

Although the Bible does not expressly say it, we believe that all its prophets were called, commissioned, or constrained by God to prophesy. Some callings were very dramatic and took place in real-world settings, often with witnesses. Examples of such callings are

- Moses at the burning bush, Exodus 3:1–4:17
- Paul on the Damascus road, Acts 26:12–18 (cf. Acts 9:3–18)
- Samuel, lying in his bed, 1 Samuel 3
- Elisha, in two stages:
  - o Called while farming, 1 Kings 19:19–21
  - o Spirit-filled at Elijah's ascension, 2 Kings 2:9–15
- Amos, as he drove a flock of sheep, Amos 7:15
- Peter, Andrew, James, and John called while fishing, Matthew 4:18–22; fully commissioned later, Mark 16:14–18, Acts 1:8
- Matthew while collecting taxes, Luke 5:27–28; fully commissioned later

Other callings took place in visions or dreams described for us by the prophets themselves:

- Isaiah, Isaiah 6
- Jeremiah, Jeremiah 1:4–19
- Ezekiel, Ezekiel 1 and 2

Some prophets were groomed for the office, either as servant-understudy disciples like Joshua, Elisha, and Jesus's apostles (q.v. all, chapter 3); or in seminaries (1 Kings 20:35–42; 2 Kings 2:3, 5, 7, 15; 4:38; 9:1–10). Neither kind of training guaranteed commissioning by God: witness Gehazi (2 Kings 4:29–31; 5:20–27) and Judas Iscariot. One prophet, Amos, made it clear that he was *not* formally trained for the office (Amos 7:14).

God secretly ordains His prophets before birth, even before conception (Jeremiah 1:5; Galatians 1:15). However, only John, the baptizer, was openly announced as a prophet before he was conceived in the womb (Luke 1:13–17).

Most music prophets who proclaimed the words of God in psalmody—and there were thousands of them—were prophets because they were born to certain Levite families, assigned to the office, and trained (1 Chronicles 23, 25). Some of these, such as Heman, Asaph, and Jeduthun (q.v., chapter 3), were clearly God-called fiducial prophets. Some, probably, were not.

As for the rest of the prophets we have little or no information about the circumstances and details of their callings. Most of the canonical prophets simply proclaim their prophecies, and do not give any personal background information. Elijah and other heroic[B] prophets suddenly appear on the scene of history as full-blown prophets. However, some prophets were anointed; and one (John) was publicly identified as a prophet even before his birth. God used some prophets to call, ordain, or commission other prophets such as Timothy (1 Timothy 1:18; 4:14), Barnabas, and Saul (Paul) (Acts 13:1–3), typically with the laying on of hands.

It has been observed that there were three offices in the Bible to which people could be anointed: prophet, priest, and king. However, there are not many biblical accounts of actual anointments; and those of prophets are downright rare. Besides Jesus, only Elisha (1 Kings 19:16), two anonymous prophets (Zechariah 4:14; cf. Revelation 11:3) and Paul, Silas, and Timothy (2 Corinthians 1:19, 21) are said to have been anointed to preach or prophesy.

There is in the New Testament the concept of Christians in general being anointed with the Holy Spirit (1 John 2:27), but it is not clear that this is specifically for prophesying.

The word *Christ* or *Messiah* means anointed; and there are ample references in both the Old and New Testaments to Jesus's anointing.[C] He was anointed as prophet, as priest, and as king. Certain Scripture refers specifically to His anointment to preach, or prophesy (Isaiah 61:1[D]; cf. Luke 4:18).

4. *Preparation for Prophethood*

God does not just call His prophets and give them messages. He also equips them to prophesy. Almost always, this involves study, education, and training; sometimes, higher education. Moses and Daniel were educated in the best universities of their times (Acts 7:22; Daniel 1:4). Paul studied under the great rabbi Gamaliel (Acts 22:3; cf. 5:34). Timothy, in turn, studied under Paul (2 Timothy 1:13). Joshua and Elisha were tutored by master prophets. The apostle prophets were educated for years by the greatest rabbi of all, Jesus Christ; and many others received at least some of His training (Luke 10:1–20; Acts 1:21–22). Apollos was "instructed in the way of the Lord" and took an important postgraduate course (Acts 18:25–26). Solomon was one of the best-educated men of his or any time (1 Kings 4:30–34).

There can be no question that all of the canonical prophets had highly honed literary skills—even Amos, who presented himself as a rustic not educated in a school of the "sons of the prophets" (Amos 7:14). We are not told where most of these writing prophets got their literary training. In the ninth century BC, schools or centers were established to train prophets (2 Kings 2:3, 5, 7, 15; 4:38). Only two of their students, however, are known to have become prophets (1 Kings 20:35–42; 2 Kings 9:1–10).

Levites by the hundreds were "instructed in the songs of the LORD" to prophesy musically (1 Chronicles 25:1–7).

Several prophets were trained for the priesthood, an office that involved teaching God's statutes (Leviticus 10:11) and so was akin to and good training for the office of prophet. Some of these were Eleazar, Ezekiel, Ezra, Iddo II, Jeremiah, Samuel, and Zechariah II (q.v. all, chapter 3).

After his vision, call, and commissioning, Ezekiel was told to go home and shut the door, presumably to digest and study further the revelation he had received. To make sure he did not start verbally prophesying before his preparation was complete, God even rendered him dumb (Ezekiel 3:24–26). Likewise, Paul, after his Damascus Road vision and call, went immediately to Arabia for three years, presumably for further study, prayer, and meditation (Galatians 1:15–18).

God also prepared prophets by life experiences—for example, David the shepherd; Amos and Elisha, farmer/ranchers; and the four fishermen who became fishers of men. Hardship and loneliness prepared prophets such as Elijah and John, the baptizer. Although Jonah was a prophet before his adventure at sea, he was certainly prepared for his mission to Nineveh in the fish's belly.

Some prophets were given special tools and were trained in their use:

- The *rod* of Moses and Aaron (Exodus 4:2–5)
- The *mantle* of Elijah and Elisha (2 Kings 2:8, 13–14)
- The *Urim* in the high priest's breastplate (Numbers 27:21; cf. Exodus 28:30)
- The *musical instruments* of David (1 Chronicles 25:1) which were used by thousands of prophets over many generations (cf. 2 Chronicles 29:25–26; Habakkuk 3:19)

The one essential preparation of any prophet is an infusion of the Holy Spirit (2 Peter 1:21). A person can get the "right" education, study under a prophet, renounce all sinful living, live in a cave, and even have the word of God (Scripture) in his mind; but without the Holy Spirit, he is no prophet. Moreover, relatively worldly or uneducated people can become at least temporary prophets if the Holy Spirit falls on them; for example, Saul (1 Samuel 10:9–13) or the seventy elders (Numbers 11:24–25).

5. *Duties and Tasks of Prophets*

The principal duty of every prophet is to faithfully proclaim God's word as revealed to him or her, whether that word is law, judgment, or gospel. This duty defines him or her as a prophet. Perhaps just as mandatory, but not expressly commanded even for fiducial prophets, is the duty to walk with God—to live a holy, righteous life and to pray. All we know of Enoch, one of the first prophets, is that he walked with God. Many prophets were called man of God. Peter calls prophets in general, "holy men of God" (2 Peter 1:21). Prophets were frequently called God's servants.

Certainly a large part of walking with God is prayer, especially intercessory prayer. Abraham, not known for verbal or written prophecy, was known as a prophet because "He will pray for you and you shall live" (Genesis 20:7). Scripture records not a few weighty prayers of prophets, including

- Hannah, 1 Samuel 2
- David, 2 Samuel 7:18–19; and several of his Psalms
- Solomon, 1 Kings 8:22–53
- Hezekiah, 2 Kings 19:14–19; 20:3
- Habakkuk, Habakkuk 3
- Daniel, Daniel 9:3–19
- Nehemiah (with fasting, tears, and mourning), Nehemiah 1:4–11
- Jesus, John 17; many others
- Paul, Ephesians 1:5–13; others

It is reported that other prophets prayed, although the content of their prayers is not published (e.g., Samuel, 1 Samuel 8:6 and Peter, Acts 10:9). It is hard to imagine that any serious fiducial prophet did not pray a great deal. Some prayed that their own prophecies would *not* come true or would be delayed—prophecies such as national or personal disasters—and sometimes, these prayers were granted! A prime example of this is Moses pleading with God to relent from His announced (through Moses) decision to annihilate Israel for their apostasy (Exodus 32:9–14).

Besides these fundamental duties to prophesy and to walk with God, which included prayer, the duties of fiducial prophets were wonderfully varied:

- **National Leader/Statesperson**. Moses, Joshua, Deborah, Samuel, David, Hezekiah, Nehemiah, and others were called upon to lead their nation (Israel or Judah) as heads of state. This usually included being commander in chief of the military.
- **State Official or Advisor**. Other prophets, while not heads of state, were privy counselors to kings, and/or held high offices, not necessarily in Israel or Judah. These include Joseph (in Egypt), Nathan, Ahijah, Elisha, Daniel (in Babylon), and Nehemiah (in Persia).
- **Anointer**. Moses anointed Aaron and his sons as priests. Samuel, Nathan, Ahijah, and Anonymous Prophet 9 (chapter 4) anointed kings. Elijah anointed Elisha to the office of prophet. John the baptizer anointed Jesus, if baptism can be considered a form of anointing. Prophets anointed

Timothy, Paul, Barnabas, and Silas through prayer, fasting, and the laying on of hands.

- **Builder**. Haggai and Zechariah were temple builders, possibly even assisting with manual labor (Ezra 5:2). Noah built a huge ship—no mean engineering or construction feat. Moses prophesied the plan of the first tabernacle and oversaw its construction. David built houses and a new tabernacle for the ark of the covenant and developed plans and stockpiled building materials for the first hard-sided temple. Nehemiah built a new wall around Jerusalem. Paul made tents.
- **Teacher**. Some prophets taught as well as proclaimed. Examples include Ezra and other prophets who were also priests, Jesus, and Paul in the school of Tyrannus at Ephesus. (Acts 19:9–10)
- **Trial Lawyer**. Some prophets were prosecutors at the bar of God, e.g., see Isaiah 3:13–14 and Micah 6:1–8. They arraigned nations (Amos 1:3, 6, 9, 11, 13; 2:1, 4, 6; Jeremiah 2:9) and kings (2 Kings 1:16; Daniel 5:26–28). Of course, this was figurative but often courtroom procedures and language were used.
- **Executioner**. Two prophets, Samuel and Elijah, were called upon to physically execute enemies of God and Israel (1 Samuel 15:32–33; 1 Kings 18:40).
- **Historian**. This was a common and important task of biblical prophets. Moses wrote most of the Bible's very ancient history before about 1500 BC. Even if the creation, fall, flood, and Babel stories are not considered rigorous history, Moses did provide a chronological genealogy with elapsed times from Adam through Abraham (Genesis 5; 11:10–26); as well as chronologically arranged lives of Abraham, Isaac, Jacob, Joseph, and himself. He also kept a journal that chronicled events during the forty-year wilderness wanderings (Exodus 17:14) and recorded, at God's specific command, all their starting points and encampments (Numbers 33). Samuel is believed to have written much of Israel's history during his own lifetime (1 Samuel).

  Many of the principal prophets during the Kingdom Era of Israel/Judah were official national historians. Samuel, Nathan, and Gad recorded the acts of David (1 Chronicles 29:29). Nathan, Ahijah, and Iddo chronicled Solomon's reign, and Iddo also recorded events in the days of Kings Rehoboam and Abijah (2 Chronicles 9:29, 12:15; 13:22). Shemaiah contributed to the history of Rehoboam's reign. Jehu wrote the acts of King Jehoshaphat (2 Chronicles 20:34). Isaiah was the biographer-historian of King Hezekiah (2 Chronicles 32:32). Manassah's wicked times were chronicled by Hozai. (2 Chronicles 33:19)

  There are important historical passages in the books of Isaiah (36–39), Jeremiah (32–44), Daniel (1–6), Ezra (all), and Nehemiah (all). In the New Testament, all four gospels are histories, although other considerations often preempt rigid chronology. Luke styles himself as a historian (Luke 1:1–4; Acts 1:1–3). The book of Acts is definitely a history.

6. *How Prophets Prophesy (Means and Media)*

> God, who at various times and in various ways spoke in times past to the fathers by the prophets, has in these last days spoken to us by His Son. (Hebrews 1:1–2)

The various ways are principally:

- **Verbal.** Proclaiming, preaching, telling, advising, glossolalia, dream interpretation, storytelling (parable).
- **Writing.** Oracle, burden, letter, verse, song, history, apocalypse, allegory, collection of sayings or sermons.
- **Music.** Singing psalms and hymns with or without accompaniment
- **Demonstration.** Clothing, hair, countenance, eating and drinking (what and how much; see also 1 Corinthians 11:26), diorama, pantomime, symbolism, portrayal—all usually in conjunction with verbal prophecy.
- **Miracle (rare).** Miracles typically confirm the divine source of, or elucidate, verbal prophecy. Some miracles, however, can be considered prophecy in themselves, e.g., the ram substituted for Isaac (Genesis 22). See also the next section, 7, on miracles.
- **Acts and Events.** Typical of patriarchal prophets such as Noah and Abraham. See also Jonah (Matthew 12:40) and Abel (Hebrews 11:4; 12:24).

This topic will not be further developed or illustrated from Scripture here. The various styles of prophesying are amply described for the various prophets in chapters 3, 4, and 6. The historical development of prophecy styles is traced in chapter 7, "The Biblical History of Prophecy."

7. *Miracles of Prophets*

Prophecy itself is miraculous. That God should speak through men and women is as supernatural, incomprehensible, and wonderful as any healing of disease or parting of waters. Thus all prophets are God's agents of miracles. Many biblical prophets were also agents of physical miracles. In fact, prophets were the *only* human agents of miracles when God chose to involve human agents. Prophecy and other miracles go hand in hand.

Miracles are usually signs that validate prophets' words as being from God and that validate the prophets as being sent from God. This principle was clearly set forth for Moses:

> Then Moses answered and said, "But suppose they will not believe me or listen to my voice; suppose they say, 'The LORD has not appeared to you.'" So the LORD said to him, "What is that in your hand?" He said, "A rod." And He said, "Cast it on the ground." So he cast it on the ground, and it became a serpent; and Moses fled from it. Then the LORD said to Moses, "Reach out your hand and take it by the tail" (and he reached out his hand and caught it, and it became a rod in his hand), "that they may believe that the LORD God of their fathers, the God of Abraham, the God of Isaac, and the God of Jacob, has appeared to you." [A second miraculous sign was given.] "Then it will be, if they do not believe you, nor heed the message of the first sign, that they may believe the message of the latter sign." (Exodus 4:1–8)

And again, for Jesus,

> Rabbi, we know that You are a teacher come from God; for no one can do these signs that you do unless God is with him. (John 3:2)

Jesus Himself stated the following principle often:

> I told you, and you do not believe. The works [miracles] that I do in My Father's name, they bear witness of Me. (John 10:25)

> If I do not do the works [miracles] of My Father, do not believe Me; but if I do, though you do not believe Me, believe the works that you may know and believe that the Father is in Me, and I in Him. (John 10:37–38)

> Believe Me . . . or else believe Me for the sake of the works themselves. (John 14:11; see also John 5:36)

There are several CAUTIONS that must be kept in mind concerning prophets and miracles:

- CAUTION! Not all prophets worked miracles. Most notably, John, the baptizer, worked no miracle (John 10:41). No miracle other than that of prophesying is associated with most of the minor canonical prophets, Jonah excepted.

- CAUTION! Not all seeming miracles are from God. The magicians of Egypt were able to duplicate or counterfeit Moses's first three miracles (Exodus 7:1–12, 20, 22; 8:5–7). Later, in prophecy given through Moses, God acknowledged satanic "miracles" and warned His people about false prophets using them (Deuteronomy 13:1–5). Passing over other examples, we come to a New Testament magician, Simon Magus of Samaria, who had a great following, for he was able to astonish people with his sorcery (Acts 8:9–11). Jesus warned that counterfeit or godless miracles would continue (Matthew 7:22–23).

- CAUTION! The physical benefits of miracles can overshadow and undermine their purpose, which is to support prophecy. Many miracles in the Bible, in addition to being signs for prophecy, had very practical and salubrious results: healings, raisings from the dead, food for the hungry, military victories, etc. Therein lies a problem: People love and want the physical benefits, not the spiritual message and the responsibilities included in the message. They say, "If You [Jesus or any prophet] can heal one person, why not abolish disease, and we will suffer no discomfort? Give us bread and meat from loaves and fishes, and we won't have to work for it. Give us invincibility instead of just one military victory, and we won't have to fight." Jesus pinpointed this problem early in His earthly ministry. After the feeding of the five thousand, He said to the crowd of new "followers," "Most assuredly, I say to you, you seek Me, not because you saw the signs, but because you ate of the loaves and were filled" (John 6:26).

- CAUTION! The more the miracles, the more are expected. Miracles can become an end in themselves. People crave miracles, even signs that have no physical benefit. "What *else* can you do?" is our question, instead of "Who sent you?" or "What does that mean?" Once some scribes and Pharisees said to Jesus, "Teacher, we want to see a sign from You." He answered, "An evil and adulterous generation seeks after a sign" (Matthew 12:38–39). Paul wrote, "It pleased God through the foolishness of the message preached to save those who believe. For the Jews request a sign, . . . but we preach Christ crucified, to the Jews a stumbling block" (1 Corinthians 1:21–22).

8. *A Prophet's Reward*

> He who receives a prophet in the name of a prophet shall receive a prophet's reward. (Matthew 10:41)

What is this "prophet's reward" Jesus speaks of? He does not tell us, and we cannot know for certain. But we can glean from other Scriptures what are some prophet's rewards and what are not.

Material Rewards

When Jesus sent His disciples out on a preaching/healing mission He told them to accept food, drink, and lodging from friendly, worthy householders, "for the laborer is worthy of his wages" (Luke 10:7; Matthew 10:11). Paul insisted on the right of prophets to receive basic material sustenance from the church although he himself usually refused it (1 Corinthians 9:3–14; 1 Timothy 5:17–18). Elijah and Elisha both accepted hospitality from worthy women (1 Kings 17:8–9; 2 Kings 4:8–10); although in Elijah's case the woman was so poor that she was about to die of starvation, and God miraculously provided for her, her son, and Elijah. (This whole incident is a perfect physical example of Jesus's aphorism quoted at the beginning of this section.)

But Scripture is clear that no prophet should get wealthy by prophesying. The Holy Spirit is not for hire or sale (Acts 18:18–20). Yes, Solomon was an exceedingly rich prophet and some other prophets were "comfortable," but they did not gain their wealth from fees or gifts for prophesying. Moses refused to profit from his position as prophet-leader of Israel (Numbers 16:15). Samuel was equally circumspect about taking "rewards" of chattel or money (1 Samuel 12:3). Elisha refused a small fortune offered by Naaman (2 Kings 5:5, 15–16), and his greedy servant Gehazi was severely punished for attempting to take some of it (2 Kings 5:20–17). Paul, a Roman citizen (Acts 21:39), born into a family that could send him away to school (Acts 22:3), lived "poor" most of his life as a prophet, and did manual labor to earn his necessities (Acts 20:33–34). Jesus had virtually no earthly possessions, not even a shack or tent to lie down in (Luke 9:58).

Material "prophet's rewards," then, are limited to receiving basic necessities such as food, clothing, and shelter from willing and worthy people.

Rewards of Respect, Honor, and Esteem

There is usually a measure of man's honor and respect given to prophets except from the prophet's own countrymen and family (Mark 6:4). In fact, God has provided special protection for His prophet people in foreign lands (Psalm 105:13–15). But the disrespect shown by those nearest often overshadows foreign honors:

> But they mocked the messengers of God, despised His words, and scoffed at His prophets. (2 Chr. 36:16)

Elijah and Jeremiah are prime examples of this kind of ill-treatment. Jeremiah received respect and fairness only from Israel's archenemy Nebuchadnezzar (Jeremiah 39:11–12). However, there is honor and reward in being ridiculed and even persecuted. Jesus told His disciples,

> Blessed are you when they revile and persecute you, and say all kinds of evil against you falsely for My sake. Rejoice and be exceeding glad, for great is your reward in heaven, for so they persecuted the prophets who were before you. (Matthew 5:11–12)

First-brother James echoed Jesus's encouragement,

> My brethren, count it all joy when you fall into various trials. (James 1:2)

Paul took pleasure "in infirmities, in reproaches, in distresses, for Christ's sake" (2 Corinthians 12:10) and said, "We also glory in tribulations" (Romans 5:3), although he looked for a greater reward (Romans 8:18).

The Reward of Heaven?

Paul's last cited statement (Romans 8:18), and that of Jesus in Matthew 5:12, may lead us to surmise that the "prophet's reward" is heaven itself—eternal life. ASSUREDLY, THIS IS NOT SO! Everlasting life is the gift of God's sheer grace only; it is never a reward for good works, not even for such excellent work as prophesying. Jesus, anticipating this error, specifically excluded entrance into the kingdom of heaven as a reward for prophesying and miracle-working (Matthew 7:21–23). [Note that in Matthew 5:12 He promised not the reward *of* heaven, but a great reward *in* heaven.]

The Reward of Martyrdom?

Could it be that a prophet's ultimate reward in this earth is dying for his Master? This seemingly cruel irony might be suggested by the fact that so many prophets were indeed martyred—prophets both before and after Jesus (Luke 11:49; Matthew 23:34; Acts 7:52). In the vernacular of our own day we sometimes speak of the death of an evildoer as his "just reward." But a prophet? Surely not. God promised Jeremiah that He would *preserve* his life, even though this prophet suffered much (Jeremiah 15:20–21). And so He did, sparing Jeremiah from martyrdom several times. Moses, Joshua, Samuel, David, Daniel—none of these great prophets was martyred, though they all suffered. Jesus spoke of His own death as that of a prophet (Luke 13:33), but it was not His "reward." It was His agony, His unwanted cup, His obedient duty, and His greatest work. Praise Him! But He did not "deserve" it for prophesying.

Spiritual Rewards

Every fiducial prophet receives the exquisite rewards of knowing the Almighty God, fellowship with the Savior of mankind, and joy in the Holy Ghost—all by virtue of being a co-laborer with the Lord. What more reward could be asked for than to be used of God in such a special way? What greater satisfaction than to hear His "well done," or just to know that you have faithfully delivered His message? A great orator or writer may receive applause, fame, and fortune; but a prophet needs no such rewards. His are better. It is enough to be in communion and partnership with the living God and to receive, handle, and deliver His living word. The prophet Solomon once wrote, "Nothing is better for a man than that he should eat and drink, and that his soul enjoy good in his labor" (Ecclesiastes 2:24). That was written about common food, drink, and work. How much more satisfaction there is in eating the scroll of God's word (Revelation 10:10–11), imbibing of His Holy Spirit (Acts 2:15–17), and laboring to deliver His message (Acts 20:18–24)! The "prophet's reward" is in the business of prophesying, and above all in the nearness of God. And God only knows what more, what special rewards, are in store for those prophets He takes to heaven (Matthew 5:12).

Addendum

God's People as Prophets

There are two Scripture passages—one in the Old Testament, one in the New—that refer to God's chosen people, collectively, as prophets to the world. They are Psalm 105:15 and 1 Corinthians 11:26.

Kingdom of God
Earth Division
Job Description

Job Title: Prophet, Prophetess

Principal Duties:

- o Receive and communicate Employer's words to designated individuals, groups, nations, or peoples
- o Pray. In particular, pray (intercede) for those to whom Employer's word is communicated
- o Perform signs and miracles as directed and enabled by Employer
- o Other tasks and responsibilities as directed

Qualifications:

o Education	}	
o Previous employment	}	
o Skills	}	as determined by Employer,
o Age	}	can vary greatly
o Nationality	}	

Salary:

None. No tips, bribes, or gifts can be accepted. Basic subsistence is guaranteed, but employee may have to do menial work to get it.

Other Benefits:

- Filling of the Holy Spirit
- Report directly to King
- Fellowship with Prince
- Satisfaction in performing assigned duties
- Honors from foreigners
- Possible rewards in heaven

Opportunities for Advancement:

None. This is the top position in the Earth Division. Also, heaven cannot be gained by performing the duties of this office.

Job Hazards:

- Rejection, ridicule, and isolation from friends, neighbors, and family
- Persecution by civil authorities, including beatings, imprisonment, etc.
- Death by stoning, burning, crucifixion, etc.

How to Apply/Hiring Procedure:

- Applications not accepted. Jobholders were chosen before birth. However, inquiries may be made directly to King, as often as desired.
- Generally, hiring ("calling") is by conscription. New jobholders *will* be notified directly. Refusal is impossible.

Endnotes for Chapter 2

A. Although the gift of prophecy was widely distributed in the apostolic-era church, few such prophets are identified. Their number is unknown.

B. See chapter 7, "The Biblical History of Prophecy."

C. Psalm 45:7; Daniel 9:24; Habakkuk 3:13; Acts 4:27; 10:38

D. Isaiah 61:1 may have first referred to Isaiah but is here taken to refer to Jesus Christ.

Part II

Listings of Biblical Prophets With Biographical Sketches and Other Information

Chapter 3 The Named True Prophets

Chapter 4 Anonymous True Prophets
1. Individuals
2. Groups

Chapter 5 False Prophets

Note: Musical prophets are included in chapters 3 and 4 and are also listed in a different way in chapter 6.

Chapter 3

The Named True Prophets in Scripture (Alphabetical Order)

Headnotes

1. Prophets are given and numbered in alphabetical order. Alternative names and spellings of prophets' names are placed in alphabetical order, but are enclosed in brackets { } and are not given numbers.
2. Notes and extrabiblical references are indicated with numeric superscripts and are given at the end of the chapter.
3. **Boldface** is used the first time another prophet is named or mentioned in the write-up of the subject *prophet.* If a review of some aspect of that other prophet is suggested, "q.v." (which see) is added.
4. Dates are approximate. They are derived from several different sources which do not always agree. For more detail on dating see the appendix to chapter 7, "The Biblical History of Prophecy."
5. The criteria for inclusion of prophets in chapter 3 are

    - any person designated in Scripture as a prophet, seer, prophetess, or man of God
    - the authors of the books of the Bible known as "The Prophets," Isaiah through Malachi; these are the so-called canonical prophets
    - any author, if known, of any other book in Scripture, e.g., Luke (All Scripture communicates the word of God to man, which is the basic definition and function of prophecy. See chapter 1, "On Prophecy.")
    - any person who is said, in Scripture, to prophesy, or to have spoken "in," "by," or under the influence of the Holy Spirit, at least once; most persons included by this criterion alone are better known by some other title or function than "prophet"
    - any Levite "singer" who was duly ordained to prophesy according to 1 Chronicles 25:1–7, including those of later generations who performed the same service

    Angels are excluded.

Prophets

1. **Aaron**, as a prophet, was primarily a surrogate. According to Scripture he was the prophet of his younger brother **Moses**. But Moses was made "as God" to Pharaoh and also to Aaron (Ex. 7:1; 4:16). Therefore Aaron, as Moses's spokesman-prophet, was in fact God's prophet. He was also a prophet in his own right (Num. 12:1-2).

There is no other arrangement *exactly* like this in the Bible. However, there are other secondary or surrogate prophets in Scripture. **Elisha** sent one of his student-prophets to deliver prophecy to Jehu (2 Ki. 9:1-10)—prophecy that, in part, Elisha had gotten from *his* former mentor, **Elijah** (1 Ki. 19:15-16). Hundreds of Levite singers prophesied with the words of Psalms written by **David**, **Asaph**, and other primary prophets (1 Chr. 25). **Jesus** sent His disciples—first the twelve, then seventy others—to prophesy words He had given them (Luke 9:1-2, 60; 10:9). Oh yes, Jesus was God; but they, most of them, knew Him at that time only as a prophet (Luke 24:19), and themselves therefore as surrogate prophets.

Aaron, then, was both Moses's prophet and God's prophet. There were instances of God's speaking directly to Aaron alone (not through or with Moses) to give him instructions about his conduct as a priest—not to give him words to prophesy (Lev. 10:8-11; Num. 18:1, 8, 20) . Aaron also received the power to perform miracles attesting to the truth and divine origin of God's prophecy. Directions to use this power, however, also came through Moses (Ex. 7:8-10, 19; 8:5, 16).

It is not known exactly how long this God-to-prophet-to-prophet arrangement lasted, but there seems to have been a gradual lessening of Moses's reticence to speak and act for himself, and therefore a diminishing use of Aaron in these functions. Even while they were still in Egypt, the text has Moses sometimes speaking directly to Pharaoh and to the people of Israel (Ex. 8:29; 9:29; 10:9, 25, 29. 11:4; 12:21). This may, however, be Scripture shorthand: Aaron's role as spokesman being by now understood.

Scripture's wording of how, or through whom, the miracles in Egypt were performed also changes. The first sign to Pharaoh and the first three plagues were all worked through Aaron (Ex. 7:8-10, 19; 8:5, 16). No human agency is mentioned for the fourth, fifth, or tenth plagues; and Moses was the immediate agent of the sixth, seventh, eighth, and ninth plagues (Ex. 9:8, 22; 10:12, 21), as well as of the parting and the closing of the Red Sea (Ex. 14:21, 26). Aaron had a "hand" in the miraculous victory over the Amalekites (Ex. 17:11-13), but no other miracle in the wilderness is connected to him . In fact, Moses seems to have taken back the rod with which many miracles were triggered—the rod which was once entrusted to Aaron (Ex. 4:2-5, 17, 30; 7:8-10, 19; 8:5; 17:5-6).

However, even in the wilderness Moses still sometimes needed Aaron to speak for him (e.g., Ex. 16:9). And Aaron also went up Mount Sinai with Moses to receive the Law the first time, before it was written on stone tablets (Ex. 19:24-20:17).

[**Joshua** went up with Moses the time they stayed forty days and the first set of tablets was given, when Aaron was left in charge of the people and succumbed to apostasy (Ex. 24:13-32:35)]. Much of the book of Leviticus—almost all direct words of God—was given to "Moses and Aaron" (Lev. 11:1; 13:1). But after the Sinai encampment, Aaron is not again mentioned as Moses's spokesman prophet.

A major disruption in the Moses-Aaron tandem occurred at the camp of Hazeroth, not long out of Sinai. Aaron and sister **Miriam** became angry with Moses over his marriage to an Ethiopian woman, "So they said, 'Has the LORD indeed spoken only through Moses? Has He not spoken through us also?'" (Num. 11:35-12:2). God straightened out this family squabble, and in the process, He clarified His way of communicating to prophets (Num. 12:4-16). Later, however, God again spoke to Aaron, both to give him specific personal directions and, together with (not through) Moses, prophecy (Num. 16:20; 18:1, 8, 20; 19:1-2).

Aaron and his siblings, Miriam and Moses, were of the tribe (family) of Levi, of the Kohath branch (1 Chr. 6:1-3). They were all born in Egypt, where Aaron and Miriam lived for approximately eighty years as slaves. They came out in the great Exodus, ca. 1450 BC. We know nothing of the life of Aaron until he was over eighty years old (Ex. 7:7), when he began to prophesy as Moses's spokesman. Within a year out of Egypt, God chose Aaron and his sons to be priests in His new creation, the nation-church Israel (Ex. 28:1 with 40:17). As high priest, Aaron was given a special way to prophesy: the Urim (and the Thummim?) on the breastplate of the ephod he wore (Ex. 28:30; Lev. 8:8). There is no record of Aaron's actual use of this oracular device although we must not rule it out.

Aaron served as high priest for nearly forty years. He died on Mount Hor in the wilderness at the age of one hundred twenty-three (Num. 33:38-39). His death was remarkable, to say the least: for God revealed the exact time and place beforehand. The text does not say how he died, but it may have been natural. The nation mourned for him thirty days (Num. 20:22-29).

2. **Abda**, also known as Obadiah (Obadiah II in this list) was a leading Levite who lived in Jerusalem after the return from Babylon of the first large party of Jews, ca. 537 BC (Neh. 11:17; 1 Chr.9:16). Abda was a direct descendent of the great musical prophet **Jeduthun** (q.v.). He is mentioned in Scripture along with **Mattaniah III** and **Bakbukiah**, both musical prophets (q.v. each). Because of these associations Abda is assumed to have been a musical prophet, one of the more than one hundred singers who celebrated the completion of the foundation of the new temple "with cymbals, to praise the LORD, according to the ordinance of **David** king of Israel" (Ez. 2:41; 3:10-11; 1 Chr. 25:1-7). Some of the words of their prophecy were,

> For He is good,
> For His mercy endures forever toward Israel. (See "The Great Refrain," pages 267-69)

3. **Abel** was the first prophet. Yes, Abel, the second son of Adam and Eve, murdered by his older brother Cain, was a prophet. He might not be recognized as a prophet at all were it not for the testimony of our Lord **Jesus** (Luke 11:50-51; Matt. 23:34-35). Abel's prophecy, according to an apostle, was this: "By faith Abel offered to God a more excellent sacrifice than Cain, through which he obtained witness that he was righteous, God testifying of his gifts; *and through it he being dead still speaks*" (Heb. 11:4). Yes, and he "speaks," ultimately, of Christ's offering of His own blood. In addition to prophesying through the blood of the firstborn of his sheep (Gen. 4:4, 10), Abel's own blood "speaks" to us from the ground (Heb. 12:24).

4. **Abraham** is the first person in the Bible to be identified by the title "prophet" in his own time (Gen. 20:7). God Himself gave Abraham this new and mysterious title. Even more interesting is the fact that God considered *intercession*—not proclamation—the defining characteristic of this prophet. In the episode at hand Abraham was not bearing a message from God to man, but was bearing one from man to God (Gen. 20:17).

Intercession was a hallmark of Abraham's entire prophetic ministry. Besides interceding for Abimelech, he interceded for wicked Sodom, pleading with God to spare that city from destruction for the sake of a few righteous persons he supposed to be in it (Gen. 18:16-33). [In the denouement only Lot was righteous, and only he and his daughters were saved (Gen. 19).] Earlier, Abraham (then Abram) had interceded for Lot by executing a daring military rescue of his nephew from captivity by Cherdolamer, et al (Gen. 14). This is not depicted as a spiritual victory, but it had to be a miracle because of the small number and lack of military training of Abram's "army." And Melchizedek correctly attributed the victory to God (Gen. 14:20).

But intercession was not the only aspect of Abraham's work as a prophet. He received many messages from God; and he must have told someone, or written them down, else we would not have them in the Bible (Gen. 12:1-3; 15; 17:1-22; 18; 22:1-2, 15-18) . Also, Abraham publicly *called on the name of the Lord* (Gen. 12:8; 13:4; 21:33). But most of all, Abraham spoke (prophesied) by acts of faith, like the righteous **Abel** (q.v.). And, like Abel, he prophesied of **Jesus** Christ; for example, when he offered up his "only begotten"[1] son as a sacrifice for sin, being convinced that God was able to raise him up from the dead (Heb. 11:17-19). Abraham, by example, prophesied a message of faith (Rom. 4; Heb. 11:8-10).

David regarded Abraham as a prophet (1 Chr. 16:7, 16, 22).

Abraham lived about two thousand years before Christ. He was born in Ur (lower Mesopotamia). He emigrated to Haran (upper Mesopotamia) with his father Terah, wife Sarai (Sarah), and nephew Lot. After Terah died there, Abraham was told by God to move on "to a land that I will show you" (Canaan). This he did, taking along Sarai, Lot, and their "people" (servants). Abraham was seventy-five years old. Because of a famine in Canaan, they did not stay long, this time, but continued on to Egypt. Returning to the land God had promised him, Abraham stayed in Canaan most of the rest of his long life; but he moved about and was always a sojourner, owning very little property. He died at the age of one hundred seventy-five (Gen. 11:26-25:10). Within this framework, quite a few details of Abraham's life are given in Scripture, especially his visions and visits from God. These episodes and visions—although the latter were not proclaimed in the manner of later prophets—form the corpus of Abraham's prophecy.

{Abram—**Abraham**}

5. **Agabus** is one of the few true prophets of the apostolic era who is both identified by name and titled a prophet. He is best known for foretelling actual events in the near future. He traveled considerable distances to bring these messages to just the right people. His two recorded predictions were of a great famine, and of **Paul's** arrest and imprisonment (Acts 11:28; 21:10-11).

6. **Agur** "uttered" the words of Proverbs 30. Verse four is particularly prophetic of Christ. Nothing else is known of Agur.

7. **Ahijah** announced God's decision to divide Israel into two kingdoms after the end of **Solomon's** reign, ca. 930 BC. He personally told Jeroboam, in both word and demonstration, that he would succeed Solomon as king of the ten northern tribes of Israel (1 Ki. 11:29-39).

In spite of this favor with God at the beginning of his reign, Jeroboam became corrupt. Years later, he did not even want to face Ahijah. So when Jeroboam's son became gravely ill and Jeroboam wanted desperately to inquire of God about him, no doubt to seek His mercy, he sent his wife to the prophet Ahijah—in disguise! By this time Ahijah was old and nearly blind, so they might have gotten away with it. But God revealed the ruse to Ahijah. When the queen walked in the door, Ahijah called her by name, and gave her more prophecy than she had come for: not only would her son die, Ahijah also prophesied the demise of the sinful house of Jeroboam (1 Ki. 14:1-18; 15:29-30).

Ahijah, who lived in Shiloh, also wrote prophecy about Solomon and possibly about Jeroboam (2 Chr. 9:29). His writings are not extant.

> Ahitophel NOTE: "Now the advice of Ahitophel, which he gave in those days, was as if one had inquired at the oracle of God. So was all the advice of Ahitophel both with **David** and with Absalom" (2 Sam. 16:23). Taken alone, this verse strongly suggests that Ahitophel was a true prophet, although the words "as if"

warn us that he may not have been. Ahitophel was a trusted privy counselor to David. But his treasonous defection to Absalom, his wicked advice to him, and his ultimate suicide (2 Sam. 15:12; 16:15, 20-22; 17:1-4, 2-3), militate against him being classified as a true prophet of God; although we must remember that evil men like **Balaam** (q.v.) did prophesy God's word. Ahitophel is not numbered among the prophets here, on the basis of the qualifying "as if" and for want of any true prophecy of his, identified as such.

8. **Amasai**, a "chief of captains" (major?) in **Saul's** army, defected to **David** and his army, ca. 1010 BC. At the moment of decision he spoke in the Spirit prophesying of David's righteous ascendency (1 Chr. 12:16-18).

9. **Amos** was a farmer from Tekoa, Judah, whom God specially called, prepared, and sent north, into Israel, to prophesy (Amos 1:1; 7:14-15). He prophesied during the reign of Israel's King Jeroboam II (793–753 BC). He not only wrote the book of Amos, but he also preached at Bethel.

Amos had five visions from God that he recorded: 1. a plague of locusts devastating Israel (7:1); 2. destruction by fire (7:4); 3. the Lord on a wall with a plumb line signifying judgment by His true standard (7:7); 4. a basket of summer fruit, signifying the end of Israel's season (8:1); and 5. the Lord standing by the altar pronouncing sentence on Israel (9:1). After each of the first two of these visions Amos, so characteristically of a good prophet, interceded for Israel, calling them by their nonpolitical name Jacob (7:2-3, 5-6). They were not of his own political nation, Judah, but they were part of God's chosen people. Both times that Amos interceded, God heard his prayers and relented of those disasters; but Israel must be punished.

Besides these visions, Amos preached and/or recorded in his book numerous direct messages or oracles from God. The first two chapters of his book are a single sermon consisting of eight "Thus says the LORD" statements (1:3, 6, 9, 11, 13; 2:1, 4, 6). Although the main subject of this sermon was Israel, God also dealt in it with seven surrounding nations including Judah. Amos continued to emphasize that he was proclaiming God's word throughout the book (3:1, 10, 11, 12; 5:3, 4, 16; 6:8; 9:1).

Amos encountered hostile resistance when he preached at Bethel. Bethel had been one of the main centers of idolatrous worship in the northern kingdom, Israel, ever since its founding by Jeroboam I [930–909 BC] (1 Ki. 12:28-33). Amaziah, a priest there, first reported Amos's "conspiring" to the king (Amos 7:10-11). Israel was at that time prosperous and had become politically prominent under Jeroboam II. Therefore Amos's message of God's displeasure and judgment, and of Israel's impending demise and captivity, was very unwelcome in Bethel. After reporting him to the king, Amaziah next tried to intimidate Amos and send him home. But Amos turned the tables on Amaziah and prophesied of God's severe judgment on him and his family (Amos 7:12-17).

Although he humbly thought of himself as a rustic farmhand, Amos was very knowledgeable about Israel's history and God's law, and he was a skilled writer. There are many memorable passages in Amos. Two that are invaluable to our understanding of biblical prophets, and prophecy, are,

> 3:7 Surely the Lord GOD does nothing,
> Unless He reveals His secret to His servants the prophets.

> 3:8b The Lord GOD has spoken!
> Who can but prophesy?

10. **Ananias**, a devout Jew and a disciple (follower) of **Jesus**, who lived in Damascus, prophesied to and about Saul (**Paul**) after receiving a vision from God and after being used to restore the apostle's eyesight (Acts 9:10-19; 22:12-16).

11. **Andrew** was one of **Jesus's** twelve original disciples who prophesied and performed healing miracles when they were sent out through the towns of Galilee and/or Judea (Luke 9:1-6; Mark 6:7-13; Matt. 10:1-8). They went in pairs, Andrew probably with his brother Simon **Peter**. Andrew was also one of the apostles who prophesied in foreign languages on a Pentecost morning in Jerusalem (Acts 2); and who "with great power . . . gave witness to the resurrection of the Lord Jesus" (Acts 4:33). Although Andrew is not named in the book of Acts beyond being listed with the disciple/apostles (Acts 1:13), or in any of the epistles of the New Testament, it is almost universally believed that he, like all of the other apostles, had an ongoing ministry of gospel prophesying. Mr. Foxe says that Andrew preached the gospel to many Asiatic nations and was crucified in Edessa, a town in Mesopotamia.[2]

Before he met Jesus, Andrew was a disciple of **John I**, the baptizer. While he was with John in Judea, upon seeing Jesus and hearing John call Him the Lamb of God, Andrew and another disciple decided to "follow" Jesus literally: to spend some time with Him, observing and hearing Him. Andrew found his brother Simon (Peter) and brought him to meet Jesus too (John 1:35-42). Jesus did not call them to follow Him as disciples until some time later, in Galilee (Matt. 4:18-20). At that time Andrew lived with Peter and his family in Capernaum (Mark 1:21, 29). They had earlier lived in Bethsaida (John 1:44). Both towns were on the Sea of Galilee.

Andrew was a "go-between" disciple who specialized in introducing people to Jesus: first, his brother; then a lad with a lunch; and also "certain Greeks" (John 1:41-42; 6:8; 12:20-22). As an apostle, we do not know what his style of prophesying was other than the one instance of glossolalia on Pentecost.

12. **Anna** was a long-term prophetess who served God with fasting and prayers night and day in the temple at Jerusalem. She was there, at age 84, when **Joseph III**

and **Mary** came to present **Jesus** to God and to offer the required atoning sacrifice for Mary forty days after childbirth. Anna bore witness to Jesus as redeemer (Luke 2:36-38). Along with **Simeon I** and **John I**, the baptizer, she was among the last Old Testament prophets.

13. **Apollos** was a gospel prophet in the times of the apostles, ca. AD 40–65. He was a powerful orator, very well-versed in the Scriptures of the Old Testament, fervent in spirit, and, when we first meet him, "instructed in the way of the Lord," yet not completely (Acts 18:24-25). We do not know how he learned about **Jesus**, or if he ever met Him. Apollos was a Jew born in Alexandria, Egypt.

Apollos had become a traveling preacher, apparently independent of **Paul**, **Barnabas**, and their sending church at Antioch. He happened to come to Ephesus just after Paul's first, brief, visit there (Acts 18:19-21). After Appolos preached in the synagogue, Priscilla and Aquila, a Christian couple who had come to Ephesus with Paul and had stayed there, took him aside, and "explained to him the way of God more accurately" (Acts 18:26-28). What he already knew and preached was edifying, but something—we do not know exactly what—was lacking. Apollos "knew only the baptism of John" (**John I**, the baptizer). That would be a baptism of repentance, with a cleansing from sin, but without the regeneration worked by the Holy Spirit (cf. John I). John the baptizer died before Jesus's death, resurrection, ascension, and the pouring out of His Holy Spirit. All of this suggests the intriguing possibility that Apollos had been a disciple of John.

Whatever had been lacking in Apollos's sermons (and heart?), it was corrected at Ephesus. He went on to become a great prophet of and for Jesus (Acts 18:27-19:1). Leaving Ephesus, Apollos went to Corinth, where he was soon regarded as the equal—and, unfortunately, the rival—of Paul and **Peter**. Paul later had to deal with this sectarianism (1 Cor. 1:12; 3:4-6, 22). It was not the fault of Apollos, but of the Corinthians themselves, that they divided into the Paul, Peter, and Apollos parties. In fact, Paul urged Apollos to go back to Corinth right away, but he was unwilling (1 Cor. 16:12). Possibly, he was committed to go elsewhere.

The last we read of Apollos was about eight years later. He was in Crete with **Titus**, still working for the Lord Jesus. And like so many prophets, he had not acquired wealth, but was in need of material support (Tit. 3:13).

14. **Asaph** is one of the leading musical prophets in Scripture. He was a Levite descended through Gershon. Asaph served as one of the three principal prophetic singers under **David** (1 Chr. 6:31-42; 15:16-19; 25:1-7). He also played the cymbals (1 Chr. 16:4-7). Many of his progeny served as musical prophets—even as late as the days of **Nehemiah** over five hundred years later! (2 Chr. 5:12; Neh. 11:17)

Asaph wrote twelve of the biblical psalms (50, 73-83). His credentials as a prophet are established by the appellation "Asaph the seer" (2 Chr. 29:30), by the phrase "Asaph, who prophesied . . ." (1 Chr. 25:2), and by his psalms. When one of his psalms is quoted in the New Testament, it is attributed to "the prophet" (Matt:13:35). Even **Jesus** quoted him (John 10:34).

Asaph was assigned the singular honor and important duty of ministering before the ark of the LORD in Jerusalem as the leader of eight other musicians while **Ethan** and **Heman** were dispatched to lead choruses in Gibeon before the original (Mosaic) tabernacle and altar (1 Chr. 16:4-5, 37-42).

15. **Asharelah**, also called Jesharelah, was a Levite musical prophet who was appointed leader of the seventh section of **David's** 288-man tabernacle choir/orchestra(s). His father was **Asaph**. Asharelah was one of the sons "who should prophesy with harps, stringed instruments, and cymbals" as well as leading a twelve-man section (1 Chr. 25:1, 2, 14).

{Azarel I—**Uzziel II**}

16. **Azarel II** was a member of a prophesying choir that was involved in the dedication of the new Jerusalem wall built under the leadership of **Nehemiah**, ca. 445 BC (Neh. 12:31-46) His choir was led by **Ezra** and used "the musical instruments of **David** the man of God" (and no doubt some of David's psalms, i.e., prophecy). As a leading Levite musician of his time, Azarel probably also served in the standing temple choir/orchestra which prophesied "according to the command of David and **Solomon** his son" (Neh. 12:45-46 [cf. 1 Chr. 25:1-7]).

17. **Azariah** was a very common Hebrew name. More than twenty-five different men in Scripture had this name. Only one, however, was a prophet. This Azariah successfully led a major reformation and covenant renewal in about 900 BC. He called upon Asa, the third king of Judah, and the people of the tribes of Judah and Benjamin to put away idols and return to the true God. They did! Even many people from the neighboring tribes in Israel, especially Ephraim, Manassah, and Simeon, came over to Asa's kingdom to join the reformation (2 Chr. 15:1-15).

18. **Azaziah** was one of the nineteen Levite musicians selected to help escort the ark of the covenant of God from Obed-Edom's house to the tabernacle prepared for it by **David** in Jerusalem (1 Chr. 15:21). He was, therefore, very likely among the 288 members of the permanent choir/orchestra(s), which definitely prophesied (1 Chr. 25). Azaziah played the octave (eight-string) harp, or lyre, tuned to (or according to, or on) Sheminith, a musical term.

{Aziel—**Jaaziel**}

{Bakbakkar—**Bakbukiah**?} (Compare 1 Chronicles 9:15 with Nehemiah 11:17)

19. **Bakbukiah** was one of the three leaders of the Levite musician-prophets ("singers") in the first large group of Jews who returned to Judah from captivity in Babylonia in about 537 BC (Neh. 12:8-9). These 148 (Neh. 7:44) or 128 (Ez. 2:41) singers were organized into two or three choirs that "stood across from" one another, apparently to sing antiphonally. At the celebration of the completion of the foundation of the new temple, they sang "according to the ordinance of **David**" (Ez. 3:10)—definitely prophesying (1 Chr. 25:1-7). Bakbukiah lived in Jerusalem (Neh. 11:1, 17).

20. **Balaam** is one of the most challenging prophets to categorize, let alone to understand. Scripture leaves no doubt that he was an evil, mercenary, false prophet (2 Pet. 2:15; Jude 11; Rev. 2:14); but the only actual prophecies of his that are recorded in Scripture are true! Indeed, he is often quoted in Christian print and pulpit, e.g., "God is not a man, that He should lie, nor a son of man, that He should repent. Has He said, and will He not do? Or has He spoken, and will He not make it good?" (Num. 23:19). Balaam even prophesied of **Jesus** Christ: "I see Him, but not now; I behold Him, but not near; a Star shall come out of Jacob; a Scepter shall rise out of Israel, and batter the brow of Moab, and destroy all the sons of tumult." (Num. 24:17). Yet the man who uttered these God-given words was the archetypical false prophet who "loved the wages of unrighteousness," taught others to sin for his own worldly gain, and was justly executed by an Israelite army under **Moses** (2 Pet. 2:15; Num. 31:8, 16).

In the world of his day, Balaam was much more than a third-rate fortune-teller from an obscure country who just happened to cross Israel's path as they advanced toward the promised land. He was world-renowned, as evidenced by King Balak's decision to summon him from a great distance and at great expense (Num. 22:5). He held a large part of the civilized world in thrall, as they believed that his curse or blessing would guarantee defeat or victory (Num. 22:6). Most importantly, his teachings were widely held. These were implicated in the affair of Peor, to Israel's great shame and harm (Num. 25, 31:16). When Jesus said (through **John II**) that Balaam "taught Balak to put a stumbling block before the children of Israel" (Rev. 2:14), He was not referring to the episode of Numbers 22–24 and Balaam's prophecies there, but to Numbers 25, the Peor affair, and Balaam's wicked doctrines including idolatry and sexual promiscuity. Balaam accumulated power and wealth by means of his unrighteous teachings. He was a "great man" on the world scene.

Balaam used sorcery and is called a diviner and a soothsayer (Num. 24:1; 22:7; Josh. 13:22). Given this, and his overall wickedness, the hardest things to understand about him are that

- o Balaam knew and respected God (Num. 22:18),
- o God spoke to Balaam (Num. 22:9, 12), and

- o God chose the wicked Balaam to reveal His words of true prophecy (Num. 23:7-10, 18-24; 24:3-9, 15-24).

We are led by the Holy Spirit to ascribe this to God's sovereignty. Just when we think we know all of His ways and, in this case, means, God surprises us and humbles our minds. Ask **Job**. A delightful parable of this is imbedded in the story about Balaam's commission to curse Israel, and God's compelling him to bless them instead. It is the donkey. Yes, just as God can make a dumb ass speak to an intelligent man (Num. 22:22-30), He can make a wicked false prophet speak His divine words of truth to a chosen people.

21. **Barnabas** is a nickname meaning "son of encouragement" given by the Apostles to a Jewish Levite Christian named Joses, from Cyprus (Acts 4:36). He is best known as the Apostle **Paul's** sponsor, friend, and missionary partner (Acts 9:26-27; 11:25-26; 12:25-13:3).

Barnabas was an important leader in the first Christian church, the one in Jerusalem. He was dispatched from there to Antioch, in Syria, to investigate the preaching of the gospel to a group of "outsiders" (Hellenists) in the new church there (Acts 11:22). While he was in Antioch, Barnabas and four others were known as "prophets and teachers" (Acts 13:1). Whether some of these were prophets and others were teachers, or some or all of them were both, is not clear in the translations. But there is other evidence that Barnabas was a prophet. He was "full of the Holy Spirit" (Acts 11:24); and he preached the gospel, along with Paul, on their first missionary journey (Acts 13:43, 46; 15:35). Barnabas's spiritual gifts clearly included giving (Acts 4:37), exhortation (4:36), apostleship 14:14), and miracles (14:3; 15:12). It seems likely that the Holy Spirit also equipped him with the gift of prophecy, especially for his missionary work. He did, after all, lead a mission trip to Cyprus, his native land, without Paul (Acts 15:39).

It is surprising, therefore, and a bit disappointing, that no writing, sermon, or prophecy in any form, specifically attributed to Barnabas alone, can be found in Scripture. The same can be said, however, about most of the original apostles, all of whom were prophets (q.v. each).

{Barsabas—**Judas IV**}

22. **Bartholomew** was one of **Jesus's** twelve disciples and one of His first eleven apostles (Matt 10:2-4; Acts 1:13). He is believed to be the same person called Nathanael in **John's** gospel.[3] As a disciple he prophesied a message given him by Jesus and performed miracles of healing, on a mission to the villages of Galilee and/or Judea (Matt. 10:1-3, 7; Mark 6:7-13). As an apostle he prophesied miraculously on a Pentecost morning and later within the assembly of believers (Acts 2:1-18; 4:32-33). He undoubtedly continued to prophesy about Jesus Christ in obedience

to Jesus's command and commission (Mark 16:14-15; Acts 1:8). Mr. Foxe writes that Bartholomew carried the gospel to India and translated the Gospel of Matthew into their language, but was eventually beaten and crucified by idolators.[4]

Nathanael (Bartholomew) was one of the first disciples of Jesus and one of the last to see Him in His resurrected body (John 1:43-51; 21:1-2). He was from the town of Cana in Galilee, which *may* explain his disdain for the nearby (and smaller?) village of Nazareth. Jesus immediately recognized him as an honest, if prejudiced, Israelite. In this first encounter, Nathanael at first was skeptical of **Philip's** claim that Jesus was the One of whom Moses and the other prophets had written, but he soon recognized Jesus as the Son of God and King of Israel.

23. **Benaiah** prophesied through music in the days of King **David**. He was one of those nineteen musicians (including David) who marched the ark of the covenant of the LORD from the house of Obed-Edom to the new tabernacle prepared for it in Jerusalem. Benaiah not only played the harp or lyre "according to Alamoth," he was also a priest who blew a trumpet, and a gatekeeper (1 Chr. 15:16-18, 20, 24).

After the ark was installed, Benaiah was one of the eight musicians under **Asaph** the seer who was permanently assigned to minister before the ark, daily. He also blew his trumpet there as a priest (1 Chr. 16:4-6, 37). As a member of this group, Benaiah participated in the premier performance of David's psalm of thanksgiving which first contained the "great refrain" [see pages 267-69] (1 Chr. 16:7-36, see vs. 34).

24. **Bukkiah** was one of the Levites "who should prophesy with harps, stringed instruments, and cymbals" and "who were instructed in the songs of the LORD" in the days of King **David** (1 Chr. 25:1-7, 13). He was a son of **Heman** and therefore a great-grandson of **Samuel** (1 Chr. 6:33). Bukkiah led the sixth twelve-man section of David's 288-man chorus. His name means "mouth of Jah."

25. **Caiaphas** was the Jewish High Priest who, in a trial before the Sanhedrin, was instrumental in "convicting" **Jesus** of capital blasphemy (Matt. 26:57-66). Thus, he helped fulfill his own prophecy that Jesus would die for the Judean nation and for the children of God scattered abroad (John 11:45-52). This account of Caiaphas's prophesying indicates that high priests were still, by virtue of their office, invested with prophetic powers. In the Old Testament this was true, through the use of the Urim and Thummim (the Lights and the Perfections) on the breastplate of the ephod (Ex. 28:30; Num. 27:21; 1 Sam. 30:7-8; Ezra 2:63). We do not know if Caiaphas used this device.

Difficult as it is to believe that such a man as Caiaphas could prophesy (speak for God) truthfully, we must accept it as infallible Scripture; remembering that King **Saul** prophesied even while he was seeking to murder **David** (1 Sam. 19:

20-24), and that the arch false prophet **Balaam** was compelled to speak God's words (Num. 23, 24).

26. **Chenaniah** (Kenaniah) was so skilled at music that he was put in charge of **Heman**, **Asaph**, **Jeduthun** (Ethan), and the others (including **David**) who sang and played as the ark of the covenant of the LORD was moved to the new tabernacle prepared for it in Jerusalem (1 Chr. 15:16, 22). Because he instructed and directed these illustrious prophets in the art of prophesying musically, Chenaniah is included in this listing of Bible prophets.

Apparently, Chenaniah's music-prophecy career was cut short, for his name does not appear again in this capacity, not even among the leaders of David's 288 tabernacle singers. A possible explanation for this is that David found him indispensable for other duties: a man with the same name, also a Levite (of the Izharites), and at the same time, was put in charge of civil affairs for Israel outside of Jerusalem (1 Chr. 26:29).

27. **Daniel** is one of the four major canonical prophets. The biblical book bearing his name contains both historical narrative and prophecy. Daniel's prophecies are primarily interpretations of symbolic dreams and visions. They are almost entirely predictive, with very little said about the sinfulness and infidelity of God's people or about judgment, punishment, repentance, or even God's mercy. Empire simply follows empire, ruler supplants ruler, until the Messiah finally is to come. Undoubtedly this was largely because Daniel prophesied at a time when Israel was already *being* punished—the nation defeated and disbanded, the temple and city of Jerusalem destroyed, the people captives in a foreign land. Hope and direction for the future, not doom, came from God through Daniel. His prophecies concerning the rise and fall of world empires and rulers, from his own time until Jesus Christ's, are unparalleled in Scripture. It is often said that the voice of God was silent (in terms of new revelation) for about four hundred years from **Malachi** until the birth of **Jesus** and the appearance of prophets like **Anna**, **Simeon**, and **John I** the baptizer. But thanks to the book of Daniel, and only this book, God was not silent *about* this intertestamental period.

Born a Jewish noble, Daniel was captured as a youth by the Chaldeans who were conquering Judah. He was taken to Babylon where he spent most of his long illustrious life. While remaining faithful to God and the Jewish religion, Daniel nevertheless submitted to the Babylonian king in general education and in civil affairs (Dan. 1, 2). He so distinguished himself that he quickly rose to one of the highest positions in Nebuchadnezzar's administration (Dan. 2:48).

Daniel was extraordinarily wise and righteous. **Ezekiel**, a contemporary, counted Daniel as one of the three most righteous men in history (Ezek. 14:14, 20). But even higher honors and accolades came to him. While Daniel was praying very earnestly about his own sin and Israel's, the angel Gabriel was sent to him personally and told Daniel that he was greatly beloved by God (Dan. 9:20-23). Still greater honor came when Jesus quoted from the book of Daniel, validated Daniel as a prophet, adopted Daniel's Messianic appellation "Son of Man," and promised to fulfill Daniel's prophecy to come back "with the clouds of heaven" (Matt. 24:16, 30; 26:64/cf. Dan. 7:13).

Daniel's life was punctuated with unforgettable adventures and miracles. While still a youth in training, he saved his and others' lives by telling, and then interpreting, Nebuchadnezzar's dream about a succession of images representing world empires (Dan. 2). In another dream interpretation, Daniel foretold Nebuchadnezzar's fantastic worldly power and glory, his insanity and humiliation, and his recovery and restoration (Dan. 4). Perhaps the best-known episode in Daniel's life, however, was when his life was miraculously preserved by God in a den of hungry lions where he had been cast for execution (Dan. 6:1-23). What is not commonly known about this episode is that Daniel was then a very old man of about ninety—not the handsome youth we see in Bible pictures!

28. **David** is best known as a hero, a king, a psalmist, a performing musician, and a forerunner of Christ both biologically and spiritually. Less known is the fact that he was a prophet—indeed, one of the foremost prophets. David himself was well aware of his prophetic gift (2 Sam. 23:2). But it was not until a thousand years after his death that David was actually called a prophet in the Bible. **Matthew**, quoting from David's Psalm 22, says it was "spoken by the prophet" (Matt. 27:35). And **Peter**, in his famous speech on the Day of Pentecost fifty days after Jesus's resurrection, explicitly says that David was a prophet (Acts 2:29-31). There are many other New Testament references to, or quotations of, psalms of David as prophecy, including some by **Jesus** Himself (e.g., Acts 1:16; Mark 12:36).

David was a prophet in life and deed; a prophet in word, especially psalm words; a prophet to himself; a musical prophet; and a patron of many prophets.

In life, David prophesied as a type and forerunner of Christ. Some examples are his zeal:

- for God (Ps. 63:1)
- for God's word (Ps. 19:7-11)
- for God's house (Ps. 69:9; 122)
- for God's people (Ps. 25:22)

David's glorious kingdom prophesied of Christ's much more glorious kingdom, although only as a worldly type (Ps. 2:6; 21:1-7). Some other ways that David's life prefigured that of Jesus were his total reliance on God (1 Sam. 17:37; 2 Sam. 15:25-26), his humiliation and suffering (2 Sam. 15:30; 16:5-8), and his return and restoration after what seemed to be final defeat at the hands of his own people, who turned against him (2 Sam. 15-19). Of course, David was but a man, a fallen and sinful man, but nevertheless a man after God's own heart (1 Sam. 13:14; Acts 13:22), who God used as much as any other man, in life as well as in word, to point the way toward His own Son.

As a writing prophet, David authored at least seventy-five of the psalms in the Book of Psalms. Because they are all part of the inspired word of God, it can be said that all of these psalms are prophecy. Some of them that are the most clearly prophetic of Christ are the eighth (Heb. 2:6-9), the sixteenth, which was quoted by Peter on Pentecost Day (Acts 2:29-31), the twenty-second, which prophesies of Jesus's suffering on the cross (Matt. 27:35, 39, 46), the sixty-eighth concerning Christ's ascension and His giving the gifts of the Holy Spirit (Eph. 4:7-8), and the hundred-tenth which was quoted by our Lord Himself as well as by some of the apostles (Luke 20:41-44).

On several occasions David acted as his own prophet-advisor, seeking and then acting upon God's word in matters of war and in other important decisions (1 Sam. 23:1-13; 30:7ff; 2 Sam.2:1-3; 5:19-20; 21:1). It might be argued that this was prayer, not prophecy; or, that Abiathar was the prophet on at least two of these occasions. However, by analogy with other kings and other prophets (2 Ki. 19:1-7; 1 Ki. 22:9), one gets the sense that the process was just as if God had sent another prophet to David, except David acted as both prophet and king.

But David as king and king-elect was far from being independent or heedless of other prophets. The first of these was of course **Samuel** (1 Sam. 16:13; 19:18). Two of them, **Gad** and **Nathan**, were official "court" prophets; but they were hardly the soothsayers and "yes-men" that most court prophets became to later kings. Gad, who prophesied to David both early and late in David's career and was called "David's seer" (1 Sam. 22:5; 2 Sam. 24:11), apparently kept his distance from the king more than Nathan did. Nevertheless Nathan (2 Sam. 7:2) stunned the sinner-king with his famous "Thou art the man" (2 Sam. 12:7). Apparently David recognized the need to have at least one true prophet of God in his cabinet as a check on his enormous political power and on spiritual presumption.

In addition to writing prophetic songs, David was a performing musical prophet. He calmed **Saul's** evil spirit (1 Sam. 16:23); played music, sang, and danced before the ark of the covenant of God as it was being moved (2 Sam. 6:5, 14, 21); and he may have sometimes conducted his prophesying choir and orchestra in Jerusalem (1 Chr. 25). David even made (invented, manufactured, developed, or dedicated) certain musical instruments for praising God (1 Chr. 23:5; 2 Chr. 7:6).

David promoted and developed the gift of musical prophecy in others, and he organized choirs and orchestras to present it (1 Chr. 6:31-47; 15; 25). Under David, prophesying was first introduced into the formal worship of God—in the form of music, psalms. Preaching, as a form of prophesying in formal worship, followed musical prophesying by at least several centuries! When David was old and about to turn over the kingdom to **Solomon**, there were four thousand Levites who praised God musically (1 Chr. 23:1-5).

29. **Deborah** was already a prophetess when she became the fourth Judge of the theocracy of Israel (Judg. 4:4-5). God gave her revelation that Israel should go to war against their Canaanite oppressors and would be victorious (Judg. 4:6-7. So great was her influence over the nation that Israel's military commander in chief, Barak, refused to go to war without her (Judg. 4:8). Although women just did *not* go into the battlefield, Deborah did agree to go; but she prophesied that a woman, not Barak, would have the glory of the victory (Judg. 4:9). In the denouement she proved to be right on every count.

Deborah, like many other prophets, was also a musician. Her celebratory lay (Judg. 5), which she sang with Barak, is not labeled as God-given prophecy, but it closely resembles **Miriam's** song (Ex. 15:21) and several Psalms.

30. **Eldad** was one of the two elders of Israel in the wilderness (the other being **Medad**) who, for some unknown reason, stayed in the camp while **Moses** took seventy other elders to the tabernacle of meeting to receive the Holy Spirit so that they could help Moses bear the burden of government. The seventy prophesied while at the tabernacle, probably as a sign of having received the Spirit, and Eldad (and Medad) prophesied too, in the camp. This was reported to Moses. **Joshua**, Moses's assistant, thought it was improper, and asked Moses to forbid the two from prophesying. But Moses was pleased, saying, "Oh, that all the LORD's people were prophets" (Num. 11:16-30).

31. **Eleazar**, the second high priest of Israel, was also a prophet—usually a surrogate one like his father **Aaron** (q.v.). During the years after Aaron's death and before **Moses's** death, Eleazar worked closely with Moses in leading Israel by God's word (Num. 31:12-32:28). God spoke to Eleazar along with Moses, and together they prophesied and carried out His commands (Num. 26:1-4). Eleazar acted as Moses's spokesman, just as his father had done (Num. 31:21-24). And Eleazar was commissioned to prophesy for **Joshua**, Moses's successor, specifically by using the Urim on the high priest's breastplate (Num. 27:18-21).

Eleazar was the third son of Aaron and his wife Elisheba (Ex. 6:23). His two older brothers, Nadab and Abihu, died as a result of profaning God's worship, probably while they were drunk (Lev. 10:1-3, 8-11). Eleazar and his younger brother Ithamar narrowly escaped a similar fate after they disobeyed God's ordinance for priests, omitting a duty, but Aaron interceded for them and they were saved (Lev. 10:12-20). Later, Eleazar was given additional responsibilities, including the oversight of all the leaders of the Levites in charge of the sanctuary (Num. 3:32). When Korah and two hundred and fifty other men of Israel challenged Moses's and Aaron's authority, and the Levites among them tried to usurp the priesthood, they were summarily dispatched by God; and Eleazar was chosen by God to gather the rebels' golden incense censers and have them beaten into a cover for the altar as an enduring reminder of the results of such rebellion (Num. 16:1-40).

It is a singular thing that Eleazar, rather than Aaron, was chosen by God for the "red heifer" rite of purification (Num. 19:1-10).

Eleazar was inaugurated high priest as his father was dying on Mount Hor in the wilderness near Kadesh (Num. 20:22-29). He served in that capacity during the remaining time of Moses and during the entire period of Joshua's leadership of Israel. He helped Joshua divide the land of Canaan among the tribes of Israel, prophesying God's will for this by the use of lots (Josh. 14:1-2; 19:51; 21:1-8). Eleazar died shortly after Joshua died (Josh. 24:29-33).

32. **Eliab** was one of the nineteen Levite musicians selected to help escort the ark of the covenant of God to the tabernacle in Jerusalem which **David** had prepared for it (1 Chr. 15:18-20). He then ministered before the ark in Jerusalem under **Asaph** the seer (1 Chr. 16:4-5, 37). It is probable that this musical group was part of the 288 Levite musicians "Who should prophesy with harps, stringed instruments, and cymbals" (1 Chr. 25:1). Eliab played a stringed instrument "according to Alamoth."

33. **Eliashib** was a singer in Jerusalem in about 455 BC. He was the only singer among the 113 Jews who at that time were found guilty of, and repented of, having pagan wives (Ezra 10:24). His designation as a prophet rests on the assumptions that he took part in the praise-prophesying "according to the ordinance of David" (1 Chr. 25:1) at the laying of the temple foundation (Ezra 4:10-11), and/or that he was a member of the permanent prophesying choir in the new temple (Neh. 12:45-46).

34. **Eliathah** was a Levite who was chosen by lot to lead the twentieth twelve-man section of **David's** 288-man chorus/orchestra (1 Chr. 25:4, 27). He was one of **Heman's** fourteen sons "who should prophesy with harps, stringed instruments, and cymbals," and who "were instructed in the songs of the LORD" (1 Chr. 25:1, 7). Eliathah was a great-grandson of the prophet **Samuel** (1 Chr. 6:33).

35. **Eliezer** prophesied about a great naval disaster that was brought on by an unholy alliance. In about 852 BC, Jehoshaphat, generally a "good" king of Judah, allied himself with the wicked King Ahaziah of Israel to build ships at Ezion Geber (on the Gulf of Aqaba). The vessels were probably "ships of Tarshish"—a class of merchant ships, rather than "ships to go to Tarshish" as some translations say.[5] These were to go to Ophir, on the Red Sea, to get gold. God disapproved of Jehoshaphat's alliance with the idolatrous son of Ahab and Jezebel. The ships all sank while still in Ezion Geber harbor, fulfilling God's word through Eliezer His prophet (2 Chr. 20:35-37). King Ahaziah tried to revive the project, but Jehoshaphat, now wiser, refused (1 Ki. 22:48-49).

Eliezer was the son of Dodavah of Mareshah—the hometown of the prophet **Micah** a century later, when it was spelled Moresheth. Eliezer was a contemporary of **Elijah**, **Micaiah**, **Jahaziel**, and possibly **Elisha**.

36. **Elijah** is one of the most famous prophets and, indeed, one of the best-known characters of the Bible. He was a man of great contrasts and conflict. To many of us Elijah is almost a caricature of a prophet: rough-hewn, long-bearded, stern, fearless, unwavering, incredibly holy, and a powerful worker of miracles. He called down fire from heaven, stopped and started the rain, and restored human life. Yet Scripture says he had a nature just like ours (James 5:17). He ran away to save his own skin—and then prayed to die (1 Ki. 19:3-4). He became discouraged, despondent, and bitter (1 Ki. 19:10). In personal relationships he antagonized kings, mocked rivals, and was abrupt with even his closest allies (1 Ki. 18:17-18, 27; 19:20). Yet his great love for others shows through. He is revered today by nearly all Christians and Jews.

Elijah was from a small place in Gilead, a part of the Kingdom of Israel east of the Jordan River (1 Ki. 17:1). He appears suddenly on the scene of history. Nothing is known of his family, his preparation, or his call. He prophesied in and to the northern kingdom (Israel) during the wicked, idolatrous reigns of Ahab and his wife Jezebel (874–853 BC), and of Ahab's son Ahaziah (874–852 BC). Elijah lived on into the reign of another of Ahab's sons, Jehoram. King Jehoshaphat reigned in Judah throughout this time. Jehoshaphat was a good king, but his son, also named Jehoram, drew Elijah's attention, wrath, and a letter of rebuke and dire prophecy (2 Chr. 21:12-15).

Contemporary prophets included **Micaiah** in Israel; **Jehu**, **Jahaziel**, and **Eliezer** in Judah; and a number of other significant, but anonymous, prophets. Interestingly, Elijah's name is never linked with any of them. Elijah anointed and trained **Elisha**, who served under him about ten years and then succeeded him (1 Ki. 19:19-21; 2 Ki. 2).

More miracles are associated with Elijah than with any other prophet before him except **Moses**, or after him except Elisha, **Jesus**, and **Paul**. Elijah's miracles include

1. a three-year drought, "at my word," said Elijah (1 Ki. 17:1; Jas. 5:17)
2. ravens bringing Elijah his necessary food (1 Ki. 17:6)
3. unlimited flour and oil supplied to a widow at Zarephath (17:16)
4. the widow's son brought back from death to life (17:22)
5. fire from heaven consumes the sacrifice (and the firewood, altar stones, dust, and water) on Mount Carmel in the sight of 850 rival prophets of Baal and Asherah and other spectators (18:38)
6. the drought is broken when Elijah prays (18:41-45; Jas. 5:18)
7. oven-fresh cake and a jar of water are provided to Elijah by an angel of God in the wilderness (1 Ki. 19:6).
8. this meal of cake and water, taken twice, sustains Elijah forty days and nights in the wilderness (19:8).
9. fire from heaven consumes two platoons of fifty-one men each, who were sent to arrest Elijah (2 Ki. 1:10-12).
10. the Jordan River parts to let Elijah and Elisha cross over (2:8).

11. horses and chariots of fire appear, as a whirlwind takes Elijah to heaven without a natural death (2:11).

In many of these signs and wonders we can see Elijah as a "type" of Jesus Christ. Indeed, miracles are a major part of his prophecies pointing to Christ:

- the inexhaustible food supply for hungry people
- the restoration of a dead child's life
- being ministered to by angels in the wilderness
- surviving in the wilderness forty days without food

Jesus forbade His disciples to replicate another Elijah miracle: consuming some inhospitable Samaritans with fire from heaven, "just as Elijah did," in the disciples' own words (Luke 9:54-55).

But it was not primarily Jesus of whom Elijah was a type and forerunner. It was **John I**, the baptizer. Jesus Himself said as much (Matt. 11:13-14; 17:11-13). Rugged, unshaven, reclusive, bombastic, stern, finger-in-the-face-of-evil-rulers, outlaw, persecuted by a wicked queen, anointing (or baptizing) his Successor—these were all characteristics and experiences of John.

Elijah's recorded verbal prophecies (1 Ki. 17:1, 14; 18:41; 21:19-24; 2 Ki. 1:3-4, 15-16; 2:10) and the one written prophecy that is preserved in Scripture (2 Chr. 21:12-15) are brief, and not obviously Messianic. Most of them are rebukes of kings (Ahab and Ahaziah of Israel, Jehoram of Judah), predictions about their deaths, and foretelling near-term events. Elijah prophesied principally with his life and miracles, not with his pen, orations, or music.

Elijah believed that his (God's) victory over 450 prophets of Baal on Mount Carmel would turn the nation back to God. This was achieved, but only temporarily (1 Ki. 18:37-39). Even the welcome relief of the drought, and Ahab's spurious repentance, failed to convince or convert Jezebel, who turned public opinion back against Elijah and God. She said that his executing the prophets of Baal was a crime, not what it really was: justice. Elijah became a fugitive once again, disillusioned, despondent, and bitter. He thought his life and career as a prophet were over, but they were not. God nursed him, chastened him (like **Job**), and gave him a new mission (1 Ki. 19). Elijah would once again confront wicked kings and prophesy (1 Ki. 21:17-19; 2 Ki. 1:3-4). He would again call down fire from heaven (2 Ki. 1:10, 12). He would anoint and train a successor, Elisha, and through him anoint other kings (1 Ki. 19:15-16; 2 Ki. 8:13; 9:1-10).

Then, as a signal honor from God for his life, work, and faith, Elijah was transported to heaven without a normal death—one of only two persons in the Bible (the other being Enoch) thus taken up by God (2 Ki. 2:11; Gen. 5:24).

Elijah remains a man of mystery and contradiction. Despite his incredible faith and victories for God, his efforts to turn the nation Israel from Baal worship back to God worship failed. His successor Elisha was more effective. Elijah's prophecies, as we have them, were mostly condemnations and predictions of terrible, painful deaths. They were not seemingly Messianic. He left no written oracle, no psalm—just one short letter. In life he typified John more than Jesus. Yet God honored him above all other prophets and almost all men by his miraculous entrance into heaven and by his recognition as "The Chariot of Israel and its Horsemen." And even greater than this was Elijah's honor of representing, along with **Moses**, all the Old Testament prophets and prophecy at the glorious transfiguration of our Lord, Jesus Christ (Luke 9:28-36; Matt. 17:1-13; Mark 9:2-13). Perhaps Elijah's unique ascension into heaven was one reason for this; for Moses also had a mysterious death and a more mysterious burial (Deut. 34:5-6). Jesus, on the mount, was talking to Moses and Elijah about His impending departure from this world (Luke 9:31).

The prophet **Malachi**, in the very last verses of the Old Testament, prophesied that Elijah would return (Mal. 4:5-6). He did—in the person of John I, the baptizer, who didn't know it and even denied it (Matt. 11:14; Mark 9:11-13; Luke 1:17; John 1:21).

Sadly, even today, the Jews in their temporary blindness of mind (Rom. 11:25) expect Elijah's return, placing a chair for him at their ceremonies, hoping that every male Jewish baby born might be him. Excepting Moses, no prophet is more honored by Jews; and, excepting Jesus, by many Christians.

37. **Elipheleh** was a Levite singer-harpist-prophet, one of the nineteen musicians selected to help escort the ark of the covenant of God from Obed-Edom's house to the tent (tabernacle) prepared for it in Jerusalem by **David** (1 Chr. 15:18, 21). Elipheleh was very likely among the 288 members of the permanent tabernacle chorus. He is listed as a prophet by analogy and extrapolation from that group, who were trained to prophesy with music (1 Chr. 25:1-7). Elipheleh played the eight-string harp, or lyre, "on the Sheminith."

{Elisius—**Elisha**}

38. **Elisha** was one of the last of the great non-writing, heroic prophets of the Kingdom Period of Israel. He was raised to be a farmer in Abel-Meholah, a place in Gilead close to **Elijah's** hometown of Tishbe. His father was a wealthy farmer (twelve yoke of oxen!), but Elisha dramatically renounced his occupation and inheritance when he was called by Elijah to be that prophet's understudy—and servant (1 Ki. 19:16, 19-21). But Elisha's ministry, his style, and his times were much different from Elijah's, though both came to be called "the chariot(s) of Israel and its (their) horsemen" (2 Ki. 2:12; 13:14).

Elisha is one of many Old Testament "types" of **Jesus** Christ, but none is more closely identified with our Lord. Their names, Elisha and Jesus, both mean "God

Saves." Their forerunners, Elijah and **John I**, the baptizer, were very similar in message and style; Jesus even identified John as "the Elijah who was to come" (Matt. 11:14). Both cured men of leprosy (2 Ki. 5; Matt. 8:1-4). On another occasion, Jesus actually referred to Elisha's curing Naaman (Luke 4:27). Other miracles wrought through Elisha were remarkably parallel to some of Jesus's:

- Elisha purified a city water supply and made other water look red in color; Jesus turned water into wine (2 Ki. 2:19-22; 3:22; Jn. 2:1-11).
- Both restored a dead boy to life—at or very near the same, exact place!– Shunem (2 Ki. 4:8, 32-37); Nain (Luke 7:11-17).
- Both fed a large crowd of men using only a few loaves of barley bread, and with plenty left over. Both used servants (disciples) to distribute the food. And when Jesus performed this miracle, men in the crowd recognized the prophet connection, saying, "This is truly the Prophet . . ." (2 Ki. 4:42-44; Jn. 6:1-14).

Elisha was even more closely connected with Elijah. He was handpicked, by God, to succeed that Great One (1 Ki. 19:15-16). Elisha completed Elijah's mission in some very specific ways, particularly the anointing of Jehu to be King of Israel and of Hazael to be King of Syria (2 Ki. 8:13; 9:1-3). Some of Elisha's miracles were almost carbon copies of Elijah's:

- Parting the waters of the Jordan River. This miracle actually manifested their spiritual continuity (2 Ki. 2:8, 14).
- Providing abundant oil to a poor widow (1 Ki. 17:16; 2 Ki. 4:1-7).
- Restoring a dead boy—each the only son of his mother—to life (1 Ki. 17:17-24; 2 Ki. 4:17-37). There is a strong inference that the mother in Elisha's case expected him to do it because she knew what Elijah had done.
- Elisha was the agent of at least sixteen miracles. Many of them were "humanitarian" in nature, such as healing (leprosy, blindness), purifying (water, poison stew), feeding and providing basic necessities (bread, oil), and restoring lost property (axe head). After Elisha's death, God used his very bones to restore life to another corpse (2 Ki. 13:20-21).

Like Elijah and other prophets of their times, Elisha prophesied principally with miracles and other acts, and accurate short-term predictions, not writings. If Elijah was the more heroic and confrontational of the two, Elisha was the more versatile and, well, "likeable"—and often more effective. Elisha used music (2 Ki. 3:15). He frequently involved others in his ministry, such as distributing the bread, gathering things, and even sending a student prophet to anoint a king (2 Ki. 4:43; 2:20; 4:3; 9:1). He made a mistake in his choice of Gehazi as his first servant/ intern, but he was extremely patient with Gehazi's failures (2 Ki. 4:11—5:27).

Elisha frequently visited the schools, or monasteries, of the "sons of the prophets" to teach and train. He probably helped Elijah found these institutions. [Just decades before, during Elijah's early ministry, all the prophets of God were murdered or driven into hiding. (1 Ki. 18:4).] Whereas Elijah had been an outlaw and a fugitive, Elisha enjoyed relatively more freedom, acceptance, and respect from the state (2 Ki. 4:13). More than once he helped King Jehoram of Israel in military crises (2 Ki. 3; 6:8-12). But when Elisha delayed intervening to lift the brutal siege of Samaria, (a judgment from God) he quickly became Jehoram's enemy (2 Ki. 6:31).

To crown his distinguished career, Elisha—the farm boy from the "other" side of the Jordan, the manservant of the great Elijah, the personable humanitarian prophet of God, and the teacher and friend of many young prophets—this Elisha became a world leader, grasping and turning the very wheel of history. He alone knew of, and probably prayed for, the great victory over Syria when all seemed lost. It was Elisha God used to put into motion His plans for justice, setting up new regimes in Israel, Syria, and Judah; and destroying forever the wicked dynasty of Ahab/Omri (2 Ki. 6-10). Truly, Elisha deserved the title, in plural form, which he himself had accorded to his master Elijah: "The chariots of Israel and their horsemen" (2 Ki. 2:12; 13:14).

Somehow, still, Elisha remains forever in the shadow of his onetime master Elijah, but from that shadow a strong light shines forward on his eternal Master, Jesus.

39. **Elizabeth** prophesied about **Jesus** while she was pregnant with **John I** (the baptizer), just when she heard her cousin **Mary** greet her (Luke 1:41-45). Later, Elizabeth faithfully revealed God's word as given to her husband, when she named her son John (Luke 1:13, 59-60).

40. **Enoch** headed the seventh generation of mankind. He "walked with God" and was a prophet (Gen. 5:19-24; Jude 14-15). The Book, *1 Enoch,* from which **Jude** quotes is considered apocryphal; but Jude is canonical and thus validates both Enoch as a prophet and this particular prophecy of Enoch's. Also, the fact that Enoch did not die a natural death but was taken to heaven by God—an honor given to only one other man, the prophet **Elijah**—militates strongly in favor of his prophethood (Heb. 11:5-6).

> Enosh—NOTE: Enosh, Adam's grandson, is mentioned in chapter 7, "The Biblical History of Prophecy," as a *possible* prophet because in his days "men began to call on the name of the Lord" (Gen. 4:26). It would appear that Enosh was one of those men. But there is no clear evidence that "calling on the name of the Lord" meant prophesying. Enosh is not counted here as a prophet.

{Esaias—**Elijah**}

{Ethan—**Jeduthun**}

41. **Ezekiel** is one of the four major prophets in the Scripture canon. He was a priest (Ezek. 1:3), but was deprived of this office by his capture and deportation from Jerusalem to Babylon in 597 BC, along with about ten thousand others (2 Ki. 24:14-16). He was preceded to Babylon by a smaller, select group of Jews, including **Daniel**, nine years earlier (Dan. 1:1-7). Left behind in Jerusalem was a third great contemporary prophet, **Jeremiah**. It is noteworthy that three of the four major prophets in Scripture prophesied during the captivity.

Ezekiel was probably about twenty-five years old when he was taken into captivity. He was thirty when he received his first prophetic vision and call "in the fifth year of Jehoiachin's captivity" (Ezek. 1:2-3), 592 BC. About seven years after his call, Ezekiel's wife died. He was forbidden by God to publicly mourn or weep for her, as a sign and example for the exiled Jews to follow when, a short time later, God's temple in Jerusalem, "The desire of your eyes, the delight of your soul," would be destroyed (Ezek. 24:15-24). We do not know how long Ezekiel lived, or where and how he died although Jewish tradition says he was put to death by the exiles in Babylon by being dragged upon the stones until his brains were dashed out.[6]

Many Christians consider Ezekiel's visions to be bizarre and his writings to be difficult. In the introduction to his commentary on Ezekiel, Matthew Henry states that "the Jewish rabbin forbade the reading of (Ezekiel) to their young men, till they came to be thirty years of age, lest by the difficulties they met with there they should be prejudiced against the scriptures."[6] Henry further observes, "Though the visions here be intricate, such as an elephant may swim in, yet the sermons are mostly plain, such as a lamb may wade in." Actually, Ezekiel's book is methodical, organized, and prosaic compared to most of the writing prophets. He carefully dates his visions and prophecies, to the day. Most are in chronological order. Less than a third of the book is in poetic form. Ezekiel uses parables, proverbs, and plain talk. His visions are carefully documented and painstakingly reported.

More than any other prophet, Ezekiel used symbolic actions and visual aids to deliver and/or to illustrate his prophecies. Some of this was necessary because God struck Ezekiel mute for a long time (Ezek. 3:26-27; 33:21-22). Often these demonstrations caused him pain, both physical and emotional. We have already mentioned his God-ordered stoicism when his young wife died. Earlier, he symbolically (not actually, as did **Jesus**) bore the iniquities of Israel and Judah by lying on his left side 390 days and on his right side forty days, a day for each year of their respective unfaithfulness to God (Ezek. 4:4-7). During all this time Ezekiel was bound with ropes (Ezek. 4:8; cf. 3:25?) and was nutritionally sustained only by a measured daily ration of 0.6 liters (about 3 glasses) of water and 220 grams (perhaps seven hundred calories) of bread, cooked over a dung fire (Ezek. 4:9-15). He also had to shave off his hair and beard (Ezek. 5:1-4). Truly, Ezekiel lived and felt, in his own body as well as his soul, the word he preached.

Ezekiel was usually addressed by God in visions as "son of man," meaning "human" and emphasizing his frailty and insignificance. This is not the same way

Daniel used the same title, "son of man," to designate Christ (Dan. 7:13). Ezekiel was humble, and honored his contemporary prophet Daniel above almost all other men of God in history (Ezek. 14:14, 20). But Ezekiel was respected by the elders in his own community, who often met at his house to inquire of God (Ezek. 8:1; 14:1; 20:1).

There are striking similarities in certain visions of Ezekiel and **John II** in the book of Revelation. These similarities are because they saw the same things, not because John copied or even was inspired by reading Ezekiel; for John clearly states, "I looked" and "I saw" (Rev. 4:1ff). Thus John validates the accuracy of Ezekiel's visions: they are true scenes of heavenly things.

In addition to the magnificent apocalypse of "living creatures" and the throne of God (seen later by John), Ezekiel's inspired pen gives us many familiar metaphors and figures: the prophet as a watchman, "sour grapes," "standing in the gap," the irresponsible shepherds, the valley of "dry bones," the river of healing waters flowing from God's temple, and "showers of blessing," to name several.

Ezekiel unabashedly juxtaposes God's sovereign, irresistible will (e.g. chapters 25–32) with man's individual responsibility (e.g. chapters 18, 33). To many minds this may seem to be an antinomy; but Ezekiel is right to hold both principles to be true, as taught throughout the Bible. Ezekiel's last, longest, and probably least understood prophetic vision was of a new temple, a new city (Jerusalem), and a new state (Israel) [Ezek. 40-48]. At first reading this appears to be God's blueprint for the new earthly Kingdom of Israel, in its restoration after Babylonian captivity—similar to His plan for the first tabernacle, given to **Moses**, and His division of the land of Canaan by lot. But Ezekiel's vision was never realized or even approached by the returning exiles under Zerubbabel, **Nehemiah**, and others. Many theologians have therefore (and for textual reasons also) concluded that this long passage in Ezekiel is a symbolic description of an ideal, heavenly kingdom. But why, then, the detailed dimensions and directions? We submit that Ezekiel's temple and its environs and its regulations remain, perhaps forever, suspended between heaven and earth—not unlike Ezekiel himself, "standing in the gap."

42. **Ezra** was a priest, a scribe, a teacher, and a national leader during the restoration of the people of Israel to the land of Judah after the Babylonian captivity (Ezra 7: 1-6, 10, 12, 28b; 8:15, 21, 24). The office of prophet may also be ascribed to Ezra purely on the basis of his authorship of a portion of God's written inspired word. He also prayed (interceded) to God for his people, part of a prophet's calling (Ezra 9:5-15); he preached (Ezra 10:10-11); and he sang in a prophesying chorus assembled by **Nehemiah** to celebrate and dedicate the new wall around Jerusalem (Neh. 12:33, 36).

Ezra led a group of about 1,750 men, plus women and children, from Babylon to Jerusalem in 458 BC—eighty years after the first large exodus of about fifty thousand persons had come, and a little while before Nehemiah came to rebuild the walls of Jerusalem and to govern the province (Ezra 7, 8). Ezra was a brilliant man, a priest and a scribe with an extraordinary allotment of spiritual gifts including teaching, leadership, and prophecy. He had a deep reverence for God's written word, and when he learned that many of the Jews had intermarried with pagans—disobeying God's Law—he was so disturbed that he pulled hair out of his head and beard, sat down astonished, and prayed for God's mercy (Ezra 9). Then he fasted and mourned, called a national convocation, and preached to all of the people in the open courtyard of the temple during a heavy downpour. There was great repentance (Ezra 10).

On another occasion Ezra read the Law of God to a large assembly of men, women, and children. Other priests and Levites also read, taught, and interpreted the Law, and a great revival broke out (Neh. 8:1-12).

43. **Gad** is known to us as a prophet to **David** and as a historian of David's deeds (1 Chr. 29:29). It is not unreasonable to surmise that he had a wider ministry, for he first appears as a full-fledged prophet when David was still young, a fugitive from Saul (1 Sam. 22:5). Gad did affiliate himself closely with David, and he might even be called a court prophet, for he is later designated "David's seer" (2 Sam. 24:11). But Gad was anything but a yes-man or a soothsayer to the king. His recorded prophecies as "David's seer" were to offer David, from God, a choice of punishments for a wrongful deed (2 Sam. 24:11-13) and to give David a message from an angel of the LORD to build an altar of sacrifice on a certain threshing floor (2 Sam. 24:18)—*which would become the site of the temple of* ***Solomon*** (2 Chr. 3:1).

44. **Gedeliah** was a Levite who prophesied with music as leader of the second twelve-man section of **David's** 288-man choir/orchestra. Gedeliah was one of **Jeduthun's** sons "who should prophesy with harps, stringed instruments, and cymbals" (1 Chr. 25:1, 3, 9).

45. **Giddalti** was another of those Levites in **David's** tabernacle choir/orchestra "who should prophesy with harps, stringed instruments, and cymbals" (1 Chr. 25:1, 4, 29). His father was **Heman**, his great-grandfather was **Samuel** (1 Chr. 6:33), and he led the twenty-second twelve-man section.

46. **Gilalai** was one of the "sons of **Asaph**" in the first of two large thanksgiving choirs that marched on top of the newly rebuilt wall of Jerusalem to celebrate its completion in about 445 BC (Neh. 12:36). It is assumed that Gilalai went on to become a member of the standing temple choir/orchestra which was patterned after the original "in the days of **David** and Asaph" (Neh. 12:45-46) and which, therefore, prophesied with music (1 Chr. 25:1).

47. **Habakkuk** is one of the "minor prophets" in the Old Testament canon. His importance is hardly minor, however. Just one fragment from his book, "But the

just shall live by his faith" (Hab. 2:4) has had a *major* influence on the apostle **Paul** (Romans 1:17), another apostle (Hebrews 10:37–38), Martin Luther, William Tyndale, and, through them and many others, almost all of Christendom.

Habakkuk lived and wrote near the end of the seventh century BC (see "The Writing Prophets" in chapter 7). It was one of the worst times in Israel/Judah's history. The many years of sins of her kings, nobles, priests, and people—sins from idolatry to injustice to plundering, violence, and drunkenness—were about to receive God's wrath. He was raising up Nebuchadnezzar of Babylon to be His rod of chastisement. Habakkuk was deeply troubled by God's apparent indifference toward His people's sufferings and His apparent tolerance of wicked, treacherous, cruel, godless nations like Assyria and Babylonia. This prophet's written dialogue with God is reminiscent of **Job's**, only much shorter. The denouement is also similar, with Habakkuk regaining his confidence in God, expressed in prayer and song.

Habakkuk was a musical prophet. Psalm-like directions are given at both the beginning and the end of the third chapter. Another verse (Hab. 2:20) is often sung in churches. He meant to have his prophecy sung by the Temple Choir, accompanied by "my" stringed instruments (Hab. 3:19)—indicating that Habakkuk was an accomplished musician whose original orchestrations were different from those of **David**, **Heman**, **Asaph**, and **Jeduthun**.

48. **Haggai** was a writing prophet and also a tireless encourager of the Jews who were rebuilding the temple in Jerusalem in 520–515 BC (Ezra 5:1-2; 6:14). His ministry is closely linked with that of the prophet **Zechariah**. They had the same mission and worked as a team. The setting for their mission was this: The people who returned from Babylonian captivity in about 537 BC had immediately built a new altar and started to offer burnt offerings to the LORD. They also began collecting money and materials for the temple, and in a year had laid its foundation (Ezra 3). But opposition arose from the surrounding peoples, and the project was shut down (Ezra 4). After about fifteen years, God sent Haggai and Zechariah to spearhead the completion of the temple (Ezra 5:1-2), which was accomplished in less than five years (Ezra 4:24 and 6:15).

Haggai's written messages from God were precisely dated and addressed (Hag. 1:1, 13; 2:1-2, 20-21). They all came in the space of just four months in 520 BC, kicking off the temple project restart. They were addressed to the king-governor, Zerubbabel; to the high priest, Joshua; and to all the people. The results were startling: within twenty-three days, work on the temple was resumed in earnest (Hag. 1:12-15).

Three months later God, through Haggai, warned the priests that the people doing the work must be pure and undefiled ceremonially. Because they weren't, God was withholding material blessings, but "from this day forward" He would bless them (Hag. 2:10-19).

Haggai also wrote, with strong Messianic overtones, about future glory for the temple and for Zerubbabel (Hag. 2:6-9, 20-23).

49. **Hanan** was a "man of God," one of Scripture's synonyms for prophet. His father was named Igdaliah. Hanan's sons, in about 605 BC, kept or lodged in one of the chambers attached to the temple in Jerusalem (Jer. 35:4). This is all that is known of him.

Some of the chambers, which were part of the original temple construction, were used for lodging Levite singer-prophets (1 Ki. 6:5; 1 Chr. 9:33). Thus Hanan's sons, and Hanan himself, may have been musical prophets.

50. **Hanani I** was one of the twenty-four Levites each appointed to lead a twelve-man section of the original tabernacle choir (ca. 1000 BC) "who should prophesy with harps, stringed instruments, and cymbals . . . in the songs of the LORD" [psalms] (1 Chr. 25:1, 4, 7, 25). He was a son of **Heman**, "the king's seer in the words of God" (1 Chr. 25:5) and a great-grandson of **Samuel** (1 Chr. 6:33). Hanani led the eighteenth course, or section, of musical prophesiers.

51. **Hanani II** was a seer who got thrown into prison for telling one of Judah's *best* kings that he had made one big mistake. King Asa, **Solomon's** great-grandson, was a strong and good king for most of his reign. He believed in God, listened to God's prophets, and carried out many reforms. Judah enjoyed peace and prosperity for thirty-four years—so much that even many people from the larger northern kingdom, Israel, came over to join Judah (2 Chr. 15). But when the king of Israel made trouble for Judah in about 873 BC, Asa turned to Syria instead of to God for help. It was a crucial mistake and amounted to spiritual apostasy since Asa knew better. God sent Hanani the seer to pronounce His judgment against Asa who became furious and imprisoned the prophet. As Hanani predicted, Asa's last five years were miserable: He was plagued with war, oppression, and disease (2 Chr. 16).

We don't know what became of Hanani. He was the father of another prophet, **Jehu** (q.v.), who was called by God to perform a similar duty (bringing a message of disapproval) toward Jehoshaphat, Asa's son and successor (2 Chr. 19:1-2).

52. **Hanani III** was in one of the great thanksgiving choirs that celebrated, "with the musical instruments of **David** the man of God," the completion of the rebuilt wall around Jerusalem in about 445 BC (Neh. 12:36, 45-46). He is assumed to have also been appointed to the temple choir/orchestra which was ordained "according to the command of David and **Solomon** his son," and which therefore (1 Chr. 25:1-7) prophesied in song.

53. **Hananiah**, a son of **Heman** "the king's seer in the words of God," led the sixteenth section of the original, 288-man tabernacle choir/orchestra appointed by

David and his captains to "prophesy with harps, stringed instruments, and cymbals . . . in the songs of the LORD" [psalms] (1 Chr. 25:1, 4, 5, 7, 23). Hananiah's great-grandfather was **Samuel** (1 Chr. 6:33).

54. **Hannah**, the mother of the great prophet **Samuel**, was a prophetess in her own right. This fact is clearly established by the content of her second prayer (1 Sam. 2: 1-10). Just how important a prophetess she was can easily be lost in her motherhood and/or her exemplary faith in God. Hannah has been, for good reason, the subject of thousands of Mothers' Day sermons and lessons in churches where this special day is observed. Her reliance upon God alone, plus her follow-through on vows made to God (1 Sam. 1), are sources of inspiration for both men and women.

But Hannah's actual prophecy, and her possibly important role in Israel's history (beyond being the mother of one of its most famous prophets), are frequently minimized or overlooked. These should not be overlooked, because certain details of her prophecy and of her first prayer are difficult to reconcile with a concept of Hannah as merely a simple, faithful mother.

In her prayer begging for a son, Hannah addresses God as "LORD of hosts" (1 Sam. 1:11). Where did she get *that*? This is a title for God as the Commander of armies in warfare, including angel-armies. Hannah is the first[7] prophet to use this title—one that is much used by later (but perhaps not greater?) prophets such as **Isaiah**, **Jeremiah**, **Zechariah**, and **Malachi**—as in, "the LORD of hosts musters the army for battle" (Isa. 13:4), one example of many such uses. Why would Hannah address God as the Commander of armies in her request to open the womb of one obscure woman? Would this take an army?

Then, we go on to her prayer-prophecy (1 Sam. 2:1-10), delivered (and, we suppose, written) well after her request for a son was granted. The first three verses are all praise, worship, and thanksgiving—with just a tinge of justified gloating? But beginning in verse four, and culminating in the cosmic victory of God in verse ten, we are shown a sovereign God engaged in warfare against the mighty of the earth and the forces and effects of evil, such as poverty and oppression. Finally, in the greatest surprise of all, Hannah alludes to an anointed king! But Israel had not yet had a king, and would not have one until Hannah's then grown son would anoint and commission **Saul**. Was God revealing through Hannah, His prophetess, much more than His ability to give children to the barren and to answer faithful prayers?

When reading this entire episode, 1:1 through 2:10, some may tend to be doubtful, even dismissive, of Hannah's prophetic office. There are several ways to deal with her second prayer and her way of addressing God in her first prayer.

1. *These passages and phrases were added to the historical narrative by the writer of 1 Samuel (or even a later editor), a "real" prophet. Hannah herself was after all "just" a mother who believed fervently in God.* This view is an easy "out," but there is no warrant for it except our own incredulity.

2. *Hannah was a "robotic" prophetess who simply said (and/or wrote) words dictated by God, without understanding it or involving her own will.* This view is sometimes held about prophets and Bible writers in general! We reject it.
3. *Hannah had "inklings," or even revelations, about her son's future and very important role in Israel's destiny. Her prayer reflected these inklings. In this respect she had much in common with* ***Elizabeth, Mary****, and Mrs. Manoah, Samson's mother. These latter three all had visions from heaven concerning their unborn sons (****John I, Jesus****, and Samson). The same cannot be said of Hannah, except by analogy and inference. For example, Hannah's vow that Samuel would be raised a Nazirite may have been a condition imposed by God during a vision, as it was for Mrs. Manoah (Judges 13:3-5) and, through* ***Zacharias****, for Elizabeth (Luke 1:11-17).*
4. *God gave to Hannah specific prophecy, or revelation, that He wanted to convey to His people through a chosen, enlightened, participating prophet. She was a prophetess on the order of* ***Deborah****, a prophet of the stature of Samuel. She was a stateswoman prophet (see chapter 7). She was gifted. She was not only an exemplary mother and the mother of a great prophet, but also the "Mother of her Country" as a kingdom. Hannah knew perfectly well, by revelation, that the "LORD of hosts" not only would give her a son, but also, through him and others, not without warfare, would bring about great changes and establish a kingdom in Israel. Hannah delivered this prophecy in the form of a polished, poetic prayer, much as* ***Habakkuk,*** *for example, would later do (Hab. 3).*

This student believes that Hannah was somewhere between 3 and 4, tending toward 4. But regardless of where *you* put her, notice must be taken that echoes of her prayer-prophecy can be heard in the prophetic song or "magnificat" of our Lord's mother, Mary (Luke 1: 46-55), who knew that her son was destined for even greater things.

55. **Hashabiah I** "was instructed in the songs of the LORD" that he "should prophesy with harps, stringed instruments, and cymbals" in the original Davidic tabernacle choir/orchestra, ca. 1000 BC. He was the son of **Jeduthun** (Ethan) and the leader of the twelve-man course of singers (1 Chr. 25:1, 3, 7, 19).

56. **Hashabiah II** was a leader of the Levite singer-prophets in a new (postexilic) temple choir, which was ordained "according to the command of **David** the man of God" (Neh. 12:24). Such choirs were "instructed in the songs of the LORD" (psalms) and "should prophesy" (1 Chr. 25:7, 1). It is not clear whether Hashabiah lived in the second generation after the return from Babylon (ca. 500-460 BC) or in the days of **Ezra** and **Nehemiah** (ca. 450-420 BC). This Hashabiah *may* be mentioned elsewhere in Scripture (Ezra 8:19, 24; Neh. 10:11), but perhaps not, for it was a common name.

57. **Heman**, "the King's seer in the words of God" (1 Chr. 25:5) was one of the three principals (with **Asaph** and **Jeduthun**) appointed by **David**, his captains, and the other Levites to lead in musical psalm prophecy, ca. 1000 BC (1 Chr. 25:1). Heman's grandfather was the great prophet **Samuel**; they were Levites descended through Kohath (1 Chr. 6:33).

Heman was earlier selected by his fellow Levites to be a lead singer and cymbal player in the musical group that escorted the ark of the covenant of the LORD to its new, special tabernacle in Jerusalem (1 Chr. 15:16-28). After this he was dispatched by David to Gibeon to help lead the music-prophecy ministry at the original (Mosaic) tabernacle and altar of burnt offering (1 Chr. 16:39-42; 21:29).

Heman had fourteen sons, all of whom became section leaders in the 288-man choir-orchestra which prophesied with "the songs of the LORD" in "the house of the LORD" (1 Chr. 25:4-7). This gave the Heman family a dominant majority in the musical prophecy department; or as Scripture so aptly puts it, Heman had fourteen sons (and three daughters) "to exalt his horn." The Heman family music-prophecy heritage continued for many generations (2 Chr. 29:14). Heman himself may have served beyond David's reign, into **Solomon's**. His name is mentioned in connection with the greatest musical event of all time, when God Himself came to the concert (2 Chr. 5:11-14).

It is inviting to identify this Heman as the librettist of Psalm 88 (see title) and/or the wise man of 1 Ki. 4:31, but in neither case does the genealogy agree with 1 Chr. 6:33. A Heman is mentioned in 1 Chr. 2:5, who seems to have connections with the Hemans of both Psalm 88 and 1 Kings 4:31, but he was Judah's grandson, hundreds of years before Heman the musical seer, and of the wrong tribe.

58. **Hezekiah**, the thirteenth king of Judah (715–686 BC) was a prophet. He is the only king of either of the divided nations, Israel and Judah (forty kings in all), who was a prophet.

Convincing evidence that Hezekiah was a prophet comes when this great reformer-king was only twenty-five years old, in the first year of his reign. He determined to cleanse and repair the two-hundred-year-old temple built by **Solomon**, which had recently been abandoned and desecrated by Hezekiah's father Ahaz, and to restore the true worship of God (2 Chr. 28:22-24; ch. 29). Hezekiah's orders to cleanse, repair, and sanctify the temple are regarded in Scripture as "the words of the LORD" (2 Chr. 29:15)—i.e., prophecy. Also, his command (along with other leaders) to keep the Passover feast was "at the word of the LORD" (2 Chr. 30:12).

A writing of Hezekiah (Isa. 38:9-20), after God had miraculously cured him of fatal disease and extended his life fifteen years, smacks of prophecy although it is not labeled as the word of God. However, in it, Hezekiah states that God had spoken to him (Isa. 38:15). His invitation to the Passover feast is also prophecylike (2 Chr. 30:6-9). Hezekiah's self-humiliation and prayers were answered with a great miracle: the withdrawal of a superior Assyrian army from Jerusalem's gates (2 Ki. 19).

Hezekiah sponsored and participated in musical prophecy. He may have actually written songs for the temple singers (Isaiah 38:20), although the translations do not all agree on the pronoun *my*. Hezekiah did restore full temple worship including a Levitical prophesying choir "according to the command of **David**, of **Gad** the king's seer, and of **Nathan** the prophet; . . . to sing praise to the LORD with the words of David and of **Asaph** the seer" (2 Chr. 29:25, 30 – cf. 1 Chr. 25).

Hezekiah was a client, an ally, and apparently a friend of the prophet **Isaiah** (Is. 37:2, 21; 38:1-8). The military miracle mentioned above was actually God's answer to the prayers of both prophets. Isaiah had foretold it in prophecy (Is. 37:5-7). When Hezekiah became deathly ill, Isaiah came to him with a heavy heart because he came with prophecy from God that Hezekiah would die. But after the king-prophet prayed and wept, God relented; and He gave through Isaiah the news (welcome to both prophets, we believe) that He would extend Hezekiah's life. God sealed this prophecy with a miracle: The earth rotated backwards ten degrees. Of course, Hezekiah recovered—a double miracle (Is. 38:1-9, 21).

Hezekiah made a stupid mistake just after his recovery, by showing off all the treasures of his kingdom to an envoy from Babylonia, then a rising nation. Sadly, Isaiah had to tell him that some day the Babylonians would be back to take away all these treasures as well as some of Hezekiah's own progeny (Is. 39). This prophecy was literally fulfilled a century later.

Historically, Hezekiah is sandwiched between his apostate father, Ahaz, and his son Manassah, who was arguably the worst king Judah ever had. But Hezekiah, the only prophet-king of Judah, was one of her best kings—perhaps *the* best.

59. **Hosea** was a "sensational" writing prophet. His shocking family life, including his marriage to a harlot, was the background for equally strong, shocking language in his message from God. Perhaps the most stunning thing of all, as we read about it today, is that God *told* Hosea to marry a harlot, to give their children names like "No Mercy" and "Not My People," and to pay for a prostitute—his own wife! For this reason, some Bible students take these accounts of Hosea's personal life allegorically, not literally. In any event, the first part of his message (chapters 1–3) is strong and clear: Israel was a spiritual harlot with other "gods" and idols; therefore, God would have no mercy on her children and would disown them, but in the end, after her punishment, God would redeem and reform His people.

Although the harlotry of Israel continues to be a major theme throughout the book, Hosea contains many other striking metaphors and figures of speech, as well as very straightforward language. Hosea was a colorful writer.

Shocking language was used to awaken and warn a decadent culture on the verge of collapse. Such was certainly the condition of Israel in Hosea's time, ca.

760–710 BC. One telling point is that the prophet deliberately omits from his introduction (Hos. 1:1) the last six kings of Israel, all of whom reigned during his ministry. Four of those six kings were assassinated by their successors. Israel had last known political peace and prosperity under Jeroboam II (793–753 BC), the only king of that nation that Hosea deigns to mention. His disrespect for the other six seems obvious.

Most prophets' messages call for repentance of the current generation, hoping to deflect God's wrath and renew His blessing. While this is not entirely absent from Hosea (6:1-3), it is definitely not the major emphasis. Instead, the restoration of Israel as a people, and God's great mercy and blessings to them *through* and *after* His judgment and punishment, is a major theme of the book.

Hosea's oracle continued into the reign of **Hezekiah** of Judah (715–686 BC), well after the final fall of Samaria and the nation Israel in722 BC. Most of its citizens were deported to Assyria and replaced with foreign immigrants (2 Ki. 17). A major part of Hosea's message is that God, while letting Israel be ruined as a political entity, still loved them as His chosen family, His people—and always would.

{Hoshea—**Joshua**} (Numbers 1:16, most translations except KJV)

60. **Hothir** was a son of **Heman** who was commissioned "to prophesy with harps, stringed instruments, and cymbals," and was "instructed in the songs of the LORD" (psalms). He was chosen by lot to lead the twenty-first twelve-man section of the tabernacle singers (1 Chr. 25:1, 4, 7, 28). His great-grandfather was **Samuel** (1 Chr. 6:33).

61. **Huldah** is one of the outstanding prophetesses in the Bible. She was chosen to declare the fate of King Josiah and his kingdom, Judah, after they came to realize that they stood condemned by God's long-overlooked written word. Like many people, even today, who know the truth about themselves for the first time, they were terrified. What would God do to them? To get an answer, they went to Huldah, an established and respected prophetess of God. She was chosen over contemporary prophets including **Zephaniah** and **Jeremiah**. Her answer was straight from God (2 Ki.22; cf. 2 Chr. 34).

Biographical information given about Huldah includes her husband's name (Shallum), his lineage, and her address: Second Quarter, Jerusalem (2 Chr. 34:22).

62. **Hozai** will be counted a prophet, but the word *Hozai* may not mean a specific person; it could mean "the seers." The translations differ, but usually give the alternative meaning in the margin or a footnote. This Hozai, if a person, was a historian prophet(seer) who wrote about King Manasseh's sin and his "foxhole" repentance (2 Chr. 33:19).

63. **Iddo I** was a seer who chronicled some of the acts of Kings **Solomon** and his heirs, Rehoboam and Abijah, all in the tenth century BC (2 Chr. 9:29; 12:15; 13:22). He also recorded his visions from God concerning Jeroboam, the first king of the breakaway nation Israel (2 Chr. 9:29). His writings are not extant, unless they are embedded in the Chronicles.

Concerning Rehoboam, Iddo wrote genealogies, possibly to prove Rehoboam's right to the crown over the upstart Jeroboam. Iddo recorded the "sayings" of King Abijah, indicating that this king possessed some of his grandfather Solomon's proclivity for proverbs and wisdom. These sayings are lost.

64. **Iddo II** was the father or grandfather of the prophet **Zechariah VI**, the canonical prophet (Zech. 1:1, 7). According to the KJV and NKJV translations, this Iddo was a prophet himself. Other translations move the word *prophet* to Zechariah or leave it ambiguous. **Nehemiah** indicates that Iddo was Zechariah's father (Neh. 12:4, 16). Zechariah describes himself as the son of Berechiah (Zech. 1:1); however, supporting **Nehemiah**, the phrase "son of Berechiah" may mean "the Berechite" (the blessed). So reads the Septuagint translation: "Zacharias the Barachite, the son of Addo (Iddo), the prophet." Father or grandfather, we will list Iddo II as a prophet with no other warrant than some translations' punctuation and word placement. It is certain that this Iddo was a "head" priest among the first large group of Jews that returned to Judah from Babylon in ca. 537 BC (Neh 12:1-7); but that does not exclude him from being a prophet – many priests were prophets.

We must differentiate Iddo II from **Iddo I**. The fact that 2 Chronicles, containing three references to Iddo I (q.v.) as a historian, was written (or completed) after Zechariah's grandfather would have lived (2 Chr. 36:22), leaves the possibility that Iddo I was Zechariah's grandfather. However, this seems highly unlikely because Iddo I had "visions concerning Jeroboam the son of Nebat" (2 Chr. 9:29)—and would a prophet have visions about a man who had lived four centuries earlier? More likely, Iddo I lived during the times of Jeroboam and could not have been Zechariah's grandfather.

65. **Isaac**, the son of **Abraham** and father of Jacob-**Israel**, is listed with the prophets although he does not *clearly* meet any single criterion set forth at the head of this list. **David** may have referred to Isaac as a prophet in Psalm 105 (cf. 1 Chr. 16:7ff.) although the direct connection of verses 9 and 15 is not certain. Other than this possibility, Scripture never calls him a prophet, seer, or man of God. Isaac does not expressly claim to speak for God or to have had a divine vision. The inspired word does not say he prophesied or was filled with the Holy Spirit. He did not write a book, oracle, or psalm in God's word.

The Scripture that compels us to see Isaac as a prophet was written by an apostle: "*By faith* Isaac blessed Jacob and Esau *concerning things to come*" (emphasis added) [Heb. 11:20]. Without that testimony, Isaac's blessings could be taken merely as a father's hopes and good wishes for his sons (Gen. 27:27-29, 39-40; 28:3-4).

There is no question that Isaac knew God, talked to Him, called upon His name, and worshipped Him (Gen. 25:21: 26:25). On at least two occasions the LORD appeared to Isaac, giving him instructions and renewing God's covenant promises to Abraham's descendants (Gen. 26:2-5, 24). Even the Philistines recognized Isaac's special standing with God (Gen. 26:26-29).

Isaac was the only son of Sarah and Abraham. His conception and birth were miraculous, occurring when Sarah was ninety years old. Most importantly, he was their "son of promise," meaning that God's chosen people, His covenant promises, and eventually **Jesus Christ**, would come through Isaac and not through his older half-brother Ishmael, who was Abraham's first-born son. **Paul** makes much of the spiritual and legal differences between Isaac and Ishmael in explaining Christianity to Christians in the AD first century (Gal. 4:21-31).

66. **Isaiah** stands first in the canon of the prophets, and many would say he stands foremost among the writing prophets, if not *all* the prophets of the Old Testament. The book Isaiah is far too large, complex, and sublime for any summary or characterization in this compendium. It is quoted more often in the New Testament than any other book of prophecy except Psalms. For example, Matthew directly quoted Isaiah at least eight times, usually with reference to the prophet by name. These include two instances of **Jesus's** quoting of Isaiah. Also, Jesus commenced His public prophetic ministry by quoting from Isaiah 61 (Luke 4:17-21). **Paul** quotes this prophet by name five times in Romans.

What sort of man was this eminent prophet? Biographical details are few but very interesting. We are told by Isaiah, no fewer than thirteen times, that he was the son of Amoz. Clearly, he honored his father greatly. (Although the chronology would fit, Amoz was not the same as **Amos** the prophet.) Isaiah was supposedly of the tribe of Judah, and he probably lived in Jerusalem. He ministered as prophet at least from the year of King Uzziah's death in 740 BC (Is. 6:1) through King **Hezekiah's** death in 686 BC (2 Chr. 32:32)—a period of fifty-four years. That is a long career for anyone, especially in the high-risk occupation of prophet.

Isaiah's commissioning (Is. 6) is one of the most dramatic, memorable, and preached-upon calls in all of Scripture. It includes his vision of the throne room of God, his conversion, and a commissioning dialogue that stands as a virtual definition of how prophets are called. Jesus even applied part of it to Himself (Matt. 13:14-15). Paul quoted this same passage at the close of his own ministry (Acts 28:25-27).

Isaiah was married and referred to his wife as "the prophetess" (Is. 8:3). They had at least two sons, one named Shear-Jashub (Is. 7:3) and the other, Maher-Shalal-Hash-Baz (Is. 8:3). These unusual names signified upcoming events that Isaiah foretold concerning Judah, Israel, Syria, and Assyria. At least one of these names, and probably both, came directly from God.

During his public ministry, Isaiah twice brought advice from God to a king of Judah during a military crisis. He—or more accurately, God's word—was accepted and heeded, with good results, both times: when King Ahaz was threatened by an alliance of Israel and Syria (Is. 7:1-9), and when King Hezekiah was threatened by Assyria under Sennacherib (2 Chr. 32:20-23). In these instances, at least, Isaiah was atypical of the prophets of his day, most of whom were ignored or even persecuted by their kings. Isaiah was somewhat of a throwback to the statesmen-prophets like **Samuel**. However, his standing in court was tenuous; tradition (not Scripture) holds that he was ultimately martyred.

Isaiah had access to King Hezekiah and was God's agent for this king's miraculous recovery from a nearly fatal illness (2 Ki. 20:1-11). However, a short time later Isaiah sharply rebuked Hezekiah for foolishly showing off Judah's treasures to an envoy from Babylon, and he pronounced God's judgment against this act (2 Ki. 20:12-19).

Some scholars hold that Isaiah was a nobleman. Aristocrat or not, Isaiah knew suffering and humiliation. In one of the more abasing demonstrations by any prophet, Isaiah was required by God to walk about naked and barefoot for three whole years! (Is. 20:2-3). *Naked* could mean stripped of his outer garments, his prophet's vestment or sackcloth. Still, it was humiliating.

In addition to being a prophet, a superb writer, a statesman, and one who suffered in his ministry, Isaiah was God's agent of several miracles. One of these was the temporary reversal of the earth's rotation by ten degrees, as a divine sign to King Hezekiah that he would recover from a grave illness (possibly a staphylococcus infection) and live another fifteen years. Connected to this cosmic miracle was the miracle of the healing itself, using a fig poultice (2 Ki. 20:7-11). Another supernatural act connected with Isaiah was the killing of one hundred eighty-five thousand enemy Assyrians in one night by an angel of the LORD, just when they were about to storm Jerusalem (2 Ki. 19). To be accurate, this miracle is attributed to the prayers of both Hezekiah and Isaiah, both prophets (2 Chr. 32:20-21).

Equally supernatural were many of Isaiah's written predictions, including the identification *by name* of Israel's benefactor-to-be, Cyrus of Persia, about 150 years in advance (Is. 44:28-45:13). This prophecy is one of the principal reasons that critical scholars have postulated that the book Isaiah was written by two or more authors, the last one as late as after the exile in Babylon—a theory rejected by conservative scholars.[8] No one is so rash as to suggest that the book of Isaiah was completed after Jesus came—yet the astounding, profound, accurate prophecies about Him are precisely the greatest miracles of this book. Isaiah contains the only physical description of our Lord Jesus in all of Scripture, including the New Testament (Is. 53:1-3). And only Isaiah describes, in rich detail, our Savior as the Suffering Servant He really was. How aptly has Isaiah's written word of prophecy been characterized as "The Gospel in the Old Testament."

67. **Israel** (Jacob), just like his father **Isaac** and grandfather **Abraham**, was the one and only person of his generation to whom and through whom God's covenant promises were given (Gen 28:13-15; 35:9-12; 48:3-4). Like them, he was the only prophet of his generation. As with Isaac, Israel's only recorded verbal prophecies were in the form of blessings and predictions concerning his sons and grandsons (Gen. 49). Those of Israel, however, were more extensive and more clearly "prophetic" in the future-telling sense. Israel's blessing/prophecy of his son Judah (Gen. 49:8-12) has, in retrospect, come to be understood as a Messianic prophecy.

Also like his father Isaac, Israel (then called Jacob) supplanted his elder brother (Esau), and returned to Haran to take a wife rather than marry a Canaanite (Gen. 27-29). And both Isaac and Israel were born as special gifts from God, if not miracles (Gen. 25:21; 21:1-3).

Jacob/Israel had dramatic visions and encounters with God. On his way to Haran to find a wife, he saw in a dream a ladder from earth to heaven, with God's angels going up and down; and God spoke to him (Gen. 28:12-13). This proved to be a prophecy of **Jesus** Christ, our Ladder to heaven (John 1:51). On his return trip many years later, Jacob's name was officially changed to Israel after he wrestled with a man (Gen. 32:22-32)—later identified by another prophet as an angel (Hos. 12:4-5)—but recognized by both as God Himself.

Like many prophets, Israel, while still named Jacob, was God's agent of a physical miracle. He caused sheep and goats to reproduce selectively so that their offsprings' colors and markings were determined by sticks (rods) placed before them during mating (Gen. 30:25-43). Some reformed Bible scholars and commentators do not consider this a miracle; others deny that Jacob really had a hand in it.[9, 10] This may be because they do not think of Jacob, "the deceiver" as a prophet of God, at least not at this stage of his life. But consider the evidence: First, God was directly responsible for the miracle; He confided in Jacob and involved him in it (Gen. 31:11-12). It was premeditated. Second, this miracle was enacted not only to provide Jacob with the means to support his large and growing family when they left Haran, but also to demonstrate Jacob's righteousness and special relationship with God, compared with Laban's deceit and idolatry (Gen. 30:27-30, 33). Third, concerning the outward means of the miracle, the sticks or rods—which seem to be a "sticking" point with some—is this any different from **Moses** putting a bronze serpent on a pole, so people who *looked* at it would not die of snakebite (Num. 21:8-9)? Or, what about Jesus making a paste of dust and spittle to "cure" blindness (John 9:6-7)? He obviously didn't need the mud; it was symbolic. Fourth, Jacob *was* a prophet! God often works miracles through His prophets, usually to make a point or validate them as His prophets.

68. **Jaaziel** (Aziel) was a Levite psalm singer and string player who was in the band that escorted the ark of the covenant of the LORD to its tabernacle in Jerusalem, ca. 1000 BC (1 Chr. 15:18-20). While Scripture does not expressly state that this group

prophesied with music, it is likely that they did; and, it is also likely that Jaaziel went on to join the 288-man tabernacle choir/orchestra "who were instructed in the songs of the LORD (psalms)" and "who should prophesy with harps, stringed instruments, and cymbals" (1 Chr. 25:7, 1).

{Jacob—**Israel**}

69. **Jahaziel** prophesied during the "good" days of Jehoshaphat, king of Judah. His prophesying encouraged this king, and the people of Judah and Jerusalem, to take a stand against aggressors from Moab, Ammon, and Seir (ca. 860 BC) [2 Chr. 20:14-17]. Not only did Judah win the battle, it was done in such a way that everyone including other nations knew that God had done it for them! (2 Chr. 20:29).

Jahaziel was a Levite descended from **Asaph** the musical seer (2 Chr. 20:14), so he may have led or been among the singers who went *before* the army of Judah singing the Great Refrain (q.v., pages 267-69), sending the enemy into confusion and a self-destructive rout (2 Chr. 20:18-23). This victory, the spoils gathered afterward, and the response of the people led to the naming of that place the "Valley of Berachah" (Blessing) [2 Chr. 20:26].

70. **James I**, a son of Zebedee, was one of **Jesus's** twelve disciples. He was filled with the Holy Spirit on the Day of Pentecost, fifty days after Jesus's resurrection. He prophesied then with other "tongues" (languages) [Acts 2:1-4]; and, we may be sure, in his own language on many other occasions (Acts 1:8; 4:33). James's first recorded experience as a prophet was when Jesus sent him out, paired with his brother **John II**, to preach and perform miracles (Matt. 10:1-8).

James and John were fishermen (Matt. 4:21). They were given the surname, or nickname, "Boanerges" (Sons of Thunder) by Jesus (Mark 3:17). They certainly fit this name when they wanted to command fire from heaven to consume a whole village of Samaritans (Luke 9:51-56). Jesus gave them preference (along with **Peter**) among His disciples (Mark 5:37; 9:2). Abetted by their mother, James and John became ambitious, much to the displeasure of the other ten disciples (Matt. 20:20-24). Jesus dealt with this jealousy as well as with James and John (Matt. 20:25-28), who remained in Jesus's "inner circle" (Mark 14:33).

James was the first apostle to be martyred for his Christian witness (prophesying) [Acts 12:1-2].

71. **James II**, a son of Alphaeus, was one of the twelve disciples/apostles (Matt. 10:3; Acts 1:12-14) who was filled with the Holy Spirit ten days after **Jesus's** ascension into heaven. At that time he was given the gift of prophesying in a foreign language (Acts 2:1-4, 14-18). We may safely assume that this James, along with the other apostles, continued to prophesy "in Jerusalem, and in all Judea and Samaria,

and to the end of the earth," according to the command of Jesus (Acts 1:8; 4:33). Earlier, during Jesus's earthly ministry, James was sent out with the other disciples (possibly teamed with **Thaddaeus**) on a preaching mission, invested with power to perform attesting miracles (Matt. 10:1-8).

Nothing else is known from Scripture about James son of Alphaeus unless, as some scholars assert, he was the same man as **James III**, the Lord's brother. This theory, put forth by Jerome in AD 383, seems weak; but if the reader prefers it, most of the comments about James III (q.v.) would apply to James of Alphaeus.

72. **James III** was **Jesus's** own (half) brother (Matt. 13:55; Gal. 1:19), although Jerome and other Christian scholars, with whom we respectfully disagree, speculate that he was really just a *cousin* and the same person as **James II**. In any case this James wrote the letter James, which is part of the Bible, God's word, making him a prophet by our definition. Furthermore, as a leader in the church in Jerusalem, James interpreted God's word and was a party to (perhaps author of) a letter which spoke for the Holy Spirit (Acts 15:13-21, 23, 28).

Jesus's brothers including James initially followed Him (John 2:12), but came to disbelieve His divinity (John 7:5) and tried to restrain Him, saying He was "out of His mind" (Mark 3:21, 31-32). But James and **Jude**, and hopefully all of His brothers, came at last to believe in Jesus as Lord and Savior (Jam. 1:1; Jude 1). James was granted a special visit by his resurrected, not-yet-ascended Brother (1 Cor. 15:7). He went on to become a prominent leader of the church in Jerusalem and was counted an apostle (Acts 12:17; Gal. 1:19; 2:9). An extrabiblical source, Heggesippus, says, "Because of his exceeding righteousness he [James] was called the Just, and Oblias, which is in Greek 'Bulwark of the People,' and Righteousness, as the prophets declare concerning him."[11] (We wonder what "prophets" were meant—probably New Testament ones!) James is said to have abstained from wine, meat (flesh), and strong drink; and to have developed thick calluses on his knees from praying for the people. According to Heggesippus, James was martyred by being thrown off the pinnacle of the temple of Jerusalem, and then his brains were bashed out with a launderer's (fuller's) club.

The book of James reflects the character of a man such as described by Heggesippus, emphasizing self-control, good works, and patience (endurance) amid trials and suffering. Worldly riches and social status are especially condemned; humility and wisdom are extolled. It is a practical book, occupying a special niche in the New Testament, and continues to inspire, inform, and guide the church of Jesus Christ.

{Jedidiah—**Solomon**} (2 Kings 12:35)

73. **Jeduthun**, alias dictus Ethan, was one of the three principal musical prophets (with **Heman** and **Asaph**) under Kings **David** and **Solomon** (1 Chr. 6:31-45;

15:16-19; 25:1). The name "Jeduthun" may have been a title or surname for Ethan because it means "a choir of praise" and because no genealogy is given for this name but is given for Ethan, who was descended from Levi through Merari (1 Chr. 6: 44-47).

Jeduthun is expressly called a "seer" in the Bible (2 Chr. 35:15).

Jeduthun was a singer, a cymbal player, and the father of six section leaders in the first tabernacle choir/orchestra "who were instructed in the songs of the LORD" and who "should prophesy with harps, stringed instruments, and cymbals" (1 Chr. 15:19; 25:1,3,7). Jeduthun himself was the "chief musician" or "choir director" to whom at least three Psalms were assigned or dedicated: two by David, one by Asaph (Psa. 39, 62, 77 titles). If Jeduthun permanently held this position, or held it a long time, up to fifty-two more Psalms were "to" him, the unnamed choir director or chief musician.

After the ark of the covenant of the LORD was placed in its new tabernacle in Jerusalem (ca. 1000 BC), the musical prophets were assigned either to it or to the Mosaic tabernacle/altar in Gibeon. Jeduthun served in the latter place where some of his sons were also gatekeepers (1 Chr. 16:37-42). Later, when the temple built by Solomon was dedicated and the ark brought into it (ca. 958 BC), Jeduthun and/or his sons participated in the greatest musical event of all time on this earth, when God Himself came (2 Chr. 5:11-14).

The music-prophecy legacy of Jeduthun (and of Asaph and Heman) lived on for at least five hundred years (2 Chr. 29:13-14; 35:15; Neh. 11:17).

74. **Jehiel I** was a string player and singer who was in the band that escorted the ark of the covenant of the LORD into Jerusalem (1 Chr. 15:18, 20), and then stayed to minister musically before the ark under **Asaph's** direction (ca. 1000 BC) [1 Chr. 16:4, 5, 37]. An elaboration about this latter ministry states that they should prophesy and were instructed in the songs of the LORD (psalms) [1 Chr. 25: 1, 7].

75. **Jehiel II** was a "son" (biologically or spiritually) of **Heman** (2 Chr. 29:14). He served in the temple ministry in the days of King **Hezekiah** (ca. 700 BC). His first assignment, however, was to help cleanse the temple, which, along with God, had been neglected and abused during the reign of Hezekiah's wicked father, Ahaz (2 Chr. 29:3-19). It is assumed that Jehiel went on to prophesy as a Levite musician (1 Chr. 25:1-7) in the choir/orchestra that was carefully reformed, according to the commandment of **David** and his prophets to "praise the LORD with the words (psalms) of David and **Asaph** the seer" (2 Chr. 29:25-30).

76. **Jehu** was a speaking prophet, a son of the prophet **Hanani** (q.v.)[1 Ki. 16:1, 12], and a writing prophet whose works are not preserved unless they are embedded in 1 Kings (2 Chr. 20:34). He prophesied in both Israel and Judah, for nearly half

a century: from the latter years of Baasha king of Israel (ca. 888 BC)[1 Ki. 16:1-7, 12] until long enough after the reign of King Jehoshaphat of Judah (872–848 BC) to write his history (2 Chr. 19:1-3; 20:34). His recorded messages from God, one for each of these kings, were not pleasant ones. Wicked Baasha was promised the bloody extermination of his whole house (family)—prophecy that was literally fulfilled in just a few years by the usurper Zimri (1 Ki. 16:1-13). Jehoshaphat, a good king for the most part, was nevertheless told by Jehu of God's wrath for his tolerance of wicked God haters, even though the king himself was godly (2 Chr. 19:2-3).

Jehu's contemporaries included **Elijah**, **Elisha**, **Micaiah**, **Jahaziel**, **Eliezer**, and several anonymous prophets; but none of them is connected to Jehu in Scripture.

{Jehoshua—**Joshua**} (Num. 13:16, 1 Chr. 7:27 KJV)

77. **Jeiel** was a gatekeeper/harpist/assumed singer who was in the band that escorted the ark of the covenant of the LORD into Jerusalem (1 Chr. 15:18, 21), and who stayed there to minister musically before the ark under the direction of **Asaph** (ca. 1000 BC)[1 Chr. 16:4-5, 37]. As described later in the Bible, this ministry was one of prophecy as well as praise and thanksgiving "in the songs of the LORD" (psalms) [1 Chr. 25:1, 7].

78. **Jeremiah**, a major writing prophet, second in the canon of prophets, has often been called the Weeping Prophet. This characterization is based on his book of Lamentations; his weeping over the slain and captives among his people (2 Chr. 35:25; Jer. 9:1; 13:17; 14:17-18; Lam. 3:48); and his periodic bouts of despair and self-pity (Jer. 15:10, 15-18; 20:7-18; Lam. 3:1-20). But, to call Jeremiah the weeping prophet, and leave it there, would be to misrepresent him.

One apt characterization of Jeremiah would be as the Going Prophet. He had a message from God that had to come out (Jer. 20:9). The people, the priests, and the rulers hated the message and would not come to Jeremiah to hear it. So God said, "For you shall *go* to all to whom I send you" (Jer. 1:7).

- Go and cry in the hearing of Jerusalem (2:2)
- Run to and fro in the streets of Jerusalem (5:1)
- Stand in the (temple) gate and proclaim (7:2)
- Go and get yourself a linen sash (13:1), and . . .
- Go to the Euphrates (13:4, 6)
- Go stand in the gates of Jerusalem, and say . . . (17:19-20)
- Arise and go down to the potter's house, and there I will cause you to hear My words. (18:1)
- Go and get a potter's flask . . . and go out to the valley of Ben-Hinnom . . . and proclaim there . . . (19:1-2)

- Then Jeremiah . . . stood in the court of the LORD's house and said to all the people . . . (19:14)
- Go down to the house of the king of Judah, and speak this word, and say . . . (22:1-2)
- Stand in the court of the LORD's house, and speak . . . (26:2)
- Go to the house of the Rechabites, speak to them, and bring them into the house of the LORD; . . . (35:2)

Yes, Jeremiah was probably the going-est of all the prophets. Jeremiah was a street preacher. He had to be. And for this, especially for prophesying in the temple court, he was arrested and almost lynched on the spot (Jer. 26:8-16). Later, he was beaten and put in stocks (Jer. 20:1-2) for his "Valley of Ben-Hinnom" (Tophet) sermon (Jer. 19). Still later, he was banished from preaching in, or even going to, the courts of the temple (Jer. 36:5). Finally, Jeremiah was arrested, beaten again, and imprisoned for a long time—all for prophesying publicly (Jer. 37:11-38:13; 38:28). For being a Going Prophet.

Where Jeremiah could not go, he sent messages. He wrote letters to the Jewish exiles in Babylon (Jer. 29; 51:59-64). He dictated to Baruch, his assistant, who wrote this prophecy on a scroll and read it in the temple court after Jeremiah was not allowed to go there (Jer. 36:1-10). And Jeremiah wrote his book, Jeremiah—for the Jews (Jer. 30:2-3), for **Daniel** (Dan. 9:2), and for us to read. It can truly be said that, in the providence of God, Jeremiah would never have written this book we so treasure, if he had been allowed to preach openly. He was a Writing Prophet.

Weeping Prophet, Going Prophet, Writing Prophet—Jeremiah was also the Prophet to False Prophets. Not since **Elijah** 250 years before, nor again until **Jesus** 650 years later, did so many false prophets claim to know the truth, and were opposed by so few true prophets of God. The book of Jeremiah abounds with sermons against false prophets and narratives of confrontations between Jeremiah and some of them (Jer. 8:10; 14:13-18; ch. 23; 26:8, 11; 27:9-10, 14-15; chs. 28, 29). Virtually everybody in Judah or exiled to Babylon—especially any "prophet" who wanted to keep his head—said, preached, and tried to believe that God would eventually save them from Nebuchadnezzar and the Chaldeans—everybody except Jeremiah. That was the crux of the matter. Jeremiah knew, and was commissioned to tell, that *this* time God had had enough and was using Nebuchadnezzar/Chaldea to punish His own chosen people. Dozens, hundreds, perhaps thousands of false prophets said otherwise: "God would relent in the end. He just wouldn't let His people, His kings descended from David, His city, His temple, go down." Jeremiah faced enormous opposition from false prophets.

A final characterization of Jeremiah, and one that seems on its face to belie the old label of Weeping Prophet (but doesn't), is the Strong Prophet. Jeremiah was very, very strong: physically, mentally, and spiritually. During his long ministry (a testimony to his strength in itself), Jeremiah endured:

- A conspiracy to take his life (11:18-21)
- Treachery of his own brothers (12:6)
- Being cursed (15:10)
- Organized opposition (18:18; 26:9)
- Being struck, beaten (20:2; 37:15)
- Being put in stocks in public (20:2)
- Derision, mocking (20:7-10; Lam. 3:14)
- Mob action, death threat (26:8)
- Accusation of capital crime (26:11)
- Being banned from temple area (36:5)
- Being a fugitive from "justice" (36:26)
- Arrest under false pretenses (37:11-14)
- Imprisonment in a dungeon for many days (37:15-16)
- Confinement with minimal food (37:21)
- Being left to die of thirst and starvation in a second dungeon, a cistern (38: 4-6, 9)
- Confinement (defenseless) when enemy army was sacking Jerusalem (38:28)
- Being carried away in chains by Chaldeans (40:1)

By the time of the fall of Jerusalem, 586 BC, Jeremiah was about sixty years old, assuming he was called at about the age of twenty, a youth (Jer. 1:2-3, 6). Truly, this Strong Prophet had endured much.

In all of his sufferings Jeremiah had very few friends, allies, or even family support. He was forbidden to marry or have children (Jer. 16:2). His own brothers turned against him (Jer. 12:6). The men of Anathoth, his hometown, sought to kill him (Jer. 11:21). **Ezekiel** and Daniel, his younger contemporaries who would surely have been his allies, were far away in Babylon. **Habakkuk**, also a younger contemporary, either operated in an entirely different "sphere" in Jerusalem, or was also carried off to Babylon. **Huldah** and **Zephaniah**, older contemporary prophets in Jerusalem, apparently were inactive (or deceased) after the reign of Josiah. Jeremiah's only known prophet ally in Jerusalem was **Urijah**, who was martyred by King Jehoiakim about midway in Jeremiah's career (Jer. 26:23). At that time Jeremiah was spared the same fate by some cooler-headed princes and elders (Jer. 26:16-19) and one friend with influence—Ahikam, a holdover official from good King Josiah's time (Jer. 26:24; 2 Ki. 22:12). The only other friends of Jeremiah mentioned in his book are Ebed-Melech the Ethiopian eunuch, who saved the prophet from death by dungeon (Jer. 38:7-13); and his good, faithful secretary, Baruch. Baruch may have helped write the book we know as Jeremiah (Jer. 36:4, 10; ch. 45). He stayed with the prophet to the end, down in Egypt (Jer. 43:6-7). Although he could hardly be listed as a friend, King Zedekiah twice spared Jeremiah from dungeons and respected the prophet (or was superstitious) enough to consult him several times (2 Chr. 36:11-12; Jer. 37:18-21; 38:10; 21:1-2; 37:3, 17; 38:14).

Perhaps the cruelest of all blows to Jeremiah was his having to watch his own prophecies come true, as his beloved people were starved, killed by the sword, and carried away to Babylon in chains (Lam. 1, 2). They could have been saved, at least from death, had they but heeded God's word through Jeremiah, to submit to the Chaldeans. A final stroke against the old prophet was his being taken to Egypt with the Jewish remnant, against his God-given advice (Jer. 43:4-7). But Jeremiah bore even this with characteristic resignation and strength.

Could not this Strong Prophet be allowed some tears, lamentations, and even self-pity, without being labeled a "weeper"? Do not these emotions show his humanity rather than his weakness? And was he not a strong man to admit his tears, fears, and despair in writing?

Jeremiah has revealed much about his personal life and his dealings with God. He was from a small town in Benjamin, where his family were priests (Jer. 1:1-2). The LORD called and commissioned him as a prophet when he was but a youth, in the year 626 BC (Jer. 1:2, 4-5).

The boy was reluctant, but God prevailed (of course!) and affirmed Jeremiah's readiness with two "test" visions: an almond branch and a boiling pot (Jer. 1: 6-14). God told the young prophet at the outset of his ministry that there would be fierce opposition, but he would be delivered from violent death (Jer. 1:8, 19). Jeremiah still had misgivings, and he accused God of deceiving His people (Jer. 4:10). Perhaps the inexperienced prophet still thought that the many false prophets *were* speaking for God, as they claimed, when they cried "Peace." The LORD soon corrected this misconception (Jer. 5:30-31).

More than once, God instructed Jeremiah to do the unthinkable for a prophet: *not* to intercede for the people (Jer. 7:16; 11:14; 14:11). Intercession is a major part of most prophets' ministries. But this case was closed. The trial was over, the sentence passed, and there were no more appeals. All that was left was the execution of the sentence. Nevertheless, God Himself would have relented in the very unlikely event of an eleventh-hour *true* repentance (Jer. 4:1-4, 14; 17:24-27; 22:1-5). But Jeremiah was told not to plead for this. Even **Moses** and **Samuel**, had they been there, could not have helped (Jer. 15:1). Still, Jeremiah contended with the LORD in the manner of **Habakkuk** (q.v.), arguing from God's righteousness, mercy, and covenant (Jer. 12:1-4; 14:19-22). God's answers were compassionate but firm (Jer. 12:5-13; 15:1-9).

Eventually, Jeremiah fell into spells of fear, despair, and self-pity but always, like **Job**, taking his troubles directly to God—even ascribing them to Him (Jer. 15:15-18; 17:14-18; 18:19-23; 20:7-10; Lam. 3). Also like the righteous Job, Jeremiah cursed his own birth(Jer. 15:10; 20:14-18). Sometimes God reassured Jeremiah, returned him to his task, and promised him protection (Jer. 15:19-21). At other times, in what are some of the most beautiful passages in the Bible, Jeremiah's complaints turn to praise (Jer. 20:11-13; Lam. 3:20-39) as he prays and realizes who God is: his "dread champion" (Jer. 20:11 NASB) and the One of

Whom we sing "Thy compassions they fail not—Great is Thy faithfulness!" (Lam. 3:22-23).

The book of Jeremiah is like a memoir, full of personal experiences and flashbacks as well as direct messages from God. It contains a great deal of history not found elsewhere in Scripture, especially chapters 39–44. However, it is not all arranged chronologically.

Much of Jeremiah's prophecy was about doom and judgment, but he also clearly conveyed God's promise of restoration *after* seventy years of captivity. In the middle chapters, after many revelations about Jerusalem's impending doom, the end of the house of **David** (at least for a time), and warnings about false prophets and Babylonian victory (Jer. 21-23; 27-29), Jeremiah finally received and recorded messages from God about Israel's and Judah's return from captivity, a remnant being saved, and future mercy, joy, and prosperity (Jer. 30-33). No wonder that he slept well that night! (Jer. 31:26).

Most of Jeremiah's prophecies are not Messianic or eschatological. The imminent punishment of Judah, the restoration after the captivity, and God's judgment of all the nations (chapters 46–51) are the main prophetic themes of Jeremiah. However, there are some notable exceptions. A Branch of David, a righteous leader, is promised (Jer. 23:5-6; 33:15-17). This was initially fulfilled in the restoration, in the persons of Zerubbabel and Joshua, combining the offices of priest and king (Zech. 3:8; 4:7; 6:12); but it ultimately refers to **Jesus** Christ, THE LORD OUR RIGHTEOUSNESS. Jeremiah also prophesies of a New Covenant of God with the house and seed of Israel (Jer. 31:31-37). This has been completely fulfilled only in the spiritual seed, Jesus Christ, and His house, His church (Gal. 3:15-25; Rom. 4:16-17).

{Jeremias (KJV)—**Jeremiah**}

{Jeremoth—**Jerimoth**}

{Jeremy (KJV)—**Jeremiah**}

79. **Jerimoth** (Jeremoth) was instructed in the songs of the LORD (psalms) to prophesy, with instrumental accompaniment, in the house (tabernacle) of the LORD. He was a son of **Heman** and was chosen by lot to lead the fifteenth twelve-man section of musical prophets (ca. 1000 BC) [1 Chr. 25:1, 4, 6-7, 22]. He was **Samuel's** great-grandson (1 Chr. 6:33).

80. **Jeshaiah** prophesied musically in the house (tabernacle) of the LORD, being instructed in the songs (psalms) of the LORD. His father was **Jeduthun**. Jeshaiah was chosen by lot to lead the eighth twelve-man section of the tabernacle choir/ orchestra which "should prophesy with harps, stringed instruments, and cymbals" (ca. 1000 BC) [1 Chr. 25:1, 3, 6-7, 15].

{Jesharelah—**Asharelah**}

{Jeshua I—**Joshua**} (Nehemiah 8:17, KJV, ASV)

81. **Jeshua II** was one of the leaders of a postexilic temple choir which sang antiphonally "according to the command of **David** the man of God" (Neh. 12:24). This title for David, "man of God," stresses his *prophetic* office, which underscores the fact that such choirs were "instructed in the songs of the LORD" (psalms) to *prophesy* with music (1 Chr. 25:1, 7). Jeshua lived either in the second generation after the return from Babylon (ca. 500–460 BC) or in the times of **Nehemiah** and **Ezra** (ca. 450–420 BC) [Neh. 12:26].[12] If the latter, this could be the same Jeshua who helped Ezra teach the Law of God to the people and who helped lead a public prayer of confession (Neh. 8:7; 9:4-5).

82. **Jesus** was the Christ, the Son of God. To say "Jesus was a prophet" risks perpetuating the very grave error made by millions (particularly Moslems, many Jews, and cults such as Jehovah's Witnesses) that He was *just* a prophet, not the divine Son of God. On the other hand, to say "Jesus was not a prophet" is contrary to Scripture. A correct statement is "Jesus, the God-man, executed the office of a prophet." That He did, and better than anyone else. He completely filled and defined the office of prophet, while at the same time fulfilling prophecy. Among His many other accomplishments while He was a man on this earth (John 21:25), *Jesus was the Perfect Prophet.* The historical significance of this is discussed at more length in chapter 7, "The Biblical History of Prophecy."

To attempt a biographical sketch of Jesus, or a summary of His messages from God and His life's work—as attempted for other prophets in this list—would be ridiculous. **Matthew**, **Mark**, **Luke**, and **John** have done that. This synopsis, therefore, is limited to: (1) a summary of specific biblical references to Jesus as a prophet, including His own statements; (2) some unique aspects of Jesus as a prophet; and (3) the unfulfilled/eschatological sayings of Jesus.

Jesus as a Prophet

When Jesus returned to His hometown, after launching His ministry in Galilee, He identified Himself with a passage from **Isaiah** that emphasized prophesying: to preach and to proclaim (Luke 4:16-21, cf. Is. 61:1-2). Then He went on to say, "No prophet is accepted in his own country," referring to Himself (Luke 4:24). Another time He said, in the same vein, "A prophet is not without honor except in his own country and in his own house" (Mat. 13:57). And as He started His last trip to Jerusalem, where He would be crucified, Jesus said, "I must journey today, tomorrow, and the day following; for it cannot be that a prophet should perish outside of Jerusalem" (Luke 13:33).

God the Father testified of Jesus's prophetic office and mission. On the Mount of Transfiguration, God's voice was heard saying, "This is My beloved

Son. *Hear* Him!" (emphasis added) [Mark 9:7]. In other words, He spoke for God: prophecy.

Many people who lived in Jesus's time on earth believed He was a prophet. Some declared it after a personal encounter with Jesus: a Samaritan woman (John 4:19), a man healed of blindness (John 9:17). Others proclaimed Jesus to be a prophet after they had witnessed a miracle: the raising of a dead man to life at Nain (Luke 7:16), the feeding of five thousand men from a few loaves and fish (John 6:14). The general populace then began to think of Jesus as a prophet, as reported by His disciples (Matt. 16:14), heard by Simon the Pharisee (Luke 7:39), proclaimed by the crowds on Palm Sunday (Matt. 21:11), and mockingly admitted by cruel Roman soldiers (Luke 22:64).

Some of the more astute Jews speculated that Jesus was "the Prophet" like **Moses**, promised by God through Moses (Deut. 18:15-19). Indeed He was this prophet (John 6:14; 7:40)—and will be still when He returns to earth, as revealed through a prophecy of **Peter** (Acts 3:19-26). Still others—temple policemen, to be specific—said Jesus's speech excelled that of all other men (John 7:46). Even after His resurrection, some of His disciples referred to Jesus as "a Prophet mighty in deed and word before God and all the people" (Luke 24:19).

In all of these citations, many of which fell upon Jesus's own ears, He never denied the designation *prophet* nor rebuked anyone for using it. Of course, we know He was much more than a prophet. Why, even **John I**, the baptizer, was "more than a prophet" (Luke 7:26), and he was not worthy to loosen Jesus's sandal strap (John 1:27). But Jesus did execute the office of a prophet, perfectly and completely, *declaring God* for our salvation (John 1:18).

Jesus a Unique Prophet

In chapter 7, "The Biblical History of Prophecy," it is observed that:

> Jesus as a prophet did not invent a new medium or language. He did not perform a new kind of miracle. He did not overwhelm, coerce, or 'pull His rank' to get His message across. When Jesus took and executed the office of a prophet He stayed within its traditional parameters.

Nevertheless, Jesus was a unique prophet. Like other prophets, He spoke and acted for God; but at the same time He *was* God. Jesus never said, "Thus saith the LORD," or got messages from God through visions and dreams like other prophets did. It was probably for this reason that Moses called Him a Prophet "like me" (Deut. 18:15), for Moses had a special face-to-face relationship with God that did not require visions and dreams (Num. 12:6-8; Deut. 34:10). Still, Moses was just a man. Jesus was God incarnate.

Another unique aspect of Jesus as a prophet is that He, Himself, was and is the main focus of prophecy (Luke 1:69-70; 4:21; 24:44; John 5:39). He fulfilled

(continued on page 124)

Jesus and Old Testament Prophets

Jesus quoted, paraphrased, or alluded to at least nineteen Old Testament prophets, not counting John I, the baptizer, who is considered by some to be the last Old Testament prophet. This is a remarkable thing in itself. While other prophets did occasionally refer to contemporary or previous seers, none did it nearly so generously, so widely, and so knowledgeably as Jesus. He made sure that we would know that He was the principal subject and the fulfillment of others' prophecies (Matt. 5:17; Luke 24:27). In quoting and alluding to other prophets, individually and categorically, Jesus also validated them.

The three prophets most frequently acknowledged by Jesus are Moses, David, and Isaiah. Moses is quoted or paraphrased by Jesus at least nineteen times in Matthew alone.[13] Excerpts from a number of David's psalms are quoted by Him including the eighth (Matthew 21:16), the twenty-second (Mark 15:34), the one hundred tenth (Luke 20:42–43), and the one hundred eighteenth (Matthew 21:42). Jesus quoted from Isaiah 6, 29, 53, 56, and 61 (cf. Luke 8:10; Matthew 15:8–9; Luke 22:37; Matthew 21:13; and Luke 4:18–19 respectively).

Other prophets' writings quoted or paraphrased by Jesus include Asaph (John 10:34); Jeremiah (Matthew 7:11, 15; 11:29); Daniel[14] (Matthew 24:15, 30; 26:64); Hosea (Matthew 9:13, 12:7; Luke 24:30); Joel (Matthew 24:29); Micah (Matthew 7:15; 10:35–36); Zechariah VI (Matthew 26:31); and Malachi (Luke 7:27; Matthew 11:13–14). Two other canonical prophets mentioned, but not quoted, by Jesus were Solomon (Luke 11:31; 12:27) and, very importantly, Jonah (Matthew 12:39–41; 16:4; Luke 11:29–30).

Jesus referred by name to several noncanonical prophets including Abel (Luke 11:51); Noah (Matthew 24:37–38); Abraham (Luke 16:22ff; John 8:56); Elijah (Luke 4:25; Matthew 11:14, 17:11–12); Elisha (Luke 4:27); and Zechariah II (Luke 11:51).

Jesus identified Himself, or let others identify Him, with certain Old Testament prophets:

Jonah: Matthew 12:39–41; 16:4; Luke 11:29–30
Elisha: Same name, meaning "Savior" or "God-Savior"
"Same" forerunner, cf. Matthew 11:7–14
Remarkably similar miracles, cf. Elisha write-up
David:[15] Luke 6:3–5; Matthew 27:46; cf. Psalm 22:1
Moses: John 6:14; Acts 3:20–23; cf. Deuteronomy 18:15

prophecy, even while He prophesied. Of all who ever bore the office and ministry of prophet, only Jesus's prophecies could be, and *had* to be, self-centered!

The apparent contradiction, or absurdity, of a prophet prophesying about himself, on his own authority, bothered many people, and still does, so Jesus dealt with it at length (e.g. John 8:13-14, 17-18). Although He did not *need* other witnesses, He had them: God the Father, John the baptizer, the works (miracles) Jesus did, and the Scriptures of the Old Testament including Moses's writings (John 5:31-47).

The Apocalypses of Jesus

All of Jesus's words and deeds when He was on earth were messages from God since He was God. Therefore, all were prophecy. However, only certain of His sayings were prophecies about things to come *after* His death and resurrection. These "foretelling" prophecies are particularly concentrated in Matthew 24 and 25; Mark 13; Luke 21:5–36; John 14:15–18 and 15:26–16:15; Acts 1:8; and the book of Revelation, which is Jesus's own revelation through His angel and through **John II** (Rev. 1:1; 22:6, 16). The main topics and themes of these "future" prophecies of Jesus are

1. The coming of His Holy Spirit to comfort, help, guide, and empower His disciples (fulfilled at Pentecost and still ongoing)
2. The spread of the gospel (ongoing)
3. The destruction of Jerusalem and the temple (historically fulfilled in AD 70)
4. Other tribulations and persecutions (ongoing)
5. The return or second coming of Christ (yet to come by most eschatological systems)
6. Final judgment (yet to come)
7. The new heavens, earth, and city (to come)

Jesus sternly warned against our speculating or calculating exactly when these things would happen, especially His return; but He did say "be ready" and "watch for signs." These warnings and exhortations guard us against laxity and fatalism.

{Jesus II—**Joshua**} (Acts 7:45, Hebrews 4:8—KJV only)

83. **Jezariah** was the director of musical prophecy in the days of **Nehemiah** (ca. 445 bc). He specifically led the combined Levite choirs which had been gathered to Jerusalem from around the country to dedicate the new city wall (Neh. 12:28, 42). Because of this, he is assumed to have also been part of the permanent temple choir which "kept the charge of their God . . . according to the command of **David** and **Solomon** his son" (Neh. 12:45)—which meant prophesying (1 Chr. 25:1).

{Jizri—**Zeri**}

84. **Joanna** prophesied to **Jesus's** disciples the words of God that had been given to her and several other women by two men (angels) in Jesus's tomb (Luke 24:10). Joanna and the other women had come there at dawn on the day after the Sabbath following Jesus's crucifixion to anoint His body (Luke 24:1-11). Their encounter with the angels is described as a vision (Luke 24:22-23), which is precisely how God gives prophecy (see chapter 1).

85. **Job**, whose spirited debates with his friends, and sometimes daring dialogues with God, comprise most of the book of Job, is counted among the prophets "who spoke in the name of the LORD" by the apostle **James III**, our Lord's brother (James 5:10-11). The book of Job itself does not contain any statements by Job of a "thus saith the LORD" form or nature. On the contrary, Job is complaining throughout most of the book that he cannot *find* God or get an audience with Him. And Job did not write the book, which would have automatically qualified him as a prophet since it is a portion of God's word.

Why, then, does James call Job a prophet? It is possible that Job prophesied in or wrote other books that were known to James, but not to us. However, the statement made by James about Job seems to derive from the book of Job itself. Job's claim to the title and office of prophet seems to be grounded in his surpassing faith and righteousness (Ez. 14:14). He was "blameless and upright, and one who feared God and shunned evil" (Job 1:1). This borders on the title "Man of God," which is one of the synonyms for prophet. Moreover, Job acted as God's agent in interceding for his sons and daughters (Job 1:4-5). Job belonged to the patriarchal era, and his "prophesying" is similar to that of **Abraham**, **Isaac**, and others then—mostly action and example, not verbatim words of God.

Notwithstanding the facts that the book of Job is not among "the Prophets" in the Scripture canon, and none of Job's statements in it purport to be God's direct messages or visions from God, there *are* some passages that smack of prophecy, whoever may have been the human author. The most famous of these, thanks to G. F. Handel, is "For I know that my Redeemer lives, and He shall stand at last on the earth."

86. **Joel** is, biographically, one of the least knowable of the writing prophets. His known lineage stops with his father Penuel. His birthplace, tribe, age, residence, marital status, any events in his life, and time in history (even the century) are all unknown. Joel is named only twice in the Bible: once in his own book (1:1), and once when quoted by **Peter** (Acts 2:16).

Joel's prophecy, however, is far from unknown. Peter quoted Joel in his great Pentecost speech (Acts 2:16-21), and used Joel-like language and imagery in his second Epistle (2 Pet. 3:10-12). **Paul**, too, quoted from Joel (Rom. 10:13).

The prophecy about frightening celestial phenomena (e.g., the sun darkening, the moon turning to blood) "before the coming of the great and awesome day of the LORD" (Joel 2:10, 30-31; 3:15-16), while not totally unique to Joel among the Old Testament prophets (cf. Is. 13:9-10; Zeph. 1:14-16), is used by **Jesus** in His Olivet Discourse (Matt. 24:29-30) and several times in the book of Revelation (6:12-13; 8:12; 9:2).

The book of Joel moves quickly and powerfully from terrible judgment and tribulation for God's people, to a call for repentance, to promises of God's lavish blessings, and to judgment of His and His people's enemies.

87. **John I**, the baptizer: "A prophet? Yes, . . . and more than a prophet. Assuredly . . . among those born of women there has not risen one greater than John the Baptist; . . . And if you are willing to receive it, he is **Elijah** who is to come" (Matt. 11:9, 11, 14). This testimony came, of course, from none other than our Lord, **Jesus** Christ.

John was God's "messenger" or "voice" promised through **Isaiah** (40:3) and **Malachi** (3:1; 4:5) to prepare the way of the Lord Jesus. His birth was announced beforehand to his father, a priest named **Zacharias**, by the angel Gabriel (Luke 1:11-19). He was to be "filled with the Holy Spirit, even from his mother's womb"—a prophecy that was manifested while he was still in that womb! (Luke 1:44).

John's name, destiny, and even mode of life were given beforehand to his parents (Luke 1:13-17, 60). His conception and the circumstances surrounding his birth were singular, if not miraculous. Both of his parents were, at different times, filled with the Holy Spirit and became prophets themselves (Luke 1:41-45; 67ff). Of his newborn son, **Zacharias** said, "And you, child, will be called the prophet of the Highest; for you will go before the face of the Lord to prepare His ways, to give knowledge of salvation to the people by the remission of their sins, . . ." (Luke 1:76-77).

John's austere, Spirit-filled life was foretold (Luke 1:15), and he adhered to it (Luke 1:80; 7:33; Matt. 3:4). His resemblance to Elijah in his lifestyle is unmistakable (compare Matt. 3:4 with 1 Ki. 17:6 and 2 Ki.1:8). Some scholars think he was a member of the Essene sect of Jews (see chapter 7, "The Biblical History of Prophecy").

John's confrontational preaching style and message also resembled Elijah's (Matt. 3:1-2; Luke 3:7-14; cf. 1 Ki. 18:21, 27; 21:17-19; 2 Ki. 1:2-4). Both of them were regarded by their governments as troublemakers, and became hated and feared by their respective kings and queens (Luke 3:19-20; Mark 6:17-20; cf. 1 Ki. 18:17; 19:1-3). Elijah barely escaped execution (1 Ki. 19:3); John was martyred by Herod and Herodias (Mark 6:22-28).

During his prophecy ministry, John gained a large following. He had his own disciples (John 1:35; 3:25; Luke 7:18). At least two of them, **Andrew** and another, left John to follow Jesus (John 1:37, 40). Others stayed with John at least until his death (Mark 6:29). John taught them to fast often (Luke 5:33) and how to pray (Luke 11:1).

John became well-known, respected, and popular (Matt. 3:5; 11:7-9). He was widely regarded as a prophet of God (Mark 11:32; Matt. 14:5), although he never performed a miracle (John 10:41).

John's core message was simple: "Repent, for the kingdom of heaven is at hand." "Confess your sins, and be baptized for the remission of sins." (Matt. 3:2; Mark 1:4-5). It struck a responsive chord with the downtrodden, sin-sick Jews in Jerusalem and all Judea. So did the simple symbolic act of baptism. Even tax collectors accepted it but not most Pharisees and lawyers (Luke 7:29-30). Despite this popularity, John knew his limits, his mission, and who he was. He was only preparing the way for something (One) even greater (John 1:19-23).

As a very popular figure to whom people listened, yet one who knew his role and his Master, John himself was perfectly prepared to announce and inaugurate the ministry of Jesus Christ (John 1:29-34). This was his purpose, his crowning moment—and he was up to it. Jesus even insisted on being baptized by John although He certainly did not need it for the remission of (His) sins. As John baptized Jesus with water, he became eyewitness to God's baptizing His Son with the Holy Spirit "descending like a dove" and earwitness to God's affirming and blessing Jesus (Matt. 3:13-17; John 1:32-34).

Although he knew, and had to tell his envious disciples, that "He [Jesus] must increase, but I [John] must decrease" (John 3:22-30), John continued his ministry of preaching and baptizing, at least until he was imprisoned by Herod (John 3:22-24). John continued, also, to witness that Jesus was God's own Son although when in prison he had doubts and needed reassurance (Matt. 11:2). The witness of John was very important to our Lord (John 5:32-33).

After John's execution, some people, including Herod his murderer, imagined that Jesus was the resurrection or "reincarnation" of John, the baptizer! (Matt. 14: 1-2; 16:13-14).

John's influence continued long after his death and even after Jesus's death and resurrection. Although John had been deceased for quite some time, the risen Christ had to remind His disciples/apostles that their own baptism would be like His, with the Holy Spirit, and not like John's with water only (Acts 1:5). Years later, during **Paul's** third mission trip to Europe (ca. AD 54), **Apollos** was preaching in Ephesus. It was obvious to two Christians there, Aquila and Priscilla, that Apollos "knew only the baptism of John," a deficiency they soon corrected (Acts 18:24-26). A short time later Paul found approximately twelve followers of John, the baptizer, in Ephesus (Acts 19:1-7).

If "the baptism of John" signifies a confession and repentance of sins, followed by a reformation of moral behavior and religious observance, but without the Spirit of Christ (the Holy Spirit), then there have probably been millions of others baptized "into John's baptism." It is a good baptism and a true baptism; but even John himself said that it is inadequate and inferior to the baptism of Jesus Christ, which includes the Holy Spirit (Acts 1:5; Matt. 3:11; Mark 1:8; John 1:30-33; 3:22-36).

88. **John II**, son of Zebedee, brother of **James I**, was one of **Jesus's** twelve disciples (Matt. 10:2) who were all filled with the Holy Spirit on a Pentecost Day and prophesied "with other tongues" (languages) [Acts 2:14-18]. But John prophesied much, much more, notably with **Peter**, as an apostolic team (Acts 3; 4:1-2, 13, 18-19; 8:14, 25) and eventually as the human author of five books of Scripture: the Gospel of John, three epistles of John, and the Revelation. The latter is the only book of self-declared prophecy in the New Testament (Rev. 1:3; 22:18-19).

Before he became a full-time disciple of Jesus, John was in the family fishing business, on the Sea of Galilee, with his father and his brother James (Matt. 4:21-22). They were partners with Simon (Peter) and **Andrew** (Luke 5:10). Apparently John was the younger brother for James is almost always named first.

These two brothers, along with Peter, became Jesus's closest disciples and companions. They alone were allowed to witness Jesus raising Jarius's daughter from death to life (Mark 5:37), and Jesus's transfiguration (Mark 9:2). They went farther with Jesus into the Garden of Gethsemane (Mark 14:22-23). John and Peter (without James) prepared the "last supper" or passover meal for Jesus and His twelve disciples (Luke 22:8). These two were also the first of the "twelve" (now eleven) to hear of Jesus's resurrection and the first to see His empty tomb (John 20:1-8). This special nearness to Jesus undoubtedly influenced John's career as a prophet.

Young John tended to be possessive and protective about his association with Jesus. He forbade people who were not with "us" (the twelve, probably) from casting out demons in Jesus's name (Luke 9:49). John, with James his brother, wanted to annihilate some Samaritans for being unfriendly toward Jesus and His disciples (Luke 9:54). These same brothers, abetted by their mother, attempted to secure superior rank in Christ's kingdom (Matt. 20:20-28). In each of these cases, John and James were rebuked by Jesus and were taught better. Jesus nicknamed them Sons of Thunder (Mark 3:17), perhaps to remind them to hold their ambition in check.

But John is also supposed to be Jesus's "beloved" disciple. To be sure, this designation comes to us only through the writings of John himself (John 13:23; 19:26; 20:2; 21:7, 20, 24). It is put in an anonymous manner; John never names himself in the Gospel of John. But then, neither does he name James, his brother. Or four other disciples,[16] for that matter. But John 21:24 identifies "the disciple Jesus loved" as the writer of this gospel, who is almost universally accepted to be John, the son of Zebedee. According to this, then, John *was* the beloved disciple. It was John to whom Jesus, from His cross, entrusted the care of His mother **Mary**. (How enticing to speculate about how John's own ambitious mother took this!)

John had a long, fruitful ministry as an apostle, preaching (prophesying), teaching, and participating in miracles. We have noted him teaming up with Peter after Pentecost Day in Jerusalem. This partnership began before Jesus was crucified (Luke 22:8), continued through Jesus' resurrection (John 20:1-8), and lasted several years after then, at least until after **Stephen** was martyred and Christ's followers (except apostles) were scattered (Acts 8:1, 14, 25). After this, we do not read again of John's movements until he was (supposedly) imprisoned or exiled on an island, Patmos, off Asia Minor in the South Aegean Sea. From John's epistles, and the locations of the seven churches addressed in Revelation 2 and 3, it is deduced that he had a significant ministry in Asia Minor, traditionally in and around Ephesus. This ministry must have commenced after **Paul's** missionary visits there (ca. AD 54), for John the apostle would not have left a cell of disciples in Ephesus who were only baptized "into **John** (the baptizer)**'s** baptism" (Acts 19:1-7).

In his second and third Epistles John calls himself "the Elder," and in the first he writes very paternalistically, calling his readers "my little children." These indications fit well with the chronology that John ministered in Asia Minor in the latter half of the first century, as a senior, if not elderly, apostle. John was one of those all-too-rare prophets who had a long career and life. According to *Foxe's Book of Martyrs*, John was the only apostle who did not suffer a violent martyr's death, although he was cast into a cauldron of boiling oil, escaping by a miracle.[17]

John's writings are an extremely important part of the "whole counsel of God." His gospel, possibly the last one of the four to be written, assumes the historical facts of Jesus's life found in Mark, Luke, and Matthew and supplies many other details not found there such as Jesus's encounter with Nicodemus which leads to that most well-known Bible verse, John 3:16. John chose to repeat many essential episodes about Jesus that are found in the synoptic gospels, such as His feeding of the five thousand and of course His death and resurrection. John is the most intimate gospel and contains several of Jesus's discourses, conversations, and prayers not found elsewhere. As to eschatological prophecy, John contains hardly a word, not even Jesus's "little apocalypse"; he seems to have saved it all for Revelation. But John's gospel contains by far the most prophecy on the promise and work of the Holy Spirit (John 14:15-28; 15:26-16:15).

The Apocalypse, or Revelation, *of* Jesus Christ, sent *by* His angel, *to* John, *for* Christ's servants—is the capstone of Holy Scripture. It is the only book in the New Testament that is labeled as sheer prophecy, and it comes at the end, just as "the Prophets" come at the end of the Old Testament. Revelation proclaims itself to be prophecy at its beginning and its ending, with blessings promised for the obedient reader and curses for anyone who would make deletions or additions (Rev. 1:3; 22:18-19).

{John III Mark—possibly **Mark** the gospel writer (q.v.); otherwise, not a prophet}

89. **Jonah** is almost always associated with the whale or "great fish" that swallowed him and then disgorged him alive after three days. But there is much more to Jonah. He was a very important prophet, historically and theologically. He was the first writing or canonical[18] prophet, chronologically. He was also the last of

the hero prophets[19] such as **Elijah** – those whose testimony was primarily in deeds and miracles. But to Christians, the most important fact about Jonah is that **Jesus** pointed to him as a sign of two things: (1) His resurrection from death and (2) the way His ministry was received (Matt. 12:38-42).

Jonah was from the village of Gath-Hepher in northwest Israel. He prophesied during or before the reign of Jeroboam II of Israel (793–753 BC), a time of prosperity and expansion for that nation. Jonah prophesied to Israel and foretold its national expansion (2 Ki. 14:25). His book, however, is not about Israel at all. It is about his preaching mission to Nineveh, the capital city of the most powerful nation in the world, Assyria. Nineveh was a wicked city, but God determined to offer them a chance to repent and be spared from His anger.

Jonah is often portrayed as a spiritual coward because he tried to run from his mission to Nineveh (Jonah 1:3); and as a spiteful ingrate because he was angry for its success (Jonah 3:10-4:1). However, he could equally be depicted as a fine example of humility, honesty, and self-deprecation for publicly (in writing) admitting his doubts, fears, and prejudice, and his trying to avoid God's call. These are things that many another prophet—perhaps all of them—think, feel, and do at times. Your view of Jonah's character pretty much hinges on whether or not he actually wrote Jonah—and there is no compelling evidence that he didn't.

The book of Jonah can be a stumbling block to the weak or pliable and is a favorite target of those who would controvert or undermine Scripture by saying that it is foolish to believe a man could live three days inside a fish. But the case may be even harder than that to swallow, for many believe that Jonah actually died in the fish and was resurrected to life! There is some internal evidence for this belief, in Jonah (2:6), but the principal reason for accepting it is Christ's own testimony (Matt. 12:40): Why would Jesus have chosen *this* event, above all other three-day events unless it *also* exemplified resurrection?

Jesus had another reason to single out the prophet Jonah as a "sign" to His generation. It is that Jonah demonstrates God's sovereign, catholic love to people and nations other than His chosen ones, signifying that although "His own received Him not" (John 1:11), Christ lived, died, and rose again for many people (including Gentiles) and for other generations (John 3:16; 10:16).

{Joses—**Barnabas**}

90. **Joseph I**, eleventh of the twelve sons of **Israel**, was the last of the patriarch prophets; and only the second prophet[20] in Scripture who clearly received messages from God about future events, which he verbally related to others.

Joseph's mother was Rachel. The stirring story of his brothers' jealousy, their selling him into slavery, his rise to power in Egypt, the world famine, God's provision through Joseph, his incognito appearances during his brothers' visits to Egypt, and the move of the whole family of Israel to Egypt—is well-known (Gen.

37; 39-47). Although these events and the deeds of Joseph can be seen as prophecy in its patriarchal form, we will pass over them to focus on what are some of the earliest examples of verbal prophecy.

The first two of these prophecies were received by the young lad Joseph in dreams about his family—dreams that his brothers took for ambition, hating Joseph for it; and dreams that his father Israel rebuked him for, but remembered. These dreams were truly prophetic, in the future-telling sense (Gen. 37:5-11).

Years later, when Joseph was unjustly imprisoned in Egypt, he gave divine interpretations of two fellow prisoners' dreams (Gen. 40:8-23). These prophecies led to Joseph's release from prison and reinstatement in Pharaoh's administration (Gen. 41:9-14). But first he had to pass another severe test: to interpret Pharaoh's dreams. Joseph made it clear that the interpretation came from God, not himself (Gen. 41:15-16, 25ff). And it came true. These two things mark it as true prophecy. Also, at that time Joseph possessed the defining attribute of a prophet: he was filled with the Spirit of God (Gen. 41:38). He was thirty years old (Gen. 41:46).

There is a disturbing statement in the Bible that Joseph "practiced divination," as if he were a magician, or sorcerer (Gen. 44:4-5). But this appears to be just part of a ruse he used to frighten his brothers through his steward. Later, Joseph stated it himself, emphatically but hypothetically (Gen. 44:15). God's law against practicing divination was not codified until four hundred years later (Deut. 18:10-14), but it seems unlikely that God would have one of His patriarch prophets practicing what was later revealed to be an abomination to Him.

Joseph's last recorded prophecy, given on his deathbed at the age of 110, predicted the Exodus of his people from Egypt and their return to the land that God promised to **Abraham** and his descendants, the land of Canaan (Gen. 50:24-26). This was fulfilled four hundred years later under **Moses** and **Joshua**.

91. **Joseph II**, a Levite, was "instructed in the songs of the LORD" to "prophesy" in "the house of God—with harps, stringed instruments, and cymbals." He was a son of **Asaph** the king's seer and was chosen by lot to lead the first of twenty-four twelve-man sections of the original tabernacle musical prophecy contingent (ca. 1000 BC) [1 Chr. 25:1-9].

92. **Joseph III**, a humble and just carpenter in Nazareth of Galilee and a descendent of Judah through King **David** (Matt. 1:2-16), prophesied with a single word: He named his wife's son **Jesus**, exactly as he was instructed by an angel of the Lord in a dream (Matt. 1:20-21, 25). Joseph received other instructions from God in dreams (Matt. 2:13, 19-20, 22), but none of them resulted in his prophesying verbally. His obedience, however, is reminiscent of patriarchal prophets such as **Abraham**.

93. **Joshbekashah** was one of the sons of **Heman**, the king's seer in the words of God, and a great-grandson of **Samuel** (1 Chr. 25:4-5; 6:33). He was leader of the

seventeenth twelve-man division of the original tabernacle singers (1 Chr. 25:24). This entire group consisted of 288 Levites "who should prophesy with harps, stringed instruments, and cymbals . . . for the service of the house of God . . . (and) who were instructed in the songs (psalms) of the LORD" (1 Chr. 25:1, 6, 7).

94. **Joshua** was God's great military prophet-general. As commander of Israel's armed forces, he led them to an amazing series of victories, conquering and/or claiming the whole promised land of Canaan. Joshua's personal character was exactly what God, **Moses**, and the people exhorted him to be: strong and courageous (Deut. 31:7, 23; Josh. 1:7, 9, 18). His real strength was his faith.

Joshua is never called a prophet, a seer, or a man of God in the Bible. But he had all the other credentials of a prophet.

- Joshua was filled with the Spirit (Num. 27:18; Deut. 34:9);
- was called and commissioned by God (Deut. 31:14);
- spoke for God (Josh. 20:1; 24:2);
- foretold future events that came to pass (Josh. 6:26; 1 Ki. 16:34)
- was God's agent and spokesman in physical miracles, including stopping the flow of the River Jordan (Josh 3:9-17) and temporarily stopping the Earth's rotation (Josh. 10:12-14);
- was God's agent and spokesman in many miraculous military victories, including the felling of the walls of Jericho (Josh. 6:20), the ambush of Ai (Josh. 8:18), and the rout/slaughter of a five-kingdom army as God sent hail from heaven (Josh. 10:8, 11) – see also Josh. 11:20, 23:3;
- wrote on stones, and read aloud, the words of God as given to Moses (Josh. 8:32,34); wrote in the Book of the Law of God (Josh. 24:26); and probably wrote much of the book of Joshua; and
- brokered covenants and established memorials and ceremonies for the people of God (Josh. 4:1-7; 5:2; 8:30-35; 24:25)

Yes, Joshua was a prophet, and a great one, although it is hard sometimes to see the prophet through the general.

Who was this unusual prophet? Scripture gives us several scenes from Joshua's life *before* he became Israel's commander in chief. Most of them deal with prophecy, not military matters, and it is worth reviewing them.

Joshua must have been born a slave in Egypt. He was given the name Oshea or Hoshea, meaning "God helps (or saves)" (Num. 13:8; 1 Chr. 7:27). His father was Nun (about whom we know nothing else) and his grandfather was Elishama, the patriarch-leader of the whole tribe of Ephraim during their wilderness wanderings (Num. 1:10; 2:18; 10:22). Moses changed Oshea's name to Joshua (Num. 13:16). Perhaps this better reflected God's personal name (YHWH or Jehovah) that had been revealed to Moses (Exodus 3). In any case it meant the same: "God (Jehovah) saves." This, of course, is the name God chose for His only begotten Son, **Jesus**. The fact that Joshua and Jesus are the same name in slightly different languages is demonstrated by this: In the only two New Testament (Greek) references to Joshua, he is called "Jesus" (Acts 7:45 and Hebrews 4:8, KJV and marginal notes in other versions).

Joshua (Oshea) probably knew Moses in Egypt before the Exodus. Surely he must have known about the ten plagues, the Passover, and the plan to escape. Very shortly after the Israelites were out of Egypt, Moses turned to young Joshua to muster a fighting force to oppose and defeat Amalek (Ex. 17:8-13). By the time they got to Sinai, three months out of Egypt, Joshua was Moses's personal assistant (Ex. 24:13). We do not know how long he served in this role, but it was an intense period of training for prophethood. The Bible gives three important episodes:

First, Joshua accompanied Moses on his seventh ascent of Mount Sinai, when Moses stayed forty days and nights and received God's plans for the tabernacle, the ark, the altars, other furniture, and the priests' garments—and two stone tablets of the Testimony (Ex. 24:13–31:18). Was Joshua with Moses on the Mount this whole time? We know he went up with Moses who told the elders of Israel, "Wait here for *us* until *we* come back to you" (Ex. 24:14). Forty days and nights later, they came down together, for Joshua heard a noise from the camp that he mistook for a war cry (Ex. 32:17). In any case, just being on the mountain where Moses was receiving directions from God must have been quite an experience for the young intern.

The second episode is even more intriguing. Just after Israel's outrageous apostasy—the golden calf incident—Moses pitched a tent *outside* the camp of Israel for anyone to pray and seek God (Ex. 33:7-11). He called it the tabernacle of meeting, but this was not the holy tabernacle of meeting that would house the ark, the lampstand, etc.—it had not yet been built (Ex. 40). When finished, it would occupy the center of the camp (Num. 2). But this first "tabernacle of meeting", probably an ordinary tent, was pitched outside the camp—far outside—because the people were polluted with idolatry. Now when Moses took his turn going out to the tabernacle of meeting, which was probably more often than most of the men, he took Joshua along with him. And everybody else watched, from a distance, standing by his own tent, for it was a spectacle and a worshipful sight. They could actually see God come to the tabernacle, in a pillar of cloud, where He spoke to Moses face-to-face. Then Moses would return to the people in camp, but *Joshua stayed in the tent of meeting*! Nothing else is said about this except that Joshua was still a young man. What did Joshua see? Hear? Why didn't he come out with Moses? Was he overcome by such close proximity with God? We can only speculate. But what an experience for this young prophet-in-training!

In the third episode during Joshua's service as Moses's personal assistant (and prophet apprenticeship), Moses took seventy elders of Israel, and Joshua, with him to the permanent tabernacle of meeting, where God gave each of them a portion of His Spirit so they could help Moses bear the responsibility of leadership (Num. 11:16-30). When God's Spirit fell on them, they prophesied—and so did two other elders who had been listed to go, but remained in camp. A young man ran from camp to tell Moses about those two prophesying. When Joshua heard it, he was incensed and asked Moses to forbid them to prophesy. Moses's wise answer, "Oh, that all the LORD's people were prophets and that the LORD would put His Spirit upon them!" (Num. 11:29) was very much like Jesus's response when His young disciple, **John II**, wanted to stop people who were "not of us" from casting out demons in Jesus's name (Mark 9:38-40). It was a lesson on prophesying that Joshua needed; and one for all overzealous "exclusivist" followers of God.

Not long after this, Joshua nearly lost his life for his faith and courage. Moses sent twelve men—one from each tribe—on a surveillance mission into the territory of Canaan, which God had promised to Israel, but which they would have to conquer (Num. 13). Joshua was chosen from Ephraim. When they returned from their mission, only Joshua and Caleb (representing the tribe of Judah) had the faith in God and the courage to recommend invasion (Num. 14:6-10). They were outvoted (or outshouted) and almost stoned to death by the rest who were afraid to attack Canaan. God's sudden appearance in the tabernacle of meeting at this very time undoubtedly saved Joshua's and Caleb's lives. Decades later these two were rewarded by being the only men of that generation to enter Canaan permanently (Num. 14:30; 32:11-12)—Joshua leading the nation in (Josh. 1:1-9).

Nothing else is said about Joshua, through all the wilderness wanderings (almost forty years), until God chooses him to succeed Moses just before the latter's death (Num. 27:15-23). What was Joshua's main qualification for this very high and difficult calling? He had the Spirit. Moses inaugurated, or commissioned, Joshua with a laying-on of hands before **Eleazar** the priest and all the congregation of Israel. Later, perhaps in this same ceremony, Moses presented the new leader-elect to the congregation and publicly exhorted them, and Joshua, to "be strong and of good courage" (Deut. 31: 1-8). This is a phrase that resounds throughout Joshua's leadership.

Just before launching into his military campaigns, after crossing the Jordan River into Canaan, Joshua had another "commissioning": a personal visit from the commander of the army of the LORD! (Josh. 5:13-15). Was this commander the archangel Michael (cf. Daniel 10:10–21; Jude 9; Revelation 12:7)? No. It was an epiphany of the Lord Himself, for He allowed Joshua to worship Him, and He declared His sovereignty and holiness.

A final question must be answered about Joshua. Was he the "prophet like me" that Moses, and God, promised would be raised up to lead the people after Moses? (Deut. 18:15-19). He was a prophet and leader of Israel. He had the Spirit (Num. 27:18). And the context of the promise of a "prophet like Moses" seems to imply an immediate successor. However, the postscript of Deuteronomy equates the "likeness" to Moses with a face-to-face relationship with God, which we are certain Joshua did not have (Num. 12:6-8), and with miracles and mighty deeds that Joshua did not match (Deut. 34:10-12). Also, the pious and religious Israelites were *still looking* for this promised Prophet over fourteen centuries later, when they asked **John I**, the baptizer, "Are you the Prophet?" (John 1:21). No, he wasn't, no more than Joshua was. That Prophet would be Jesus, the namesake of Joshua! (Luke 7:16; 24:19; John 6:14).

95. **Jotham** prophesied with a fable (Judg. 9:7-15). Fables are fictitious stories, whose characters are usually animals (in this case, trees), that teach moral truth. They are rare in Scripture. Jotham's fable is deemed to be prophecy, partly on the basis that contains a prediction that came true (Judg. 9:15b, 20, 45-52). Fulfillment of a prediction is one test of prophecy (Deut. 18:21-22), but it is not conclusive. In fact, we are warned that it can be a false indicator (Deut. 13:1-3). But Jotham's fable was obviously from God, so Jotham was a prophet.

Jotham was Gideon's youngest son. He narrowly escaped being murdered by his half brother Abimelech who killed Gideon's other sons, seventy in all, in order to claim kingship over Israel (ca. thirteenth century BC). Jotham climbed up on Mount Gerizim, a special place designated by God for declaring His *blessings* (Deut. 27:12), to pronounce instead a *curse* on the men of Shechem for supporting bloody Abimelech. After delivering his fable and curse, Jotham ran for his life and went to Beer (Judg. 9:1-21). He is not heard from again.

96. **Judah** is a very common name in Scripture, being that of the fourth son and ultimately the dominant tribe of Israel, and the name by which the Southern Kingdom and eventually the only Kingdom of Israel was called. But the only Judah (by this spelling) who was a prophet was not even of this tribe. He was a Levite singer (musician) who was appointed to the choir that celebrated the completion of the rebuilt Jerusalem wall in about 445 BC "with the instruments of **David** the man of God" (Neh. 12:36). It can be assumed that Judah was also one of the regular temple singers who "kept the charge of their God . . . according to the command of David . . . " (Neh. 12:45). These references to the instruments and commands of David, the man of God (prophet), tell us that the music was psalmody and prophecy (1 Chr. 25).

{Judas I—**Thaddaeus**} (Compare Luke 6:16 and Acts 1:13 with Matthew 10:2–4 and Mark 3:16–19. See also John 14:22.)

{Judas II—**Jude**} (Mark 6:3)

97. **Judas III** Iscariot brings us face-to-face with the disturbing truth that evil persons can, at times, prophesy God's truth. Just as Judas is the most despised character in all history, so **Balaam** was the vilest in Old Testament history (2 Pet. 2:15). Yet each one of them was at one point in his life a true prophet of God (Matt. 10:1-8; Num. 23:5-10, 16-24; 24:2-9, 15-25).

Jesus stated that many who will say to Him, at the judgment, "Lord, Lord, have we not prophesied in Your name, cast out demons in Your name, and done many wonders in Your name?"—many of these will not enter the kingdom of heaven (Matt. 7:21-23). Jesus did not condemn or discredit their works, including prophecy, but their hearts. Although Jesus said *many*, we find but a few clear examples of such people in Scripture: Judas, Balaam, **Saul**, and **Caiaphas** come to mind. Nebuchadnezzar also comes to mind although he cannot be considered a prophet (see note at "Nebuchadnezzar" in this list). **Paul** complained that Demas, a fellow worker in the gospel, had forsaken him, loving this present world (2 Tim. 4:9). **Peter**, **Jude**, and others condemned and warned about false prophets in the church, some of whom may have started well but became apostates (2 Pet. 2; Jude). Both of these apostles compare them with fallen angels. In the Old Testament, without citing specific passages, there are implications that some of the false court prophets (soothsayers) started well, but forsook the truth out of greed or fear.

As for Judas, he certainly fit Jesus's description of a false-hearted prophet, cited above, for he prophesied in Jesus's name, cast out demons in Jesus's name, and did wonders in Jesus's name (Matt. 10:1-8; Luke 9:1-6). He did this when he was sent out by Jesus, probably paired with **Simon II** Zealotes, to preach, cast out demons, and heal bodily diseases. Peter said Judas "was numbered with us and obtained a part in this ministry" (Acts 1:15-17). Yet Judas himself is condemned (Acts 1: 18-20).

It is also worth noting that Judas fulfilled prophecy about himself. He was chosen by Jesus, who knew what Judas would do to Him (John 6:70-71). And he was spoken of by Old Testament prophets (Zech 11:12-13 [cf. Matt 26:14-15; 27:3-10]; Ps. 41:9 [cf. John 13:18-19]).

98. **Judas IV**, also named Barsabas, was a prophet and a leader in the apostolic church in Jerusalem, ca. AD 48. Judas and **Silas** were chosen by the apostles and elders and the whole church to personally deliver a decree concerning circumcision to the church in Antioch, Syria. They stayed in Antioch for a while and "themselves being prophets also, exhorted and strengthened the brethren with many words." Judas then returned to Jerusalem (Acts 15:22-34).

99. **Jude** conveys to us the word of God in the form of the epistle (book) that bears his name. Besides its main messages—warnings against ungodly teachers and exhortations to keep the true faith—Jude contains several interesting insights into the subject of prophets and prophecy. In Scripture, Jude alone identifies **Enoch** as a prophet (Jude 14). Only Jude tells about the archangel Michael contending with the devil about the body of **Moses**, the great prophet (Jude 9). And Jude recognizes the fulfillment of a predictive prophecy of other apostles of **Jesus** (Jude 17-18).

Jude was the brother of a certain James (Jude 1), most likely **James III**, the half-brother of Jesus (Gal. 1:19). This, then, would make Jude also our Lord's half-brother. Indeed, a Jude (Judas) is listed among Jesus's brothers (Matt. 13:55). None of His brothers, including Jude, believed Jesus's claims to deity until after His resurrection (John 7:5), but later they became leading evangelists, ranking with the apostles (1 Cor. 9:5).

{Kenaniah—**Chenaniah**}

{Lebbaeus—**Thaddaeus**} (Matthew 10:3)

100. **Lemuel** wrote a portion of the inspired word of God (Proverbs 31), which his mother taught him! Thus he is a sort of surrogate prophet, like **Aaron** was when he spoke for Moses. Lemuel's chapter in the book of Proverbs contains certain advice given to him as a future king, but its main section extols the ideal "virtuous wife." This passage is a classic and much-loved description of a truly good woman.

Lemuel was a king—of what nation we are not told, but we know it was not Israel or Judah. This fact underscores the universality of the Scripture wisdom he wrote. But make no mistake, this is not universal*ism*; for the truly virtuous woman is one who, above all, *fears the Lord* (Prov. 31:30).

{Levi—**Matthew**}

{Lucas—**Luke**}

101. **Lucius** was one of the five "prophets and teachers" who ministered in the Christian church in Antioch, Syria, in about AD 45 (Acts 13:1). It is not known whether some were prophets and some were teachers, or all five were both. But the two we know the most about, **Barnabas** and Saul or **Paul**, were certainly prophets as well as teachers. We can assume that Lucius and the rest were too.

The only other fact given about Lucius is that he was from Cyrene, North Africa—also the home of Simon who bore Jesus's cross to Golgotha (Mark 15:21). Cyrene was a seedbed of Jewish and Christian activists (Acts 6:9; 11:20).

102. **Luke** prophesied by conveying to man God's word in two books of the Bible, Luke and Acts. Also, Luke probably took his turns at preaching (prophesying) verbally when he travelled with **Paul** and others on foreign mission trips (Philem. 24).

Luke is named only three times in Scripture—all by Paul and all rather incidentally. We know from these references that Luke was a physician (Col. 4:14) and that he remained loyal when all others on Paul's team had abandoned him (2 Tim. 4:11). Luke was a Gentile, not a Jew, for Paul clearly excludes him from the other fellow workers who were "of the circumcision" (Col. 4:10-11, 14). And Luke (Greek, Loukas; Latin, Lucas) is not a Hebrew name. The only other biographical information about Luke is that which can be derived from the "we" sections of Acts (16:10-17; 20:5-15; 21:1-18; 27:1–28:16); but Luke never tells about his own role or actions, only that he was there.

Luke's Gospel is based on careful research as well as divine inspiration (Luke 1:1-4). He may never have met **Jesus** in the flesh, but he certainly knew Him well in the Spirit. Luke had ample opportunity to hear firsthand, eyewitness accounts of Jesus's life from the apostles. He probably spent a lot of time in Palestine, e.g., during Paul's imprisonment under Felix and Festus (AD 58–60). Luke also spent time on the mission field with John Mark (Col. 4:10, 14; Philem. 24), although it is not at all certain that John Mark wrote the second Gospel (see **Mark**). It is often speculated that one of Luke's sources was **Mary**, Jesus's mother. He does give, in his Gospel, the fullest account of Jesus's birth and childhood.

Luke contains many things not found in the other Gospels, including these pertaining to prophets and prophecy: Only Luke tells about the prophetess **Anna** and the prophet **Simeon I**. Only Luke contains the prophetic utterances of **Zacharias**, **Elizabeth**, and Mary. It is Luke that most often and most clearly highlights the prophetic office of Jesus (Luke 4:17-24; 13:33; 24:19). Only Luke reports that Jesus said that His death and resurrection accomplished things "written by the prophets" (Luke 18:31), and that the Law, the Prophets, and the Psalms all spoke of Him (Luke 24:27, 44-45).

Luke's second Bible book, the Acts of the Apostles, is based partly on research, partly on personal experience and entirely on the inspiration of the Holy Spirit. Luke was with Paul (and others) on certain missionary journeys or portions thereof and on Paul's voyage as a prisoner, to Rome. The value and importance of Acts to Christians is inestimable. It provides the historical framework for much of the apostolic era and the New Testament epistles. It chronicles the work of the Holy Spirit in establishing and spreading the church.

Like his Gospel book, Luke's Acts provides much invaluable material on prophets and prophecy beginning with Jesus's last words to His apostles just before His ascension (Acts 1:4-8). Luke gives the *only* account of Pentecost Day, when prophecy really broke out among Christ's followers fulfilling **Joel's** prophecy that "your sons and your daughters shall prophesy" (Acts 2:17, cf. Joel 2:28). Next there are **Peter's** sermons, full of references to the prophets of old and how their prophecies were fulfilled in Christ and were now being fulfilled by His Holy Spirit through the apostles and others (Acts 2:14-39; 3:12-26; 4:8-12). Paul's only two recorded verbal sermons are in Acts (Acts 13:16-41; 17:22-31). The first of these, addressed to Jews in Antioch, Pisidia, is also full of prophecy and references to prophecy.

In Acts we meet many other Christian prophets in addition to the original apostles: **Stephen**, Paul, **Barnabas**, **Ananias**, **Agabus**, **Simeon I**, **Lucius**, **Manaen**, **Judas IV**, **Silas**, **Timothy**, and **Philip II** and his daughters. And we meet some apostolic-era false prophets including Simon the sorcerer and Bar-Jesus (Acts 8:9; 13:6).

In summary, Luke was not only a prophet himself; his writings have also provided a great deal of information on prophets, on the history of prophecy, and on the subject of prophecy.

103. **Maai** prophesied "with the musical instruments of **David** the man of God," as a member of a large choir celebrating the completion of the new Jerusalem wall, ca. 445 BC (Neh. 12:36); and then, it may be assumed, as a regular temple singer "according to the command of David and of **Solomon** his son" (Neh. 12:45-46; 1 Chr. 25:1-7). Maai and other Levite singers who had settled in the villages around Jerusalem were brought to the city to serve in the temple (Neh. 12:27-29).

104. **Maaseiah** was one of **David's** first singer-musician-prophets; he prophesied "with strings according to Alamoth" (1 Chr. 15:20). Maaseiah was appointed by the Levite leaders to help escort the ark of the covenant of the LORD to Jerusalem from the house of Obed-Edom (ca. 1000 BC) [1 Chr. 15:16-28]. Later, David and his captains appointed 288 musicians to "prophesy with harps, stringed instruments, and cymbals" in the house (tabernacle) of the LORD, singing the songs of the LORD (psalms) [1 Chr. 25:1, 6, 7). It is assumed that Maaseiah was one of these.

105. **Mahazioth** was one of the sons of **Heman**, the king's (**David's**) seer in the words of God who "should prophesy . . . in the house of the LORD . . . in the songs of the LORD" (1 Chr. 25:1, 4, 6-7). Mahazioth was a great-grandson of **Samuel** (1 Chr. 6:33). He was chosen by lot to lead the twenty-third twelve-man course of musical prophets (ca. 1000 BC.)[1 Chr. 25:30].

106. **Malachi** was a writing prophet whose "burden" is the last book of the Old Testament (Mal. 1:1). Biographical data about Malachi are even scarcer than about **Joel**. We do not have his father's name, his hometown, or his tribe. For this and other reasons some scholars believe there was no such person, but that Malachi means angel or messenger, or that some other person wrote this book. Malachi is considered a real person in this listing. In any case the message itself is an important part of God's word.

Malachi prophesied in the middle to last half of the fifth century BC. After this there was no new revelation from God for about four hundred years until He visited **Zachariah** the father of **John I**, the baptizer.

Malachi prophesied about John, calling him "**Elijah**" (Mal. 3:1a; 4:5-6 [cf. Matt. 11:9-14]). The Jews of John's and **Jesus's** day were expecting Malachi's "Elijah" (John 1:21). Sadly, many are still waiting. Malachi also prophesied distinctly of Jesus (3:1b; 4:2).

As for the people of Malachi's own time: God, through this prophet, upbraided them for corruption in the priesthood, for failure to tithe, for marital infidelity and divorce, and for lack of respect for what should be holy. These very topics are uncomfortably relevant today. Malachi also conveyed God's message of His sovereign love and His promise of a Righteous Savior (1:2-3; 3:1-7; 4:1-3).

107. **Mallothi** was leader of the nineteenth twelve-man course of singers who "should prophesy with harps, (etc.) . . . in the house of the LORD . . . (being) instructed in the songs of the LORD." (ca. 1000 BC) [1 Chr. 25:1, 4-7, 26]. He was one of the sons of **Heman** "the king's seer in the words of God," and a great-grandson of the prophet **Samuel** (1 Chr. 6:33).

108. **Manaen** ministered in the burgeoning church of Antioch, Syria, in about AD 45. He was one of five "prophets and teachers" who were there at that time (Acts 13:1). Some of them had come from Jerusalem (Acts 11:27). The five are all assumed to have been both prophets and teachers (see under **Lucius**).

Manaen had been raised with Herod the tetrarch (Acts. 13:1). This interesting fact is worth exploring on two fronts—one concerning Herod and one concerning Manaen.

Herod (Antipas), one of the sons of Herod the Great, was tetrarch (governor of one-fourth) of Galilee and Peraea. He is the one who—in a cowardly way, at that—had **John I**, the baptizer, beheaded (Matt. 14:1-12). He wanted to kill **Jesus,** too, and Jesus called him "that fox" (Luke 13:31-32). Pontius Pilate tried to "pass the buck" to Herod when Jesus was accused before him; but when Herod could get no answers from our Lord, he mocked and abused Him and sent Him back to Pilate (Luke 23:6-12). This weak and evil man, Herod Antipas, enemy of Christ, was brought up with Manaen, one of the first Christian prophets!

As for Manaen, being raised up with (some say, the foster brother of) a prince, he must have been high up the socioeconomic scale and well-educated. At least two more of the five "prophets and teachers" at Antioch, **Barnabas** and Saul **(Paul**), had significant worldly advantages and/or accomplishments—not that they counted these any more than filthy rags compared with knowing Christ. But this bit of background information about Manaen and the others should put to rest any notion that all the early Christians, including prophets, were a bunch of riffraff. To be sure, many of these Christians and prophets were social nobodies, poor of wealth, and even uneducated in a formal way; but some were not. From the very first, Christ was building His church from all social, political, racial, gender, age, and other human variations.

109. **Mark** prophesied by writing the Gospel of Mark, and possibly in other ways as well. The question is: Who was this Mark? The human author of Mark's Gospel is commonly believed to be the same person as *John* Mark, **Barnabas's** nephew and sometime assistant to **Paul** and/or Barnabas; but there is no clear Scriptural warrant for this identification.

There is a very strong tradition in early Christian literature that Mark the Evangelist was "the interpreter of **Peter**." Peter refers to a "Mark" as his son, either biological or spiritual (1 Pet. 5:13). There are internal indications in Mark (if you are looking for them!) that Peter was a primary source. The only biblical connection of *John* Mark with Peter is when the apostle, just freed by God's angel from prison, went to Mark's mother's house (Acts 12:12). On the other hand, *John* Mark is associated primarily with Uncle Barnabas and Paul—who usually operated in a totally different part of the world from Peter (Acts 12:25; 13:5, 13; 15:37-39; Col. 4:10; Philem. 24; 2 Tim. 4:11).

Still, John Mark did come from, and left the mission field to return to, Jerusalem where Peter ministered (Acts 12:12; 13:13).

Whether Mark the Evangelist was John Mark or not, whether he was Peter's interpreter or not, his Gospel is God's word and he is a major prophet. Many scholars believe that Mark was the first Gospel written, and was a resource for others, particularly Matthew and Luke. It is the most compact and action-oriented Gospel. One distinctive that is significant regarding the subject of prophecy is Mark's version of Jesus's Great Commission and its outworking. It speaks of signs and wonders that will be performed by the apostles to confirm their message—just like many prophets of old (Mark 16:14-20).

110. **Mary I**, **Jesus's** mother, prophesied poetically, possibly in song, while she was visiting her cousin **Elizabeth** during Elizabeth's third trimester of pregnancy with **John**, the baptizer-to-be (Luke 1:46-55). Mary's oracle, called the Magnificat, contains several key elements of true prophecy:

- It conveys to others, words of God given particularly to her (through Gabriel in this case) [vv. 48-49; see vv. 26-38].
- It is about Christ.
- It predicted something that would take place and has indeed come to pass (v. 48b).
- It represents and/or interprets God's previously written word, in this case the prayer of **Hannah** (1 Sam. 2:1-10).

We might ask if Mary extemporaneously spoke or sang this carefully worded sonnet. Certainly the Holy Spirit in her could do that: we read of King-elect **Saul,** with no known musical or literary training, spontaneously prophesying with a group of musical prophets (1 Sam. 10:5-13). But in Mary's case, **Luke** points out, just here (v. 56), that she spent three whole months with Elizabeth. They weren't knitting booties or having baby showers *all* that time! There was ample time for reflection on Gabriel's words and for composition of this sonnet.

To our knowledge Mary prophesied only that once. However, she was very involved with Jesus's ministry (including His prophetic office) and, after His death, in the church. Mary knew, probably better than anyone else including John the baptizer, who Jesus really was (Luke 1:26-38). During His infancy and childhood she observed many special things about Him, which she kept and pondered in her heart (Luke 2:19, 51). Knowing something of Jesus's supernatural powers, Mary had a major part in launching His public ministry, at a wedding in the town of Cana, near Nazareth their hometown (John 2:1-11). She accompanied or followed her Son to other towns (John 2:12; Luke 8:19), and He visited her in Nazareth (Luke 4:16; Mark 6:1-3). Mary was with Jesus at the end, His crucifixion; when He, although in extreme agony, saw her need and made arrangements for her welfare (John 19:25-27).

Apparently Mary did not go to the tomb with the other women to anoint Jesus's body (Mark 16:1; Luke 24:9-10). Therefore, Jesus's mother did not see His vacated tomb, nor did she hear an angel there announce that Jesus had risen from the dead. If she saw her son after His resurrection, before His ascension, Scripture does not record it. What is certain is that Mary continued to participate in Christ's work. We last see her at a prayer meeting with His disciples, after His ascension (Acts 1:14).

111. **Mary II**, surnamed Magdalene, was one of several women who came to **Jesus's** tomb just after sunrise on the day after the Sabbath following His crucifixion. She is the only one who is mentioned by name in all four Gospel accounts of this event (Matt. 28:1; Mark 16:1; Luke 20:1-10; John 20:1). She saw at least one, probably two angels at the tomb (Matt. 28:2-7; Mark 16:5-7; Luke 24:4-7; John 20:12), in what is later described as a vision (Luke 24:22-23). The angel(s) gave her a message from God, which she told (prophesied) to the disciples.

Mary Magdalene was also, on that same morning, the very first person to see the risen Jesus (Mark 16:9-11), although others saw Him at almost the same time or shortly thereafter (Matt. 28:9-10). In any event, Mary Magdalene gave the disciples Jesus's message for them, words of prophecy (John 20:18). They did not believe her (Mark 16:11)—not unusual for a prophet!

112. **Mary III**, the "other" Mary, identified as the mother of James and Joses, was one of the women who came to **Jesus's** tomb at dawn after the Sabbath following His crucifixion (Matt. 27:56; 28:1-8; Mark 15:47-16:8; Luke 23:55-24:11).

She and the others saw angels who gave them a message from God, and they told (prophesied) that message to the disciples. It is significant that their encounter with the angel(s) was described as a vision (Luke 24:22-23)—see "How God Gives Prophecy" in chapter 1.

Could this Mary have been the same person as **Mary I**, Jesus's mother? The arguments in favor of this theory are the following:

1. Out of her natural maternal love and instincts, Jesus's mother would have wanted to go to His tomb with the other women; but she is not mentioned unless she is the "other" Mary.

2. **James** and Joses are also the names of two of Jesus's half brothers, sons of Mary I (Matt. 13:55; Mark 6:3).

But against these arguments come the compelling questions:

1. Why would Jesus's mother be identified so obliquely, by all three synoptic evangelists, without reference to Him?
2. Why would Jesus's other brothers, Judas (**Jude**) and Simon, not be mentioned in Matthew 27:56, if this was Jesus's mother?

Mary III is therefore to be considered a distinctly different person—and prophetess—than Jesus's mother Mary.

113. **Mattaniah I** was a Levite who was separated to prophesy with music, specifically the songs of the LORD (psalms), in the house of the LORD, during **David's** kingship (ca. 1000 BC) [1 Chr. 25:1-7]. He was one of **Heman's** sons and a great-grandson of **Samuel** (1 Chr. 6:33). Mattaniah was chosen by lot to lead the ninth twelve-man course of tabernacle prophesiers (1 Chr. 25:16).

114. **Mattaniah II**, a Levite, was a descendent of **Asaph** and lived during the reign of King **Hezekiah** of Judah (ca. 700 BC) [2 Chr. 29:1, 12-13]. He "arose" (volunteered?) to help clean out the temple, which had been neglected and abused (along with the worship of God) during the wicked reign of Hezekiah's father Ahaz. After the temple had been cleansed and sanctified by the priests and Levites, proper sacrifices and offerings were made to God; and the king "stationed the Levites in the house of the LORD with cymbals, with stringed instruments, and with harps, according to the commandments of **David**, of **Gad** the king's seer, and of **Nathan** the prophet, for thus was the commandment of the LORD by His prophets" (2 Chr. 29:25). Such music was prophecy (1 Chr. 25). Mattaniah, being a "son" of Asaph, whether biologically or musically, can be assumed to have been one of those Levites who were commanded "to sing praise to the LORD with the words of David and of Asaph the seer" (psalms) [2 Chr. 29:30].

115. **Mattaniah III** "led the thanksgiving psalms" for the first large party of Jews who returned to Judah from captivity in Babylon in 537 BC (Neh. 12:1, 8). There were 128 (or 148) male Levite singers among the 42,360 returning Jewish exiles, along with two hundred (or 245) other singers, servants, women as well as men (Ezra 2:41, 64-65; Neh. 7:44, 66-67). When the foundation of the new temple was completed (ca. 536 BC), the Levite singers sang responsively, or antiphonally, "according to the ordinance of **David,**" the Great Refrain (see pages 267-69):

> For He is good,
> For His mercy endures forever toward Israel.—Ez. 3:10-11

This was a form of prophesying (1 Chr. 25:1). And it fulfilled a specific prophecy of Jeremiah (33:10-11).

A Mattaniah, the son of Micha, is mentioned in connection with the people who dwelt in Jerusalem rather than in the outlying villages (Neh. 11:1-24). This was some eighty years later, in the time of **Nehemiah**; but the fact that he had a grown grandson by then (Neh. 11:22) means that he could have been, quite possibly was, the same person who sang the Great Refrain with the first returning exiles. We also learn that Mattaniah was a biological descendent of **Asaph** (1 Chr. 9:15; Neh. 11:17, 22; 12:35) and that when he led the thanksgiving music, he began with prayer (Neh. 11:17).

116. **Matthew**, a.k.a. Levi[21], was one of **Jesus's** twelve disciples and original apostles (Matt. 10:1-4; Mark 3:14-19). All of them were commissioned prophets (Luke 9:1-2; Matt. 28:16-20), and they all (except **Judas**) prophesied by the Holy Spirit on the Pentecost Day just after Jesus's death and resurrection (Acts 2:1-4). In addition, Matthew prophesied by writing down God's word to man: the Gospel-book that bears his name.

Matthew (Levi) was a son of Alpheus (Mark 2:14); if this was the same Alpheus, Matthew was the brother or half-brother of another disciple/apostle and prophet, **James II**.

Matthew's calling by Jesus was surprising and dramatic, for he was a tax collector, a despised Roman agent (Mark 2:14; Luke 5:27-28; Matt. 9:9). This occupation probably made him a man of some means, too. To his credit, Matthew the new recruit held a big dinner for Jesus and His other disciples, and he invited many other tax gatherers and sinners to meet and hear Jesus (Matt. 9:10-13; Mark 2:15-17; Luke 5:29-32). This led to open criticism of Jesus by the Pharisees: "Why does your Teacher eat with tax collectors and sinners?" Jesus's well-known response was, "Those who are well have no need of a physician, but those who are sick. I did not come to call the righteous, but sinners, to repentance." We have no other biographical details or anecdotes about Matthew in Scripture. He may have been the twelfth disciple called by Jesus; he *is* the last whose calling is described.

His book, Matthew, opens the New Testament. One of its signature characteristics, compared with the other three Gospels, is the repeated use of phrases like "that it might be fulfilled, which was written in . . ." or "as written by the prophet . . ." Matthew definitely had a burden to tell his readers that Jesus was fulfilling Old Testament prophecy.

117. **Matthias** was chosen by **Jesus's** disciples to replace traitor-suicide **Judas** (Acts 1:21-26). Thus he was one of those who, a few days later, "were filled with the Holy Spirit and began to speak with other tongues" (languages) "as the Spirit gave them utterance," i.e., to prophesy (Acts 2:1-4). This was probably not the last time Matthias prophesied, nor the first. When he was chosen to replace Judas, **Peter** had

proposed, "Therefore, of these men who have accompanied us all the time that the Lord Jesus went in and out among us, beginning from the baptism of **John** to that day when He was taken up from us, one of these must become a witness with us of His resurrection" (Acts 1:21-22). Matthias, therefore, would likely have been one of the seventy disciples who had been sent out to proclaim the kingdom of God (prophesy) in cities and other places where Jesus was about to go (Luke 10:1-20).

118. **Mattithiah** was a Levite singer-harpist-prophet in about 1000 BC. We find him serving

1. in the band that escorted the ark of the covenant of the LORD to its special new tabernacle in Jerusalem (1 Chr. 15:16, 18, 21);
2. under **Asaph**, to minister before the ark in Jerusalem (1 Chr. 16:4-5); and
3. as leader of the fourteenth twelve-man section of musicians "who should prophesy . . . in the house of the LORD . . . in the songs of the LORD" (1 Chr. 25:1-7, 21).

Mattithiah was one of the sons of **Jeduthun** (1 Chr. 25:3).

119. **Medad** was one of two elders of Israel in the wilderness (ca. 1450 BC), who inexplicably stayed in camp while **Moses** took seventy other elders to the "tent of meeting" to receive a portion of God's Holy Spirit so they could help Moses govern. When the Holy Spirit rested on the seventy, they prophesied. So did Medad (and **Eldad**, the other elder who stayed in camp). A young man ran and told Moses about them; and **Joshua**, Moses's personal assistant, asked Moses to forbid Eldad and Medad to prophesy. But Moses rebuked Joshua, saying, "Oh, that all the LORD's people were prophets and that the LORD would put His Spirit upon them!" (Num. 11:16-30). A similar situation occurred over 1,400 years later when **Jesus** rebuked His disciple, **John II**, for wanting to forbid "outsiders" to cast out demons in Jesus's name (Luke 9:49-50). **Joel** prophesied that Moses's heartfelt desire for all of God's people to be Spirit-filled and to prophesy would actually take place (Joel 2:28-29), and Peter declared that the outpouring of the Holy Spirit and prophesying on that certain Pentecost Day was in fulfillment of Joel's prophecy (Acts 2:16).

120. **Micah** is one of the twelve "minor" prophets whose writings are in the Scripture canon. He prophesied during the latter eighth and early seventh centuries BC—a period that saw the final defeat of Israel (the northern kingdom) and the reduction of Judah by Assyria. Micah's prophecies concern both Samaria and Jerusalem, capitals of Israel and Judah, respectively (Mic. 1:1).

Micah was a contemporary of **Isaiah**, and to some extent he seems to have dwelt in the shadow of that great prophet. It was Isaiah who was consulted by

Judah's King **Hezekiah** and was deeply involved in that country's national affairs (2 Ki. 19:1-4, 20). It was Isaiah who was God's agent in miraculously extending Hezekiah's life by fifteen years. *But it is Micah's prophesying, not Isaiah's that is credited with turning Hezekiah's nation back to God!* (Jer. 26:18-19).

Micah was from the town of Moresheth in the foothills of Judah southwest of Jerusalem. The name Micah is short for Micaiah, which means "who is like Jah (Jehovah)?" Micah faithfully delivered God's messages, many of which were severe judgments on His people and brought the prophet no pleasure. He felt personal anguish over the people's sin (Mic. 7:1-7). He lamented (1:8b). He suffered humiliation and discomfort by going about stripped (Septuagint "barefoot") and naked (possibly, without the outer garment of sackcloth) [1:8a]. Micah also suffered the rejection of his message and opposition by lying false prophets (2:6; 3:5-7). Despite his personal feelings, pain, humiliation, rejection, and opposition, Micah was confident in his message and calling from God (3:8).

The book of Micah may be a collection or abstract of sermons the prophet preached over a period of three decades or more. However, it is cohesive, organized, and balanced. The basic form of the book is the sentencing or judgment of Samaria/Israel, Jerusalem/Judah, and their leaders— who have been found guilty in a covenant lawsuit (1:2, 5; 3:1, 8). However, the trial is still underway—perhaps testimony is still being taken for the sentencing phase (6:1-3). God's judgment is severe, irrevocable, and just (1:3-7; 3:9-12; 6:14-15). Yet He makes it abundantly clear that punishment of both nations is for their own good and restoration; God is just *and* merciful. Zion shall rise again (4:6-13). A new Ruler (Messiah) shall come forth (5:2). Israel's present conquerors and enemies shall be punished (5:5b-15). God will pardon iniquity, have compassion, cast out sins, and give mercy to "Abraham" (7:18-20).

Within this framework, the book of Micah contains many memorable gems of predictive prophecy. Probably the best-known of these is the prediction, found only in Micah, that the Messiah would come from Bethlehem (5:2). Herod the Great was told of this and tried to use the information to destroy the baby **Jesus** (Matt. 2:1-18). Micah also prophesied the Jews' exile to Babylon (Mic. 4:10), which in his time was only a second-rate power compared to Assyria; the dispersion of the Jews in Gentile lands (5:7-8); and the gathering of a remnant of them to reestablish Zion (4:6-8).

One of the most cherished verses in all of Scripture is Micah 6:8:

> He has shown you, O man, what is good:
> And what does the Lord require of you
> But to do justly,
> To love mercy,
> And to walk humbly with your God?

This is one of the most concise, yet complete and balanced, statements of God's will for man ever penned. Millions of people have memorized it and used it to guide their lives. It has been set to music. Countless sermons have been preached on it. Great leaders have quoted it in speeches and heeded it in their own lives. Theodore Roosevelt called it the "Micah Mandate" and had it inscribed in pocket New Testaments given to American soldiers. He said, "The whole teaching of the New Testament [is] foreshadowed in Micah's verse."[22] George Washington, several other presidents, and Winston Churchill used it in speeches. The list goes on—preachers, patriots, and ordinary people. But the most important affirmation is Jesus' parallel statement about the "weightier matters of the law: justice, mercy, and faith" (Matt. 23:23).

121. **Micaiah**, a contemporary of **Elijah,** stood as one man of God against about four hundred false prophets—very similar to Elijah's contest with false prophets at Mount Carmel a few years earlier. Micaiah's opponents "guaranteed" a victory over Syria for Kings Ahab of Israel and Jehoshaphat of Judah, who had become temporary allies. Only Micaiah knew and dared to tell of the impending military disaster for the allies, and of Ahab's death in the battle (1Ki. 22).

We have no biographical information about Micaiah except for this single defining episode in his life. Apparently at this time, ca. 853 BC, Elijah was persona non grata in Samaria, Ahab's capital. He had recently condemned Ahab, who called Elijah "my enemy" (1Ki. 21:17-24). Several other prophets of God passed through Ahab's life (1Ki. 20:13, 28, 41), but only Micaiah managed to stay within reach of the king although Ahab hated him (1 Ki. 22:7-8).

One of the most interesting glimpses in Scripture of the inner workings of God's court—and one that challenges some of our beliefs—was revealed to Micaiah in a vision (1 Ki. 22:19-23). God actually asked His court for suggestions on how to convince Ahab to go into this battle, in which he would be killed, and then He approved of a plan to do it by putting a lying spirit in all of Ahab's court prophets! We are reminded of the scene and events in heaven in the book of Job (1:6-12; 2:1-6), and of the biblical assertions that God put a distressing (evil) spirit in **Saul** (1 Sam. 16:14) and that He hardened Pharaoh's heart (Ex. 11:10). All of these may disturb us, but they cannot be ignored.

Micaiah lied to Ahab too, at first. But it must have been done so sarcastically that even Ahab, who desperately wanted to hear "good" prophecy about himself, knew Micaiah wasn't serious (1 Ki. 22:15-16).

Micaiah suffered for his faithful prophesying. He was struck on the face by a leader of the false prophets named Zedekiah (1 Ki. 22:11, 24). Then Ahab sentenced him to prison with a starvation, bread-and-water diet, "until I" (Ahab) "come in peace" (1 Ki. 22:26-27). If this sentence was carried out, Micaiah died there in prison, for Ahab never came back. Micaiah knew his probable fate, for he alone knew that Ahab would not return. Yet his last words in Scripture were to warn other people—not to try to save himself (1 Ki. 22:28).

122. **Mikneiah** was one of **David's** prophesying Levite musicians who marched with the ark of the covenant of the LORD into Jerusalem in about 1000 BC (1 Chr. 15:18, 21). He was "to direct with harps on the Sheminith." It is assumed that he went on to prophesy in the tabernacle as part of the 288-man Levite chorus, instructed in the songs of the LORD (1 Chr. 25:1-7).

123. **Milalai** was in one of the two thanksgiving choirs assembled by **Nehemiah** to help celebrate and dedicate the new Jerusalem wall by marching on that wall to the temple, where they "sang loudly," being accompanied by "the musical instruments of **David** the man of God" (Neh. 12:31-36; 42b). The title "man of God" refers to David's prophetic office (see chapter 2), and the choirs undoubtedly sang some of his psalms. Milalai probably then became a member of the regular temple choir that prophesied "according to the command of David (1 Chr. 25) and **Solomon** his son" (Neh. 12:45-46).

124. **Miriam** was the first prophetess, one of the first musical prophets, and the "first sister" of the greatest prophet of the Old Testament, **Moses**. In some ways, she is to prophetesses what Moses is to male prophets: an example, a leader, a prototype.

Miriam's only known recorded prophecy is very short. It is a song or hymn praising God for victory over Pharaoh's army at the Red Sea. It was accompanied by the music and dancing of other women (Ex. 15:20-21). But brief as this one sample is, there is evidence that Miriam prophesied many times over a period of nearly four decades. This is suggested, albeit negatively, in her rebellion (with **Aaron** and against Moses) at camp Hazeroth (Num. 12). She and Aaron said, "Has the LORD indeed spoken only through Moses? Has He not spoken through us also?"(v. 2). Yes, He had. After all, Miriam was known as "the prophetess" (Ex. 15:20), not just as Moses's sister who spuriously prophesied once or twice. Even more convincing is the fact that God, speaking through **Micah**, places Miriam alongside her brothers as His agents (Micah 6:4).

Miriam was born from Hebrew slaves in Egypt, Amram and Jochabed, of the tribe of Levi (Num. 26:59; 1 Chr. 6:3). Her name probably means fat or thick. Her first appearance in Scripture is anonymous: as Moses's older sister watching over her baby brother in the bulrushes and guiding Pharaoh's daughter to hire their mother as wet nurse (Ex. 2:1-10). We believe that this was Miriam because she is the only sister mentioned in the genealogies.

From the bulrush episode, in which Miriam is called a maiden (Ex. 2:8) and in which she acted quite cleverly, we surmise that she was perhaps ten years old. Thus, since Moses was eighty just before the Exodus (Ex. 7:7), Miriam was about ninety when she and all Israel left Egypt and when she delivered her musical prophecy. So much for our fancies of Miriam as a lithe young maiden with a tambourine doing a victory dance!

The one stain on Miriam's reputation is her behavior at camp Hazeroth in the wilderness (Num. 12). From a purely human point of view (which is exactly the way she and Aaron were acting), her jealousy of Moses is quite understandable. Older siblings are naturally resentful of preferment shown to a younger brother or sister. Scripture is replete with other examples of this, from Cain to Esau to **Joseph's** brothers to the prodigal son's elder brother. But being and acting natural and human does not excuse sin; in most cases, as in Miriam's, it is *why* we sin. God severely punished her, with leprosy.[23] Only because of Moses's intercession was she restored to physical and, apparently, spiritual health. The latter is indicated by the endorsement in Micah (6:4) and by Miriam's honorable funeral (Num. 20:1).

The Hazeroth episode produced benefits. Because of it, God revealed just how He normally gives prophecy to prophets: dreams and visions (Num. 12:6; and see chapter 1). This event also gave the Israelites an example of how to manage leprosy by isolation and sacrificial intercession (for Moses did risk, and would have sacrificed, his own standing with God, for her sake) [Deut. 24:8-9; cf. Lev. 14].

Miriam died and was buried at Kadesh, almost forty years out of Egypt (Num. 20:1). Since her younger brother Aaron died at the age of 123 at the next encampment (Num. 33:36-39), she must have been about 130 when she died.. Her given name, Miriam, is shared by only one obscure person in Scripture (1 Chr. 4:17). But its Greek equivalent, Mary, was given to several women in the New Testament including **Jesus**'s mother. Like Miriam, **Mary** and several other prophetesses of the Bible are believed to have prophesied in song.

125. **Moses**, if prophets could be ranked, was the greatest one in the Old Testament and the greatest prophet of all except **Jesus** and **John I**, the baptizer (John 11:1). Many historians would agree that Moses was one of the greatest *men* of all time—such an outstanding leader and pioneer that it is easy to forget that he was primarily a prophet. Robert Young wrote,

> As a historian, an orator, a leader, a statesman, a legislator, a patriot, and a man, Moses stands pre-eminent. But no mere genius could have made him the originator of sound jurisprudence—the great teacher of monotheism and sound morality—except he had also been a prophet of the Most High, supernaturally guided and aided in his work.[24]

The fact that Moses was a prophet, first and foremost, cannot be missed in Scripture:

> By a prophet the LORD brought Israel out of Egypt, and by a prophet he was preserved. –Hosea 12:13

> But since then there has not arisen in Israel a prophet like Moses, whom the LORD knew face to face . . . –Deuteronomy 34:10

> This is that Moses who said to the children of Israel, "The LORD your God will raise up for you a Prophet like me from your brethren. Him you shall hear." This is he who was in the congregation in the wilderness with the angel who spoke to him on Mount Sinai, and with our fathers, the one who received the living oracles to give to us. –Acts 7:37-38

> You [God] spoke by Your servant Moses, –1 Kings 8:53

Early Life

Moses's lowly birth to slaves in Egypt (Ex. 2:1-2; 6:20); his mother Jochabed's desperate plan to save his life from Pharaoh's edict of mass ethnic infanticide; the bulrushes and sister **Miriam's** ploy; his adoption by Pharaoh's daughter (Ex. 1:22-2:10); his success as an Egyptian (Acts 7:22); and his exile to Midian as a fugitive from justice for killing an Egyptian (Ex. 2:11-15)—all this is well known from our Sunday school lessons and will not be rehearsed in detail here. Two points from this period of Moses's life (his first forty years) that are not at first obvious and have a bearing on his career and character as a prophet, are as follows:

The first is that Moses meant to deliver his Israelite brethren even before he was called by God to do so. He thought that his high position as a prince of Egypt, plus his great knowledge and skill, would enable him to deliver them "by his (own) hand" (Acts 7:25). He couldn't—not until God called and empowered him forty years later—but he tried.

The second point about Moses' nativity and early life relates to the fact that he was a descendent of Levi (Ex. 6:16-20). The Levites had a genetic disposition toward fierce anger and cruelty—so much that they were *cursed* in **Jacob's** prophecy concerning his sons (Gen. 49:5-7). Moses inherited these traits and killed a man in anger himself (Ex. 2:12). However, he later became the *meekest* of men (Num. 12:3 KJV). And, through Moses, God elevated the tribe of Levi to be His priests and special servants in Israel (Deut. 10:8-9; 33:8-11). This was undoubtedly an honor and a blessing for them. However, Jacob's curse was not technically repealed in one sense: the Levites remained scattered in Israel.

Moses's parents were *both* Levites (Num. 26:58-59). His father Amram lived 137 years (Ex. 6:20), but it is not known whether or not he was in the Exodus. He may have died in Egypt. In the wilderness, the patriarch of Moses's family, the Kohathites, was one Elizaphan (Num. 3:30). Moses's sister Miriam was several years older than he, and **Aaron**, his brother, was three years older than Moses (Ex. 7:7).

Moses's name, given him by Pharaoh's daughter, ironically and prophetically means "draw out." He was drawn out of the Nile river (Ex. 2:10). In Midian, he drew out water for Jethro's flock (Ex. 2:16-19). He drew Israel out of Egypt.

Moses left Egypt when he was "full forty years old" as a fugitive from justice (Acts 7:23). He went to Midian, probably east of the Sinai Peninsula, beyond the Gulf of Aqaba. There he met and married Zipporah, a Midianite priest's daughter (Ex. 2:16-21). Their meeting—at a well—is reminiscent of Jacob's meeting Rachel at a well (Gen. 29:1-14) and of **Isaac's** marriage-broker meeting Rebekah at a well (Gen. 24:1-28). [How Hebrew boys meet girls in a foreign country?] Moses settled into an obscure life of tending the sheep of his father-in-law, Jethro, a.k.a. Reuel (Ex. 3:1). Moses and Zipporah had two sons, Gershon (Gershom) and Eliezer (Ex. 18:3-4). Moses failed to do his duty as an Israelite father, circumcise his son(s) [Ex. 4:24-26]. This indicates that Moses thought he would never return to his own people. Then, out of the blue, the call came from God.

The Call

Moses's call (Ex. 3:1-4:17) came when he was eighty years old (Acts 7:23, 30; Ex. 7:7)—a mature man, then; elderly, by today's reckoning. God spoke to Moses from, of all things, a bush that burned without being consumed. He initially called Moses to bring Israel out of Egypt but did not say how. In the denouement, Moses led Israel out as a prophet: with only God's word and miracles, not with a rebel army or even with diplomacy and persuasion.

Moses was a true original, the Prototype Prophet. No Israelite had prophesied since **Joseph** interpreted Pharaoh's dreams about four hundred years earlier (Ex. 12:40). Moreover, all previous prophesiers were patriarchs first, prophets incidentally. Of them only **Abraham** (q.v.) was *called* a prophet, and that only once. Moses was the second son in an obscure family in an accursed tribe of an enslaved people, but the first full-time prophet of God! Furthermore, since the days when they were a small family or tribe under a patriarch, no one had ever been the leader, or chief, of all these Hebrews. Moses had little idea of what he was getting into when his call came. There were no "former prophets," or even former national leaders, on which to model himself.

Moses tried to duck his call—not just once or twice, or three or four times, but five times! (Ex. 3:11, 13; 4:1, 10, 13). God met each of Moses's objections: first, by promising not to abandon him; second, by telling Moses His personal name and disclosing His overall plan for freeing Israel; third, by giving Moses three signs (miracles) with which to convince the Israelites that his commission was from God; fourth, by promising Moses speaking ability; and finally, angered by Moses's continued unwillingness to go despite all these promises, God promised him a spokesman, Aaron.

Moses's speech problem is doubly interesting: first, because it is a major handicap for a prophet and second, because before he left Egypt the first time he was "mighty in words and deeds" (Acts 7:22). What happened? Had he forgotten the Egyptian language (with which to speak to Pharaoh) during those forty years in Midian? Or did he not know the dialect of the Hebrews, with which to speak to them, since he was not raised among them? The latter seems to be implied after

Moses's first efforts to gain a holiday backfired and the children of Israel "did not heed Moses" (Ex. 6:9, 12). He complained that he had "uncircumcised" lips. Or had Moses simply developed a stammering or other speech problem in Midian? The Bible does not say. Eventually, Moses seems to have overcome any problem he may have had in communicating with the people of Israel, relying less and less on Aaron.

Family Man

Moses took his wife and two young sons with him on his mission to Egypt, but when things got sticky there he sent them back to Midian, to his father-in-law Jethro (Ex. 18:2-3). After all, they were not Israelite slaves; this was not their fight. Following the dramatic Exodus of Israel from Egypt, when they got to Sinai, Jethro brought Moses's wife and sons to him (Ex. 18:1-6). There, as Moses told him the details about God's mighty acts to free Israel, Jethro became a believer. He had been a Midianitish priest who believed in "all the gods." Now he brought offerings and sacrifices to God and worshipped Him. In testimony to his sincerity, he was honored by a dinner with Aaron and the elders of Israel (Ex. 18:7-12). Then Jethro gave Moses some very good advice about how to govern Israel, and returned to Midian (Ex. 18:13-27). Hobab, Moses's brother-in-law (Jethro's son), was persuaded to stay with the Israelites as a wilderness guide (Num. 10:29-32).

We do not know what became of Moses's wife Zipporah. Both of her sons, Gershom and Eliezer, were "reckoned to the tribe of Levi" (1 Chr. 23:13-17). They made no claim to inherit their father's special position in Israel. They and their progeny were assigned Levitical duties including the oversight of the treasuries of dedicated things (1 Chr. 26:23-28).

Moses later married an Ethiopian woman. This fueled a huge rift between Moses and his sibling prophets, Aaron and Miriam (Num. 12). The latter two contended that this marriage compromised Moses's prophetic authority and, by comparison, elevated theirs. Their carping at Moses angered God, who suddenly called all three to His office, the tent of meeting. *God's words in support of Moses on this occasion comprise one of the Bible's most definitive statements on the subject of prophets and prophecy* (Num. 12:6-8). Miriam was punished with leprosy. Aaron was devastated by her punishment and his own shame. Only after Moses interceded for them were they restored to health and grace.

Moses's Ministry of Prophecy

The scope and grandeur of Moses's prophetic ministry, and its impact on mankind to this day and as long as the world shall last (Matt. 5:17-18), cannot be exaggerated. We plead lack of words to express it. A few major aspects will be barely touched upon in the following paragraphs. It is well to remember that these splendid achievements were all of God's doing; Moses was simply His mouthpiece, and even for that he needed Aaron's help. Granted that Moses was a brilliant, educated, skilled, and righteous man, he did nothing great without God. When called by God, Moses was a fugitive who was trying to live a quiet life in a faraway country. Yes, Moses was patriotic and compassionate toward Israel when he was younger (Ex. 2:11; Acts 7:23-25), but he had given up and was most reluctant to take up their cause again. And Moses, despite his brilliance and skill, could never have come up with the successful plan, and the means, to free Israel from Egypt and to govern them in the wilderness.

Miracles

Over twenty-five miracles were worked through Moses and his subprophet Aaron, more than through any other prophet except **Jesus**. The times were so spiritually impoverished, and the children of Israel's faith in God was so weak, that miracles were needed to get their attention, to make them believe, and to rescue them. Besides the ten plagues in Egypt (Ex. 7:14-12:30), there were the three signs God gave Moses to convince the Israelites (and Pharaoh) of the divinity of his mission: the rod that turned into a snake, the leprous hand, and the turning of river water into blood (Ex. 4:1-9). The rod somehow became Aaron's and was used many more times in connection with other miracles.

The most significant miracle associated with Moses—although Moses has very little to do with it other than to announce God's plan and instructions—was when death "passed over" the houses of all the Israelites who had sacrificed a perfect lamb and put its blood on their door posts and lintels while the Egyptians' firstborn were all killed (Ex. 12:1-30). Jews still celebrate this Passover event. But the far greater significance of this first Passover is prophetic: for as millions of Christians know, "Christ, our Passover, was sacrificed for us" (1 Cor. 5:7). Eternal death passes over those for whom Jesus died, who appropriate His blood to the "door posts and lintels" of their earthly tabernacles (bodies and souls), the blood of the Lamb.

The parting and closing of the waters of the Red Sea (Ex. 14:21-29) is one of the best-known miracles associated with Moses. It had several purposes:

1. To save Israel from the Egyptian army, in hot pursuit—Ex. 14:13-14
2. To teach the Egyptians a lesson—14:17-18
3. To make it difficult for Israel to return to Egypt—13:17
4. To make Israel fear God, and to believe Him and His prophet Moses—14:31.

This miracle also inspired the writing and singing of the first psalm prophecy in Scripture (Ex. 15:1-18). And it inspired the first prophetess, Miriam, to prophesy, also in song (Ex. 15:20-21).

About as many miracles were performed through Moses in the wilderness over the next forty years as had been done in Egypt and at its border. All have Messianic overtones, but the two most obvious in this respect were the giving of manna and the bronze serpent. The manna miracle (Ex. 16) foreshadowed and was totally eclipsed by Jesus Christ, the Bread of Life (John 6:30-58). The bronze serpent, raised on a pole, gave healing to Israelites who merely looked at it after they had been bitten by poisonous snakes because they grumbled against God and Moses (Num. 21:4-9). Fifteen hundred years later Jesus said

> And as Moses lifted up the serpent in the wilderness, even so must the Son of Man be lifted up, that whoever believes in Him should not perish but have eternal life.—John 3:14-15

Birth of a Nation through Prophecy

Moses was not only the first full-time prophet, he was also the first Head of State in Israel.[25] Before Moses there was no nation of Israel—only a family, a race, a people. When Jacob moved his whole family to Egypt, Israel consisted of seventy males plus wives and daughters (Gen. 46:27). Now, 430 years later, there were about 600,000[26] men of military age, not counting Levites (Ex. 12:37; Num. 1:46-47). They had their tribes, their families, their elders, and their officers (foremen) [Ex. 5:14]; but they did not have a sovereign nation with a government of their own. They were slaves. No wonder Moses asked God, "But suppose they will not believe me or listen to my voice; suppose they say, 'The LORD has not appeared to you'" (Ex. 4:1). But after they saw the three signs and heard the words of God, the elders and all the people believed that God would deliver them with Moses as their leader (Ex. 4:29-31).

Moses and Aaron first went to Pharaoh acting more like labor leaders negotiating for a holiday, than rebels demanding independence (Ex. 5). And Pharaoh responded as a tough owner-manager, insisting on keeping the same production quota while adding more work and refusing the holiday. Pharaoh won. The people turned against Moses. Moses lost heart. But this was only round one. It was all part of God's plan. He encouraged and redirected Moses. He sent the plagues. The people came over again, to God and to Moses, and we know the outcome: not only were they freed from slavery and got out of Egypt, but a brand new nation was born, all through prophecy and miracles.

There was much more to be done, of course. Within just a few months this nation would have its own laws (Deuteronomy), military (Num. 2), religion (Leviticus), and government (Ex. 18:25-26). There were officials all the way from "rulers of tens" up to Moses, a total of about 78,600. All of this, too, God worked through His prophets Moses, Aaron, and Miriam—principally Moses.

The Law

The new nation, Israel, would be a constitutional theocracy. It would be governed by law and by God Himself. Moses was not a dictator, he was a prophet. In fact, God dictated the Law through Moses. God had more in mind than the nation of Israel when He gave them the moral Law. Most of the world would know and admire this Law, if not keep it. And it will be in force until the end of time (Matt. 5:18).

Moses has been called the Great Legislator. Actually he did not author or pass a single law. It all came from God, but it did come through Moses as prophecy.

Religion

In just a few short months, not only a new nation and its laws, but also a new religion was prophesied into existence through Moses (Leviticus and parts of Exodus, Numbers, and Deuteronomy). This religion, with its sacrifices, feasts, offerings, Sabbaths, priesthood, architecture, ceremonies, and rules for living, is all about God's oneness, purity, and holiness; plus it deals with man's greatest problems, sin and guilt, through the rituals of atonement. No so-called religion, in all the world and in all history, has ever been as good as this one was. But it was primarily a "copy and a shadow of the heavenly things" (Heb. 8:5). Pure Christianity is its fulfillment:

Jesus Christ is the ultimate and final Sacrifice for sins –Heb. 10:12
He is the high and only Priest and Mediator (Intercessor) between God and man –Heb. 7:24-25
He is Sabbath Rest –Heb. 4:10; Matt. 11:28-29
He is the great Feast –John 6:35ff
and He serves in a "greater and more perfect tabernacle not made with hands" –Heb. 9:11

Moses did not invent Judaism any more than he thought up the ten plagues, created the nation Israel, or authored the Law. His ministry was to prophesy the words of God faithfully and fully as he received them on the Mount, from the cloud, and in the tabernacle. And as he prophesied this new religion, he also prophesied of Christ.

Writings

Moses is not classified as a "writing prophet" in the canon of Scripture. But in point of fact, he was the most prolific Scripture writer of all the prophets. The Pentateuch (Genesis through Deuteronomy), nearly fifteen percent of the Bible, is primarily attributed to Moses, although there are some obvious additions by others, such as Deuteronomy 34. Moses also wrote several rather lengthy songs, one of which appears outside the Pentateuch (Ex. 15; Deut. 32; Psalm 90). One tradition holds that he also wrote the story line of Job (chapters 1 and 2 and the end of 42), although there is no clear Scriptural warrant for this.

Shortly after the Exodus from Egypt, Moses was expressly told by God to write in "the book", possibly a journal (Ex. 17:14). After his first extended audience with God on Mount Sinai, Moses told the people God's "words and judgments," including the Ten Commandments. Then he wrote them down as "the Book of the Covenant," which he read publicly (Ex. 24:3-8). The people agreed to obey it, and this covenant was sealed with blood (v. 8). It is interesting that this prophet wrote the very first copy of the Ten Commandments (and other words of God); the stone tablets written by the finger of God, even the first set, came later (Ex. 24:13; 31:18). Then, after these tablets were broken and Moses returned to the Mount for a second forty-day period, while God wrote on the second set of stone tablets, He instructed Moses to produce another copy, presumably on paper (papyrus?) or clay (Ex. 34:27-28). These documents are probably the bases for parts of Exodus and Deuteronomy, but not Leviticus or Numbers.

Leviticus, except for some short narrative passages, was dictated by God from the tabernacle of meeting where He was wont to appear and speak either in the door or from above the mercy seat (Lev. 1:1; Num. 12:5; Lev. 16:2). More verbatim words of God (prophecy) appear in Leviticus than in any other book of the Bible. God also commanded Moses to keep a log of the wilderness journey's starting points (Num. 33:1-2). This log was probably a source document for much of the book of Numbers.

Moses's complete exposition of God's Law (possibly much like the book of Deuteronomy) was delivered to the elders and the Levitical priesthood of Israel shortly before his death (Deut. 31:9-13, 24-26). He commanded them to keep this book of the Law in the holiest part of the tabernacle, right next to (but not inside) the ark of the covenant of the LORD. He also enjoined them to read it publicly, in its entirety, every seven years. Joshua cited and obediently read this "book of the Law of Moses" (Josh. 1:7-8; 8:34; 23:6); he even added to it a record of the covenant renewal at Shechem (Josh. 24:1-28, see v. 26). Apparently, however, the seventh-year readings were later neglected although the book itself was preserved. Almost nine centuries later, workers repairing the temple found it (2 Ki. 22:3-13)—leading to a period of reformation under King Josiah (2 Ki. 23:1-25). Even later, at least a thousand years after it was first written, and *after* the Babylonian captivity through which it had been preserved, **Ezra** stood upon a wooden platform and publicly read the book of the Law of Moses to the Jews rebuilding Jerusalem; and again, a revival broke out (Neh. 8:1-12).

The "Best" of Moses

He was given awesome political power over a nation, and a very important role in world history, but Moses never exalted himself. He never sought to be king, pharaoh, or sheikh. He did not abrogate the authority of the tribal/family leaders, the elders; rather, he encouraged it. He delegated authority, especially to his brother Aaron who became High Priest. The only title Moses took was "prophet." Even in that he was "very humble, more than all men" (Num. 12:3).

Moreover, Moses never sought or amassed wealth for himself. No luxury personal tabernacle, no harem, no flocks and herds, and no crown jewels. Indeed,

Moses did not take even one donkey from the people for himself (Num. 16:15). How easy it would have been for Moses to acquire personal wealth. In fact, he did collect enormous riches from those wandering ex-slaves (Ex. 25:1-9; 35:4-9, 20-29); but it all went into the tabernacle, with its clasps and overlays of gold, sockets of silver, and fine tapestries and curtains; the furniture including the golden lampstand, the gold-overlaid ark, and the mercy seat and cherubim of pure gold; and the priest's vestments including the ephod and breastplate studded with precious stones (Ex. 25:10-28:43; ch. 37-39). All of this was ordained by God for His worship and glory, nothing for Moses. Future prophet-kings of Israel like **David** and **Solomon** would have great palaces and vast personal estates; not Moses.

Far from assuming Lordship or amassing wealth, Moses humbled himself and, like most prophets, suffered for being God's servant. On at least two occasions he endured very long periods of starvation and thirst on Mount Sinai (Deut. 9:9, 18). When the children of Israel had a setback or hardship they usually blamed Moses, forgetting that he did not choose this assignment (Ex. 5:20-21; 16:2-3; 17:3). Some were envious of Moses's standing with God (though he did not seek or choose it) [Num. 16]. His own sister and brother accused him (falsely) of Lording it over them, and tried to displace him (Num. 12:1-3).

Moses's character shone the brightest when, more than once, God was ready to destroy, abandon, or very severely punish the people for their faithlessness, constant complaining, and outright rebellion against Him. God is exceedingly long-suffering, beyond all human comprehension; but He does have a limit, and these incorrigible reprobates deserved to be cast out. To keep His covenant promises to Abraham, **Isaac**, and Jacob (**Israel**), God was prepared to start over with just Moses (Num. 14:12). *But over and over again, Moses interceded for the people!* He begged for more mercy, basing his plea on God's honor and glory and putting his own standing with God on the line (Ex. 32:30-35; 33:3, 12-17; Num. 11:1-2; 14:11-20). Such radical intercession, especially on behalf of sinful, unrepentant, undeserving people, was not in the terms of Moses's call to prophesy. It came from Moses's character, his heart, his love for his people, and his concern for God's honor. Moses could have stood back and accepted God's gracious offer to start over with just him (Deut. 9:13-14), but he didn't!

While Moses's character shone in his humility, poverty, and intercessory love, his face literally shone just after he talked face-to-face with God (Ex. 34:29-35). Some of God's physical, visible glory was temporarily transferred to Moses's face! This never happened to any other Old Testament prophet, for none but Moses and Jesus ever spoke with God *vis-à-vis* (Num.12:7-8; Deut. 34:10).

Moses died at the age of 120 (Deut. 34:7). He was disappointed at being denied the privilege of leading Israel across the Jordan River into Canaan, but he accepted this as justice from God and his faith was not diminished. Also, "His eyes were not dim nor his natural vigor diminished" (34:7). He died because it was time to die, "according to the word of the LORD" (34:5). He was buried in a valley in Moab, but his grave was not marked and never found (34:6). The archangel Michael argued with the devil over Moses's body (Jude 9).

But Moses did finally make it into the promised land, both figuratively and geographically. For, his greatest moment of glory came some 1,500 years later when he once again appeared bodily, with another prophet, **Elijah**, talking with Jesus his Lord on a mountain somewhere in Judea or Galilee (Luke 9:28-36).

126. **Nahum** is one of the most obscure personalities among the canonical prophets. Just before addressing his congregation, a preacher may pray, "God, please hide me and let Yourself show through." Nahum exemplified this ideal. His name is given only once in all Scripture, and the only biographical detail is that he was an Elkoshite. If Elkosh was a place, modern scholars have not found it.

Nahum's book is a "burden against Nineveh" (Nah. 1:1) written after Assyria (i.e., Nineveh) had destroyed Israel in 722 BC, and before that city-nation's fall to Babylonia (Chaldea) in 612 BC. Remarkably, this is the second book of Scripture devoted entirely to Nineveh, the other being Jonah. No other Gentile empire gets that kind of canonical attention. About a century before Nahum wrote, Nineveh repented at the preaching of **Jonah** and was spared by God. Not so this time: in Nahum the cruel, evil city and its empire (Assyria) are judged, found guilty, and sentenced to utter annihilation (Nah. 1:14; 2:13; 3:1-4, 19).

The first part of Nahum is a powerful and soaring description of God Almighty, and is not "against Nineveh" or anyone else in particular (Nah. 1:2-10). This beautiful passage transcends all "Ninevehs," past and future. Nahum gradually zeroes in on Nineveh but does not even mention that place by name until halfway through his prophecy (Nah. 2:8), except of course in the introduction. Besides being a judgment of Nineveh, Nahum's vision was a comfort to Judah (just then being oppressed by Nineveh), as it is to any of God's people who are tyrannized.

127. **Nathan** appears historically four times in Scripture, over a period of about thirty years (1000–970 BC), all four times in connection with King **David**. The first was soon after David had defeated his internal and external enemies, united the kingdom of Israel, made his capital at Jerusalem, brought the ark of the covenant there, and settled down in his own new house. David began to dream of building a permanent structure to house the ark of the covenant of the LORD, instead of the tabernacle (tent) he had erected for it (2 Sam. 6:17). David shared this desire with Nathan (2 Sam. 7:1-2), who first agreed to it (2 Sam. 7:3). But that very night Nathan had a vision from God with other directions: David's seed (son), who would succeed him, would build "a house for My name" (2 Sam. 7:4-17; cf. 1 Chr. 17:3-15)). This complete prophecy was about much more than buildings of stone and wood. In it, God promised that *He* would build *David* a house (dynasty) and that "your house and your kingdom shall be established forever before you. Your throne shall be established forever." It was an unconditional covenant promise,

similar to those God made to **Abraham**, **Isaac**, and Jacob/**Israel**! Little did Nathan know that this was ultimately speaking of **Jesus Christ** (David's seed in the flesh) and His everlasting kingdom. David must have grasped something of its ultimate meaning when he wrote psalms such as the 110th.

This first glimpse of Nathan shows that David trusted and confided in him. These were the best of times for prophets. From **Samuel** to **Ahijah**, for over one hundred years, prophets of God were highly esteemed. Kings were prophets, and, more importantly, they honored and even submitted to prophets. This honor would be severely tested in Nathan's next appearance: He was sent by God to confront David about his sin in the affair of Bathsheba and Uriah (2 Sam. 12:1-15). In spite of his high esteem in David's eyes, Nathan had to use extreme tact—and a parable—to convict David. His sudden revelation, "Thou art the man!"(v. 7, KJV) is one of the high-drama points of Scripture. It was immediately followed by a tongue lashing and a sentence of punishment against David from God through His prophet Nathan. In any other times and with any other king, Nathan may have been arrested, banished, imprisoned, or even executed for this effrontery. But the episode ends with a simple "then Nathan departed to his house." One of the most compelling psalms of David, the fifty-first, arose from this encounter; Nathan is named in its title.

In his third appearance Nathan is sent by God to rename David's child, **Solomon**, "Jedidiah" (beloved of the LORD) [2 Sam. 12:24-25]. Inexplicably, this name did not stick.

Lastly, Nathan masterminded the transfer of David's kingship to Solomon, just when it seemed that the throne had been seized by another son, Adonijah (1 Ki. 1). Following the example of **Samuel**, the prophet who anointed both Saul and David, Nathan the prophet (along with Zadok the priest), anointed Solomon the third king of Israel. Nathan's career as a prophet continued during Solomon's reign although he is not mentioned except as a historian of that period (2 Chr. 9:29). If Nathan lived to the end of Solomon's reign, his career would have spanned an unlikely seventy years.

Nothing is known of Nathan's background or his personal life. His name, meaning "gift," is also embedded in other names such as *Jonathan* (Jah is given) and *Nathanael* (gift of God). It is enticing to speculate that David named one of his own sons—Solomon's brother—after his favorite prophet (1 Chr. 3:5; 14:4).

Nathan wrote a book, or books, about David and about Solomon (1 Chr. 29:29; 2 Chr. 9:29. He was also deeply involved in the establishment of musical prophecy (2 Chr. 29:25; see also chapter 6 and David in this chapter). Nathan was a more accomplished and multifaceted prophet than is generally recognized.

{Nathanael—**Bartholomew**}(supposed)

Nebuchadnezzar NOTE: Nebuchadnezzar is not included in our list of prophets despite his prophecylike utterances in Daniel 4:3 and 34–37. His omission is *not* because he had been an unrighteous pagan, for **Balaam** was a God-hating pagan, yet God used him to prophesy truth. Even **Judas III** Iscariot prophesied. Nebuchadnezzar, the worldly, ruthless, idolatrous king; the one who decimated Judah, razed Jerusalem, and took thousands of Jews into captivity; this same Nebuchadnezzar praised and honored God (Dan. 4) after he had been humiliated, degraded, and then restored to health and power. We long to know if Nebuchadnezzar's conversion was genuine and permanent, especially in light of his spurious "rocky ground" conversion after he witnessed God's miraculous deliverance of Shadrack *et. al.* from the fiery furnace (Dan. 3:28-30). But the Bible does not tell us. It speaks no more of Nebuchadnezzar after his humiliation and restoration.

However, none of this matters with regard to Nebuchadnezzar's status as a nonprophet. Fully converted or not, he cannot be listed as a prophet here simply because he fails to meet any of the criteria (see headnotes). His hymn of praise and his confessions—admittedly worthy of a prophet—are nowhere called prophecy or words of God, or are said to have been given Nebuchadnezzar by God in dream or vision. He is not said to have prophesied or spoken under the influence of the Holy Spirit. Nebuchadnezzar is not called a prophet, seer, or man of God, and he was not a human author of Scripture (God's word)—**Daniel** merely reports his words. We hope we have not done Nebuchadnezzar a disservice. Perhaps he was in fact filled with the Holy Spirit, and prophesied; but the evidence is not there.

128. **Nehemiah**, that brilliant project manager (the wall) and twice governor of the restored nation Judah (445–433 BC [Neh. 5:14] and an undated second term [Neh. 13:6ff]), was also a prophet. He served in the office of prophet by being author of a portion of God's written word, the book bearing his name (Neh. 1:1). Also, he interceded with God for the children of Israel, as prophets intercede (Neh. 1:5-11). Further, if Nehemiah was the author of the magnificent psalm-prayer of praise, confession, and thanksgiving, which was then prophesied by a Levite choir (Neh. 9), this adds to his credentials as a prophet.

But Nehemiah needs no other credentials than that of Scripture writer. He was a man of action and few words. All that is known of his family is his father's name, Hachaliah (1:1). Perhaps they were of Judah's tribe. Nehemiah was endowed by God with extraordinary abilities. As an exile in Susa, a Persian capital, he rose to the trusted position of king's cupbearer. He used this leverage to gain the king's permission to go to Judah to rebuild Jerusalem after being told by his brother Hanani and others of its disrepair and of the people's poverty—and after much prayer. Although his main project, to rebuild the city wall, was completed in only fifty-two days (Neh. 6:15), Nehemiah stayed on as governor for twelve years. The servant cupbearer proved to be a man of enormous leadership ability and a great man of God, rebuilding not only walls and buildings but reforming the morals and religion of the Jewish people twice! Besides civil governance, during his first term Nehemiah organized the priests and Levites into their original Mosaic and Davidic configurations, as much as possible (Neh. 12:27-47). This included ordaining choral prophecy choirs "according to the command of **David** and **Solomon** . . . and **Asaph**." Together with **Ezra** and others, Nehemiah led a great revival of morals and religion (Neh. 8, 9, 10).

But after Nehemiah returned to the king's service in Persia, things in Jerusalem went downhill, due in part to a corrupt priest named Eliashib. Nehemiah came back to Jerusalem "after certain days" (probably years) and had to start the reformation process all over again (Neh. 13). We do not know how long his second term as governor lasted, but the reformation was again successful (v. 30).

129. **Nethanel** was one of the Levites who prophesied "with the musical instruments of **David** the man of God" (Neh. 12:36) during **Nehemiah's** governance of the Jews who had returned to Jerusalem from Babylonia/Persia and were living there in the second half of the fifth century BC. He is named among the members of the choir commissioned for the new wall's dedication parade, which ended in the temple (Neh. 12:40). It can be assumed that he was also appointed a regular Levite temple singer ordained to prophesy according to the command of David and Solomon—and Asaph (Neh. 12:45-46) "in the songs of the LORD" (1 Chr. 25:1-7).

130. **Nethaniah** was one of the sons of **Asaph** who was separated to prophesy with music "for the service of the house of God" in Jerusalem, being "instructed in the songs of the LORD." He was chosen by lot to lead the fifth twelve-man section of the 288 tabernacle singers (1 Chr. 25:1-8, 12).

131. **Noah** was a "preacher of righteousness," according to the apostle-prophet **Peter** (2 Pet. 2:5). That is an apt characterization of any prophet. But, oh! What illumination these three words infuse into our understanding of Noah. We had seen him as a righteous, obedient man, like **Job** and **Daniel** (Ezek. 14:14). We also knew Noah as a shipbuilder, a zookeeper, the second progenitor of mankind, and even as a "prophet" from his predictions[27] about the races that would spring from his sons (Gen. 9:25-27). But "preacher of righteousness" brings Noah into focus for us. He was *not* a religious recluse isolating his little clan from an evil world while he surreptitiously built an ark to save them from the wrath to come. No! Rather, he was out there preaching, prophesying, trying his best to save anyone who would repent and call upon the name of God. That none did repent was not Noah's fault. The world was never more evil (Gen. 6:5). Noah preached righteousness anyway. He was all alone in this, certainly the loneliest prophet of all time. **Elijah** thought he was all alone in God's service, and he despaired (1 Ki. 19:14); yet in Elijah's day, God had reserved seven thousand souls to

Himself (1 Ki. 19:18). Noah really was alone, but he did not despair of preaching righteousness and obeying God.

As the only prophet in the entire world, Noah could not preach to everyone. Not every soul heard about God and was offered a chance to repent and follow Him. Perhaps that is what is behind Peter's remarkable revelation[28] about **Jesus's** preaching to spirits who were imprisoned during, or ever since, the days of Noah (1 Pet. 3:19-20).

We have no sermons of Noah. We do have his predictions about his sons (Gen. 9:25-27). We also have the amazing account of his life, some events in which are prophecies in themselves; for example, the flood is a prophetic type of Christian baptism (1 Pet. 3:20-21), which itself symbolizes cleansing from sin.

Noah was historically the third prophet, after **Abel** and **Enoch**. He was by far the longest-lived prophet—950 years. In addition to being a preacher, a shipbuilder, and a zookeeper, Noah became a farmer (Gen. 9:20).

132. **Obadiah I** could be called the least of the minor prophets because he wrote the shortest book of the Old Testament, just twenty-one verses. Of course this does not make him less important, any more than the minor prophets are inferior to those who wrote longer books. Biographically, nothing is known of Obadiah except his name.

Obadiah's prophecy concerns the judgment of Edom, Israel's brother nation. Jacob(**Israel**) and Esau, **Isaac's** twin sons, transmuted into the nations of Israel and Edom, respectively (Gen. 36:1). Although the brothers themselves made peace with one another (Gen. 33; 35:29), the two nations became bitter rivals (Ex. 15:13-15; 1 Sam. 14:47). Edom was founded as a nation well before Israel (Gen. 36:31). After the Israelites escaped from Egypt as a fledging, wandering nation, Edom coldly refused their brothers' passage through their territory (Num. 20: 14-21). Later, when Israel became a strong nation under **David**, they subdued Edom (2 Sam. 8:14) just as predicted by **Balaam** (Num. 24:18). After about 150 years Edom revolted against Israel and gained independence again (2 Ki. 8:20-22).

Edom's fatal crime against Israel, for which God through Obadiah condemned them, was their gloating over and abetting their brothers' defeat at the hands of foreigners, probably Babylonia (Ob. 10-14). God did not condemn Edom for their fight for independence from Israel, nor for direct conflicts; but when their brother nation was being reduced by outsiders they should have closed family ranks. Their unbrotherly, completely callous behavior toward Israel would not be tolerated by God, and this is the main message of Obadiah.

Obadiah's dire predictions about Edom (Ob. 15-16, 18b) were partially fulfilled when the Edomites were pushed out of their ancestral territory by Arabs in the sixth century BC (see Obadiah in chapter 7). Survivors founded Idumea ("New Edom") in southern Judea, but there is no known remnant today; Obadiah's prophecy has been fulfilled. Obadiah's prophecy goes much beyond Edom's demise, however, in foretelling a future and greater glory for "the house of Jacob . . . and the house of **Joseph** . . . And the kingdom shall be the LORD's." (Ob. 17-21).

{Obadiah II—**Abda**} (1 Chronicles 9:16; Nehemiah 11:17)

133. **Obed-Edom** was a Levite music prophet serving under King **David** in about 1000 BC. He was a harpist "on the Sheminith" when the ark of the covenant of the LORD was brought into Jerusalem (1 Chr. 15:21). Afterwards, he stayed in Jerusalem to minister before the ark under **Asaph** the chief music prophet (1 Chr. 16:4-5). As reported in more detail later in Scripture (1 Chr. 25:1, 7), these musicians "prophesied . . . in the songs of the LORD."

There may have been two or more men named Obed-Edom who were connected with the ark and the tabernacle service at that time. Obed-Edom the Gittite kept the ark at his house for three months (2 Sam. 6:11). Gittites in general were foreigners to Israel, Philistines[29] (Josh. 13:3; 2 Sam. 15:18; 21:19); so it is not likely that this man was the same as the Levite music prophet Obed-Edom.

Obed-Edom was also the name of a Levite gatekeeper/doorkeeper (1 Chr. 15:18, 24; 16:38, 42). We will assume that this was the same music prophet, especially because he was a son of **Jeduthun**, one of the three principle singers and a choir director (1 Chr. 25:1, 3). It appears that Jeduthun's sons and grandsons had double duties as gatekeepers and musicians (1 Chr. 16:42). Sixty-two of Obed-Edom's progeny were gatekeepers (1 Chr. 26:1, 8, 15).

134. **Oded I** is identified both as a prophet (2 Chr. 15:8) and the father of the prophet **Azariah** (2 Chr. 15:1), in the days of King Asa of Judah (910–869 BC). Oded and/or his son brought God's word to Asa, who instituted a major reformation of Judah/Benjamin back to the true God, to a teaching priesthood, and to the Law of God (2 Chr. 15:3, 12). Many commentators (and some manuscripts) discount 2 Chr. 15:8, or rephrase it in a way that does not identify Oded as a prophet himself, but only as the father of Azariah. This is appealing, but we will accept the literal meaning found in the KJV, NKJV, NASB, NIV, and others, counting him a prophet.

135. **Oded II** was one of the last prophets of God in the northern kingdom, Israel. He was in its capital, Samaria, when the army of Israel returned there from a major victory over Judah (ca. 732 BC). This defeat was God's judgment against Judah for forsaking Him. But Israel went too far (2 Chr. 28:5-15).

God, through Oded, convicted Israel of their own sin in the affair: they had needlessly slaughtered men of Judah "in a rage that reaches up to heaven." Then they brought back to Samaria two hundred thousand Judean women and children, planning to make slaves of them. Some were even brought back naked. These atrocities went far beyond God's judgment of Judah. Some of the leaders of Israel (Ephraim) heeded Oded's prophecy. They convinced the army to return the captives, even clothing the naked ones. It was one of the last decent moments in Israel. About ten years later they were defeated, occupied, and scattered by Assyria, never to rise again (at least in biblical times) as a separate nation.

{Oshea—**Joshua**} (Numbers 13:16, KJV)

136. **Paul** was and is the second greatest prophet to the church of **Jesus** Christ—after only Christ Himself. Given a good understanding of "prophet," that simple statement says as much about Paul as any analysis of his education, character, intellect, sufferings, or circumstances can say—and many such analyses, some very fine, have been made. Paul was chosen by God even before he was born, dramatically called, given heavenly visions, revelations of God's word, the necessary gifts, and a target audience. Paul delivered God's messages faithfully, lived with many hardships, performed miracles, was opposed by the powerful of this world, and suffered persecutions for his ministry—just like many another great prophet, from **Moses** to **Elijah** to **Isaiah**. Not much separates Paul from these prophets except time and circumstances. But there is one important difference: Paul's greater, fuller revelation from God. His Son had at last come, lived, taught, suffered, and died for His elect, been resurrected to life, ascended to heaven, and given His Holy Spirit to His followers. Much has been made of Paul's education, culture, and intellect. They were formidable indeed, but Paul himself denied that they were important to his calling: God's prophet to the nations!

A "Full-Service" Prophet

Paul styled himself an apostle, a teacher, and a preacher (1 Tim. 2:7). Nowhere in Scripture is he called a prophet or seer, except by inclusion in a list of "prophets and teachers" at Antioch (Acts 13:1). But it would be a huge mistake to omit Paul from even the shortest list of biblical prophets.

Paul's credentials as a prophet now rest primarily on his letters to churches and individuals, thirteen of which are Holy Scripture, God's word. But he saw himself not primarily as a writer but as a man who came face-to-face with the risen Jesus and was called, yea, *compelled* to go into all the world with His gospel message (1 Cor. 9:16; Acts 18:5). In the book of Acts we see not a writer but an active, fully engaged prophet: going where sent, preaching, planting churches, having not just one but several heavenly visions, performing miracles, singing, undergoing hardship and peril, and being beaten, stoned, and imprisoned for prophesying. Paul prophesied in deeds, spoken word, song, and written word.

As to miracles, an almost sure mark of a prophet, Paul has a prominent place among the prophets. Eight specific miracles are attributed to Paul in Acts (13:11-12; 14:9-10; 16:16-18; 16:26ff; 19:6; 20:9-12; 28:3-6; 28:8) . And it is noted in the Bible that he was God's instrument of *many other* signs and wonders, some jointly with **Barnabas** (Acts 14:3; 15:12; 19:11-12; 28:9; Rom. 15:18-19; 2 Cor. 12:12). Miracles were a regular part of his ministry, authenticating his gospel message. Paul's miracles included many healings, one case of inflicting blindness on a sorcerer, casting out evil spirits, escape from prison, speaking in tongues if that be a miracle (it was also a spiritual gift), reviving a dead boy, and immunity from deadly snake venom.

Another mark of a prophet—a necessary one—is receiving revelation from God in dreams and/or visions (Num. 12:6). Paul had many visions that are documented, and probably more that are not (Acts 9:12; 16:9; 18:9; 23:11; 26:19; 27:23; 2 Cor. 12:1-4).

Biographical Notes

A thorough biographical sketch of Paul for this compendium is both impractical and unnecessary. **Luke**, in the Book of Acts, has provided an unusually extensive (for Scripture)[30] life of Paul. In addition, in his letters Paul has filled in many details about his life, including spiritual experiences, anecdotes, personal plans, feelings, and news about churches and coworkers (e.g. Rom. 11:1; 2 Cor. 1:8-2:13; Gal. 1:11-2:21). Modern writers have collected and collated these and many other Scriptures, sometimes adding other sources and inferences, forming expanded biographies of Paul. One of the best of these is *The Apostle* by John Pollock.[31] Others have delved more particularly into Paul's character and personality with remarkably divergent and sometimes unflattering results.[32]

A few biographical details and personal characteristics that pertain directly to Paul's office of prophet will be considered in the following sections.

Jew and Pharisee

The facts that Paul was a Jew, and a Pharisee, were significant to his office of prophet. The apostle to the Gentiles was indeed a Jew (Acts 22:3), "circumcised the eighth day, of the stock of Israel, of the tribe of Benjamin, a Hebrew of the Hebrews" (Philip. 3:5); the seed of **Abraham** according to the flesh (2 Cor. 11:22). His Hebrew name, Saul, was proudly that of Israel's first king, also a Benjamite. So, what is remarkable about a prophet being a Jew? Almost every prophet in this compendium was a Jew, Israelite, or descendent of Abraham—including Jesus. But in Paul's case, because he prophesied mainly to Gentiles, it made a difference.

It is obvious to anyone acquainted with Paul's ministry that God planned that His premier missionary-prophet to the Gentile world should be a Jew. It gained Paul access to the synagogues where both Jews and God-fearing Gentiles gathered (Acts 13:42-44) and which were the launching pads for Christianity in almost all the cities Paul visited. Being a Jew afforded him fluency in Aramaic Hebrew, which was not only useful in some synagogues but also in the temple in Jerusalem (Acts 21:40). Paul also spoke Greek fluently (Acts 21:37; 17:22)) and probably knew Latin. Paul's Hebrew heritage and education gave him a solid background in the Scriptures—indispensable for his ministry. The Holy Spirit revealed to him, again and again, that Old Testament prophecy was fulfilled in Jesus Christ; was being fulfilled in the spread of His gospel, particularly to Gentiles; and would be fulfilled in the future (e.g. Rom. 11:25-27; 16:25-26; 2 Cor. 3:12-18). Paul called this "the revelation of the mystery," and he often quoted Scripture to that effect.

Paul's kinship and natural love toward his native race prompted one of his own most important prophetic passages, in his letter to the mixed Jewish/Gentile church in Rome (Rom 9-11). But being a Jew caused Paul terrible physical suffering more than a Gentile prophet in his place would have received. He was whipped by the Jews five times with thirty-nine lashes each time (2 Cor. 11:24)—one stripe shy of the maximum penalty for blasphemy and other crimes supposedly committed against Judaism (Deut. 25:3). No Gentile would be thus punished. These whippings were so painful and bloody that they could kill; they were also humiliating beyond measure. Neither Paul nor Luke tells when these lashings occurred. Some scholars put them during Paul's years in his hometown of Tarsus after he was run out of both Damascus and Jerusalem for preaching Christ (Acts 9:20-30) and before he came to Antioch to begin his western missionary career (Acts 11:25-26).

Paul also took physical abuse from Gentiles just for being a Jew—or that was their excuse (Acts 16:20-23). He was jailed in Philippi (Acts 16:20-23) and put in peril of being killed by a mob in Ephesus (Acts 19:28-34), at least in part because of Gentile prejudice against Jews.

Paul was not an ordinary Jew; he was a member of Judaism's strictest sect, the Pharisees (Acts 26:5). His father was a Pharisee (Acts 23:6) and sent his young son to Jerusalem to be educated by the illustrious rabbi, Gamaliel (Acts 22:3). Paul was a very apt pupil, becoming an outstanding and zealous Pharisee. Even as a mature Christian he retained this affiliation (Acts 23:6). In addition to having a profound effect on his life and making his conversion to Christ even more amazing, Paul's Pharisaic training colored his prophecy. It gave him the razor-sharp distinction between works/religion and faith/grace that is so characteristic of his writings (e.g. Rom. 1-8). And, it helped Paul to understand and refute the Judaizers who came in to corrupt and take over churches he had founded (Philip. 3:2ff; Gal. 3:1-4; 4:21ff).

Gentile Connections

Equally important as his Jewishness to Paul's prophetic ministry, were his Gentile roots and connections. Paul was born in Tarsus (Acts 21:39), where he lived until being sent to school in Jerusalem, and again for several years as a grown man and a Christian (Acts 9:30; 11:25-26). Tarsus was "no mean city" in the Roman province of Cilicia/Syria in southeastern Asia Minor (modern Turkey) just west of Syria proper. Tarsus was a large city, a cosmopolitan city, a cultural and commercial center, and allegedly a very wicked city.[33] Greek was spoken there, and Greek history and mythology were embedded in the culture. Paul was born a Roman citizen (Acts 22:27-28), supposedly because his father had earned or purchased this status for his family.[34] Paul's Latin name, or part of it, was Paullus, meaning "little"; hence Paul was the name he began to use on his first missionary trip out of Antioch.

All of these factors contributed to Paul's presentation of the gospel prophecy given him by God. Although he was a Jew, steeped in the Hebrew Scriptures, trained in the Law, and called by Jesus Christ (another Jew), Paul could genuinely relate to Gentiles. He preached in Greek and debated with Greek philosophers at the Aereopagus (Mars Hill) in Athens (Acts 17:16-34), quoting from Greek poets (v. 28). In Paul's epistles there are allusions to other Greek writers.[35] Paul is the only prophet who speaks of *citizenship* (a Greek concept) in God's kingdom (Philip. 3:20; Eph. 2:19). Also, Paul knew all too well about the prevalent evil practices of pagan Gentiles, and he frequently addressed them head-on (Rom. 1; 1 Cor. 5:11; 6:8-11; Col. 3:5-7). He was particularly concerned with idolatry (1 Cor. 10:14; 12:2; Acts 17:16), which was no longer a common Jewish practice but a prevalent pagan one.

Family

The only relatives of Paul who are even obliquely mentioned in the Bible are his father, his sister, and his nephew (Acts 23:6, 16). While Paul insisted on his right to take along "a believing wife" on his missions (1 Cor. 9:5), he apparently did not have one (or was celibate) at the time he wrote to the Corinthian church about marriage (1 Cor. 7). However, in the latter part of this passage (vv. 25-40), Paul departs from prophesying God's revealed word and gives his own opinion "as one whom the Lord has made trustworthy"—the voice of marital experience?

The family trade was tentmaking (Acts 18:3). This work supported Paul at Corinth for a year and a half (Acts 18:11) and possibly for over two years at Ephesus (Acts 19:8-10; 20:34-35), where he had earlier left his fellow Christian tentmakers Aquila and Priscilla.

Physical Suffering

Paul suffered in his body (short of death) more than any other prophet in the Bible! This may seem to be a bold assertion considering the severe treatment of so many of God's prophets.[36] For example, **Jeremiah** could say to God, with perfect integrity, "Why is my pain perpetual and my wound incurable, which refuses to be healed? . . . Cursed be the day in which I was born!" (Jer. 15:18/20:14). A list of Jeremiah's sufferings (including mental and emotional) can be found under his name. Jeremiah was indeed the most abused prophet of the Old Testament. But based on documented instances, Paul's physical sufferings were even worse.

A partial list of Paul's physical sufferings is given in his second letter to the church at Corinth (11:22-33):

- stripes (whippings) without measure including at least five times with thirty-nine stripes
- frequent imprisonment
- three beatings with rods

- o stoned, with intent to kill, and left for dead (Acts 14:19)
- o three shipwrecks—once being overboard for a whole night and day
- o exhaustion
- o sleeplessness
- o hunger and thirst (starvation)
- o cold, nakedness

This list does not include Paul's famous "thorn in flesh" (2 Cor. 12:7-8) which was quite possibly a physical disease or infirmity. Nor does it include, if different from the thorn, the physical infirmity Paul called a "trial . . . in my flesh" (Gal. 4:13-14)—possibly a disease such as malaria—that detained him in Galatia (to the Galatians' great benefit!). Small wonder, then, that Paul engaged a physician, Luke, to accompany him on subsequent mission trips.

The list of sufferings in 2 Corinthians was incomplete also because Paul still had at least a decade of ministry—and suffering—ahead of him. We do not know all that happened to Paul in these latter years, but it included being:

- o manhandled (roughed up) by an angry mob that tried to kill him (Acts 21: 30-31)
- o put in chains (Acts 21:33)
- o bound with leather thongs in preparation for torture by scourging (which was averted) [Acts 22:24-25]
- o imprisoned, or under "house arrest" much of the rest of his life, quite a few years (Acts 23:35; 24:23, 27; 25:14; 26:29; 27:1, 42; 28:16-20; 2 Tim. 1:8)
- o in a fourth shipwreck or grounding, after a terrible two-week storm at sea (Acts 27:13-44)

What shall we say then (to use a little Pauline rhetoric)? Was Paul a masochist? A daredevil? God forbid! For Paul avoided physical confrontation and abuse whenever he could—escaping Damascus in a basket and also escaping Jerusalem when his life was threatened (Acts 9:23-30), leaving Antioch and Iconium and Thessalonica and Berea when things got hot (Acts 13:50; 14:5-6; 17:10, 14), heeding his friends' advice not to go into danger at the temple of Diana in Ephesus (Acts 19:30) and leaving that city (Acts 20:1), invoking his Roman citizenship to avoid a scourging (Acts 22:24-25), informing a Roman centurion of a secret plot to murder him (Acts 23:12-24), and appealing to Caesar when faced with a Jewish kangaroo trial and probable death sentence (Acts 25:9-12). *No, Paul did not seek danger or pain.* As he wrote to the Galatians, "From now on let no one trouble me, for I bear in my body the marks of the Lord Jesus" (6:17). Sadly, much more suffering was yet to come. But Paul would not and did not back down from the gospel, nor from preaching it whenever he could, nor from following the leading of the Holy Spirit—and for these, he suffered.

Paul's attitude about all his suffering for the sake of the gospel was straight out of Jesus's playbook, and of **James III's** as well:

> Blessed are you when they revile and persecute you, . . . Rejoice and be exceeding glad, for great is your reward in heaven, for so they persecuted the prophets who were before you.—Matt. 5:11-12

> My brethren, count it all joy when you fall into various trials.—Jas. 1:2

Paul rather gloried in his sufferings, though he did not seek them:

> Therefore I take pleasure in infirmities, in reproaches, in distresses, for Christ's sake.—2 Cor. 12:10

> We also glory in tribulations.—Rom. 5:3; cf. 8:18

> Who shall separate us from the love of Christ? Shall tribulation, or distress, or persecution, or famine, or nakedness, or peril, or sword? As it is written:
> 'For your sake we are killed all day long;
> We are accounted as sheep for the slaughter.'
> Yet in all these things we are more than conquerors through Him who loved us.—Rom. 8:35-37

Paul believed and preached the concept that Christian suffering was fellowship with Christ Jesus:

> For to you it has been granted on behalf of Christ, not only to believe in Him, but also to suffer for His sake.—Philip. 1:29

> That I may know Him . . . and the fellowship of His sufferings.—Philip. 3:10

> For as the sufferings of Christ abound in us, so our consolation also abounds through Christ.—2 Cor. 1:5

The Moses of the New Testament

In many ways Paul was to the church of Jesus Christ what Moses was to Israel. By God's Spirit and word, Paul built up the church, led her, interceded with God for her, taught her, organized her, disciplined her, and trained and appointed new leaders for her—all things that Moses did for Israel.

Both Paul and Moses were prepared for their exceedingly difficult missions with cross-cultural backgrounds: Moses in Egypt, Paul in Cilicia. Each was a Hebrew by birth and a citizen of a foreign nation (Moses, of Egypt; Paul, of Rome). Paul's Damascus-Road conversion/call was singular and unforgettable; so was Moses's burning bush call. Both prophets encountered God in person, saw His light, heard His voice. Both went into self-imposed exile to the same general desert wilderness (Midian was in Arabia) [Ex. 2:15; Gal. 1:17]. Each of their first efforts to save

God's people was unsuccessful (Acts 7:25; 9:23-30). After years of preparation, each entered his main ministry a mature man, past the midpoint of his lifespan.

Both prophets used no force beyond God's word and Spirit—helped with not a few miracles—to forge a new nation (church) of believers. Like Moses, Paul never exalted himself, or took material gain (Num. 16:15; Acts 20:33), or claimed any title other than prophet or apostle (and even these, only as servants). John Pollock points out that "Like Moses, (Paul) was prepared to be blotted out of God's book as the price of (their kinsmen's) reconciliation"[37] (Rom. 9:3; Ex. 32:32) Both prophets suffered for their efforts, yet both were fabulously successful—although the glory is all God's.

Each of these remarkably parallel prophets had much revelation from God about prophecy itself—virtually defining it for their particular institutions (1 Cor. 14; Num. 11:6; Deut. 13). How wonderfully alike are these statements—Moses: "Oh, that all the LORD's people were prophets and that the LORD would put His Spirit upon them" (Num. 11:29); Paul: "Pursue love, and desire spiritual gifts, but especially that you may prophesy . . . I wish you all spoke with tongues, but even more that you prophesied" (1 Cor. 14:1/5).

Both prophets died before their respective fledgling communities had found their places in the world. But their prophecies are still very much alive, guiding God's people.

Prophecy

Neither a summary nor an analysis of Paul's prophecy (writings and speeches) is within this book's scope, or our ability. There is certainly no lack of such work in the literature. Nevertheless, certain characteristics of Pauline prophecy, that set it apart from other prophecy, should be mentioned.

Substance

Paul's written prophecy covers a vast range of subjects, from soaring praises of God's wisdom and sovereignty, right down to detailed instructions about eating and head coverings; from the beauty of Christlike love (agape), to the ugliness of ungodliness and unrighteousness (Rom. 11:33, 36; 1 Tim. 1:17; 3:16; 1 Cor. 10:27-11:7; 11:33-34; 1 Cor. 13; Rom 1:18-32).

The overarching purpose of Paul's written prophecy is to encourage and instruct Christian believers, churches, and church leaders. Following is a brief list of major themes, without Scripture references because there are so many:

Justification by faith
Freedom from bondage; Christian liberty
Regeneration (new life in Christ)
Inclusiveness of the gospel and the Church,
 e.g., Jew-Gentile, rich-poor, male-female
Reconciliation

- Simplicity and power of the gospel
- The resurrection
- Spiritual gifts
- Adoption
- Christian living, including,
    - Love one another
    - Imitate Christ
    - Be circumspect, respectful, moderate
    - Hospitality
    - Generosity/stewardship
    - Diligence
    - Self-denial
    - Resist, flee from sin
    - Endure suffering (for the gospel; for your faith)
- Church leadership and government
- Christian marriage, family, home

There is eschatology, too, in Paul's written prophecy including the most complete revelation in Scripture of God's ultimate plan for the Hebrew people (1 Thess. 5: 1-10; 2 Thess. 2:1-12; Rom. 9-11).

In contrast to his writings, Paul's spoken prophecy (sermons, speeches) were much more evangelistic: directed to nonbelievers. Speaking in a synagogue in Pisidian Antioch (Acts 13:16-41), he began with a review of Israel's history, culminating in Jesus—the very same "sermon" outline used by **Stephen** when Paul (then Saul) watched him die as he preached it! (Acts 7). Paul closed with a strong appeal to believe in Jesus as the Christ, the Son of God, and a warning to those who did not believe. This sermon outline was probably used often (e.g., Acts 17:1-3). But in Athens, speaking to Greeks only (Acts 17:22-31), Paul adapted his gospel message to their cultural heritage, yet still ending on Christ's resurrection from the dead. In Jerusalem and Caesarea, under arrest for "disturbing the peace" after some Jews from Asia started a riot by accusing Paul of blasphemy and temple defilement (Acts 21:27-36), he spoke to several groups and individuals in his own defense (Acts 22:1-21; 23:1, 6; 24:10-21; 26:1-29). But Paul's defense was also gospel prophecy based largely upon Christ's resurrection and upon Paul's own encounter with Jesus near Damascus. Risking his freedom or his life, Paul "almost persuaded" King Agrippa to become a Christian.

Style

The epistolary format of Paul's written prophecy accounts in part for its intensely personal style—but not entirely: the epistles of James, **Peter, Jude,** and the writer of Hebrews are not nearly so personal as Paul's. Paul frequently uses terms such as "brethren" and "my beloved children." He can also use stern personal language such as "O foolish Galatians!" (Gal. 3:1). He addresses specific groups in churches including children, fathers, slaves, masters, wives, husbands, Jews, and Gentiles. And he names names—not only the renowned individuals to whom letters are addressed, namely, **Timothy**, **Titus**, and Philemon, but also ordinary persons in churches (Philip. 4:2-3; 1 Cor. 1:11, 14).

Some of Paul's expressions are full of personal feeling:

> Shall I come to you with a rod, or in love and in a spirit of gentleness?—1 Cor. 4:21

> For God is my witness, how greatly I long for you all with the affection of Jesus Christ.—Philip. 1:8

> But we were gentle among you, just as a nursing mother cherishes her own children. So, affectionately longing for you, we were well pleased to impart to you not only the gospel of God, but also our own lives, because you had become dear to us.—1 Thess. 2:7-8

In addition to his familiar tone, Paul's letters of prophecy are made even more personal by an extraordinary emphasis on himself. He uses the personal pronoun *I* countless times.[38] He tells of his own feelings, his thoughts, his plans, his lifestyle, his hardships and painful sufferings, and his conversion. Paul urges others to follow his own example (1 Cor. 4:16; Philip. 3:17). He often defends his apostleship and authority (e.g., 1 Cor. 9:1-2). The most stunning example is Paul's "fool's speech" (2 Cor. 11:22—12:10). None of this is manifestation of conceit, self-centeredness, or narcissism although it can temporarily seem so, especially to modern readers who do not know Paul personally. Actually, Paul was a most humble person, like Moses. But he used himself as a foil. And he *had* to defend his apostolic authority when false apostles and prophets were coming to the very churches that the Holy Spirit through Paul had established, after Paul was gone, attacking Paul's authority and, thereby, the true gospel of Jesus Christ.

The self-exposing, personal style of prophecy is quite characteristic of Paul but not unique among prophets. The prophecies of David in certain psalms he wrote; of Jeremiah; and even of Moses—though he writes in the third person—come immediately to mind. There is a certain compelling power to this style. There is also a danger that the reader/hearer will be prone to "write off" the message as vanity, personal opinion, or emotional manipulation. Just so we may not be thus misled concerning Pauline prophecy, consider these passages:

> I received from the Lord that which I also delivered to you.—1 Cor. 11:23

> But we speak the wisdom of God in a mystery . . . The things which God has prepared for those who love Him . . . But God has revealed them to us through

> His Spirit . . . These things we also speak, not in words which man's wisdom teaches but which the Holy Spirit teaches.—1 Cor. 2:7-13

> But I make known unto you, brethren, that the gospel which was preached by me is not according to man, nor was I taught it, but it came through the revelation of Jesus Christ.—Gal. 1:11-12

> By revelation He made known to me the mystery . . . as it has now been revealed by the Spirit to His holy apostles and prophets . . . of which I became a minister according to the gift of the grace of God given to me by the effective working of His power.—Eph. 3:3-7

> Now the Spirit expressly says that in latter times . . .—1 Tim. 4:1

> But [God] has in due time manifested His word through preaching, which was committed to me according to the commandment of God our Savior.—Titus 1:3

Paul does not use the classic Old Testament expressions for introducing prophecy such as "thus saith the LORD," "the word of the LORD that came to" (**Hosea**), or "the vision of" (**Isaiah**). Instead, he begins each epistle with an expression like "Paul, an apostle (and/or) bondservant of Jesus Christ, called by (or according to the will of) God, to . . . ; Grace to you and peace from God our Father and the Lord Jesus Christ." These are not just formal salutations; they also establish Paul's prophetic authority and source, which carry throughout the letter and identify as God's word later passages which may be introduced with only "I say." Occasionally Paul does give his own opinion, but he is careful to label it as such (1 Cor. 7:25; 2 Cor. 11:17).

In addition to the very personal "you—me" style of Paul's written prophecy, a second noteworthy characteristic is that it is often very tightly and brilliantly reasoned, taking on a forensic style complete with rhetorical questions and *therefores*. The best example of this is Romans 1–8. (Romans is a treatise within a personal letter.) Such a style of prophecy is not unknown elsewhere in Scripture, even in the Old Testament (e.g., Mal. 3:7-15), but it is distinctively Pauline. Paul made a conscious and usually successful effort to suppress his natural genius and great learning (Acts 26:24; 1 Cor. 2:1-5), especially in his verbal prophecy, in order that "your faith should not be in the wisdom of men but in the power of God." But his tremendous intellect does often come through in his written prophecy. Paul was, after all, one of the greatest thinkers, as well as doers, of his time and of all time.

Summary: Who was Paul?

In the words of Robert Young,

> (Paul's) speeches and epistles convey to us the truest impression of him. In these we perceive the warmth and ardour of his nature, his affectionate disposition,

the tenderness of his sense of honor, the courtesy and personal dignity of his bearing, and his perfect frankness. We see also the rare combination of subtility, tenacity, and versatility existing in his intellect, with a practical wisdom generally associated with a cooler temperament than his, and a forbearance and tolerance seldom united with such impetuous convictions as he entertained."[39]

In the words of Paul (Rom. 1:1-5),

> Paul (was) a bondservant of Jesus Christ, called to be an apostle, separated to the gospel of God which He promised before through His prophets in the Holy Scriptures, concerning Jesus Christ who was born of the seed of David according to the flesh, and declared to be the Son of God with power according to the Spirit of holiness, by the resurrection from the dead. Through Him (Paul) received grace and apostleship for obedience to the faith among all nations for His name.

137. **Peter** is generally listed foremost among the twelve disciples/apostles of **Jesus**. He was also a *prophet* of the first rank—in spoken words of God, written words of God, and miracles of God. Peter was the first prophet of Christ's church.

The name Peter is a translation of the Greek word transliterated Cephas, meaning "rock" or "stone". It was given by Jesus as a surname or nickname to Simon, son of Jonas or John, a Jewish commercial fisherman from Galilee (John 1:42; Matt. 4:18). The names "Peter, "Simon Peter" and "Cephas" are all used for him in the New Testament. Only John reports as history the occasion in Judea when Jesus surnamed Simon "Peter." The three synoptic Gospels all acknowledge the name change, however (Matt. 10:2; Mark 3:16; Luke 6:14). In fact, at the first mention of our prophet in Matthew, it was "Simon called Peter"—*already* called Peter (Matt. 4:18). So also in Luke, albeit after several "Simons" (Luke 5:3-8).

The book of Acts records five God-given sermons of Peter. He wrote two epistles in the Bible, God's word to men, and he is supposed by many to have been the principal human source of the Gospel of Mark. Peter was the agent of many miraculous healings and other signs. Together these sermons, writings, and signs add up to a body of prophecy ranking in volume only after those of **Paul**, **Luke**, and **John II** in the New Testament (Jesus excepted). But prophets cannot be ranked in importance by volume of words or deeds. Peter's importance as a prophet derives from his special calling, training, and commissioning by Jesus Christ; from his all-so-human lapses of faith and behavior which were overcome at last by Christ's prayers; from his leadership as a disciple, apostle, and prophet; and from his prophecies (sermons and letters) that are classic and yet still alive and powerful.

Peter's External Life

There is a considerable amount of biographical information about Peter in the Bible. As in the case of Paul, scholars and novelists have written "lives of Peter" which, accurate or not, have colored many a modern Christian's view of the man. The basic biblical facts are these:

Simon, a son of Jonas, was originally from the town of Bethsaida (John 1:44) on the north shore of the Sea of Galilee. He made his living as a commercial fisherman. In this business he partnered with his brother **Andrew** (Mark 1:16) and with two brothers of another family, **James I** and John II (Luke 5:10). Peter moved from Bethsaida to Capernaum,[40] another seaside town about three miles away. Peter shared his house in Capernaum with his wife (although she is not mentioned as being there on the occasion reported)[41] and family, including his mother-in-law (who *is* mentioned), and his brother Andrew, possibly a bachelor (Mark 1:21, 29-31). Our Lord may have made Peter's house His regular residence in Capernaum, a town He often visited (Mark 2:1; 9:33; Matt. 4:13; 17:24-25).

Peter had a son named Mark (1 Pet. 5:13). Scholars disagree as to whether this was his biological or spiritual son and, if the latter, whether it was John Mark and/or the author of Mark (see **Mark**). He may have had other biological or adopted sons and daughters—we don't know.

After Jesus's death and resurrection, and Peter's investiture with the Holy Spirit, the apostle apparently moved his home, or at least his headquarters, from Capernaum to Jerusalem (Gal. 1:18; 2:1/9; Acts 8:1; 15:6-7) where he was a leader for many years in the new church. But Peter traveled extensively. He took at least one missionary journey from Jerusalem to Samaria (Acts 8:14-25), another to the Mediterranean coast (Acts 9:32-10:48), and yet another to Antioch in Syria (Gal. 2:11). If the addressees of 1 Peter were churches Peter had visited, then he had traveled extensively in Asia Minor—"Paul's country." Paul acknowledges Peter's missionary travels in an oblique way (1 Cor. 9:5). Peter's first biblical epistle was apparently written from Rome (code word Babylon?) [1 Pet. 5:13]; and the second was written shortly before his death, which tradition holds took place (by crucifixion) in Rome (2 Pet. 1:14).

Peter spent some time in jail after he became an apostle/prophet because he *was* an apostle/prophet. Shortly after Pentecost, he and John II were taken into custody by the temple officials in Jerusalem (Acts 4:1-22). Soon after, all the apostles were rounded up and detained in prison (Acts 5:17-19). Years later, King Herod Agrippa I imprisoned Peter and put him under armed guards, but an angel of God freed him (Acts 12:1-11). And if Peter was crucified in Rome, he must have been a prisoner there too.

Peter teamed up with his old fishing partner John II after Jesus's death and resurrection. They were the first of Jesus's disciples to His empty tomb (John 20: 1-10). They are found praying and working together just after that next Pentecost day, and they were arrested together (Acts 3, 4). Some time later these two were sent, as a team, by the church in Jerusalem to help with the great spiritual awakening started by **Philip** in Samaria (Acts8:14-25).

These are externals of Peter's life. Some aspects of Peter's spiritual life are briefly treated in the following sections.

Calling, Naming, and Commissioning

Peter's calling, naming, and commissioning(s) by Jesus Christ are fascinating and worthy of much more exposition than we can offer here. Simon first met Jesus in Judea, not Galilee—near the Jordan River where **John I**, the baptizer, was prophesying and baptizing (John 1:35-42). He was introduced to Jesus by his brother Andrew who was then a disciple of John. It is not known whether Simon was in Judea just then to see this baptizer and to visit Andrew, perhaps with a notion to join them, or whether Andrew fetched Simon all the way from Galilee just to see Jesus. In any case it was at this very first meeting that Jesus surnamed Simon "Cephas" (Peter). But Jesus did not call Peter to follow Him at this time. That was to come later, on the shores of Galilee, when the four fishing partners Peter, Andrew, James I, and John II were called to become "fishers of men" (Mark 1:16-20; Luke 5:1-11). They had had time to think and talk about Jesus since Andrew and Peter and probably John had met Him in Judea; and they immediately dropped everything else for the opportunity to follow Him.

Part of Peter's call was a name change. The surname "Peter" given by Jesus is wonderfully nuanced. Peter's natural character was more like shifting sand than rock. He was a rock at Caesarea Philippi (Matt. 16:13-19), but soon turned to sand (Matt. 16:22-23). Then we recall his well-known denial of Christ during His arraignment (Luke 22:54-62) and some of his other blunders. Jesus revealed that Satan had requested permission to sift Peter like wheat (or sand?) [Luke 22:31]. One wonders if Jesus's parable about houses built on rock versus sand (Matt. 7: 24-27) had a special application to Peter. Non-igneous rock consists of grains of sand, coalesced by tremendous forces. From Simon's sand, Jesus forged Peter, the rock-strong leader and first prophet of His church (Acts 2:14-39).

A special anointing or commissioning by Jesus came to Peter after his famous confession, "Thou art the Christ, the Son of the living God," on a road in northern Galilee (Matt. 16:13-19). Jesus blessed Peter for this answer, which came from God (one of Peter's first prophecies). Jesus reiterated the surname "Peter" and gave it new meaning. He promised Peter the keys of the kingdom of heaven.

Just before Jesus's death, when He knew that Peter was going to be sifted by Satan, our Lord revealed that He had prayed that Peter's faith would not utterly fail—that he would return to Christ—and that he would then *strengthen his brethren*: another commissioning, of a sort (Luke 22:31-32).

Finally, Jesus re-commissioned Peter shortly after His resurrection, beside the Sea of Galilee,[42] possibly near the very spot He first called Peter to be a man-fisher (John 21:15-19). This was in one sense a restoration of Peter to grace, following his recent denial of Jesus. But it was also a completely new commission: to become a shepherd of men, not only a fisher of men. It is interesting that Jesus used Peter's original family name, Simon son of Jonas, instead of the surname "Peter" on this last occasion.

Of course Peter, in addition to being singled out by Jesus for a special place and work in His kingdom, was also included in the commissions Jesus gave all

His disciples (John 20:21-23; Matt. 28:18-20; Luke 9:1-5), in His prayers for them (John 17:6-19; Acts 1:4-8), and in the outpouring of His Spirit on them (Acts 2:1-4).

Peter—The Leader

Peter appears to have been a natural leader of men. Jesus used and developed this quality. In almost every biblical list of disciples or apostles, whether twelve or two, Peter is first named.[43] **Matthew** even says "first, Peter" when he lists the twelve.

Whether officially appointed by Jesus or not, Peter was unquestionably the leader of the twelve disciples and in some secular ways, of all thirteen men including Jesus! For when the tax collector wanted to get to Jesus, he came through Peter (Matt. 17:24). When Jesus disappeared to pray, Peter led a search for Him (Mark 1:36). Peter was always included—and named first—in the "inner circle" of three disciples (Mark 5:37; 9:2-3; 14:32-33). Jesus sent Peter (and John II) to prepare His last Passover meal (Luke 22:8). Peter took a sword to Gethsemane and defended Jesus with it (John 18:10). Peter would have been the first disciple to reach the empty tomb of Jesus, had he been able to run faster than John. As it was, Peter was the first to set foot inside the tomb (John 20:1-8). Peter was the first disciple to see the resurrected Christ (Luke 24:33-34). After Jesus's ascension, it was Peter who organized a meeting of the disciples to replace **Judas** (Acts 1:15ff.).

As an apostle, Peter took the lead in addressing the crowd on that special Pentecost morning (Acts 2:14-39). Peter may have been in charge of receiving and distributing the community property that the first body of believers shared, for he confronted Ananias and Sapphira for lying about their contribution (Acts 4: 32-5:11). A few years after his own conversion to Christ, Paul regarded Peter as the leader of the church, then headquartered in Jerusalem (Gal. 1:18). Peter was given, by the Holy Spirit, the pioneering work of opening up the gospel to the Gentiles (Acts 10; 15:7). Fourteen years after Paul's first visit with him, Peter was still a leader in the Jerusalem church (Gal. 2:1-10; Acts 15:6-14).

Not much spiritual leadership can be attributed to Peter's natural ability, nor to any aggressive desire of his to be first in all things. As we have noted already, Jesus openly declared Peter, or Peter's God-given faith, to be the "rock" on which He would build His church. And He promised Peter the keys of the kingdom of heaven and the power that whatever Peter should bind and loose on earth would be bound or loosed in heaven. No one comes by that kind of authority naturally or by earthly or political means. Jesus prayed for Peter, that his faith should not fail, and told him to strengthen his brethren. Finally, Jesus gave Peter oversight responsibility for His "sheep". Yes, Peter was Jesus's designated leader.

What has all this leadership business to do with Peter as a prophet? Much. Like the other apostles, Peter became a lifetime prophet ten days after Jesus's ascension on a Pentecost morning.[44] But Peter was the first to speak, the first prophet of the apostolic era. He was already accustomed to taking the lead, which he did, most admirably and eloquently, though *all* were filled with the Holy Spirit. And people were already disposed to listen to Peter, the acknowledged leader of the twelve, when he began to speak for God. God established at the very outset that in His newest creation, the church of Jesus Christ, its leaders should be prophets; and its prophets, leaders. Years later, Peter's epistles were accepted by the church as God's word (prophecy), in part because they came from her Christ-appointed leader.

Impetuous Peter

Peter was given to rash or bold—our characterization depending on the outcome—statements and behavior. Sometimes this impetuosity affected his becoming a prophet; once, it *was* prophecy! Perhaps this trait was entirely unaffected, or perhaps it was sometimes brought out by his leadership position, whereby he felt obligated to answer or act first. It does tend to "humanize" Peter and endear him to us. But once Peter became a fully invested prophet, at Pentecost, his impetuosity seems to have all but disappeared.

A few examples of what we are writing about will be given. Peter challenged Jesus to make him, too, walk on water. Peter did, but then sank as his faith wavered (Matt. 14:28-31). Peter once rebuked Jesus (!) for talking about His impending suffering and death (Mark 8:32). Peter impulsively proposed to build tabernacles for Jesus, **Moses**, and **Elijah** on the Mount of Transfiguration (Mark 9:5-6). Mark, possibly writing Peter's own memoir, makes it clear that Peter made this ridiculous suggestion just because he didn't know what else to say! Peter refused to let Jesus wash his feet (John 13:8). Peter vehemently declared his loyalty to Jesus—and shortly thereafter fell asleep on guard duty in Gethsemane and denied that he knew Jesus, three times (Mark 14:29-42; 66-72). Quick-triggered Peter cut off Malchus's ear in Gethsemane (John 18:10-11). Jesus and/or God rebuked Peter for some of these rash outbursts and lapses of faith, but the Lord promised His disciple that, after Satan had thoroughly sifted him, his faith would not fail again (Luke 22:31-32). And this is the Peter we see after Christ's ascension and Pentecost: a rock-faithful prophet.

Some of Peter's outbursts were good. When Jesus miraculously filled the boats with fish, only Peter spontaneously confessed his sinfulness before Christ (Luke 5:8). When many of Jesus's followers were leaving Him, after His "hard teaching," it was Peter who had just the right response to Jesus's offer to release the twelve also: "Lord, to whom shall we go? You have the words of eternal life. Also we have come to believe that You are the Christ, the Son of the living God" (John 6:66-69). Another "rash" statement of Peter's, that brought Jesus's warm commendation and that Christ declared to be prophecy, was that same confession on another occasion when Jesus asked His disciples, "But who do you say that I am?" (Matt. 16:15-17).

Peter's Prophecy

Peter's first two sermons (Acts 2:14-40; 3:12-26)—the first two by any prophet after Jesus's death, resurrection, and ascension—are the *Magna Carta* of all Christian preaching. They remain models and sources of inspiration for preachers, but of course they cannot be replicated because of the special circumstances under which they were preached. Both of these sermons were set up by unplanned, unexpected miracles. Both were extemporaneous on Peter's part but under the direct and strong influence of the Holy Spirit. Both produced amazing results among the hearers: The number of believers in Jesus Christ grew by the thousands. Both messages were full of Old Testament prophecy and full of Christ. They were convicting, calling for repentance; yet encouraging, promising grace, salvation, and blessing.

Peter continued speaking in this same vein while on trial before the Sanhedrin, and he continued prophesying mightily and often in those first weeks and months of apostleship (Acts 4:5-22, 31, 33; 5:17-21, 42; 6:2, 7; 8:25; 9:32). The last verbal prophecy of Peter's that is recorded in Scripture was some time later, at Cornelius's house in Caesarea (Acts 10:34-48). Peter had lost none of his spiritual power in preaching. The Holy Spirit fell on Gentiles, for the first time, as Peter preached to them.

As with many other prophets, Peter's verbal prophesying was often preceded or accompanied by miracles, attesting to its truth and godly origin. We cannot count the number of signs associated with Peter, for Luke reports that "they brought the sick out into the streets and laid them on beds and couches, that at least the shadow of Peter might fall on some of them. And they were all healed" (Acts 5: 15-16). Specific miracles wrought through Peter, or upon Peter—some with other apostles also involved—include the language miracle on Pentecost (Acts 2:5-12), the healing of a forty-year-old man lame from birth (Acts 3:1-10; 4:22), the deaths of Ananias and Sapphira (Acts 5:1-11), two releases from prison(Acts 5:17-20; 12:5-10), the healing of Aeneas in Lydda (Acts. 9:32-35), bringing Dorcas from death back to life (Acts 9:36-42), and the sign of tongues-speaking in Caesarea (Acts 10:44-46).

Peter's written prophecies—the two biblical epistles that bear his name—are addressed to believers, not to unbelievers like his speeches and sermons (1 Pet. 1:1-2; 2 Pet. 1:1). The first letter deals primarily with persecution. It was originally written to "pilgrims" (or sojourners) "of the dispersion" throughout Asia Minor (modern Turkey) in about the seventh decade of the AD first century; but it has spoken deeply to Christians throughout the world for almost two thousand years. Silvanus (**Silas**), another prophet, helped Peter write this letter (1 Pet. 5:12)—a fact, some scholars say, that accounts for its superior Greek. Certain passages parallel Paul's prophecy in Ephesians and Colossians[45] (e.g. 1 Pet. 3:1-7, cf. Eph. 5:22-25).

The second epistle of Peter deals primarily with false teaching and false prophets within the visible church as well as with a wrong perception that Christ's second coming was somehow delayed. It is a general epistle written to "those who have obtained like precious faith with us." Its place of origin is not known although Rome is supposed because Peter sensed that his death was imminent (2 Pet. 1:14). Second Peter is remarkably similar to Jude.

Both of Peter's letters contain important passages on the subject of prophets and prophecy (1 Pet. 1:10-12; 2:6-10; 2 Pet. 1:19-2:1; 3:1-10), including one frequently quoted in this and other works: "For prophecy never came by the will of man, but holy men of God spoke as they were moved by the Holy Spirit" (2 Pet. 1:21). Peter received revelation about **Noah** and about **Balaam** not found elsewhere in Scripture (1 Pet. 3:18-22; 2 Pet. 2:5, 15). He especially illuminates Noah's ministry ("preacher of righteousness"), the symbolism of the flood, and Balaam's true character and teaching. And Peter alone tells us of Christ's going to preach to imprisoned spirits who were disobedient in the days of Noah, while the ark was being built (1 Pet. 3:19-20).

138. **Philip I** was one of **Jesus's** twelve disciples (Luke 6:14) and one of the eleven who became His apostles (Acts 1:13). There is no biblical record of any prophecy specific and unique to Philip. However, he was one of those disciples sent out by Jesus to "preach the kingdom of God" (prophesy) and to "heal the sick" (perform miracles) in Galilee (Luke 9:1-6). He was also one of the apostles who on that certain Pentecost Day "were all filled with the Holy Spirit and began to speak with other tongues, as the Spirit gave them utterance . . . 'speaking in (many) tongues the wonderful works of God" (Acts 2:4, 11). As **Peter** understood and explained to the crowd, this amazing phenomenon was prophesying, foretold by the prophet **Joel** (Acts 2:14-18). This is all we know of Philip as a prophet although he undoubtedly preached and told gospel prophecy after Pentecost (Acts 4:33). Mr. Foxe says he labored in Asia (Minor) and was martyred there by crucifixion in AD 54.[46]

Philip was the first disciple explicitly called by Jesus to follow Him, and he was instrumental in recruiting **Nathanael** (John 1:43-46). As seen in this passage, Philip was steeped in Scripture. He was from the same fishing village in Galilee as Peter and **Andrew**, Bethsaida. For these reasons he was almost surely a Jew although Philip is a Greek name meaning "horse-lover." Perhaps because of his name, and/or for other reasons, Philip was once approached by "certain Greeks" asking for an introduction to Jesus (John 12:20-22).

Philip's belief in Jesus's divinity and power was tested, and found wanting, by Jesus on at least two occasions: the feeding of the five thousand (John 6:5-7) and again at the last supper (John 14:7-9). But we sense that he was representative of all twelve in both instances and that his faith was not especially weaker than that of the others.

139. **Philip II** was one of the seven men "of good reputation, full of the Holy Spirit and of wisdom" in the primordial church of **Jesus** Christ at Jerusalem, who were chosen by the church and ordained by the apostles to distribute food fairly and equitably among the thousands of new converts, or at least among the widows (Acts 6:1-6). Philip presumably performed his duties as a deacon in Jerusalem, but God also had other important plans for him. After the church (except the apostles)[47]

scattered from Jerusalem throughout Judea and Samaria (Acts 8:1), Philip is next found in Samaria preaching God's word and doing miracles—the very signature of a prophet (Acts 8:5-7). Philip is later called an "evangelist, who was one of the seven" (Acts 21:8), distinguishing him from **Philip I**.

Philip the deacon/evangelist/prophet, like his namesake the disciple/apostle/prophet, was a Jew with a Greek name. We know his ethnicity from the list of deacons (Acts 6:5), which contains just one proselyte, Nicolas.[48]

Philip was as effective as any apostle in proclaiming Jesus Christ, the very Word of God. He had a pioneering spirit. It was Philip who first obeyed Jesus's mandate to be His witness in Samaria (Acts 1:8). Christ Himself had worked in Sychar, Samaria (John 4:1-42), and Philip found nearby Samaria City to be a fertile field for the gospel. Philip also worked many miracles there, healing especially the lame, the paralyzed, and the mentally deranged (Acts 8:5-8). Philip was the first non-apostle reported to have administered the sacrament of Christian baptism (Acts 8:12). He was the first prophet of the apostolic era to have a direct confrontation with a false prophet, one Simon, a sorcerer. Philip actually won him over, although Simon's conversion proved to be shallow if not false (Acts 8:9-13, 21).

Philip was full of the Holy Spirit and truth. In Samaria, "the multitudes with one accord heeded the things spoken by Philip" (Acts 8:6). But something was missing in the church being founded there. Machen adroitly summarizes the next development:

> The conversions wrought by the preaching of Philip were genuine conversions. They were sealed by the sacrament of baptism. But one thing was lacking. The Holy Spirit had not been given. That does not mean that the Spirit of God had not been operative in Samaria. He had attended the preaching of Philip and had created faith in the hearts of the hearers. It is rather the special, miraculous manifestation of the Spirit's presence that seems to be meant. That manifestation was connected especially with the apostles. It was not till Peter and John came down from Jerusalem that the Samaritans "received the Holy Spirit." In that way the unity of the church was preserved. The apostles were in possession of a divine authority.[49]

The situation in Samaria just before **Peter** and **John II** arrived is strikingly similar to that in Ephesus, many miles and years away, just before Paul came there (Acts 19:1-7). There was a group of Christian converts called "disciples" in Ephesus—true believers, duly baptized; but the Holy Spirit did not "fall on them" until an *apostle* came and laid hands on them.

Philip had a divine vision, or angelic visit, (another characteristic experience of prophets, although not exclusive to them) telling him to leave Samaria and head south toward Gaza (Acts 8:26). On the road he overtook a wealthy, high-ranking Ethiopian. This man was a proselyte to Judaism, for he was returning from a religious pilgrimage to Jerusalem and was reading the Jewish Scriptures. With the Holy Spirit's urging and unction, Philip witnessed to the Ethiopian, who then believed in Jesus as the Son of God and was baptized by Philip (Acts 8:27-39). This episode indicates the depth of Philip's knowledge of Scripture. It is also a literal fulfillment of a passage in Isaiah located not far from the place the Ethiopian had just been reading; a passage he must have known and cherished, for he was a eunuch, as well as a foreigner:

> Do not let the son of a foreigner who has joined himself to the LORD speak, saying, "The LORD has utterly separated me from His people"; Nor let the eunuch say, "Here I am, a dry tree." For thus says the LORD: "To the eunuchs who keep My Sabbaths, and choose what pleases Me, and hold fast My covenant, even to them I will give in My house and within My walls a place and a name better than that of sons and daughters; I will give them an everlasting name that shall not be cut off.—Is. 56:3-5

Philip then continued to prophesy as an evangelist along the Mediterranean coastal region, ending up in Caesarea (Acts 8:40), where many years later he hosted **Paul** and party on their way to Jerusalem (Acts 21:8-13). It would appear that Philip settled down in Caesarea, married, and had children, for he had a house there and four virgin daughters who were prophetesses. Paul stayed with Philip many days. During his visit, they were joined by another famous prophet, **Agabus**. So at one time, in this private home, there were at least eight prophets: Philip, Paul, **Luke**, Agabus, and Philip's four daughters. Imagine the conversation at the breakfast table!

140. **Romanti-ezer** was the last (twenty-fourth) musical prophet chosen by lot to lead a twelve-man section of **David's** prophesying chorus/orchestra. He was one of the fourteen sons of **Heman** the seer who "should prophesy with harps, stringed instruments, and cymbals . . . in the house of the LORD . . . in the songs of the LORD" (1 Chr. 25:1, 4, 6-8, 21). His great-grandfather was **Samuel** (1 Chr. 6:33).

141. **Salome** was among the women who brought spices to anoint **Jesus's** body in His tomb at dawn after the Sabbath following His crucifixion (Mark 16: 1-8). Instead of Jesus's body they saw, in a vision (Luke 24:22-23), a young man[50] (elsewhere called an angel) who gave them a message from God. Although the gospel (Mark) in which Salome is named says that "they said nothing to anyone," their silence was short-lived according to the other two synoptic evangelists (Matt. 28:8; Luke 24:9). Thus Salome, along with the other women, in telling forth a message from God that was received in a vision, did prophesy.

142. **Samuel** is one of the most important of all the prophets. He ushered in the "golden age" of prophets in the Old Testament. He initiated Israel's monarchy,

anointed her first two kings, and installed the first one. Samuel was one of the two most respected, honored, and powerful prophet-leaders in Old Testament history, the other being **Moses**.

Samuel was not the first prophet, as some say. Nor was he even the second, after Moses, as our beloved Dr. Young avers. But he was, in Young's words, "the first of . . . a class of men who continued till **Malachi** and **John**."[51] Samuel was the vanguard prophet of the kingdom period (ca. 1100-450 BC), which produced by far the largest number of prophets and the most recorded prophecy in the Old Testament (see chapter 7). Samuel was the first man known in Israel, and to us, *primarily* as a prophet (1 Sam. 3:20) although several men and women before him bore the title and/or executed the office, on occasion. It is true that Moses was primarily a prophet, indeed, the prototype and arguably the greatest prophet of the Old Testament; but we often *perceive* of him more as a legislator, a nation builder, and a great leader.

A Prophet—and More

Samuel, although first and foremost a prophet, had other very important offices and duties. He was not exclusively a prophet like, say, **Elijah** and John the baptizer. Samuel was a judge, the national leader of Israel before **Saul** became king (1 Sam. 7:15-17). Even after Saul became king, Samuel was the more powerful figure: for he, with impunity, severely chastised King Saul and pronounced his disestablishment (1 Sam. 13:13-14). Samuel was the last and perhaps best judge of Israel during their theocracy period (ca. 1400–1050 BC). He was, reluctantly at first, a kingmaker who anointed Israel's first kings. He was also a kingbreaker, with regard to Saul.

Not only was this vanguard prophet a judge-statesman, he appears to have executed the office of priest. We must be cautious here. Only **Aaron's** direct descendants were to be priests (Ex. 29:9). Samuel was a Levite[52] (1 Chr. 6:33-38), but *not* a descendent of Aaron. We are reminded that Korah, also a Levite and an ancestor of Samuel, died at God's hand for his presumption to the priesthood (Num. 16, 17); and that Gideon, a great judge, made a grave error in usurping priesthood by making an ephod (Judg. 8:22-27). But here we have Samuel offering sacrifices on an altar to the LORD (1 Sam. 7:9; 10:8)—and reproving Saul for doing the same! (1 Sam 13:9-13). Samuel even built an altar in his hometown of Ramah (1 Sam. 7:17). Yet just before the Judges Era, Israel nearly went to civil war over the building of an altar "beside(s) the altar of the LORD which is before His tabernacle" (Josh. 22:19, 29). In Samuel's time the tabernacle and altar were in Shiloh (1 Sam. 1:3; 2:12-14; 4:3-4), and then perhaps in Bethel (1 Sam. 10:3), Gilgal (1 Sam. 10:8; 11:14; 15:21), and Nob (1 Sam. 21:1-9); but it was probably never in Ramah.

There are several plausible explanations, or at least mitigating factors, for these apparent departures from God's Law on Samuel's part:

1. In fulfillment of God's judgment of Eli the high priest and his family, Eli's priestly line was cut off (1 Sam. 2:27-36; 3:11-14; 4:11, 18). There was suddenly a discontinuity in the priestly succession, which apparently was not filled for years. Samuel filled the vacuum. The next Aaronic priest mentioned in Scripture after Eli is Ahijah, when Saul was king (1 Sam. 14:3). But he was Eli's great-grandson and therefore disestablished. A valid line, or rather two lines, were established by the time **David** was king, at least forty years after the demise of Eli and sons (2 Sam. 8:17; 1 Chr. 24:1-3).
2. Samuel was raised as a priest or priest's helper even though he was not of priestly descent. He even wore, as a boy, priestly or priestlike garments (1 Sam 2:18; 3:1). Eli himself unwittingly prepared Samuel to be an "acting" priest after his own demise, until a new line from Aaron could be established.
3. When Samuel offered sacrifices to God (e.g., 1 Sam. 7:9; 10:8) it is possible that legitimate Aaronic priests were involved, though they are not named. It is not uncommon for Scripture to say that so-and-so, not a priest, made an offering to the LORD—the priest's part is taken for granted. However, the account of *Saul's* unlawful sacrifice (1 Sam. 13:9-14) strongly suggests that Samuel could lawfully offer sacrifices while Saul could not. If Aaronic priests were involved at Gilgal, Saul's sacrifice might have been lawful.
4. Finally, the "Melchizedek factor" could be invoked. Melchizedek and **Jesus** Christ were priests *not of Aaron's order* (Heb. 7), yet indeed lawful, ordained by God. Other prophets not of Aaronic descent, under certain circumstances, had priestly functions commissioned by God: for example, Elijah built an altar and sacrificed a bull on it at Mount Carmel (1 Ki. 18:20-28). Samuel could have been ordained by God to act as His priest under the special circumstances that prevailed after the demise of Eli's house.

These relatively rare exceptions to the exclusiveness of Aaron's family as priests in Israel seem to foreshadow the day, now fully come, when all believers are priests (1 Pet. 2:9; Rev. 1:6) and Christ alone is our permanent High Priest.

Samuel's Life

The life of Samuel is sketched in Scripture from before birth to death and even a (much debated) after-death appearance. He was a child of promise (1 Sam. 1), as were **Isaac** (Gen. 18:1-15), Samson (Judg. 13), **John I** (Luke 1), and Jesus (Luke 1). The story of his mother **Hannah's** barrenness, humiliation, answered prayer, and gratitude to God is well-known (1 Sam. 1:1-2:10). She named her baby Samuel, "Heard of God," for God had heard her prayer for him (1:20). She dedicated and literally gave him to the LORD to serve in the tabernacle of God under Eli the high priest (1:22-28; 2:11).

The young boy Samuel thrived in the tabernacle serving God and Eli. While thus employed he became a prophet (1 Sam. 3:11-18). There are several important aspects of his childhood with regard to the subject of prophets and prophecy:

1. Samuel is one of three child prophets in Scripture. Jesus's every word was God's word, and therefore it was prophecy; a specific instance was His parlance with the temple rabbis (Luke 2:41-50, esp. v. 47). The third young prophet was **Joseph**, who was actually seventeen years old when he had a prophetic dream and told it (prophesied) [Gen. 37:2-11].
2. "And the word of the LORD was rare in those days; there was no widespread revelation" (1 Sam. 3:1). This verse from Samuel's childhood signals the ending of a dark period of history and the dawning of an age of enlightenment by revelation (prophecy). Given this background, Eli's perception that it was God speaking to Samuel (1 Sam. 3:8) is altogether remarkable.
3. The account of Samuel's childhood prophecy (1 Sam. 3) shows just how simply and effortlessly on man's part, prophecy and a prophet can be born. Yes, an **Isaiah** or a David can labor diligently to produce a prophetic poem or psalm, and these, too, are God's doing. But He demonstrates with the boy Samuel that He can and will communicate His word to us through even an unsuspecting, ignorant, half-educated lad who thereby becomes His prophet as surely as Moses. "Samuel did not yet know the LORD, nor was the word of the LORD yet revealed to him" (1 Sam. 3:7).
4. Samuel entered adulthood firmly established as a prophet, famed in all Israel (1 Sam. 3:19-21). We know of no other career prophet so famous as a prophet, so early in life, except possibly **Daniel** (Dan. 1:3-4; 2:19-45). Even Jesus was not widely known until He began His public ministry at the age of thirty.

Despite Samuel's fame and the fact that "the word of Samuel came to all Israel," the nation stumbled badly (1 Sam. 4). The ark of the covenant of the LORD was captured by the Philistines. Eli and his sons perished in accordance with God's justice, as prophesied. Apparently the very institution of the priesthood went into eclipse, and God was not worshipped properly. Israel fell into subjection to the Philistines, and, worse, into sin—especially idolatry. After twenty years of this, Samuel the prophet stepped up and became Israel's judge deliverer as well as her interim chief priest (1 Sam. 7:2-17). The Philistines were subdued, there was peace all around, and Samuel was the nation's judge-governor-priest-prophet for some years.

But just like his spiritual mentor Eli, Samuel when he was old fell victim to the sins of his own two sons. He had set them up as deputy judges in southern Israel, but they were corrupt (1 Sam. 8:1-3). Because Samuel was old and had no worthy successor in his family, Israel demanded new leadership—a king (1 Sam. 8:4). This angered Samuel, for a human kingdom would mean that the constitutional theocracy (Lex rex, Deus rex), instituted by Moses and continued, albeit badly at times, through the judges period, had failed. It was an enormous constitutional, political, and theological crisis!

In perhaps his finest hour, Samuel did the right thing: He prayed (1 Sam. 8:6). And, although he did not like God's answer, he obeyed. Samuel prayed and obeyed, and Israel was stayed as a nation. God accepted Israel's rejection of Him as king and agreed to an earthly kingdom with a human king. But He warned them, through Samuel His prophet, about the burdens and pitfalls of an earthly kingdom such as taxes and military conscription (1 Sam. 8:7-22).

God also used His prophet Samuel to secretly anoint and then publicly proclaim Israel's first king (1 Sam. 9, 10). Saul was a tall, handsome, rugged man from a prosperous Benjamite family. It is at this time we first learn of groups of musical prophets in Israel possibly trained by Samuel and led by him on some occasions (1 Sam. 10:5; 19:20). Although David is credited with the great surge of musical prophecy, it appears that Samuel had something to do with it. We also see that at this late stage in his life Samuel was still known as a prophet (1 Sam. 9:6-9), despite the fact that he had been Israel's principal judge-leader for many years and would continue in that office until he died (1 Sam. 7:15).

Samuel's extended speech and dialogue with the people at Saul's coronation (1 Sam. 12) is one of the finest orations ever given. It is poignant, edifying, challenging, and encouraging. It is historically important, marking the end of theocracy and the beginning of monarchy in Israel. It clearly sets forth the only pathway to success for the king and for the nation, namely, fear the LORD, serve Him in truth with all your heart, and keep His commandments. Make your new government a *constitutional* monarchy, under God's Law. Samuel's speech also clearly states the dire consequences of not doing these things. The speech itself is not alleged to be prophecy, but it was affirmed by God with a miracle of thunder and rain, at Samuel's call (1 Sam. 12:18).

Samuel did not fade away like an old soldier but continued to vigorously serve God and the nation after Saul was crowned. At least twice during Saul's reign, Samuel had to rebuke him for disobeying God's commands through His prophet (1 Sam. 13:1-14; chapter 15). On both of these occasions, the LORD revealed to Samuel, and through him to Saul, that Saul's dynasty would be short-lived. Another king, of another family, a man after God's heart, would succeed Saul. After the second offense, Samuel himself had to carry out the order that Saul had disobeyed: to execute an evil king. Samuel did this with a sword even though he must have been quite elderly, for he was already old before Saul became king (1 Sam. 8:1). After this, Samuel had nothing more to do with Saul, but he mourned for him (1 Sam. 15:35). Then God told Samuel to stop mourning for Saul and to go and anoint the new king "whom I have chosen" (1 Sam. 16:1-3). This would be David.

The old prophet had little known contact with David after anointing him. But when David escaped from the murderous Saul, he fled to Samuel in Ramah. Together they went to Naioth-in-Ramah, which may have been a nearby seminary, lodge, or camp for prophets (1 Sam. 19:18). When Saul sent "messengers" there to arrest David, they found a group of prophets prophesying (musically?) under Samuel's direction. The Holy Spirit fell upon these messengers, and they, too, prophesied—three groups of them. Finally Saul himself came, and likewise prophesied, and subjected himself to Samuel (1 Sam. 19:19-24). David escaped. Perhaps this experience helped convince David to include musical prophecy in formal worship when he became king! (1 Chr. 25).

Samuel died at what must have been a very advanced age: it was toward the end of Saul's forty-year reign, and Samuel was described as old before that reign began (1 Sam. 8:1). All Israel mourned and gathered at Ramah to bury Samuel (1 Sam. 25:1). It is possible that both Saul and David came to the funeral, the occasion being so momentous that they put aside their enmity for it.

There is a postscript to Samuel's life. A medium or witch is said to have "brought (conjured) up" Samuel in a séance ordered by Saul (1 Sam. 28:3-20). There is great controversy among Bible scholars, both Jewish and Christian, about whether this was a real appearance of Samuel, or a trick of Satan and the witch.

Samuel's Prophecy

The recorded verbal prophecies of Samuel have been alluded to in the above sketch of his life. To summarize, they are

1. his boyhood prophecy about Eli, 1 Sam. 3;
2. his first charge to Israel as their judge deliverer, 1 Sam. 7:3;
3. God's word concerning a king for Israel, 1 Sam. 8;
4. the anointment speech and instructions to Saul, 1 Sam. 10:1-8;
5. the proclamation to Israel about Saul, 1 Sam. 10:18-19;
6. the first rebuke of Saul, 1 Sam. 13:13-14;
7. God's command to Saul to destroy Amalek, 1 Sam. 15:2-3; and
8. the second rebuke of Saul, 1 Sam 15:16-19, 22-23, 28.

In addition to these specific prophecies, "the LORD was with him and let none of his words fall to the ground. And all Israel from Dan to Beersheba knew that Samuel had been established as a prophet of the LORD. Then the LORD appeared again in Shiloh. For the LORD revealed Himself to Samuel in Shiloh by the word of the LORD. And the word of Samuel came to all Israel" (1 Sam. 3:19-4:1a). And again, "All that he says surely comes to pass" (1 Sam. 9:6). So Samuel verbally prophesied much more than we see recorded in the Bible.

Samuel was also a writer (1 Sam. 10:25; 1 Chr. 29:29). How much he contributed to the Bible cannot be determined. Judges, Ruth, and part of 1 Samuel are often attributed to him. He obviously could not have written any part of 2 Samuel, for it all occurred after his death. The naming of that book for him is quite a tribute to his continuing influence on the age.

As a prophet Samuel performed, or was God's agent for, miracles. Two of them involved thunder, once with rain (1 Sam. 7:9-11; 12:16-18). The signs that Samuel gave Saul to prove the divine origin of his anointing were miracles (1 Sam. 10:1-12).

The spontaneous, spurious prophesying of Saul and his "messengers" under Samuel's influence (1 Sam. 19:20-24) can be considered miraculous.

Samuel's Legacy

When Samuel was a boy, God's word was rare. There was no widespread prophecy (1 Sam. 3:1). Before he died there were groups of prophets in Israel—possibly schools or camps (1 Sam. 10:5, 10-11; 19:20). Prophets (not only Samuel) were consulted for guidance (1 Sam. 9:9; 28:6). Other outstanding, named prophets such as **Gad** were emerging (1 Sam. 22:5). Saul and others prophesied spuriously (1 Sam. 10:10; 19:20-24). David, one of God's most prolific prophets, began to prophesy in song (psalm).[53] "Prophet" had become a calling and a lifelong career for numbers of people, not just a rare and temporary phenomenon. The explosion of prophecy had been ignited. Samuel was God's detonator.

When Samuel was born, Israel was technically a theocracy, with written laws, a permanent priesthood, and *ad hoc* judge deliverers; but the Law was being widely ignored, and the priesthood and nation were decaying from sin within. When Samuel died Israel was a monarchy on the verge of her most glorious epoch under Kings David and Solomon. Samuel was God's bridge: Israel's last judge and first kingmaker. And mark it well, he instituted a *constitutional-theocratic* monarchy, the Law of God and God Himself being supreme over king and people alike (1 Sam. 12:13-15, 19-25). *Lex rex, Deus rex.*

When Samuel was young, true religion was at a low ebb. Priests were corrupt; they did not know God. Men despised holy things (1 Sam. 2:12, 17). After the established priesthood was decimated according to God's righteous judgment, and before new priestly lines from Aaron were established, Samuel acted as interim priest before God. He prayed for and taught Israel (1 Sam. 12:23). Samuel saw to it that Israel kept the Passover Feast; he was the last leader to do so for many generations including even David and Solomon (2 Chr. 35:18). He appointed Levites to their tabernacle duties (1 Chr. 9:22). He started the practice of dedicating the spoils of war to maintaining the tabernacle of God (1 Chr. 26:28).

For most of his long life, Samuel was the most powerful man in Israel. He was the second most revered, respected, and feared national prophet in Israel's political history, after Moses. Samuel was one of those prophets in biblical history who was not opposed and/or persecuted by his own government. For much of his career, he *was* the government, and he made kings of both Saul and David. Still, as a prophet, Samuel suffered and mourned (1 Sam. 8; 15:35). It just goes with the office.

143. **Saul**—is he also among the prophets? According to our criteria (see headnotes), he is (1 Sam. 10:1-13; 19:19-24). But criteria aside, how amazing it is that this question is still alive and well—and pertinent—three thousand years after it was originally asked! The essence of the question is still the same and is often asked about others than Saul: Is someone who prophesies just once or twice, under

or because of a strong external manifestation of the Spirit, a prophet? Wasn't he or she just caught up in the excitement of the music and swaying and shouting? Was it just a manifestation of group psychology, a sort of frenzy or spiritual intoxication? Or did God really speak through him, her, or me?

Well, in Saul's case we have some additional information. First, God had given him another heart (1 Sam. 10:9). That is important. He was a changed man, *before* he prophesied. Never mind that he later changed back. The gift of prophecy is not necessarily permanent. Neither is the office of prophet. Another significant fact about Saul is that, when he finished prophesying, he went straightway to a place of worship (1 Sam. 10:13). He knew that the LORD was in this thing, and he wanted to worship Him.

The report of the second instance of Saul's prophesying, at Naioth in Ramah, contains only one clue as to his spiritual condition when he was prophesying: He removed his regal robes and bowed before **Samuel**, God's representative (1 Sam. 19:24). Prior to this, Saul had disobeyed God and been disenfranchised as king, although he still held the title and office (1 Sam. 15:10-29). After **David** was anointed to eventually replace him, "the Spirit of the LORD departed from Saul, and a distressing (or evil) spirit from the LORD troubled him" (1 Sam. 16:14). When he came to Naioth-Ramah seeking to kill David he was changed again, if only temporarily—again. This is evidenced by his removing his kingly garments and prostrating himself before Samuel to acknowledge his sinfulness and inferiority before God. Yes, he really prophesied. After all, the Bible says so. But not everybody who was there or who heard of it was convinced, and the same question was asked again: "Is Saul also among the prophets?"

{Saul II—**Paul**}

144. **Shebuel** (Shubael) was a Levite musician chosen by **David** and the captains of the army to prophesy with harps, stringed instruments, and cymbals (ca. 1000 BC) [1 Chr. 25:1-7]. He was a son of **Heman** "the king's seer in the words of God," and a great-grandson of **Samuel** the prophet (1 Chr. 6:33). Shebuel was one of the 288 skilled musicians who were instructed to prophesy in the songs of the LORD (psalms). He was chosen by lot to lead the thirteenth twelve-man section (1 Chr. 25:20).

145. **Shemaiah I** was God's prophet to King Rehoboam (930–913 BC) and to what was left of his kingdom. After **Solomon's** death, most of the Kingdom of Israel rebelled against the house of **David** (1 Ki. 12:19) leaving David's grandson Rehoboam with just the tribal territories of Judah and Benjamin (1 Ki. 12:21), plus most of the Levites (2 Chr. 11:13-14). Rehoboam mustered an army of one hundred and eighty thousand warriors to subdue the rebels and forcibly reunite the kingdom under himself. But God sent Shemaiah, "the man of God," with His direct orders for Rehoboam and the people of Judah and Benjamin: Disband

the army, and do not fight against the rebels (1 Ki. 12:21-24; cf. 2 Chr. 11:1-4). Wonder of wonders, they obeyed!

After three good years as king (2 Chr. 11:17), Rehoboam forsook the Law of God "and all Israel[54] with him" (2 Chr. 12:1). So God sent an army from Egypt to discipline them (12:2-4). He also sent Shemaiah, the prophet, to tell them why this was happening. Once again, they actually listened! (12:5-6). The king and leaders of Israel[54] humbled themselves and returned to God, who spared their lives. Although Egypt gained dominion over Judah and took away her treasures, the little kingdom was allowed to exist and actually prospered (12:9-12).

Shemaiah was also a writing prophet who chronicled Rehoboam's reign (2 Chr. 12:15), but we do not have his book. It may be a source for 1 Kings and 2 Chronicles.

146. **Shemaiah II** was a Levite who, in the days of King **Hezekiah** (715–686 BC), was called upon to help clean out the temple of God, which had fallen into disuse, disrepair, and filth (2 Chr. 29:3-14). Because he is identified as a "son" of **Jeduthun** (q.v.), it may be reasonably assumed that Shemaiah was one of those who were subsequently commanded "to sing praise to the LORD with the words of **David** and of **Asaph** the seer" (2 Chr. 29:25-29), i.e., to prophesy musically (1 Chr. 25:1-7).

147. **Shemaiah III** was one of the Levite singer-musicians in the double choir that celebrated the new wall of Jerusalem built under **Nehemiah** (445 BC) [Neh. 12:36; 40-42]. He was, therefore, in all likelihood, a member of the temple choir (Neh. 12:45-46) that prophesied "according to the command of **David** and **Solomon** . . . and **Asaph** . . . songs of praise and thanksgiving to God" (Neh. 12:45-46). Such singing was prophesying (1 Chr. 25:1-7).

148. **Shemiramoth** was a Levite musician, a string player, who was in the marching orchestra that escorted the ark of the covenant of the LORD into Jerusalem (ca. 1000 BC) [1 Chr. 15:16- 20) . It is therefore probable that he later became one of the two hundred eighty-eight musicians ordained to prophesy in the house of God with the songs of God (1 Chr. 25:1-7).

149. **Sherebiah** was a leading Levite singer in the days of Joiakim the priest (second generation after the return of the first group of Jews from Babylonian captivity in 537 BC); and in the days of **Nehemiah** and **Ezra** (458 BC ff) [Neh. 12:24, 26]. Shemaiah and his brethren sang antiphonally "according to the command of **David** the man of God"[55]; therefore, they prophesied (1 Chr. 25:1-7).

150. **Shimei I** was one of the six sons of **Jeduthun** who were separated by **David** and his army captains to prophesy "in the songs of the LORD" in the house of God

(ca. 1000 BC) [1 Chr. 25:1-7]. He was selected by lot for the tenth twelve-man section of the 288 prophesying musicians (1 Chr. 25:17).

151. **Shimei II** was one of six Levites who "arose" under King **Hezekiah** (715–686 BC) to clean up the temple of God (2 Chr. 29:12-14). The temple—and God Himself—had long been neglected. Because Shimei is identified as a descendent of **Heman** the great singer-prophet, it is assumed that he took his place with the musicians who prophesied "according to the commandment of **David**" (1 Chr. 25:1-7) in the cleansed temple (2 Chr. 29:25-29).

{Shubael—**Shebuel**}

152. **Silas** (a.k.a. Silvanus) is one of the few New Testament, apostolic-era Christians who is actually called a prophet in the Bible. He is named a prophet for prophesying verbally (Acts 15:32). He also contributed written, canonical prophecy, by assisting both **Paul** and **Peter** with letters that became Scripture (1 and 2 Thess. 1:1; 1 Pet. 5:12).

Silas was a leader in the church at Jerusalem some fifteen to twenty years after the persecution that had scattered this original congregation, excepting apostles (Acts 8:1). Silas and **Judas IV**, another leader and prophet in the Jerusalem church, were dispatched with Paul and **Barnabas** to Antioch, Syria, to deliver a letter from "the apostles, the elders, and the brethren" at Jerusalem (Acts 15:22-23). The letter concerned Gentile circumcision and other matters. Silas and Judas IV had the highest of credentials—besides being prophets, they had risked their lives for the name of the Lord **Jesus Christ** (Acts 15:25-26). While at Antioch, these two emissaries from Jerusalem prophesied "with many words" for some time (Acts 15:32).

Both prophets were sent back to Jerusalem with greetings of peace from Antioch; but Silas elected to stay in Antioch (Acts 15:33-34). Here we see God's providential hand at work, for when Barnabas and Paul parted ways over John Mark, Silas became Paul's new missionary partner, duly commissioned by the church (Acts 15:39-40).

It was a good partnership. Like Paul, Silas was a Roman citizen (Acts 16:37-38). He prophesied frequently on the mission field (Acts 16:19-21, 25; 2 Cor. 1:19), but no specific message or sermon of Silas alone has been preserved in Scripture. Silas and Paul shared in physical suffering for the cause of Christ in Philippi. And they shared in a miraculous release from the Philippi jail after praying and singing together (Acts 16:19-34). At times it appears that Silas and Paul had equal footing. For example, these two were arrested in Philippi while team members **Timothy** and **Luke** were not(Acts 16:19). Again, Paul and Silas were co-leaders in Thessalonica and were sent away from there when trouble arose while the others in their party were allowed to stay (Acts 17:4, 10). At other times it is clear that Paul was the leader of the two, especially in the ministry of the word (e.g., Acts 16:14; 17:2, 13-14; 18:5).

Silas disappears from the narrative in Acts at Corinth. He had rejoined Paul there after being separated in Berea (Acts 17:14-15; 18:5). Paul stayed in Corinth for over eighteen months (Acts 18:11), but there is no further mention of Silas in the book of Acts. However, we know he preached to the newfound Corinth church (2 Cor. 1:19). Also, while he was in Corinth, Silas co-authored or co-sent, with Paul, the two letters to Thessalonica that are in the Bible. These were supposedly written in AD 50 or 51.

Silas eventually joined Peter, probably in Rome, and helped him compose his first general epistle (1 Pet. 5:12), probably in the 60s. Some scholars attribute the superior writing style of 1 Peter as compared with 2 Peter to the hand of Silas the prophet.

{Silvanus—**Silas**}

153. **Simeon I**, a devout Jew, saw the baby **Jesus** (just forty days old) being presented by his parents to the LORD in the temple, in Jerusalem. The Holy Spirit revealed to Simeon that this Child was the Lord's Christ. Simeon took Him up in his arms and prophesied about Him (Luke 2:25-32). His formal prophecy is called the *Nunc Dimittis*, its first words in Latin. Simeon then blessed **Joseph** and **Mary** but prophetically warned Mary that her child would upset all Israel and that her own soul would be pierced because of Him.

{Simeon II—Simon **Peter**, or less likely, **Simeon I**}—Acts 15:14 only, most versions.

154. **Simeon III**, called Niger (black), was one of five "prophets and teachers" who were in the Christian church at Antioch, Syria, in about AD 45 (Acts 13:1). Some may have been prophets and others, teachers; but we assume all five were both prophets and teachers because at least two of them, **Barnabas** and **Saul**, were both. As these five ministered and fasted, the Holy Spirit separated Saul and Barnabas for His special mission. Simeon and the other two, **Lucius** and **Manaen**, then fasted and prayed and laid hands on Barnabas and Saul to commission them (Acts 13:2-3).

We find no warrant in Scripture for speculation that this Simeon was Simon of Cyrene, who carried Jesus's cross (Mark 15:21); although that possibility cannot be ruled out.

{Simon I—**Peter**}

155. **Simon II**, "the Zealot" or "the Cananite,"[56] was one of **Jesus's** twelve disciples. As such, he prophesied and performed miracles when first sent out by Jesus (Matt.

10:5-10; cf. Luke 9:1-6). Simon was also one of the apostles who prophesied on the morning of Pentecost after Jesus was risen from death (Acts 1:13; 2:1-13); and who continued to prophesy in the newborn church (Acts 2:42-43; 4:33). There is no further record of Simon in the Bible. Mr. Foxe says he preached in Africa and also in Britain, where he was crucified.[57]

156. **Solomon** was one of the wealthiest men of all time. He was the brilliant king of a prominent nation. He was educated beyond measure. Even to **Jesus**, he was the epitome of human earthly glory (Matt. 6:29). And he was a prophet!—an important, longtime, prolific prophet. Thus, Solomon is the very antithesis of one common stereotype of the biblical prophet: rustic, poor, and persecuted.

Actually, Solomon was the last and most glorious of a long line of prophets during an era when most prophets were at or near the pinnacle of government and culture, from **Abraham** the father of nations through **Joseph** the highest civil officer in Egypt through **Moses** the nation builder through **Joshua** the general through **Deborah** the judge through **Samuel** the kingmaker through **David** the king. After Solomon, there were precious few who combined the offices of God's prophet and man's political leader—only **Hezekiah** and **Nehemiah** come to mind. Most true prophets were not honored in their own country. Many were unpopular. Some were persecuted and even killed for being prophets. But not Solomon.

Solomon's Prophecy

Solomon is the human author of a very large amount of written prophecy: Ecclesiastes, Song of Solomon, most of Proverbs, and Psalms 72 and 127. Some of this prophecy is decidedly Messianic, as Psalm 72. The entire Song of Solomon is held by many to be an allegory of Christ's relationship with His church. Some of Solomon's prophecy is musical, including the Song (Canticles) of Solomon. He wrote one thousand and five songs (1 Ki. 4:32), most of which are not in Holy Scripture and therefore cannot be considered prophecy. Solomon's best-known written prophecy is the wisdom embodied in the books of Proverbs and Ecclesiastes.

Solomon was not only a writer of prophecy but also a speaker of it. He styled himself "the preacher" (Ecc. 1:1). Much of his written prophecy may have been originally preached by him. Proverbs 1–9, for example, reads like a sermon or series of sermons for youthful hearers. Solomon's magnificent speeches and prayers at the dedication of the temple building and the installation of the ark of the covenant therein (1 Ki. 8; cf. 2 Chr. 6) are not identified as prophecy *per se* but have many earmarks of it.

Solomon received direct, personal revelation from God on three occasions. The first was in a dream, when God asked the young king what He should give him, and Solomon requested wisdom (1 Ki. 3:5, 9). The second, just after the temple was built, was a conditional covenant: (to paraphrase) "Walk uprightly before Me and keep My statutes and commandments, and your kingdom will prosper forever;

but if you or your sons turn away from Me, I will take away your kingdom, cut off Israel, and cast away this temple you have built for Me" (1 Ki. 9:1-9). The third revelation from God was after Solomon, in his later years, failed to keep his part of the covenant by countenancing and even embracing the idolatry of his many foreign wives. God judged Solomon and passed sentence: that the kingdom of Israel, except for one tribe, would be torn away from the house of David/Solomon (1 Ki. 11:9-13). These three divine revelations correspond to the three phases of Solomon's reign as king: (1) a humble, wise, and good beginning; (2) a fabulous middle including the building of the temple, expansion of the kingdom, and accumulation of great wealth, knowledge, and fame; and (3) a decadent ending, full of strife.

Scripture does not tell if there was a third party, another prophet, involved in any of these three revelations—as was usually the case with other kings, especially when the prophecy was God's judgment against the king. Apparently there was no such prophet. It is a singular fact that so few other prophets or prophesiers are mentioned during Solomon's entire forty-year reign. **Nathan** was instrumental in securing the throne for Solomon against much opposition, and anointed him (1 Ki. 1:11-40). But Nathan was David's prophet and is not heard from again except as historian. **Ahijah** and **Iddo I** are also mentioned as historians (2 Chr. 9:29). Ahijah did prophesy near the end of Solomon's reign, but it was to Jeroboam, not directly to Solomon (1 Ki. 11:29 ff). The only other prophet identified in the Bible as actively prophesying during Solomon's reign is *Solomon himself!* Solomon did support the formal prophesying by the Levite musicians as started by his father David (1 Chr. 25); and he brought this mode of prophesying into the newly built temple (2 Chr. 5:12-14).

Solomon's Life

Solomon was the second[58] child of David and Bathsheba, whom David had married after his illicit affair with her and the murder of her husband, and after the infant death of their firstborn who was conceived out of wedlock (2 Sam. 12:15-23). They named their second child Solomon, meaning "peace." Then, after God sent word through Nathan the prophet of His love for the child, he was also named Jedidiah, meaning "beloved of the LORD" (2 Sam. 12:24-25). For some reason only the name *Solomon* stuck, at least with the biblical writers. But God loved Solomon by any name, and God chose him to succeed David as king (1 Chr. 28:5), over the claim of his older brother, Adonijah (1 Ki. 1). God also endowed Solomon with surpassing gifts and made him His prophet (1 Ki. 3:11-13).

When he was still a young man—perhaps about eighteen—Solomon's accession to the throne of Israel was engineered by Nathan and Bathsheba (1 Ki. 1). It was a dangerous and highly dramatic event despite the fact that God had ordained it. David died soon thereafter but not before he charged Solomon to follow God in all his ways—and to punish two wrongdoers whom David had spared, hinting that execution might be in order (1 Ki. 2:1-9). Solomon obeyed, and also had to execute his rival brother Adonijah who continued to offend (1 Ki. 2:13-46). David had also charged Solomon to build a magnificent temple for God and His worship (1 Chr. 28:10). David had drawn up its plans and amassed a great store of materials and craftsmen to build it (1 Chr. 22; 28:11-19).

Before Solomon got started on the temple project, he went to worship God at the "high place"[59] at Gibeon (1 Ki. 3:4-15; cf. 2 Chr. 1:1-12), at that time the site of the Mosaic tabernacle and altar (but not of the ark of the covenant, which David had placed in another tabernacle in Jerusalem) [1 Chr. 15:1]. There at Gibeon, God spoke to Solomon in a dream and Solomon made his famous request for an understanding heart with which to rule Israel. God granted this request and added much, much more (1 Ki. 3:1-15).

We will pass over the building of the temple and Solomon's administration, wise judgment, and fabulous wealth and accomplishments (1 Ki. 3:16-10:9; cf. 2 Chr. 1:13-9:28)—although these do provide an experiential basis for, and much insight into, his written prophecy, especially Proverbs and Ecclesiastes. But we cannot pass over what took place just after the temple was built. Solomon's speeches and prayers at the dedication of the temple (2 Chr. 6; cf. 1 Ki. 8) mark a high point in his career as a prophet. Although they are not identified as prophecy per se, these words were acknowledged by God Himself, as he twice filled the new temple with His real, palpable presence in the forms of cloud, fire, and glory! (2 Chr. 5; 7:1-3) It was the first time since the days of Moses, some four hundred years before (Ex. 40:34-35), that God had come down to actually dwell among men—this time in the temple built by Solomon. It was the last time God so filled His house and dwelt with men 'til Jesus came almost a thousand years later.

Then, God had His second "little visit" with Solomon, this time to encourage him but also to warn him of the dire consequences of apostasy (1 Ki. 9:1-9; cf. 2 Chr. 7:12-22). Solomon heeded the warnings, worshipped God alone, and prospered greatly for many years.

Family Man?

Solomon "had seven hundred wives . . . and three hundred concubines" (1 Ki. 11:3). Yet the only one who is actually *named* in Scripture, and that quite incidentally, is Naamah the mother of Rehoboam (1 Ki. 14:21, 31). Even the dusky beauty in the Song of Solomon is not named or otherwise identified. The only other wife who is identified—and that not by name—is Pharaoh's daughter (1 Ki. 3:1). This was a political marriage; apparently she did not even live in Jerusalem for long (1 Ki. 9:24).

Equally remarkable, given Solomon's large number of wives and concubines, is the small number of his children who are identified. Only one son, Rehoboam (1 Ki. 14:21), and two daughters, Taphath and Basemath, are named (1 Ki. 4:11, 15). It is possible that there actually were not any, or just a few, other children. If so, this could lead to a lot of speculation about Solomon's ability to sire children.

It might be one reason for his many wives. And it could explain why Rehoboam, the son of an Ammonitess, succeeded Solomon to the throne of Israel without a conflict from within the family.

Nevertheless, Solomon the prophet had the highest regard for the family unit, for mothers, and for fidelity in marriage.

> Let your fountain be blessed,
> And rejoice with the wife of your youth.
> As a loving deer and a graceful doe,
> Let her breasts satisfy you at all times;
> And always be enraptured with her love.
> For why should you, my son, be enraptured by an immoral woman,
> And be embraced in the arms of a seductress?—Prov. 5:18-20
> An excellent wife is the crown of her husband.—Prov. 12:4
> He who finds a wife finds a good thing,
> And obtains favor from the LORD.—Prov. 18:22

(See also Proverbs 1:8; 6:20–22; 10:1; 15:20; 17:6, 25; 19:14; 20:20; 23:22, 25; 29:15)

Solomon also had a deep disdain for loose women, adulteresses—and for adulterers.

> Can a man take fire to his bosom,
> And his clothes not be burned? . . .
> So is he who goes in to his neighbor's wife;
> Whoever touches her shall not be innocent.—Prov. 6:27, 29

(See also Proverbs 5; 6:20–7:27)

Solomon's tragic downfall came through his foreign wives when he was getting older—and foolish (1 Ki. 11). Specifically, a combination of his forbidden excesses such as multiplying horses (Deut. 17:14-17), silver and gold, and wives, and his succumbing to the idolatry of his wives, finally caught up with him. Solomon sunk so low that he, once a glorious prophet himself, tried to thwart God's word of prophecy (1 Ki. 11:29-31, 40).

Solomon's end was sad—even worse than sad because it brought division, civil war, and much suffering to all Israel. We can learn much from this tragedy: especially that experience, knowledge, and age do not protect us from the devil's snares. But we should not let Solomon's downfall—nor his extreme wealth, power, and fame—diminish in the least his prophecy, a major portion of God's written word.

157. **Stephen** was one of the most consequential prophets of the New Testament although his ministry was short-lived.

- o He was the first prophet who was not an apostle, to be named in Scripture after **Jesus's** resurrection (Acts 6:8), and he was the first martyred.
- o His death (murder by stoning) [Acts 7:57-60] triggered the spread of the church, and gospel, outside Jerusalem (Acts 8:1-4; 11:19).
- o His life and dying witness had a profound influence on **Paul**, both on his conscience and on his preaching (prophesying) style.

Stephen was among the seven[60] outstanding men chosen by the first Christian congregation to help the apostles by distributing food among the believers, paying particular attention to Hellenistic (Greek-speaking) widows (Acts 6:1-7). The qualifications for this office, set forth by the apostles, were that they be "men of good reputation, full of the Holy Spirit and of wisdom." Stephen was particularly Spirit-filled and is the first one named. Like the other six, his name is Greek; they were probably all Hellenists, chosen in deference to the offended minority.

Stephen did not stop at "serving tables," as necessary and as important as that was. He preached God's word about Jesus and, like many prophets, performed great miracles although we do not have a specific example. His prophesying soon got him into disputes with a certain group of foreign Jews who, being unable to understand or overcome the Holy Spirit by whom Stephen spoke, secretly induced false witnesses to bring trumped-up charges against Stephen in the Jewish high court, the Sanhedrin[61] (Acts 6:8-15).

Stephen's defense before the Sanhedrin (Acts 7) is one of the important speeches in Scripture. He began it with a review of Hebrew-Jewish history, starting with **Abraham**. It is a *tour de force* of God's faithfulness to Israel, Israel's unfaithfulness, and events leading up to Jesus Christ including Moses's prophecy about Him (v. 37). Subtly at first, beginning with **Joseph**, Stephen pointed out their forefathers' proclivity to reject and persecute righteous prophets including **Moses** (vv. 9, 20-41). Suddenly and dramatically Stephen turned the tables and put the whole Sanhedrin on trial for Jesus's murder! (vv. 51-53). They were teeth-gnashing, table-pounding angry about this (v. 54), but refrained from taking action against Stephen until after one of the most singular moments in the history of prophecy.

Standing before the angry Sanhedrin, Stephen had a vision of heaven, seeing the glory of God and Jesus standing at the right hand of God (vv. 55-56). This he described "live" to the Sanhedrin *as it was taking place!* This was unusual—perhaps unique—in the annals of prophecy. It was too much for the blind, proud hearts of the Jewish elders to bear. They took Stephen outside of the city and stoned him to death (vv. 57-60).

Saul (later Paul) was there for the stoning (Acts 7:58, 8:1). He never forgot it (Acts 22:20; 26:9-10). Possibly, Paul was a member or a clerk or other officer of the Sanhedrin and had heard Stephen's speech. Paul's first missionary sermon outline (Acts 13:16-41) was remarkably similar to that of Stephen's defense speech!

The church of Jesus Christ has also never forgotten Stephen's trial, prophecy, and death: for it took this tragedy to force the church to begin obeying Jesus's mandate to spread His gospel everywhere (Acts 1:8; 8:1; 11:19-21).

158. **Thaddaeus**, the surname of Lebbaeus, was one of **Jesus's** twelve disciples (Matt. 10:3) and one of His apostles. These facts alone ensure that he was a prophet, for all of Jesus's disciples prophesied and performed miracles of healing during their training mission(s?) [Matt. 10:5-15; cf. Mark 6:7-12, Luke 9:1-6]; and all of His first apostles prophesied at least on Pentecost Day (Acts 2:1-4, 15-17), and much more (Acts 4:33; 5:17-32). Foxe says Thaddaeus was crucified at Edessa in AD 72,[62] which would have given him a long career and would indicate that he died because of his prophesying about Jesus.

Lebbaeus Thaddaeus apparently had yet another name, Jude or Judas, by which he is called in **Luke's** two listings of the disciples (Luke 6:16; Acts 1:13). Comparing Luke's lists with those of **Matthew** and **Mark**, Judas almost *has* to be Thaddaeus, for we know with certainty that there were twelve and only twelve principal disciples (eleven without **Judas Iscariot**) [John 6:67, 70; Matt. 19:28]. The only way Judas could *not* be Thaddaeus would be that the latter defected or died and was replaced with Judas. Such an important event would certainly have been reported in the gospels. Besides, we have Jesus's own testimony that He chose only twelve, not thirteen. **John II**, who does not list all twelve disciples, does mention the disciple named Judas (not Iscariot) who asked Jesus an important question (John 14:22).

Judas/Lebbaeus Thaddaeus was related to one James (Luke 6:16; Acts 1:13). All of the more modern English versions of the Bible including the NKJV put him as the son of James; but the 1611 Authorized Version (KJV) has him as the brother of James. The KJV interpretation (really, interpolation, for the original merely says "Judas [of] James) suggests the possibility that he was **Jude** the human author of the epistle of that name—also a brother of a "James" (Jude 1). But the James referred to in Jude 1 is almost universally believed to be Jesus's half-brother, and neither he nor his brother Jude could have been Jesus' disciple (John 7:5; Mark 3:21, 31-32). Judas the disciple (Lebbaeus Thaddaeus) and Jude the epistle writer were separate prophets.

159. **Thomas** "the Twin" (Didymus) [John 21:2], one of the twelve disciples, was sent out by **Jesus** to prophesy about the kingdom of heaven and to work miracles of healing (Matt. 10:1-10). On that mission he was probably teamed up with **Matthew**. This same Thomas, as an apostle, was commissioned by Jesus to preach the gospel wherever he could and to whomever he could throughout the whole

world—with attendant miracles (Mark 16:15-18; Acts 1:8). He prophesied in a way that was a miracle in itself, one Pentecost morning in Jerusalem (Acts 2:1-17). And he probably prophesied much more in the next few days and weeks in Jerusalem, and later elsewhere (Acts 4:33; 5:17-32). Mr. Foxe says he went east, to Parthia (Iran/Afghanistan) and India, and was martyred.[63]

Thomas has long been characterized as "doubting." Roget lists "doubting Thomas" as a synonym for "skeptic."[64] This caricature is so ingrained in our culture that it is unlikely to ever change, even though it may not be a true representation. A. B. Bruce prefers to call Thomas "the melancholy disciple."[65] He cites Thomas's gloomy statement when Jesus decided to go to Judea despite the great danger facing Him there: "Let us also go, that we may die with Him" (John 11:16). Also, Bruce points to Thomas's despairing comment about not knowing the way to heaven (John 14:1-6). Thomas was not the only disciple who doubted Jesus's resurrection, even after some time had passed (Matt. 28:17).

What has all this, about Thomas's personality, to do with him as a prophet? Two things:

1. Thomas's outlook as a disciple—whether skeptical, depressed, or pessimistic—illustrates Jesus's choice and use of all manner of people to carry out His mission of gospel prophecy.
2. We must remember that "doubting" or "melancholy" Thomas could not have retained such a personality after Pentecost, when he was filled with the Holy Spirit. He became another Thomas, Thomas the apostle, whom we do not know as well. Thomas was no more downcast than the other six disciples to whom the risen Jesus appeared in Galilee (John 21:1-2, 12), and he did not express any doubts on that occasion; furthermore, that was *before* Pentecost, indicating that Thomas's doubts or gloominess were already fading away.

{Timotheus—**Timothy**}

160. **Timothy**, the protégé of **Paul**, was a prophet . . . or was he? The Bible records not one sermon, word of prophecy, vision, or written prophecy of Timothy's. It does not say he spoke by, or under the direct influence of, the Holy Spirit. It does not call him a prophet or seer. He performed no miracle we know of. However, based on the testimony and exhortations of Paul in God's word, Timothy was indeed a prophet. In fact, he, along with **Titus**, were the biblical prototypes of the postapostolic pastor/preacher-prophet as we know that office today.

In his epistles to other Christians (churches) Paul represented Timothy as his equal: "My fellow worker" (Rom. 16:21), "brother" (2 Cor. 1:1), a full-fledged member of the great preaching team in Corinth, along with two apostles(!) [2 Cor. 1:19]; a bondservant of **Jesus** Christ, with Paul (Philip. 1:1); "like-minded" to Paul

(Philip. 2:20); "minister of God, and our fellow laborer in the gospel of Christ" (1 Thes. 3:2).

It is only in Paul's personal letters to Timothy, which were probably not originally intended for publication, that we see Timothy as a weak vessel in need of much exhortation and instruction; a youth easily intimidated by older persons in the church he was supposed to be leading (1 Tim. 4:12); a young Christian whose faith might waver in the face of false teaching (1 Tim. 6:11); one who does not know how to behave in church (1 Tim. 3:15); and an immature leader who must show some personal progress to his own "followers" (1 Tim. 4:15). Paul *wanted* Timothy to be a "man of God" (a biblical phrase synonymous with *prophet*) but he does not quite fully accord him that title, in his instructional letters (1 Tim. 6:11; 2 Tim. 3:16-17).

Who was the "real" Timothy—Paul's colleague and peer, or his immature student? All we can say is—both, according to Scripture. And the Bible does not tell us what Timothy became, or what his works were, after Paul.[66] He did have the spiritual wisdom and foresight to preserve the two personal letters from Paul and possibly to make them public. So we can give Timothy some of the human "credit" for their existence. These letters contain important doctrine that the Holy Spirit has given to the church, including: qualifications of elders and deacons (1 Tim. 3:1-13), some of the most important teaching in the Bible about itself (2 Tim. 3:15-17), and a timeless exhortation to preachers (2 Tim. 4:1-5).

Timothy was well-prepared for the ministry of the word of God. His mother and grandmother were believers (2 Tim. 1:5), probably converted to Christ on Paul's first visits to their town, Lystra (Acts 14:8-23). Even before then, Timothy was steeped in Holy Scripture (2 Tim. 3:15), his mother being a devout Jewess. Later, Paul became his teacher (2 Tim. 1:13-14). Timothy was the product of prophecy (1 Tim. 1:18). He was ordained for Christian gospel service "by prophecy with the laying on of the hands of the eldership" including Paul's hands (1 Tim. 4:14; 2 Tim. 1:6). At that time Timothy received a spiritual gift. Scripture does not say if this was the gift of prophecy, one of the other leadership gifts, or simply the gift of the Holy Spirit Himself. In Lystra/Derbe, on Paul's second mission trip there, Timothy was circumcised (because of the Jews there), and joined the Paul/Silas mission team. Timothy was already a disciple of Jesus, one who was well spoken-of (Acts 16:1-5).

Timothy stands as a biblical prototype of the postapostolic Christian pastor/preacher prophet, the kind still serving the church of Jesus Christ. He was not an apostle. He was not an eyewitness of Jesus Christ's ministry, death, or resurrection. He was not at the Pentecost event. He was a native of Asia Minor and may have never traveled to Judea or Galilee. He was prepared for the gospel ministry, first in a Christian home (at least on his mother's side), then in his home church (where he probably was converted), and then under Paul (from whom he received at least the equivalent of a seminary education). He "confessed the good confession in the presence of many witnesses" (1 Tim. 6:12). He was duly ordained to the gospel ministry by the laying on of the hands of the presbytery (elders). He was given a (the?) gift of the Spirit. Upon "graduation" and commissioning, he entered the foreign mission field, traveling with a team, working, and learning. Later he became pastor of a local church, where his duties included administration, training, and discipline as well as evangelistic preaching (1 and 2 Tim.). At some time he was imprisoned and then set free (Heb. 13:23). Truly, Timothy and Titus (q.v.) were the first "modern" preacher/pastor prophets.

161. **Titus** was a prophet of the same order as **Timothy**. We have no sermon or fragment of prophecy from his lips or pen; no title such as prophet, seer, or man of God attached to him; no miracle worked through him; and no clear evidence of his speaking or acting under the immediate, felt, or seen influence of the Holy Spirit—as the apostles on Pentecost Day. Yet **Paul** in Holy Scripture describes Titus to the Corinthian church as his brother (2 Cor. 2:13), his partner and fellow worker (2 Cor. 8:23), and one who walked in the same spirit and same steps as Paul (2 Cor. 12:18). In his personal letter to Titus, Paul urged him to "speak the things which are proper for sound doctrine" (Tit. 2:1) and to "speak these things" (about **Jesus** Christ and Christian living), "exhort, and rebuke with all authority" in Crete (Tit. 2:15). As God's spokesman in Crete and elsewhere, Titus was a prophet.

Before Crete, Titus ministered in Corinth, being sent there by Paul along with another, unnamed, brother. Actually, Titus volunteered to go (2 Cor. 8:16-18). It was an important mission, for the church in Corinth was in trouble (2 Cor. 1:15-2:11; 6:14-7:1). Also, Titus was to collect the Corinthian church's offering for the impoverished church in Judea (2 Cor. 8). Titus returned to Paul somewhere in Macedonia, having failed to meet him in Troas (2 Cor. 2:12-13), with good news about the Corinthian church (2 Cor. 7:6-7, 13-15; 8:6).

Titus once traveled with Paul and **Barnabas** to Jerusalem (Gal. 2:1). Later, Titus was left on the Mediterranean island of Crete to follow up the work started there by Paul[67] (Tit. 1:5). He was in Crete when Paul wrote him the letter that is now Scripture, in ca. AD 62–64. Titus had the wisdom to preserve this personal letter, which has edified the whole Church of Jesus Christ to this day.

At Crete we see Titus as a "modern" church pastor involved in the government, discipline, and deportment of a local Christian congregation, as well as in the continued ministry of God's word, including the refutation of false teachers within the church (Tit. 1:5-16; Ch. 2; 3:1-11).

Titus actually prototypifies the modern Christian pastor-prophet even more completely than does Timothy, in that he was not a Jew or partly Jewish, as was Timothy. Titus was perhaps the first—certainly one of the first—physically uncircumcised preacher-pastor prophet (Gal. 2:1-3).

162. **Unni I** was a string player who was selected for the marching orchestra that helped conduct the ark of the covenant of the LORD into its new tabernacle in

David's new capital, Jerusalem, ca. 1000 BC (1 Chr. 15:16-20, 28). It is assumed that he went on to become one of the 288 Levites who prophesied with voices and musical instruments in the house of the LORD in the songs of the LORD (psalms written by David, **Asaph**, and others) [1 Chr. 25:1-7].

163. **Unni II** was one of the leading Levite singers of prophecy who returned to Judea from Babylon with the first large contingent of Jews in 537 BC. He and **Bakbukiah** and their brethren "stood across" from **Mattaniah** the psalm leader with his brethren, probably singing antiphonally (Neh. 12:1, 8-9). There were over one hundred singers in the group (Ez. 2:41; Neh. 7:44). They were generically named "sons of **Asaph,**" probably for their consecration to musical prophecy rather than for their genealogy.

{Uriah—**Urijah**}

164. **Urijah** was the only other prophet who dared to stand with **Jeremiah** against all the false prophets and soothsayers in Judah who kept telling King Jehoiakim (609–598 BC) that God would save Judah from Nebuchadnezzar (Jer. 26:20-23). Only Urijah and Jeremiah knew and/or dared to tell the truth that Judah would surely fall and be carried into captivity. King Jehoiakim so hated to hear this truth that he ran Urijah out of the country into Egypt. Then Jehoiakim sent men to Egypt, brought Urijah back, publicly executed him, and gave him an ignominious burial. Jeremiah's own life was barely spared through the efforts of good Ahiakim (Jer. 26:24), a high-ranking official held over from the administration of a much better king, Josiah (2 Ki. 22:12). Poor Urijah had no such friends in high places.

165. **Uzziel I**, a.k.a. Azarel, was one of **Heman's** sons who "should prophesy with harps, stringed instruments, and cymbals." He was separated for this service by **David** and his captains (1 Chr. 25:1-7) and chosen by lot to lead the eleventh twelve-man section of a large musical contingent (ca. 1000 BC) [1 Chr. 25:8, 18). Like the 287 others, Uzziel was instructed in the songs of the LORD (psalms of David, **Asaph**, and others). Uzziel was a great-grandson of **Samuel** (1 Chr. 6:33).

166. **Uzziel II** was a Levite in the days of King **Hezekiah** of Judah (715–686 BC). He arose (volunteered?) to help clean out the temple built under **Solomon**, which had fallen into shameful disuse, disrepair, and dirtiness during the reign of Hezekiah's wicked father Ahaz (2 Chr. 29:3-14; 28:24). When the temple was cleaned, repaired, and sanctified, proper worship of God was restored. This included musical prophesying "according to the commandment of **David**, of **Gad** the king's seer, and of **Nathan** the prophet" (2 Chr. 29:25-26). When "the song of the LORD also began, with trumpets and with the instruments of David . . . (and) . . . the singers sang . . . to sing praise to the Lord with the words of David and of

Asaph the seer" (2 Chr. 29:25-30), Uzziel was in all likelihood in the prophesying chorus (1 Chr. 25:1), for he was a "son of **Jeduthun**" (q.v.).

167. **Zaccur** was the leader of the third twelve-man division of **David's** 288 musical prophesiers (ca. 1000 BC). He was a Levite, a son of **Asaph**. All the tabernacle musicians were "instructed in the songs of the LORD" to prophesy "under the direction of Asaph, who prophesied according to the order of the king" (1 Chr. 25:1-8, 10).

Over five hundred years later, Zaccur was still remembered as the ancestor of **Zechariah V** (Neh. 12:35).

{Zacharias I—**Zechariah II**, in Matthew 23:35 and Luke 11:51, KJV}

168. **Zacharias II**, the father of **John I**, the baptizer, was filled with the Holy Spirit and prophesied in verse about his newborn son and about **Jesus** (Luke 1:67-79). Zacharias had had a vision, a visit from the angel Gabriel (Luke 1:11-22). He was involved in (but did not "work") two miracles: the conception of his son in his wife **Elizabeth**, who "was barren and . . . well advanced in years" (Luke 1:7, 24); and his own sudden muteness and recovery (Luke 1:20, 64).

Zacharias was a regular temple priest of the eighth division, named the Abijah Division (Luke 1:5) after Abijah of **David's** time (1 Chr. 24:1, 10). He and his wife Elizabeth were righteous people, but they were childless and old (Luke 1:6-7). Still, they prayed for a child (Luke 1:13). In the second year before the birth of Jesus while Zacharias was in the temple burning incense and a large number of people were praying outside, Gabriel announced to him that Elizabeth would conceive and bear a son whom they should name John and who would be filled with the Holy Spirit. Gabriel also prescribed John's lifestyle and mission. Zacharias was slow to believe Gabriel and asked for a sign, which he promptly got: He became mute (Luke 1:10-22). When the boy was born and his parents named him "John" in obedience to God, Zacharias was instantly cured of being mute. He praised God (Luke 1:57-64). Then he prophesied.

169. **Zadok** was called by **David** a "seer" (2 Sam. 15:27)—proof enough that this high priest was a prophet. Zadok had an illustrious career as chief priest during David's and **Solomon's** reigns (2 Sam. 8:15-17; 1 Ki. 4:1-4). He was a pivotal figure in David's overcoming Absalom's rebellion (2 Sam. 15:11-36; 17:15ff.), and in Solomon's highly-contended accession to the throne (1 Ki. 1).

We do not know if David's remark to Zadok, "Are you not a seer?" referred only to his use of the urim and thummin to discern God's will, in his office of chief priest (Ex. 28:29-30; Num. 27:21; Neh. 7:65), or to a wider scope of prophetic vision. We have no written or verbal prophecy attributable to Zadok.

{Zaphnath-Paaneah—**Joseph** I, Genesis 41:45}

170. **Zechariah I**, the first of six prophets with this name,[68] was a musical prophet in the days of King **David** (1010–970 BC). He was a string player in the group of Levites chosen to escort the ark of the covenant of the LORD into the tabernacle built for it in Jerusalem (1 Chr. 15:16-18, 20). Then, he was appointed a minister of music next to **Asaph** the chief musician before the ark in the tabernacle (1 Chr. 16:4-5). This means that he was among the 288 musicians who prophesied "in the songs of the LORD . . . in the house of the LORD" (1 Chr. 25:1-7).

171. **Zechariah II** was a priest during the later years of King Joash of Judah (835–796 BC). After he had prophesied against the apostasy of Joash and of all Judah, Zechariah was stoned to death, right in the temple courtyard (2 Chr. 24:20-22). It was probably this Zechariah that **Jesus** meant when He was rebuking the Pharisees, lawyers, and scribes of His day for following in the footsteps of their fathers who murdered God's prophets "from . . . **Abel** to . . . Zechariah who perished between the altar and the temple"[69] (Luke 11:51).

Zechariah was the son of one of the truly admirable married couples of the Bible, the priest Jehoiada and his wife Jehoshabeath, a princess. The male royal line of **David** was almost extinguished when King Jehoram killed all his brothers and other princes (2 Chr. 21:4); then, after he died, his wicked wife Athaliah killed his (and her own!) sons and grandsons so she could reign as queen (2 Chr. 22:10). But she missed one, because Jehoshabeath, a daughter of Jehoram, stole her infant nephew Joash away from among those sons who were being murdered. She and her husband Jehoida hid Joash for six years (2 Chr. 22:11-12). When the boy was seven, Jehoida engineered a *coup d'état* (2 Chr. 23). Athaliah was killed and Joash became boy king; but good Jehoida the priest was the real power behind the throne. When he grew up, Joash "did what was right in the sight of the LORD" (2 Chr. 24:2), but after Jehoida died he turned away from God. All manner of wickedness returned to Judah (2 Chr. 24:15-19). It was then that Zechariah, Jehoida's son, prophesied against them and was stoned to death in the courtyard of the temple where he undoubtedly served as priest (2 Chr. 24:20-22). Like **Stephen**, the first Christian martyr, Zechariah had some dying, prophetic words for his killers: "The LORD look on it, and repay!" God did repay, ultimately cleansing the nation with the Babylonian defeat and captivity; but the guilt of Zechariah's murder, and of the murders of many other prophets, remained on the Jewish fathers and their sons—as evidenced by Jesus's indictment of them.

172. **Zechariah III** was a prophet in the days of King Uzziah of Judah (796–740 BC). He "had understanding in the visions of God" (2 Chr. 26:5). This highly succinct account of him—one verse—implies that he counseled Uzziah and had a very good influence on the nation. Sadly, the considerable successes of Uzziah, both militarily and at home, increased his pride and led to his downfall (2 Chr. 26:6-23).

We do not know if Zechariah had died, or Uzziah simply stopped listening to him and the LORD.

173. **Zechariah IV** was a Levite, a "son" of **Asaph**, in the days of **Hezekiah** king of Judah (715–686 BC). Good King Hezekiah, a prophet himself, determined to clean out and fix up the temple and return to the worship of God (2 Chr. 29), both of which had been neglected by his wicked father King Ahaz (2 Chr. 28: 22-25). Zechariah was one of fourteen Levites who arose (volunteered?) to lead the temple restoration project. After this, proper Mosaic-Davidic worship of God was resumed, including prophesying in music "according to the commandment of **David** (1 Chr. 25:1-7), of **Gad** the king's seer, and of **Nathan** the prophet" (2 Chr. 29:25). Zechariah, being one of the sons of Asaph, can be assumed to have been in the prophesying chorus of his day when "the song of the LORD also began . . . (and) . . . the singers sang . . . praise to the LORD with the words of David and of Asaph the seer" (2 Chr. 29:27-30).

174. **Zechariah V** was a musician who prophesied in that medium in the days of **Nehemiah**, ca. 445 BC. He was a member of one of the two thanksgiving choirs that marched atop the newly completed Jerusalem wall at its dedication ceremony (Neh. 12:31, 35). His claim to prophethood, however, rests on the high likelihood that he and his musical brethren went on to be singer musicians in the temple "according to the command of **David** and **Solomon** his son. For in the days of David and **Asaph** of old there were chiefs of the singers and songs of praise and thanksgiving to God" (Neh. 12:45-46). This was prophesying (1 Chr. 25:1-7). Zechariah was a direct biological descendent of Asaph. Besides increasing the likelihood that he was a (musical) prophet, this shows that he was not a priest's son as could be erroneously inferred from Nehemiah 12:35, especially in the KJV and NKJV. The NIV has it right.

175. **Zechariah VI** was the prophet who wrote the book of Zechariah in the Bible (Zech. 1:1). Besides being the human author of a portion of God's written word, Zechariah was a powerful speaking prophet who came to Jerusalem during the rebuilding of the temple (535–515 BC) and whose prophesying was one of the main reasons for its successful, timely completion (Ez. 5:1; 6:14). In this capacity Zechariah, along with **Haggai**, was a "project" prophet, a builder and exhorter. Yet in his book he goes far beyond the immediate enterprise into visions similar to those in Daniel and Ezekiel. Themes in Zechariah include the coming Messiah (Branch) [Zech. 3:8-10; 6:12-13; 9:9], the ideal Jerusalem (Zech. 8), and the Day of the LORD or the "end times" (Zech. 14).

We know but little of Zechariah's personal life history. He was the son, or possibly grandson,[69] of another prophet, **Iddo II** (q.v.) [Ez. 5:1], who was a priest or Levite that returned from Babylon in the first big influx to Judah, 537 BC (Neh.

12:1, 4). He came to Jerusalem with his father and/or grandfather Iddo, or soon thereafter (Neh. 12:16). Soon he was a head of his Levitical (possibly priestly) "house" (Zech. 12:12, 16)

Zechariah and Haggai began to prophesy the temple toward completion only after the project had stalled, about fifteen years after its groundbreaking (Ez. 5:1; 6:14). This is consistent with Nehemiah 12:1–16 which puts Zechariah in the second generation of re-settlers. Zechariah dates his first revelation from God in the second year of Darius (Zech. 1:1)—about 520 BC. The temple was completed four years and four months later (Ez. 6:15). The last dated revelation to Zechariah came two years and one month after the first one (Zech. 7:1). But there were other, perhaps subsequent, undated words and burdens given to him (7:8; 8:1; 9:1; 12:1).

Besides His words, God gave Zechariah symbolic, prophetic acts to carry out, in the manner of **Ezekiel** (q.v.) [Zech. 11:4-16].

The book of Zechariah is the second longest, and arguably the most complex, of the minor prophets. No attempt will be made to summarize it here. Like Revelation, Daniel, and Ezekiel, the other so-called apocalyptic books of the Bible, Zechariah can be confusing in the study and controversial among its interpreters. But all these books, it is said, are best understood by, and very comforting to, God's people when they are being threatened, oppressed, or persecuted—as the original readers were. A few distinctive aspects of Zechariah are considered below.

First, this book contains some startlingly detailed revelations concerning **Jesus**, written five centuries before His birth:

> Then they will look on Me whom they pierced.—Zech. 12:10; cf. John 19: 34-37.

> Throw it to the potter—that princely price they set on me. So I took the thirty pieces of silver and threw them into the house of the LORD for the potter.—Zech. 11:12-13; cf. Matt. 27:3-10.

and that Palm Sunday standard,

> Rejoice greatly, O daughter of Zion!
> Shout, O daughter of Jerusalem!
> Behold, your King is coming to you;
> He is just and having salvation,
> Lowly and riding on a donkey,
> A colt, the foal of a donkey.—Zech. 9:9; cf. Matt. 21:1-9.

Second, Zechariah contains a passage very much like Micah 6:8, Matthew 7:12 (the golden rule), and Matthew 22:39 (the second great commandment)—all of which succinctly state God's expectations of men. In Zechariah it is,

Execute true justice,
Show mercy and compassion
Everyone to his brother.
Do not oppress the widow or the fatherless,
The alien or the poor.—Zech. 7:9-10.

Finally, of special interest here, Zechariah contains some pertinent passages about prophets:

- Former true prophets who were not heard or heeded—Zech. 1:4-6; 7:7, 12.
- Contemporary prophets including Zechariah—Zech. 7:1-3; 8:9.
- Future false prophets who will be killed by their own parents or will be exposed and ashamed, and will "come clean"—Zech. 13:2-6.

176. **Zephaniah** is a canonical prophet. The word of God came to him in the days of King Josiah of Judah (640–609 BC), just decades before the complete defeat and destruction of that nation by Nebuchadnezzar of Babylon (Zeph. 1:1). Zephaniah may have been a direct descendent of **Hezekiah**, the last good king before Josiah and a prophet himself. If so, he was of the tribe of Judah and had royal blood. But this is speculation. Nothing else is known of Zephaniah except his written prophecies. His contemporaries included several other prophets: **Nahum**, **Huldah**, and (probably) **Jeremiah** and **Habakkuk**.

Josiah was a good king and instigated many reforms in Judah (2 Chr. 34, 35). But it was too late. Judah already stood condemned before God because of her abject wickedness during the reigns of Manassah and other kings and because of ongoing sin. Thus, while encouraging individual repentance in his prophecy (Zeph. 2:1-3), Zephaniah was absolutely sure of the imminent destruction of Judah and her neighboring nations (Zeph. 1; 2:4-15).

This doomsday message must have seemed exceedingly unfair and onerous to the Jews if it was delivered while they were in the midst of a period of reformation and renewal under Josiah. On the other hand, it may have been delivered during the first twelve years of Josiah's reign, before the reforms began (2 Chr. 34:3)—and it could have helped bring on those reforms. There is no indication that Zephaniah was persecuted or martyred. Just a few years later, under the next king, other prophets with the same message were persecuted (Jeremiah) and killed (**Urijah**). It seems likely that Zephaniah, being a bit earlier, and more ahead of the actual time of Judah's chastisement, was "merely" ridiculed and ignored. He was opposed by false prophets (Zeph. 3:4). Apparently the reforms of Josiah had not yet taken effect when Zephaniah prophesied, or these reforms were not thoroughgoing enough (Zeph. 3:1-7).

Six years after the reforms were started, workers repairing the temple discovered a copy of God's Law, which had long been forgotten (2 Chr. 34:8-18). Huldah the prophetess was asked to inquire of God about the fate of the nation, in view of God's wrath against them for not keeping His word (2 Chr. 34:19-22). She verbally delivered the same prophecy as Zephaniah wrote: Judah *will* be destroyed as a nation; this judgment was final and irrevocable. She (rather, God) added that Josiah himself, and his generation, would be spared because he had humbled himself and wept before God when he heard His word (2 Chr. 34:23-28).

Zephaniah ends his prophecy on a very high note of hope and promise. After the chastisement (defeat and captivity by Babylon), there would be a meek and humble remnant of Israelites, and captives would return to their homeland (Zeph. 3:12-13; 20). God would dwell with them once again; there would be much joy on their part—and His! (Zeph. 3:14-17). "He will quiet you with His love."

177. **Zeri**, a.k.a. Jizri, was one of the 288 Levites who were set apart to prophesy in the songs of the LORD in the house of the LORD during the reign of **David**, ca. 1000 BC (1 Chr. 25:1-7). Zeri was a son of **Jeduthun**, the choir director (Ps. 39, 62, 77 titles). He was chosen by lot to lead the fourth twelve-man course of tabernacle singers (1 Chr. 25:11).

Endnotes and References for Chapter 3

1. Ishmael was also biologically begotten of Abraham. Perhaps the writer of Hebrews used the phrase "only begotten" to suggest the spiritual connection with the sacrifice of God's only begotten Son, and/or to emphasize the unique status of Isaac as Abraham's only son of promise.

2. John Foxe, *Foxe's Book of Martyrs*, ed. William Byron Forbush, D.D. (John C. Winston, Pub., 1926; assigned to Zondervan Pub., 1967), 3.

3. The Scriptural basis for this is rather involved and will not be presented here.

4. Foxe, ibid., 4.

5. See 1 Kings 10:22.

6. Matthew Henry, *Commentary on the Whole Bible*, vol. IV, *Isaiah to Malachi* (Old Tappan, NJ: Fleming H. Revell Company, early 18th century, Puritan Reformed reprint, n.d.), 747.

7. To be sure, the phrase "LORD of hosts" is used by the author of 1 Samuel (Samuel himself?) previously in this very same chapter, verse 3; but in history, his use followed Hannah's. Also, it is recognized that the concept was not a new one (cf. Genesis 32:2, KJV and Exodus 12:41, KJV); and the appellation itself had been indirectly ascribed to God (Joshua 5:14, 15, KJV).

8. *New Geneva Study Bible, "Isaiah—Interpretive Difficulties"* (Nashville: ThomasNelson, 1995), 1020.

9. *New Geneva Study Bible, Note on Genesis 30:31–34* (Nashville:Thomas Nelson, 1995), 60.

10. Matthew Henry, *Commentary on the Whole Bible,* vol. I, *Genesis to Deuteronomy* (Old Tappan, NJ: Fleming H. Revell Co., early 18th century, Puritan Reformed reprint, n.d.), 183.

11. Hegesippus was quoted by Eusebius in his *Historia Ecclisiastica* (AD 330), quoted in William Barclay, *The Letters of James and Peter* (Philadelphia: Westminster Press, 1958; rev. 1976), 12–13.

12. The Jeshua mentioned in Neh. 12:26 (some translations) is not the prophet Jeshua; he is a leader in the first group of Jews who returned to Israel from Babylon (Neh. 12:1).

13. See Matthew 4:4, 7; 5:21, 27, 33, 38, 43; 8:4; 12:15; 15:4; 18:16; 19:4,5, 18–19a, 19b; 22:32, 37, 39; 26:14.

14. Jesus adopted the appellation "Son of Man" first revealed through the prophet Daniel (Daniel 7:13); see [e.g.] Matthew 8:20; 9:6; 10:23; 11:19; 12:8, 40; 13:37, 41; 16:13, 27, 28; 17:9, 12, 22; 18:11; 19:28; 20:18, 28; 24:27, 30a, 30b, 37, 39, 44; 25:13, 31; 26:2, 24a, 24b, 45, 64. It was His favorite title.

15. However, Jesus did not seek or validate the appellation "Son of David." He did not rebuke those who insisted on using it (e.g. Matthew 21:9), but He explained to some Pharisees that it was improper (Matthew 22:41–45).

16. Matthew (Levi), James the son of Alpheus, Simon Zelotes, Bartholomew

17. John Foxe, *Foxe's Book of Martyrs*, ed. William Byron Forbush, DD, (n.p.: John C. Winston, Pub., 1926; assigned to Zondervan, 1967), 5.

18. See "The Writing Prophets" in chapter 7, The Biblical History of Prophecy.

19. See "Prophet Types and Clusters (Kingdom Period)" in chapter 7, The Biblical History of Prophecy.

20. The first being Noah (q.v.).

21. The alias is established by comparing Matt. 9:9-13 with Luke 5:27-32.

22. This quote and other material in this paragraph are from George Grant, *The Micah Mandate* (Chicago: Moody Press, 1995).

23. Aaron's punishment may have been more severe, or at least longer lasting: the guilt and shame of seeing his beloved sister stricken for the sin he shared with her. Miriam did not plea for her clemency—Aaron did!

24. Robert Young, *Analytical Concordance*, (19th century; Grand Rapids, MI: Associated Publishers and Authors, n.d.), 670.

25. Other heads of state who were also prophets include Joshua, Deborah, Samuel, David, Solomon, and Hezekiah.

26. Skeptics ridicule this number, but it is well-documented in both Exodus 1:7–9 and Numbers 2:46. Growth from seventy to six hundred thousand in 430 years requires doubling every 33–1/3 years—not unreasonable, especially with large families.

27. "Prophet" is put in quotation marks here as a reminder that predictions, even ones that come true, do not necessarily make a person a true prophet (See Chapter 1).

28. Peter seems to have possessed extraordinary knowledge about Noah. Perhaps he had access to sermons of Noah then still extant, or perhaps Jesus told him more about Noah.

29. How remarkable it is that, if Obed-Edom the Gittite was indeed a Philistine, he was so greatly blessed by the presence of the ark in his house; see 2 Samuel 6:11–12.

30. The Bible contains more detail about Paul's life than about any other prophet except Jesus, Moses, and David.

31. John Pollack, *The Apostle* (Wheaton, Ill.: Victor Books, 1972).

32. For example, Nietzche called Paul "one of the most ambitious of men, whose superstition was only equaled by his cunning; a much tortured, much to be pitied man, an exceedingly unpleasant person both to himself and to others" (quoted in Pollack, op. cit., preface). This opinion may say more about Nietzche than about Paul.

33. Pollack, op. cit., 35.

34. Pollack, op. cit., 5.

35. Pollack, op. cit., 35.

36. We cannot assess or even imagine the pain Jesus suffered for our sakes on the cross and before that. Jesus's sufferings must be excluded from comparison, for His were unique.

37. Pollack, op. cit., 181.

38. Sixteen times, plus two *my*'s, a *me*, and three *we*'s in just the love chapter, 1 Cor. 13!

39. Robert Young, *Analytical Concordance* (first published 19th century; repr., Grand Rapids, MI: Associated Publishers and Authors, n.d.), 735.

40. Although it is physically possible that Jesus went from the synagogue in Capernaum to a house belonging to Peter in Bethsaida on a certain Sabbath day (Luke 4:31–38; Mark

1:21–29), this is highly unlikely: it would have been more than a legal "Sabbath day's journey" (about 1100 meters), and Jesus was careful not to resume His healing ministry until after sunset that day (Mark 1:32). The casting out of an unclean spirit and the healing of Peter's mother-in-law on that Sabbath were acts of mercy, completely justified.

41. That Peter's wife was still living many years later is mentioned by Paul in 1 Corinthians 9:5.

42. The Sea of Tiberias is the same as the Sea of Galilee, John 6:1.

43. Matthew 4:18; 10:2–4; 17:1; 26:37; Mark 3:14–19; 5:37; 13:3; Luke 6:13–16; 8:45; 22:8; John 18:15; 20:2; 21:2; Acts 1:13; 2:37; 3:1

44. Peter had previously prophesied when sent out by Jesus on a short-term preaching mission; and, inadvertently, in his confession of Jesus's deity (Luke 9:1–6; Matthew 16:16–17).

45. In his second epistle, Peter warmly commends Paul's letters (2 Pet. 3:15–16); he obviously had read them.

46. John Foxe, *Foxe's Book of Martyrs*, ed. W. B. Forbush, DD (J. C. Winston Pub., 1926; Zondervan, 1967), 3.

47. The phrase "except the apostles" in Acts 8:1 shows that the Philip in the rest of chapter 8 was the deacon, not the apostle.

48. All six Jewish deacons had Greek names, which may have had something to do with the fact that their new office resulted from a complaint by the Hellenists in the church. Hellenists were Jews who spoke Greek and adopted more Greek culture than the "Hebrew" Jews.

49. J. Gresham Machen, *The New Testament: An Introduction to Its Literature and History* (Edinburgh, Banner of Truth, 1976), 75.

50. The fact that Luke (24:4) and John (20:12) mention *two* "men" (angels) is not necessarily inconsistent with Mark's account of one. Mark, as supposedly also the women who told about it, could have focused on the one on the right side, who did most of the speaking.

51. Robert Young, *Analytical Concordance* (19th century; repr. Grand Rapids, MI: Associated Publishers and Authors, n.d.), 834.

52. In 1 Sam. 1:1, Samuel's great-great-grandfather is called an Ephraimite—possibly referring to his homeland, not his tribe.

53. Psalm 34 title (cf. 1 Samuel 21:10–15); Psalm 52 title (cf. 1 Samuel 22:9); Psalm 54 title (cf. 1 Samuel 23:19); Psalm 56 title (cf. 1 Samuel 21:11); Psalm 57 title (cf. 1 Samuel 22:1); Psalm 59 title (cf. 1 Samuel 19:11); Psalm 142 title (cf. 1 Samuel 22:1).

54. Judah; see 2 Chr. 12:5.

55. The phrase "man of God" signifies David as a prophet, not as a king.

56. In Hebrew "canna" means "zealous"—Robert Young, op. cit.

57. John Foxe, *Foxe's Book of Martyrs* (J. C. Winston, 1926; assigned to Zondervan, 1967), 5.

58. The lists of David's offspring in 2 Samuel 5:14 and 1 Chronicles 3:5 and 14:4 are not in birth order, in light of 2 Samuel 12:15–24.

59. Although they were later misused by the Israelites and disavowed by God, "high places" of worship were established, probably by Samuel, after the ark of the covenant was removed from the tabernacle, the priesthood was disrupted, and the Levites were scattered. (See under Samuel.)

60. The fact that seven outstanding men were needed for this task testifies not only to its importance, but also to the large numbers of believers already in Jerusalem.

61. Ironically, the seventy-member Sanhedrin is ultimately related to the seventy elders who were selected to help Moses govern Israel in the wilderness, and who, like Stephen, were all filled with the Holy Spirit in preparation for their office, and prophesied (Numbers 11:16–30). Stephen may have made an oblique reference to this in his dying speech (Acts 7:44).

62. John Foxe, *Foxe's Book of Martyrs* (J. C. Winston, 1926; assigned to Zonderban, 1967), page 4.

63. ibid.

64. Peter Roget, *The New Roget's Thesaurus* in Dictionary form, ed. Norman Lewis (Garden City, NY: Garden City Books, 1961), 442.

65. A. B. Bruce, *The Training of the Twelve*, (Grand Rapids: Kregel, 1971), 391-392.

66. An extrabiblical source says that Timothy became bishop of Ephesus, where he governed the church until AD 97, some thirty years after Paul's death; and that he was murdered there by an angry mob of pagans— John Foxe, *Foxe's Book of Martyrs* (J. C. Winston, 1926; assigned to Zondervan, Grand Rapids, 1967), 7.

67. Crete is not mentioned in any of Paul's three missionary journeys chronicled in Acts. A fourth journey that included Crete has been postulated.

68. Twenty-seven people in the Bible had this popular name, according to Robert Young, op. cit. page 1087.

69. Certainly this identity is consistent with the location of the murder. Also, this Zechariah was the last prophet martyr in the Hebrew Bible canon, of which 2 Chronicles is the last book. Thus, Abel and Zechariah were the first and last martyred prophets in Scripture—not in time. The only problem with this identity of Jesus's Zechariah is that in the parallel passage, Matthew 23:35, he is also called the son of Berechiah. The writing prophet, **Zechariah VI**, was the son of Berechiah (Zechariah 1:1). But there is no record, biblical or otherwise, that Zechariah VI was murdered. Some solutions to this problem—none completely satisfying—have been proposed. One is that the words "son of Berechiah" were inserted by an early copyist of Matthew who knew only Zechariah VI as a prophet. Another, suggested by Henry, is that Berechiah signifies much the same as Jehoida the father of Zechariah II, or may have been a second name of Jehoida [Matthew Henry, *Commentary on the Whole Bible*, vol. V, *Matthew to John* (Old Tappan, NJ: Fleming H. Revell Company, n.d.), 342]. The most satisfying solution is that the Septuagint Bible has the correct sense of Zechariah 1:1, "Zacharias (Zechariah) the Barachite (Blessed), the son of Addo (Iddo II) . . ." This is perfectly consistent with Ezra 5:1 and Nehemiah 12:16, both of which have Iddo II as Zechariah VI's father, with no mention of any Berechiah. [Some material for this note is taken from a footnote on Matthew 23:35 in the New Geneva Study Bible.]

Chapter 4

Anonymous True Prophets in Scripture (Chronological Order)

1. Anonymous Individual Prophets

Headnotes

1. Anonymous prophets are listed in chronological order.
2. Headnotes 2, 3, and 4 for chapter 3 apply.
3. Headnote 5, chapter 3, applies except anonymous Levite singers are *not* included.

Anonymous Prophets

1. **The Judge Prophet** (Judg. 6:7-10). During the Judges period of Israel, in ca. 1300 BC, a prophet was sent by the Lord to remind the nation, now fallen into sin and oppressed by Midian, that He had redeemed them from slavery in Egypt, fought their enemies, and driven out the Canaanites from their promised land—only to be disobeyed. This prophet then disappears from the narrative, but God raised up Gideon to deliver and judge Israel (Judg. 6:11-8:35).

2. **Eli's Censurer** (1 Sam. 2:12-36). Near the end of the Judges period, ca. 1100 BC, the sons of Eli the high priest, Hophni and Phineas, became exceedingly corrupt priests. They desecrated sacrifices, taking the best meat for themselves (vv. 12-17). They were fornicators (v. 22). Eli rebuked them, but did not restrain them (vv. 23-25). Finally, a prophet was sent to censure Eli and his house (family), announcing that the priesthood would be removed from them forever (vv. 27-36). Furthermore, all of Eli's male descendants would die young, "in the flower of their age." The priesthood would be given to another branch of **Aaron's** descendents, through his third son **Eleazar** (1 Chr. 6:3-15). Even worse, God told Eli, "And you will see an enemy in My dwelling place."

Later, God confirmed this anonymous prophet's condemnation of Eli's house through the boy prophet **Samuel** (q.v.) [1 Sam. 3:11-14]; and He began to carry it out in Eli's lifetime, with the capture of the ark by the Philistines and the sudden violent deaths of Hophni and Phineas (1 Sam. 4:1-11).

3. **The Split-Altar Prophet** (1 Ki. 13). A man of God, a prophet from Judah, was sent by God to the Northern Kingdom (Israel) to prophesy against its first king, Jeroboam I, and his illegal, idolatrous altar in Bethel (ca. 930 BC). This prophet made a chilling and stunningly accurate prediction: that someday a "child . . . born to the house of **David**" (i.e., a future king of Judah) named Josiah would burn men's bones on that altar. The prophet then announced a miraculous sign to validate his message: The altar[1] would split apart and the ashes would spill out. Jeroboam, standing right there at the altar, pointed to the prophet and commanded, "Arrest him!" whereupon not only did the altar split, but also Jeroboam's hand shriveled up and stiffened.

Presumably the altar was later repaired, for the prophet's prediction of its final use did come true (2 Ki. 23:15-18). The king's immediate concern, of course, was for his hand. He begged the prophet to pray to "your" God for its restoration. He did, and it was! The grateful king then wanted to entertain the prophet and give him a reward, but either of these would have violated God's direct orders. The prophet immediately set out for home, somewhere in Judah, taking a different way, as he had been instructed by God.

This anonymous but important prophet's life then took a tragic, heart-wrenching turn. After faithfully delivering his message from God, working a miracle, standing up to powerful King Jeroboam, interceding with God for him, and refusing the king's rewards, he broke faith with God when he succumbed to the adulation—or was it disguised envy?—of an old prophet living in Bethel, who lied that God had told *him* to detain the prophet and give him a nice meal. At the meal, the old liar got a *real* revelation from God: His guest, our prophet, would die before he reached Judah, because he had disobeyed God's direct command not to eat in Bethel. And so it was; our prophet was killed by a lion on his way home.

This Judean prophet's prediction—that a Davidic king named Josiah would burn men's bones on that very altar—was fulfilled to the letter *three hundred* years later! This ranks with, or actually outranks, in its specificity and time-lapse, Isaiah's more celebrated prediction about Cyrus, king of Persia, some 150 years in advance (Is. 44:28-45:1).

4. **The Lying Old Prophet of Bethel** (1 Ki. 13:11-32). Here is a prophet who is truly difficult to characterize, but whose life is poignant to ponder. The Bible calls him a prophet, without qualification—but what true man of God would lie about revelation? If the Bible were fiction, this prophet could be called a literary device used to turn the story of the **Split-Altar Prophet** (q.v.). But his grave was real, and he was remembered as a real person (2 Ki. 23:17-18).

It appears that the lying prophet had served God in former times, and was not now a false prophet in Jeroboam's employ. He had probably served during the "better" times of **Solomon** or even **David**, since he was old during the days of Solomon's immediate successor. From the fact that the Judean prophet so readily believed him, it would seem that the old prophet was well-known and of good repute among prophets. But these considerations only intensify the offense of his lie. It is easy to forgive or overlook the sins and indiscretions of youth, even in a prophet; take **Moses** and **Israel** as examples. It is harder, but still possible, to accept that spiritual giants and heroes in the Bible may have midlife, midcareer spiritual/moral lapses as David and **Jonah** did. But for an elderly, experienced prophet, a longtime man of God, to fabricate revelation from God is almost beyond belief, or what we want to believe. Perhaps this whole episode is a lesson for us about man's ultimate fallibility—as seen in both prophets.

What was the old prophet's motive for wanting to parlay with the Split-Altar Prophet so much that he would tell such a damnable lie? Was it admiration? Envy? Desperation for godly company in what had become a godless nation? Or was he, after all, a satanic false prophet? Scripture does not say. In any event he must be included in this list of prophets because he had at least one true revelation from God, which he told, about the other prophet's mistake and fate (1 Ki. 13:20-22). And to his credit, he was truly remorseful about his lie and its tragic consequences. He recovered the Judean prophet's corpse and buried it in his own tomb. He mourned for his brother. And he so admired that other prophet that he told his sons to bury their father, when he died, in the same tomb, bone to bone. They did.

5. **The Prophet Who Surprised** (1 Ki. 20:13-22). This anonymous prophet surprised King Ahab of Israel (874–853 BC) by suddenly approaching him in the midst of a council of war. He also surprises us by promising, from God, a victory for this wicked king. Had Ahab reformed, if only temporarily, after **Elijah's** stunning victory for God over the prophets of Baal and Asherah? Or had God decided to use Ahab to chasten an even more wicked regime in Syria? Neither of the above. God did this so that "you shall know that I am the LORD" (v. 13).

The Surprise Prophet not only guaranteed victory, he also told Ahab how to deploy his forces and prosecute the battle. And after the rout, the prophet returned to the king and told him to get ready: Ben-Hadad (Syria) would be back next spring (v. 22).

6. **The "Plain" Prophet** (1 Ki. 20:23-34). Sure enough, the next spring (see the end of the synopsis on "**The Prophet Who Surprised**"), Ben-Hadad of Syria reorganized his war department and mustered another overwhelmingly large army to reduce Israel. But this time they would fight in the plain, on level ground; for Ben-Hadad and his advisors superstitiously and erroneously believed that Israel had won the previous battle only because "their gods are gods of the hills . . . but if we fight in the plain, surely we will be stronger than they" (v. 23).

"Then a man of God came and spoke to the king of Israel, and said, 'Thus says the LORD: "Because the Syrians have said, 'The LORD is God of the hills, but He is not God of the valleys,' therefore I will deliver all this great multitude into your hand, and you shall know that I am the LORD"'" (v. 28). And so it was. This time Ben-Hadad did not escape but was taken prisoner. But when he begged for mercy, pledged to make reparations for previous war crimes, and made a treaty, Ahab let him go—big mistake! (See next prophet.)

7. **The Wounded Prophet** (1 Ki. 20:35-43). God sent to Ahab a third anonymous prophet in a row; this time to condemn him for releasing Ben-Hadad (see synopsis of "**The 'Plain' Prophet**"). How the prophet accomplished this mission is a short, fascinating read. There is no need to summarize this already-concise story; suffice it to say that this prophet suffered *before* delivering his message, not afterward as is more often the case. It was a rough, almost slapstick form of parable that the prophet used to convict a powerful superior of sin (cf. **Nathan's** nonviolent form of such a parable, 2 Sam. 12:1-15).

Of special interest to this book, on the general subject of prophets, is the fact that the Wounded Prophet is called both a "man of the sons of the prophets" (v. 35) and a "prophet" (v. 38). This establishes a strong link, if not an equivalency, between these terms. This is the first use of the term "sons of the prophets" in the Bible. Later it is associated with the denizens of certain seminaries or abbeys visited by **Elijah** and **Elisha** (2 Ki. 2:3, 5, 15; 4:1, 38). The "sons" were not necessarily youths. They may have been one or more orders or communities of prophets that derived from the two groups of fifty prophets saved by Obadiah from Jezebel's massacre (1 Ki. 18:4). If Elijah founded these institutions, the Wounded Prophet indicates that the work had been started after Elijah returned to Israel from his flight to the wilderness (1 Ki. 19:4ff.) and before he confronted Ahab again (1 Ki. 21:17-29). During the Syrian wars, God used these three anonymous prophets to tend to Ahab.

8. **The Insured Prophet** (2 Ki. 4:1-7). A certain one of the sons of the prophets, who was known to **Elisha**, died. His widow applied to Elisha for "life insurance benefits." She and her sons received a generous settlement because the prophet's policy was paid up, secured by his fear of the LORD. Elisha was the Insurer's (God's) agent.

9. **The Surrogate Prophet** (2 Ki. 9:1-13). One of the sons of the prophets (see "**The Wounded Prophet**," second paragraph), a young man, a servant of **Elisha**, was given an important prophet's mission by Elisha. He was sent to Ramoth in Gilead to anoint Jehu as future king of Israel and to prophesy about the fall of the house of Ahab and God's vengeance for the murders of His prophets by Jezebel. Ahab had been killed in battle in Ramoth in 853 BC (1 Ki. 22:29-35). His equally

wicked son Ahaziah reigned two years, 853–852 BC, dying from complications of an accidental fall (2 Ki. 1:2-17). Now, another son of Ahab, Joram (a.k.a Jehoram), was king of Israel. And the very evil Queen Mother Jezebel hovered in the background. It was finally time to carry out God's command to **Elijah** to anoint Jehu as king over Israel—a command issued at least fifteen years earlier (1 Ki. 19:16).

Surely Elijah had passed this command on to his protégé and spiritual successor Elisha, for the time to execute it was not yet ripe in Elijah's own lifetime (1 Ki. 21:28-29). But why did Elisha delegate such an important task to an unnamed servant, an intern? Scripture simply does not say, and we can only speculate (always dangerous). Perhaps Elisha was ill. Perhaps Jehu would have recognized him and not admitted him to his military compound. Or perhaps Elisha was watched; a trip by him to Ramoth would have been noticed in Samaria, Joram's capital. We don't know.

But we do know that the Surrogate Prophet carried out his mission, and in so doing turned the very wheel of history. He was a true prophet, even though he did not receive his revelation directly from God. In a similar way **Aaron** was **Moses**'s prophet, his mouthpiece (Ex. 7:1-2).

10a, b, c, … n. **The Sent Prophets** (2 Chr. 23, 24). Joash (835-796 BC) was a good king in Judah—until his champion and mentor, the worthy priest Jehoiada, died. Then Joash took bad advice. He, and all Judah with him, abandoned God's house and turned to idols. God's wrath fell on Judah and Jerusalem; but He also graciously sent prophets, to bring them back to Him (24:19). The people refused to listen to these anonymous prophets, and thus rose the prophet **Zechariah II** (q.v.), famously stoned to death in the temple courtyard. Zechariah was, ironically, the son of Joash's mentor Jehoida, and the two may have been raised together.

The sent prophets are listed as anonymous because the only named prophets of that time, ca. 800 BC, were Zechariah, **Jonah**, and **Amos**. There is no record or indication that either Jonah or Amos prophesied in Judah or to Joash. Zechariah may have been one of the sent prophets, but there was at least one other, possibly several. It seems unlikely that they prophesied in concert, as a group, so they are listed here as an unknown number of individuals.

11. **The Prophet Who Warned Against Mercenaries** (2 Chr. 25:5-13). Amaziah, king of Judah from 796 to 767 BC, mustered an army of three hundred thousand men to make war against Edom.[2] He also hired one hundred thousand mercenaries from Israel. A man of God, a prophet, came to warn Amaziah that the use of the mercenaries would cause him to lose the war, because "The LORD is not with Israel" (v. 7). The king should rely on God, not Israelite mercenaries. To his credit (and he needs it, considering the stupid things he did later, see next prophet), Amaziah heeded the word of God spoken by this anonymous prophet, discharged the mercenaries (with pay), and won a resounding victory over Edom.

12. **The Prophet Who Warned Against Idols** (2 Chr. 25:14-16). (Story continued from previous prophet) After defeating Edom with the help of God, not mercenaries, King Amaziah did one of the stupidest and most ungrateful things imaginable. He actually brought home the gods (idols) of the people of Seir (Edom) and began to worship them! This, from a direct descendent of **David**, in the City of David, where stood God's temple built by **Solomon**! And after having just been blessed with victory in war, by God! An angry God sent a prophet to rebuke Amaziah. Instead of heeding this man of God, as he had the previous one, Amaziah threatened to kill him if he didn't shut up! So the anonymous prophet ceased to prophesy but only after telling Amaziah that he was doomed for not heeding his advice, his prophecy from God. Amaziah did additional stupid things and led Judah into defeat and subjection by Israel (2 Chr. 25:17-24).

13. **Isaiah's Wife** (Is. 8:3). Her only known witness for the LORD was to bear a son and name him Maher-Shalal-Hash-Baz (speed the spoil, hasten the booty), in about 730 BC. But **Isaiah** identified her as a prophetess, a title used elsewhere in Scripture exclusively for women that prophesied, never for the wife of a prophet.

> NOTE: Anonymous prophets condemned Judah and Jerusalem for following King Manassah (697–642 BC) into all manner of wickedness and sin (2 Ki. 21, see v. 10). Because these prophets spoke as one on this occasion, probably with a joint proclamation, they are listed as a group (group 14) in part 2 of this chapter.

14–17. **Four Daughters** (Acts 21:8-9). **Philip II**, the deacon/evangelist (not the disciple/apostle), had four virgin daughters who prophesied. There is no indication that they were a musical group or otherwise prophesied in concert, so they are considered individual, anonymous, prophetesses.

> NOTE: Many in the apostolic-era church had the gift of prophecy and prophesied—see for example Acts 2:16-18; 1 Cor. 12:7-10; Eph. 4:11; 1 Pet. 4:10-11. But other than the named ones in chapter 3, Philip's daughters (above) and the Jerusalem prophets who went to Antioch (next), there are no specific instances of their prophesying, or prophecies, recorded in the Bible. They are listed as anonymous groups, according to their churches, in part 2 of this chapter.

18. **The Jerusalem/Antioch Prophet(s)** (Acts 11:27). "And in these days prophets came from Jerusalem to Antioch" (ca. AD 45–46). One of them was **Agabus**. The others are anonymous. We do not know how many there were in addition to Agabus; the minimum is one.

19, 20. **The Two Witnesses** (Rev. 11:3-12). **Jesus**, in His Revelation given through **John II**, identifies two witnesses who "will prophesy one thousand two hundred and sixty days." During this time these two "olive trees and . . . lampstands standing before the God of the earth" are given absolute protection from all enemies. They are also given miraculous powers including some of the exact ones given to **Elijah** and **Moses**. After their three and one-half years of unimpeded testimony, the satanic beast from the bottomless pit kills them and puts their corpses on public display for three and one-half days. Then God breathes life into them again, to the terror and dismay of their tormentors, and they ascend to heaven in full view.

Eschatologists of various persuasions place these events at different times or in the future. Some have even named these prophets. But as far as the Book of Revelation is concerned, and this book, they are anonymous.

21, 22, 23, etc. **The Authors** (human) of Scripture who are not named or otherwise known are prophets, for they are proclaimers of God's word to man. This includes the authors of Judges, Ruth, 1 and 2 Kings, 1 and 2 Chronicles, Esther, Job, certain Psalms, and portions of other books of the Bible. Of course, human authors have been postulated for most of these Scriptures, such as **Ezra** (Chronicles) and **Moses** (Job). But even if any of these proposals be true, there remain an unknown number of anonymous author-prophets.

2. Groups of Anonymous Prophets

Headnotes

1. Anonymous prophet groups are listed in chronological order.
2. Headnotes 2, 3, and 4 for chapter 3 apply.
3. The criteria for inclusion of groups of prophets are,

    - Any group designated in Scripture as "prophets," except as excluded in note 4 below.
    - Any group that is said, in Scripture, to prophesy; or to have delivered a message from God or under the influence of the Holy Spirit except as excluded in notes 4 or 5 below.

4. This section does not include the musical prophecy groups first organized under David in about 1000 BC (1 Chronicles 25) and continuing through the Jews' return from Babylonian exile and their reformation under Nehemiah in about 430 BC (Nehemiah 12:45–46). Musical prophecy groups and anonymous musical prophets in the Bible far outnumber nonmusical ones and are listed in chapter 6. One of the groups listed below in this chapter had a musical component (group 2) and is also listed in chapter 6.
5. Angelic groups are excluded.

Anonymous Prophet Groups

1. **Num. 11:16-25. Seventy Elders** gathered around the tabernacle of meeting in the wilderness (ca. 1440 BC) and prophesied, just this once, when God came down in the cloud of His presence and placed His Spirit upon them. This singular event was apparently not meant to give the seventy some new revelation from God that would be proclaimed later to others. Rather, it was a sign that God was investing them with powers and responsibilities in order that they could share with **Moses** the burden of governing the people. Still, *they prophesied.*

2. **1 Sam. 10:5-13. A Group of Prophets** at "the hill where the Philistine garrison is" came down from the high place (worship center) prophesying in a sort of parade led by a musical band. When **Saul** met them, the Spirit of God came upon him and he prophesied too! This was a sign to Saul of the divine origin of his recent anointing by **Samuel** to be king of Israel, ca. 1050 BC.

3. **1 Sam. 19:18-20. A Second Group of Prophets** was led by **Samuel** himself in or near his hometown of Ramah, where **David** was hiding from **Saul** in about 1030 BC. This anonymous group was instrumental in saving David from being taken prisoner by Saul's minions, groups 4-6. They also led Saul to prophesying again, quenching his jealous rage at that time.

4-6. **1 Sam. 19:20-21. Three Groups of Messengers** were sent by **Saul** to arrest **David** at Naioth-in-Ramah; but instead of taking David into custody, each group, in turn, joined group 3 by prophesying as the Spirit of God came upon them.

7. **1 Sam. 28:6. The Prophets Inquired of by Saul** in his last desperate weeks were apparently true prophets of God. Saul may have convened them as a group in order to get some direction from the LORD, but he got no answer.

8. **1 Ki. 18:4. Jezebel's Massacre.** A large number of prophets of the LORD was executed by Jezebel in about 870 BC.

9. **1 Ki. 18:4, 13. One Hundred Prophets** of the LORD were saved from Jezebel's massacre by a man named Obadiah, a high ranking official under Ahab/Jezebel. Obadiah hid them in two caves, fifty in each, and fed them with bread and water. These survivors of Jezebel's massacre may have been the nuclei of groups 10-13.

10. **1 Ki. 20:35. The Sons of the Prophets,** who were referred to during Ahab's reign in about 860 BC, may have been an organized group such as an abbey or learning center like we find a few years later (groups 11-13). If so, this group was

probably an underground cell, because of Jezebel; but Ahab recognized one of them as a prophet (1 Ki. 20:41). That at least some of them—certainly the **Wounded Prophet** in 1 Ki. 20:35-42—were indeed prophets and not just "sons" in any sense, is evident in this story.

11. **2 Ki. 2:3. "The Sons of the Prophets Who Were at Bethel"** spoke to **Elisha** when he and **Elijah** came through Bethel on their way to Elijah's miraculous ascension to heaven in about 850 BC. This was one of several monasteries or schools of prophets possibly founded and certainly supported by Elijah and/or Elisha. These centers of prophecy may have sprung from the **One Hundred Prophets,** group 9. Were all of the "sons" in these groups actual Prophets? Probably not, but at least one—the **Surrogate Prophet** (q.v.)—executed the office of prophet.

12. **2 Ki. 2:5-17. "The Sons of the Prophets Who Were at Jericho"** also spoke to **Elisha** about **Elijah's** imminent departure from life on earth, about 850 BC. For more about these groups (11-13) in general, see under group 11 above. The group at Jericho was more involved than the other two in Elijah's ascension and in the transfer of his mantle to Elisha, both literally and figuratively. Fifty of them continued with the two great prophets to a vantage point near the Jordan River, from whence they witnessed the river's waters part: first for Elijah as he crossed over to the east side, with Elisha; and then for Elisha alone, coming back to the west bank. Thus, these anonymous sons of prophets, including, we believe, at least some true prophets of God, were the first people to know and declare that "the spirit of Elijah rests on Elisha." Then, fifty of them (not necessarily the same fifty) formed a search party that looked for Elijah for three days, to no avail.

13. **2 Ki. 4:38. The Sons of the Prophets at Gilgal** were in another school or priory of prophets, visited by **Elisha** on several occasions. Elisha apparently had a residence on this campus, and he may have stayed there most of the time. For more about these groups in general, see groups 11 and 12.

The Gilgal center was the first stop on, or the starting point of, the circuit followed by **Elijah** and Elisha on the way to Elijah's ascension and Elisha's investiture, ca. 850 BC (2 Ki. 2:1). Later, during a famine, Elisha returned to the Gilgal campus where he ministered to the desperate need of these "sons of the prophets" by means of two food miracles. First, God through Elisha detoxified a pot of poison stew that the sons of the prophets had made (2 Ki. 4:38-41). Later He fed them all (about a hundred)—with plenty left over—from twenty loaves of barley and some grain (2 Ki. 4:42-44).

On another occasion a group of the sons of the prophets at "the place where we dwell with you" (Elisha)—probably Gilgal—went to the Jordan River forest (swamp?) to cut some beams for a larger dwelling (2 Ki. 6:1-7). This indicates that this group of prophets was growing.

14. **2 Ki. 21:10-15. God's Servants the Prophets** spoke against the wickedness of King Manassah (697-642 BC) and against Jerusalem and Judah, which had been thoroughly corrupted during Manassah's administration. It appears that these prophets jointly wrote, or at least signed, the condemnation from God that appears verbatim in 2 Kings 21:11-15. The idea that it was but one message, from several seers, is also implied in 2 Chr. 33:18. Chronologically, this group could have included a young **Isaiah**, a young **Micah**, **Oded, Nahum,** and **Hozai**; but the Holy Spirit chose to keep it anonymous.

15. **2 Ki. 23:1-2. Prophets Living in Jerusalem** were called to the temple, along with priests, elders, and "all the people," by King Josiah in 622 BC. There, they heard a public reading of the entire Book of the Covenant (see under **Moses,** *Writings,* in chapter 3), which had long been neglected and lost. The prophets in this gathering could have included **Jeremiah, Zephaniah, Huldah,** and any number of anonymous prophets.

16. **Luke 2:8-17. Certain Shepherds,** abiding in fields, had a vision or a visit from God one night, ca. 4 BC. An angel from God gave them a message from God about Jesus' birth. After they had seen the Babe Jesus, they prophesied.

17. **Luke 10:1-20. Seventy Disciples** of **Jesus** were sent out in pairs to cities Jesus planned to visit Himself. Although they were only His "advance teams," so to speak, they were given miraculous powers of healing and a particular message straight from God the Son—two sure marks of genuine prophets.

18. **Luke 23:55 – 24:11. Certain Women** arrived at **Jesus's** tomb early in the morning after the Sabbath following His death and burial, ca. AD 30. There, they saw a vision of angels (24:22-23) who told them that Jesus was alive! This message from God they told (prophesied) to the disciples and "all the rest" of Jesus's followers. Besides **Mary Magdalene, Joanna, Mary** the mother of **James**, and **Salome** (Mark 16:1), this group included certain other, anonymous, women (Luke 24:10).

19. **Acts 4:31. A Group of Believers**, companions of the apostles, "were all filled with the Holy Spirit, and they spoke the word of God with boldness." They had assembled at a place, probably a house, to hear a report from **Peter** and **John** about their arrest, trial, and release by the Jewish council. At the meeting they quoted Old Testament prophecy (4:25-26), rejoiced, prayed mightily, and prophesied. The very building shook. This took place ca. AD 30.

20, 21, 22, ... n. **Certain Members of Apostolic-era Churches** received and exercised the Spiritual gift of prophecy as described in Rom. 12:6; 1 Cor. 11:4-

5, 12:4-10, 14:1-5 and 31-32; Eph. 4:11-12; 1 Thess. 5:19-20; 1 Pet. 4:10-11. These Christians, both men and women, prophesied individually; but we have few specific cases other than the ones named in chapter 3 and the anonymous individuals numbered 14-18 in part 1 of this chapter. Therefore these prophets are listed as groups according to their churches. One such group of about twelve men was in the church at Ephesus (Acts 19:1-7). Another group, not a church yet, probably prophesied at Cornelius's house (Acts 10:44-46). Each church likely included *some* members with the gift of prophecy. There may have been hundreds or even thousands during this Apostolic Era, roughly AD 30-100.

Endnotes for Chapter 4

1. Although Jeroboam stood at an altar "to burn incense" (verse 1), the altar that was split was probably a large one used for animal sacrifices to the gold-calf idol, not just a small incense altar because "the ashes poured out" (verse 5) and because it was used later to calcine men's skeletons (2 Kings 23:16).

2. The particular reason for this war is not known. King **David** had put Edom under subjection (2 Samuel 8:14); Edom revolted against Judah's authority in the days of King Jehoram, 848–841 BC (2 Kings 8:20).

Chapter 5

False Prophets in the Bible

Introduction

False prophets fall into two groups: prophets of a false god or idol such as Baal and those who claim to be prophets of God but are not. Both types are motivated by greed and ambition. Satan, who exploits them, has another agenda: to turn people away from God the Father, His Son, and Their Spirit.

There are probably more false prophets referred to in Scripture than true prophets, but their number cannot be determined. Relatively few false prophets are identified; most of them are described as nebulous, nefarious groups. They certainly deserve no more. Some biblical terms for these miscreants are

false prophet
liar; a prophet with a lying spirit
soothsayer ("sooth" is an archaic word for "truth," but in "soothsayer," it now means the opposite)
sorcerer
magician; magi; one who practices magic arts
wizard
conjurer; one who conjures spells
medium
spiritist
necromancer; one who calls up the dead, as in a séance, to prophesy
diviner; practicer of divination
enchanter; enchanter with drugs
interpreter of omens
charmer
observer of times
belly speaker

consulter with familiar spirits
one that practiseth augury
trance speaker
astrologer
Chaldean
wise man

Many of these terms are from various English translations of Deuteronomy 18:10–14. The terms *prophet* and *prophetess* are sometimes used in the Bible for false prophets and prophetesses, but only in connection with a false god (e.g., prophet of Baal), or when the context makes it clear that a false prophet is meant (e.g., 1 Kings 22:6, 12, 13).

Demon-possessed persons are not usually false prophets. Only one such case is known: the girl in Philippi (Acts 16:16). Demon possession is typically manifested by muteness, seizures, self-destructiveness, and the like. False prophets, on the other hand, are generally healthy and sane. They know what they are doing and are capable of exchanging their lies for the truth. Few ever do, although most of them know about God. Some deny Him. Others try to syncretize Him with their false god, idol, or system. Still others claim to speak for Him, but their so-called prophecy is the invention of their own hearts.

List of False Prophets: Named and Anonymous Individuals and Groups (Chronological Order)

1. **Egyptian Magicians and Wise Men** flourished during the time of **Joseph I**, the eleventh son of Israel who was sold into slavery by his brothers and eventually emerged as the highest civil officer of Egypt (ca. 1700s BC). These false prophets could not interpret Pharaoh's dreams (Gen. 41:8, 24). At least they admitted their inability. God, in prophecy given through Joseph, did reveal the meaning of the dreams (Gen. 41:25-32); and that led to Joseph's promotion to Egypt's highest executive officer (Gen. 41:39-41).

Scripture does not tell how Egyptian magicians fared during Joseph's tenure as CEO of Egypt. Not too well, we presume. But Joseph, in order to temporarily conceal his identity from his visiting brothers, pretended to be a person who practiced divination (Gen. 44:5, 15). This is patently untrue of him (cf. Joseph I in chapter 3). His ruse does show that divination was still being practiced at that time.

2. **The Wise Men and Sorcerers of Egypt** at the time of **Moses**'s return there (ca. 1440 BC) were also called magicians. Their number is uncertain. Pharaoh summoned them to answer Moses and **Aaron's** "proof miracle": a rod becoming a serpent. These magicians were able to counterfeit or duplicate it although their serpents were swallowed up by Aaron's (Ex. 7:11-13). They also replicated the first two plagues wrought by God through Moses and Aaron: bloodying the river and producing a frog infestation (Ex. 7:19-22; 8:5-7). But they failed to match the third plague, lice, and conceded the contest to Moses and Aaron, even admitting that it was God's doing (Ex. 8:16-19). It is interesting that they admitted knowing of God. Most false prophets do, but they deny Him publicly.

3. **Jannes** opposed or resisted **Moses** (2 Tim. 3:8). According to tradition he was one of the magicians of Egypt, number 2 above. Whether he was or not, he is counted with those of all times who resist the truth, have corrupt minds, and are disapproved concerning the faith.

4. **Jambres**: same description as Jannes, number 3.

5. **Balaam** is listed both here and in chapter 3 because he prophesied both truth and falsehood. He was at heart a most false prophet, but God constrained him to prophesy His truth in four oracles (Num. 22-24). The irony of this, plus Balaam's background, character, and his truthful prophecies are reviewed in chapter 3 (q.v.) and will not be repeated here. His false prophecy and the "affair of Peor" are considered below in more detail.

The sordid episode of Baal-Peor, ca. 1400 BC, was one of the lowest points in Israel's history (Num. 25). It cost the young, small nation twenty-four thousand[1] lives and was terribly shameful. Although God's wrath was turned back after the plague that followed their sin in Acacia Grove, Israel never got completely over it.[2] Its memory even carried over into the Christian church.[3] The whole thing came about "through the counsel of Balaam" (Num. 31:16).

What was this "counsel of Balaam"? Some suggest that it was only his advice to the Moabites and Midianites, that they use their women to seduce the men of Israel.[4] But it would appear that his involvement was personal, that he actually joined in with the Moabites and Midianites, or was one of them and that his "counsel" included all his wicked teachings—his false prophecy, if you will. Thwarted in their attempts to curse Israel through sorcery (Num. 23:23; 24:1), Balak and Balaam conspired to seduce them into sin (Rev. 2:14). The doctrine of Balaam included open sexual immorality (fornication), eating the meat of animals that had been sacrificed to idols and to the dead[5] (Ps. 106:28), and the worship of Baal-Peor (Num. 25:2-3; Hos. 9:10). Baal-Peor ("Lord Peor") may have simply been named after nearby Mount Peor (Num. 23:28). An etymology for this false god's name that is more germane to Israel's sin may be inferred from the meaning of *peor*, "opening" or "the Moabite god of uncleanness."[6] Etymology aside, the whole affair was full of uncleanness, both sexual and spiritual (Num. 25:1, 6; 31:16).

It can be inferred from Scripture that the mysterious plague that killed so many thousands of Israelites was a venereal or other loathsome disease which, although the epidemic was stopped, never completely left the people of Israel (Josh. 22:17). Further evidence of such a disease is the extraordinary extent to which Israel had to cleanse themselves from all contact with the Midianites after they later took vengeance (for the LORD) on them, in war (Num. 31:1-24). Even the captured Midianite women who had known a man intimately had to be killed. All clothing, weapons, and other articles that may have been in contact with Midianites had to be cleansed with water or fire.

As for Balaam, his true colors and "prophecy" were revealed in Acacia Grove (Shittim) near Mount Peor. He was a combination of both types of false prophet—those of other gods (Baalim) and those purporting to be prophets of God. Although God did speak to and through Balaam (for His own sovereign purposes), this false prophet took money for "divining" (Num. 22:7-8) and later reverted to Baal worship and evil doctrine. Shortly after the affair of Peor, Balaam was killed by an Israelite army sent by God to prosecute His vengeance against Midian (Num. 25:16-18; 31:3-8; Josh. 13:22).

The true Church—both in its Old Testament form and its full Christian form—never forgot or, really, forgave Balaam (2 Pet. 2:12-15; Rev. 2:14). He stands as the archetypical false prophet. His name is forever linked with avarice, licentiousness, and the seduction of God's people to do evil.

8. **The Medium of En-dor** is the first false prophetess named in the Bible. She was employed by King **Saul** to give him guidance—primarily military—after

God had refused it (1 Sam. 28:3-25). Saul was desperate. The Philistines were threatening to conquer Israel, **David** had drawn away many of Saul's supporters, and **Samuel**, God's prophet to Saul and Israel, had died. This was Saul's situation in about 1010 BC.

Saul specifically sought a woman medium, perhaps because that gender specialized in séances to raise the spirits of the dead, and Saul wanted to talk to Samuel. Samuel—or possibly an accomplice of the medium dressed as Samuel (note the emphasis on his mantle, verse 14)—did appear and talked to Saul—or did he?[7] There is an ongoing controversy among theologians about this. The medium, on her part, was or pretended to be alarmed by the appearing of Samuel, and she was unquestionably afraid of Saul (1 Sam. 28:12). After the séance, she tried to strengthen Saul's body with food and to mollify his expected reprisals against her (1 Sam. 28:22-25).

> NOTE: During the next eighty years, the reigns of David and Solomon, we read of no false prophets. But they must have been there, lurking. The false gods Ashtoreth, Milcom, Chemosh, Molech, and others that Solomon turned to in his later years as king (1 Ki. 11:5-8), must have had their "prophets." Likewise, just after Solomon, there were probably false prophets associated with the idols and false priesthood that King Jeroboam set up in Israel (1 Ki. 12:28-33). Those who advised Jeroboam to do so (verse 28) were false prophets if they claimed some kind of supernatural revelation to warrant this apostasy.

9. **The Lying Old Prophet of Bethel** is also in the list of anonymous true prophets, chapter 4, part 1, number 4. He and **Balaam** (number 5, this list; number 20, chapter 3) are the only two prophets listed as both false and true, at different times. The case for the Lying Prophet being a true prophet who committed an egregious error is found in chapter 4 (q.v.). The fact that he issued one vile, false prophecy, an invention of his own heart, is undeniable (1 Ki. 13:18). This happened after King Jeroboam had secured the northern kingdom of Israel and had set up idols for people to worship at Dan and Bethel, ca. 920 BC.

10. **Four Hundred and Fifty Prophets of Baal** opposed **Elijah** in a showdown on Mount Carmel in about 870 BC (1 Ki. 18:19-40). Baal worship became the official religion in Israel after its King Ahab married Jezebel, a Baalist from Sidon (1 Ki. 16:30-33). Jezebel executed most of God's prophets, who were apparently numerous in those days, although we have but few names. Those who survived, about one hundred, were hiding in caves (1 Ki. 18:4). Elijah, one prophet of God who had gone into hiding by himself (1 Ki. 17:2-3), came out and challenged four hundred fifty prophets of Baal and four hundred prophets of Asherah (next entry, number 11) to bring down fire from the sky. The false prophets prayed to Baal, leaped about the altar they had made, cut themselves with knives and lances, and

prophesied from morning until about three o'clock in the afternoon—all to no avail. When Elijah's God did send fire in abundance, the Baalists were defeated and the crowd of onlookers acknowledged and worshipped the one and true God. Their defeat was complete, but God was not finished with these evil prophets; Elijah personally executed all 450 prophets of Baal.

11. **Four Hundred Prophets of Asherah**[8] (1 Ki. 18:19) were in league with the prophets of Baal (number 10 above) who were challenged, defeated, and executed by **Elijah**, God's prophet. They are not expressly mentioned as active participants in the contest, but they may be included in the phrase "prophets of Baal" after verse 19. If so, they also lost their lives.

12. **About Four Hundred Prophets**, who proved to be false, were gathered together by King Ahab of Israel to inquire of the LORD concerning war against Syria (1 Ki. 22:1-6). Ahab had formed an alliance with King Jehoshaphat of Judah to wage this war. Righteous Jehoshaphat was the one who requested that they seek God's word before going to war. Ahab agreed and called these four hundred prophets together, but they were court prophets and basically yes-men. This was in 853 BC, the last year of Ahab, who was killed in the ensuing battle.

These prophets were not a remnant or resurgence of the prophets of Baal and Asherah, numbers 10 and 11 above, for they were asked to inquire of the LORD, not Baal. Nevertheless they were false prophets who told the kings what they thought they wanted to hear: that they would be victorious. Their deceitfulness can be sensed in their manner of answering, to wit: they were asked to inquire of the LORD (YHWH, Jehovah), but their prophecy promised the protection of the Lord (Adonai, master; more generic than LORD). Their outright false prophecy came, surprisingly, from a "spirit" sent by God Himself (1 Ki. 22:19-23). God allowed it in order to entice Ahab into the battle in which he would die. See also **Micaiah**, chapter 3, number 121.

We are not told what became of the Four Hundred. Ahab was soon dead, so he could not punish them for lying to him. His son Ahaziah worshipped Baalim (1 Ki.: 22:53)—particularly Baal-Zebub (2 Ki. 1:2)—and probably had no interest in prophets who purported to speak for God, especially since they were already found to be unreliable.

13. **Zedekiah I** was one of the principal false prophets of the Four Hundred, number 12 above. He was certainly the most audacious. First he made a foolish exhibition of himself while he purported to prophesy for the LORD (1 KI. 22:11). Then, he mocked God's prophet **Micaiah** and struck him on the cheek (1 Ki. 22:24). He reminds us of the soldiers who struck and mocked **Jesus** (Luke 22: 63-64). Micaiah had an answer for Zedekiah (1 Ki. 22:25), which we trust came to pass.

14. **The "Peace" Prophets** of **Micah's** time, ca. 740–700 BC, divined for money, prophesied about alcohol (or were they "in their cups"?—cf. Isaiah 28:7), strove against those rulers who did not feed or pay them, and made the people stray from God and truth (Mic. 2:11; 3:5-7, 11). It is difficult to discern whether these particular false prophets were in Judah, Israel, or both. Micah prophesied to both nations (Mic. 1:1). The end of the political nation of Israel in 722 BC was very near. See also the following note.

> NOTE: At the end of the political nation of Israel in 722 BC at the hands of Assyria, the holy historian summarizes the reasons for God's just punishment (2 Ki. 17:7-18). Included in this postmortem indictment are Israel's failure to hear God's prophets or to keep His commandments and also her embracing of false prophets:
>
> And they caused their sons and daughters to pass through the fire, practiced witchcraft and soothsaying, and sold themselves to do evil in the sight of the LORD, to provoke Him to anger. 2 Ki. 17:17; cf. Deut. 18:10

15. **Manassah** (697-642 BC), arguably the worst king of Judah (2 Chr. 33:9), considered himself a prophet, for he personally practiced soothsaying, witchcraft, and sorcery, and caused his sons to pass through the fire (2 Chr. 33:6). Of course these practices made him a false prophet (Deut. 18:10). He also consulted mediums and spiritists, number 16 below.

16. **Mediums and Spiritists** flourished in Judah and Jerusalem during Manassah's wicked reign (2 Chr. 33:6). It seems likely that they would have continued to prosper during the reign of his not-much-better son Amon, 642–640 BC (2 Chr. 33:21-23). We can only speculate what happened to them during good King Josiah's reign, 640–609 BC. Suffice it to say that we do not read of these particular kinds of false prophets again in the Bible.

17. **Jeremiah's Adversaries** were an unspecified number of false prophets in Jerusalem during the last decades of Judah, say, 610–590 BC. Jeremiah wrote scathing indictments of the prophets of his day who claimed to have revelation from God but misled the people into a false sense of security, saying, "Peace, peace," when there was no peace. He compared them with the prophets of Baal in Samaria, Israel—now a "former" nation (Jer. 23:13-14). There are many, many references to these false prophets in Jeremiah. One particular passage, Jer. 23:9-40, contains some of Scripture's best characterizations of false prophets, including the following, in which God is speaking:

> Do not listen to the words of the prophets who prophesy to you. They make you worthless;

They speak a vision of their own heart,
Not from the mouth of the LORD. —v. 16

I have not sent these prophets, yet they ran. I have not spoken to them, yet they prophesied. —v. 21

I have heard what the prophets have said who prophesy lies in My name, saying, "I have dreamed, I have dreamed!" How long will this be in the heart of the prophets who prophesy lies? Indeed they are prophets of the deceit of their own heart, who try to make My people forget My name by their dreams which everyone tells his neighbor, as their fathers forgot My name for Baal.—vv. 25-27

"Therefore behold, I am against the prophets," says the LORD, "who steal My words every one from his neighbor. Behold, I am against the prophets," says the LORD, "who use their tongues and say, 'He says.' Behold, I am against those who prophesy false dreams," says the LORD, "and tell them, and cause My people to err by their lies and by their recklessness. Yet I did not send them or command them; therefore they shall not profit this people at all," says the LORD.—vv. 30-32

The conflict between Jeremiah and the false prophets went far beyond words. In about 609 BC, after he had prophesied publicly in the temple courtyard, a group of false prophets and corrupt priests seized Jeremy and would have lynched him then and there, but for the intervention of some noblemen and other people (Jer. 26:1-19).

Jeremy later took the case to Zedekiah,[9] the last king of Judah, in 593 BC, saying,

Therefore do not listen to your prophets, your diviners, your dreamers, your soothsayers, or your sorcerers, who speak to you, saying, "You shall not serve the king of Babylon." For they prophesy a lie to you.—Jer. 27:9-10

18. **"Prophets" in Edom, Moab, Ammon, Tyre, and Sidon** were indicted for prophesying falsely, in a message **Jeremiah** sent to the kings of each of these places (Jer. 27:1-11). The messages were carried back to their countries by ambassadors or envoys who had come to Jerusalem from those nations. They also took, or wore, symbolic yokes fashioned by Jeremiah, and they were *commanded* (!) by him to say to each of their kings that God, the ruler of the universe, had decreed that Nebuchadnezzar is going to take over your territory, one way or another. If you, King, accept his "yoke", your nation will survive; if not, you will be destroyed. And so, King,

Therefore do not listen to your prophets, your diviners, your dreamers, your soothsayers, or your sorcerers, who speak to you, saying, "You shall not serve the king of Babylon." For they prophesy a lie to you.—vv. 9-10a

It was gracious of God to warn these five territories, all of them Judah's neighbors, all having been enemies or rivals of Judah, and all having practiced false religions with false prophets. We do not know which, if any, of those kings heeded God's warning given through His prophet Jeremiah.

Although there were five nations, all of their false prophets, diviners, etc. are being treated as one group here because of their common error (lie) and because no distinctions are made in Scripture except nationality.

19. **Hananiah** (false) was a leader Of Jeremiah's Adversaries in Jerusalem (No. 17 above). In 593 BC Hananiah directly opposed **Jeremiah's** true prophecies, claiming that God had told *him*, Hananiah, that Judah would be restored from damages already incurred, and that Nebuchadnezzar would be defeated within two years (Jer. 28). Jeremiah publicly confronted Hananiah—rather sarcastically, we think. Hananiah then took the yoke—symbolic of Nebuchadnezzar's coming rule—off of Jeremiah's neck and broke it, while reiterating his own "prophecy." Jeremiah left. Later, God gave Jeremiah prophecy about Nebuchadnezzar specifically for Hananiah, and He also condemned Hananiah to die within the year. This sentence was soon carried out; we are spared the details.

The Hananiah affair contains two interesting sidelights. First, Hananiah is called a prophet throughout—not a false prophet, although he certainly was one, and definitely not a diviner or sorcerer, or a prophet of Baal or some other false god. He purported to speak for God. His public debate with Jeremiah ended up, for Hananiah, no worse than a draw and in his mind, a victory, since Jeremiah walked away. This is the worst type of false prophet and the hardest to detect: one who claims to speak for God. They are still with us.

Second, Hananiah is introduced to us as "the son of Azur the prophet, who was from Gibeon" (v. 1). Azur is not listed in this book for want of other information about him. Was he also a false prophet, yet accepted by many as a true prophet of God, like Hananiah? Or was he indeed a true prophet? Was he also the father of another prominent man in Jerusalem at this time (Ezek. 11:1)? We don't know.

20. **False Jewish Prophets in Babylon** were with the first large group of Jews exiled there in the eighth year of Nebuchadnezzar, 597 BC (2 Ki. 24:10-16). **Jeremiah** contended with these false prophets at long distance by letters from Jerusalem (Jer. 29). Three of them are named and are listed as numbers 21, 22, and 23 below.

21. **Ahab,** son of Kolaiah, was a false Jewish prophet living among the captives in Babylon in the 590s BC. He and Zedekiah (number 22) not only prophesied lies that they claimed to be from God, but they also committed adultery with their neighbors' wives. Their principal lie was that the Babylonian captivity would be

short-lived and God would soon restore the Jews to Jerusalem. **Jeremiah** prophesied in a letter that Ahab and Zedekiah would be slain by Nebuchadnezzar and that their names would be used as a curse by the captives in Babylon. This must have come to pass, because Jeremiah truly spoke for God (Jer. 29:21-23).

22. Zedekiah II, son of Maaseiah, was a false Jewish prophet in Babylon with exactly the same profile as Ahab, number 21 (q.v.). He is not to be confused with Zedekiah, last king of Judah, a contemporary, nor with Zedekiah I, false prophet number 13, who lived over two hundred fifty years earlier (Jer. 29:21-23).

23. Shemaiah I (false), the Nehelamite, was yet another false Jewish prophet in Babylon in the 590s BC (see numbers 20, 21, and 22 above). Shemaiah was not content to prophesy lies to the exiles in Babylon. He also sent letters to the priests and others in Jerusalem urging them to rebuke, humiliate, and imprison Jeremiah for prophesying the truth in his letters to Babylon (Jer. 29:24-28). Shemaiah insinuated that Jeremiah was demented, and accused him of being a false prophet! Jeremiah was expressly told by God to send another letter to Babylon exposing Shemaiah as the real false prophet and sentencing him and his family to banishment from the Jewish community (Jer. 29:24-32).

24. **False Prophets of Israel** against whom **Ezekiel** contended in his written prophecy (Ezek. 7:26; ch. 13; 22:25, 28) may have included many of the same ones who opposed **Jeremiah** in both Jerusalem (number 17) and Babylon (numbers 20–23) in the 590s BC. However, Ezekiel, who was living near Babylon but was sometimes transported in visions to Jerusalem (Ezek. 8:3), had a different perspective than Jeremiah and may have had certain other false prophets in view. For example, Ezekiel specifically mentions false prophetesses (13:17) while Jeremiah does not. Thus a separate group is listed here.

Most of Ezekiel's prophecy about false prophets is found in chapter 13 of his book. God calls them "foolish prophets, who follow their own spirit and have seen nothing (v. 3) . . . who envision futility and who divine lies . . . (v. 9) and who "have seduced My people, saying, 'Peace!' when there is no peace." (v. 10). These words are very similar to God's statements about false prophets in Jeremiah (see number 17). But in Ezekiel a metaphor is added, comparing their false prophecy with a (poorly built) wall covered with untempered plaster, both of which will wash away in the coming storm (vv. 10b-16; cf. 22:28).

God, through Ezekiel, took particular notice of false prophetesses, "Who prophesy out of their own heart . . . who sew magic charms on their sleeves and make veils for the heads of people of every height to hunt souls" (vv. 17-18). The phrase "of every height" may mean that they corrupted even children. God promised to tear away the arm charms and veils from these prophetesses' victims and to set them free (vv. 20-21).

25. **Chaldeans** is one term, along with *astrologers, magi, sorcerers, soothsayers, and wise men,* that **Daniel** (and only Daniel) used to identify false prophets in Babylonia when he lived there in the sixth century BC (Dan. 2:2, 4, 5, 10, 13; 4:7; 5:11). Other Scriptures use the word Chaldean to refer to citizens of Chaldea, at that time equivalent to Babylonia (Ezek. 23:23; Is. 13:19). To confuse this matter slightly more, Daniel also sometimes used Chaldean as a nationality (Dan. 5:30; 9:1).

By whatever names, these Chaldeans/seers, whose principal gods were Bel and Marduk (Jer. 50:2; 51:44), found themselves in a tight spot when King Nebuchadnezzar demanded that they tell him not only the interpretation of his dream, but also its very content! The king promised them death if they failed and great rewards if they succeeded. When the Chaldeans tried to stall, Nebuchadnezzar saw through their tactic and began to execute them (Dan. 2:1-13).

We remember that God then revealed the dream *and* its interpretation through Daniel. What we may not remember is that Daniel and certain other young Jewish intellectuals had been placed under the tutelage of Chaldeans (wise men) and were considered part of their corpus (1:3-6; 2:18); that Daniel actually interceded for these false prophets and saved their lives (2:24) as well as the lives of his Jewish companions and himself; and that as a result of his prophecy (from God) about Nebuchadnezzar's dream, Daniel was made *chief* of the wise men—the magicians, astrologers, Chaldeans, and soothsayers! (2:48; 5:11). There can hardly be a greater irony about prophets in all of Scripture. Daniel, the man of God, became the chief administrator of a band of false prophets. Rather than executing them, as **Elijah** had righteously done to the false prophets of Baal three hundred years earlier (cf. number 10, this list), Daniel rescued and ruled them. We speculate that he neutralized their lies with God's truth, reeducated them, and—who knows?—may have converted some. Yes, it is widely believed that the wise men or magi from the East who came to worship the Child **Jesus** centuries later (Matt. 2:1-2) were the spiritual progeny of the wise men of Daniel's time. Daniel had predicted the coming Messiah (9:25). Were the magi who came to Jesus not only "wise" in science but also spiritually wise, thanks to Daniel's influence on their forefathers who were formerly false prophets?

NOTE: Other canonical prophets referred to false prophets in their books but without enough specificity to list them here as identifiable groups or individuals (Is. 2:6; 9:15; 30:9-10; 47:9-14 [Babylonian]; Hos. 9:7-8; Mic. 5:12; Zeph. 3:4; Zech. 10:2; Mal. 3:5). Isaiah 28:7 gives a special reason for some false prophecy: certain "prophets" were stinking drunk!

26. **Shemaiah II** (false) tried to deceive **Nehemiah**, a true prophet, into a position of cowardice and weakness about the rebuilding of Jerusalem's wall, by means of false prophecy (Neh. 6:10-13). Shemaiah, a Jew, was actually a spy for the Jews'

enemies who were trying to disrupt the wall project (Neh. 6:1-14). The year was 445 BC.

27. **Noadiah** was a false prophetess who tried to undermine the Jerusalem wall project, like Shemaiah II (false), number 26. From her name, which means "Jah (YHWH) assembles," it appears that she was a Jewess.

28. Other **Prophets of Fear** were in cahoots with Noadiah (number 27) and Shemaiah II (number 26) to make a coward of **Nehemiah** (Neh. 6:14). They all failed.

> NOTE: This completes the list of Old Testament false prophets. Before listing specific false prophets in the New Testament, some general remarks and teachings of **Jesus** and His apostles concerning false prophets will be summarized.
>
> Jesus solemnly warned His disciples about false prophets that would rise up during their ministries. There would be many. They would deceive many people, especially concerning the return of Christ. They would spread rumors. They would be able to show great signs and wonders in order to deceive even the elect, if they could (Matt. 7:15-23; 24:11, 23-26; Mark 13:22; Rev. 13:13). Since Christ has not yet returned, these warnings are still very much in effect. Jesus also spoke of Old Testament false prophets who received the praise of men, comparing them to the rich and comfortable of His own day (Luke 6:26).
>
> The apostles encountered false prophets just as Jesus had predicted. Many of them reiterated to the church Jesus's general warnings about false prophets. For example, **James III** called false prophecy "Wisdom" (that) "does not descend from above, but is earthly, sensual, demonic" (Jas. 3:15). **Peter** devoted a major part of his second epistle to false prophets (2 Pet. 2). He spoke of the former (Old Testament) false prophets and their present and future equivalents, false teachers who would deny even the Lord who bought them. These false prophets were in the visible church in the AD first century; and from their description it appears that they still plague the church. They are adulterous, covetous revelers who follow "the way of **Balaam**" (number 5 above), and whose doom is certain.
>
> The entire book of **Jude** is about apostates in the visible church who are very depraved and have become false teachers and prophets. Jude compares them with Balaam, Cain, and Korah (v. 11). He calls them

clouds without water, carried about by the winds; late autumn trees without fruit, twice dead, pulled up by the roots; raging waves of the sea, foaming up their own shame; wandering stars for whom is reserved the blackness of darkness forever. —12b-13

John II calls false prophets antichrists who deny that Jesus is the Christ (1 John 2:18-23; 4:1-6; 2 John 7-10). Many false prophets had, by the time John wrote these things,[10] gone out from the church into the world, spreading lies and deception.

Paul wrote of depraved men and women "who suppress the truth in unrighteousness" and who "professing to be wise, . . . became fools" (Rom. 1:18-22). He urged the church in Rome to

note those who cause divisions and offences, contrary to the doctrine which you learned, and avoid them. For those who are such do not serve our Lord Jesus Christ, but their own belly, and by smooth words and flattering speech deceive the hearts of the simple. —Rom. 16:17-18

To those in the church at Corinth, Paul marked out

those who desire an opportunity to be regarded just as we are in the things of which they boast. For such are false apostles, deceitful workers, transforming themselves into apostles of Christ. —2 Cor. 11:12b-13

Paul wrote to the Galatian church:

There are some who trouble you and want to pervert the gospel of Christ —Gal. 1:7

and

O foolish Galatians! Who has bewitched you . . .? —Gal. 3:1

Paul admonished Ephesian Christians to put on spiritual armor to stand against the wiles of the devil: among other things, "against spiritual hosts of wickedness in the heavenly places" (Eph. 6:11-12). Paul told the Philippian Christians to beware of dogs, evil workers, the mutilation (Philip. 3:2). He and **Timothy** warned the Christians in Colossae and Laodicea (Col. 2:1; 4:16) to

> beware lest anyone cheat you through philosophy and empty deceit, according to the tradition of men, according to the basic principles of the world, and not according to Christ. —Col. 2:8

Paul reminded the Thessalonian church that false prophets say, "Peace and safety," when in fact their own destruction is imminent (1 Thess. 5:3). Liars, false prophets, were telling these Christians that Christ had already returned (2 Thess. 2:1-12). But, Paul reminded them, much more had to happen first, including the coming of a lawless one,

> according to the working of Satan, with all power, signs, and lying wonders, and with all unrighteous deception among those who perish, because they did not receive the love of the truth, that they might be saved. —2 Thess. 2:9-10

All of these apostolic references to false prophets are general, even if they are addressed to a particular church. However, the false prophets Paul wrote about to **Titus** and **Timothy** were localized in Crete and Ephesus, respectively, so they will be listed as discrete groups: numbers 33 and 34 below.

The Listing of Identifiable False Prophets is Now Resumed

29. **Simon the Sorcerer** is the first false prophet named in the New Testament. It is interesting that no false prophets are named in any of the four Gospels.

For some time before we meet him in the early AD 30s, Simon had had a thriving sorcery business in the ancient city of Samaria.[11] (Acts 8:9-11). **Jesus** had ministered and stayed two days in nearby Sychar (John 4:1-43), but He did not encounter Simon then. That would come later, through several of Jesus's prophets and His Holy Spirit.

Simon was not an insignificant false prophet, nor a flash in the pan. He had duped the Samaritans for a long time and they thought his powers (actually magic arts) came from God. In fact, they said, "This man is the great power of God." But when **Philip** the deacon-turned-evangelist/prophet came to Samaria with the power of the gospel and real miracles to back up his message, the multitude quickly saw the difference, accepted Jesus as Lord and Savior, and were baptized (Acts 8:5-8, 12). Even Simon believed, was baptized, and joined Philip (Acts 8:13). But his was a rocky-ground (Luke 8:13) conversion. When the apostles **Peter** and **John II** came down from Jerusalem to check out the phenomenal work of Philip in Samaria, Simon tried to buy the Holy Spirit with money (Acts 8:18-19)—of which he must have had plenty from his former trade, sorcery. Not for sale! said Peter, who exposed Simon's still-wicked heart. Scripture leaves this false prophet afraid and begging for a reprieve but not necessarily repentant (Acts 8:20-24).

30. **Bar-Jesus** opposed **Paul** and **Barnabas** in about AD 46 on their first foreign mission trip out of Antioch, in the first country they visited, Cyprus (Acts 13:6-12). Bar-Jesus, a.k.a. Elymas, was a sorcerer or "wise man" who had managed to get on the staff or in the court of Cyprus's top official, procounsel Paulus. Bar-Jesus quickly recognized that his position was seriously threatened by the truth of the gospel, so he decided to directly oppose Paul and Barnabas in front of Paulus. Paul, full of the Holy Spirit, leveled Bar-Jesus with a scathing indictment of the false prophet and a sentence of temporary blindness, which commenced immediately. The Bible leaves

Drug-induced False Prophecy

The New Testament Greek words *pharmakos*, *pharmakeus*, and *pharmakeia* are translated "sorcerer(s)," "witchcraft," "magic," and "magic arts" in the English-language translations of the Bible that were consulted[12] (see Galatians 5:20; Revelation 9:21; 18:23; 21:8; and 22:15). These English words convey the idea of false prophecy. However, for some reason none of the translators chose to convey the obvious connection with drugs. *Pharmakeia* literally means "enchantment with drugs"[13] or simply "drugging."[14, 15]

Clearly, then, drugs were used by some biblical false prophets, at least in the New Testament—drugs either taken by them, or administered to their clients (victims), or both. We do not know what drugs were used. No specific individuals practicing drug-related false prophecy are identified. This practice is attributed to "Babylon the great" in Revelation 18:23 (cf. 17:3–5 and 18:2, 21). It may have been more widespread toward the end of the AD first century. Four of the five uses of the word *pharmakeia* are in the book of Revelation, probably written around AD 95; however, the other is in Galatians, written ca. AD 50. Drug-induced false prophecy is typically included in lists of heinous sins including murder, fornication, idolatry, stealing, and lying.

It should be noted that sorcery, witchcraft, magic arts, etc., are not necessarily pharmakeia (drug induced). In the KJV the Greek word *mageia* (magic) and its variants are translated *sorcery* and its variants four times—the same number of times *pharmakeia* is so translated.[16] Of course *mageia* *could* have been drug related. The Hebrew (Old Testament) words translated sorcery, witchcraft, etc., do not appear to have a drug connotation although this is not precluded.[17] Certainly false prophecy does not *require* the use of drugs. Drugs were used in some cases.

this second New Testament false prophet much like the first, Simon the Sorcerer—grasping and gasping.

31. **A Slave Girl** possessed with a spirit of divination bothered **Paul** and his mission team when they came to Philippi, Macedonia, in about AD 49 (Acts 16:16-19). It is noteworthy that the missionaries encountered a false prophet in the first location they visited in this new mission field, Europe—just as the first mission team encountered the false prophet Bar-Jesus in the first Asian place visited, Cyprus, and as **Philip** encountered the false prophet Simon in the first gospel sortie out of Jerusalem.

This slave girl, although she was indeed a false prophetess, elicits our sympathy. First, she was demon-possessed and could not help herself. Second, she was being shamelessly exploited by some men who made money from her divination, or fortune-telling. Third, she did prophesy the truth about the Christian missionaries, although it was of demonic origin and very irritating. After many days of putting up with her following the missionaries and mocking them with true words spoken in a false spirit, Paul cast the demon out of her. At the very least she was freed of the evil spirit that had possessed her; hopefully she also became a Christian. Her emancipation was costly; it caused Paul and Silas to be arrested, dreadfully beaten, and imprisoned (Acts 16:19-24).

32. **Many Ephesian Magicians** burned their sorcery books during a great revival when new believers confessed and renounced their past sins, including the practice of magic (Acts 19:19). This happened in about AD 55 during **Paul's** extended ministry in and around Ephesus (Acts 19:8-10).

33. **Cretan Deceivers** were active within the visible church in Crete in about AD 63 (Titus 1:10-16; 3:9-11). **Paul**, in a letter, urged **Titus** to confront and excommunicate (reject) them. They were both Jews and Gentiles. These detestable persons are not expressly called false prophets, but they had the earmarks. They professed to know God, but their actions denied Him. They taught fables, "commandments of men who turn from the truth," and impurity—all for the sake of dishonest gain. The only thing lacking is a statement that they called themselves prophets or claimed divine revelation of their teachings. But they must have at least implied such authority in order to oppose Paul, Titus, and the gospel.

In writing about the Cretan deceivers, Paul alludes to a former Cretan prophet (Titus 1:12). This was probably Epimenides, who had lived centuries earlier.[18] He is not listed as a true or false prophet in this book because he is not actually identified in the Bible; and based on Paul's reference alone, this Cretan prophet is impossible to classify or characterize.

The deceivers in the visible church of Crete emerged after the church was founded—an event not recorded in Scripture. Scholars postulate that Paul and

Titus started this church during a fourth Pauline missionary journey between AD 62 and 64. According to this scenario, Paul left Titus in Crete and wrote the letter Titus shortly thereafter.[19]

34. **Ephesian False Prophets** plagued the church at Ephesus when **Timothy** was bishop there during the AD 60s. **Paul** warned about them in both of his pastoral letters to Timothy, which were probably written several years apart (1 Tim. 1:7; 6:3-4; 2 Tim. 3:1-8). These Ephesian deceivers are called teachers, but *false prophets* is a perfectly apt term for them. They are compared with Jannes and Jambres (2 Tim. 3:8), false prophets who resisted **Moses** (numbers 3 and 4 in this list). They were channels of "deceiving spirits and doctrines of demons" (1 Tim. 4:1). They sought financial gain from their church affiliation (1 Tim. 6:5). They crept into households and made captives of gullible women loaded down with sins (2 Tim. 3:6). Paul told Timothy,

> Now the Spirit expressly says that in latter times[20] some will depart from the faith, giving heed to deceiving spirits and doctrines of demons, speaking lies in hypocrisy, having their own conscience seared with a hot iron, forbidding to marry, and commanding to abstain from foods which God created to be received with thanksgiving by those who believe and know the truth. —1 Tim. 4:1-3

They would subvert and obfuscate the truth, the gospel of **Jesus** Christ, with fables and endless genealogies (1 Tim. 1:4), arguments over words (1 Tim. 6:3-5; 2 Tim. 2:14), wranglings, and profane idle babble (2 Tim. 2:16). They were exceedingly vile men (2 Tim. 3:1-9). And they were in the visible church!

Three of these Ephesian false prophets, apostates from the Christian faith, are named and listed below as numbers 35, 36, and 37.

35. **Hymenaeus** was one of the Ephesian apostates who strayed from the truth, saying that the bodily resurrection of Christians was a thing of the past, thereby overthrowing the faith of some (2 Tim. 2:17-18). **Paul** had "delivered him over to Satan" (excommunicated him?) [1 Tim. 1:20] when he (Paul) was still at Ephesus, possibly on a third or fourth visit there in about AD 62.[21] But Hymenaeus was apparently back at it again, with another ally, when Paul wrote his second letter to **Timothy** several years later.[22]

36. **Alexander** was another Ephesian apostate who, like Hymenaeus (number 35 above), had been "delivered over to Satan" by **Paul** in about ad 62.[23] (1 Tim. 1:20) But several years later[24] he was still a threat to **Timothy** and the church at Ephesus (2 Tim. 4:14-15). Alexander was a coppersmith by trade, but he must have also had extraordinary powers of persuasion, for he did Paul much harm, and greatly resisted the gospel. For these reasons he is listed as a false prophet who

actively told falsehoods in the church, instead of just being a passive member who lost his faith.

37. **Philetus** was another apostate who upset the Ephesian church with profane and idle babblings that were spreading like cancer in the AD mid-60s.[25] He preached that the resurrection of Christians was over, thereby overthrowing the faith of some members of the church (2 Tim. 2:17-18). He is not mentioned in **Paul's** first letter to **Timothy**, but he was known to Paul as a ringleader of the false teachers at Ephesus. Therefore Philetus, like Hymenaeus and Alexander (numbers 35 and 36), must have been in that church when Paul was there in about AD 62.[26]

38. **Nicolaitans** were found in at least two churches in Asia Minor late in the AD first century. One church, at Ephesus, hated and rejected them; the other, at Pergamus, tolerated them (Rev. 2:6, 15). The risen **Jesus,** speaking through **John II**, hated their doctrines and deeds. We do not know the origin or the details of this false doctrine or prophecy. Presumably Nicolaitans were a sect within the visible church, founded or named after somebody named Nicholas or Nicolai, who would be a false prophet in this listing if we knew something about him. Many Bible expositors believe that the doctrines and deeds of Nicolaitans were similar to those of the Balaamites (see number 39 below), including fornication and idolatry.

39. **Balaamites** polluted the late first century church at Pergamos in Asia Minor. Our risen **Jesus**, speaking through **John II**, held it against that church that these ungodly people were tolerated. They may not have called themselves followers of Balaam, but Jesus did because they held Balaam's doctrines of sexual immorality and eating things sacrificed to idols (Rev. 2:14).

It is remarkable to see the name of Balaam, false prophet number 5 (q.v.), turn up in connection with the church of Jesus Christ some fourteen centuries after he lived.

Presumably there was at least one false prophet in the visible church in the late first century who preached Balaam's doctrines. He or she may have been the founder of the Nicolaitans (see number 38); and "those who follow the doctrine of Balaam" may have been the Nicolaitans.

40. **Jezebel** was a false prophetess who functioned in the church of Thyratira, Asia Minor, near the end of the AD first century. Her prophecy included sexual immorality (fornication) and eating things sacrificed to idols as an act of homage to, or affirmation of, those idols (Rev. 2:20-24). These are exactly the sins that **Jesus**, through **John II**, condemned in Pergamos, where He associated them with Balaam (see number 39). These parallel sins—idolatry is, after all, spiritual fornication—were a major problem for the church of Jesus Christ throughout the first century (Acts 15:20, 29; 1 Cor. 5:1; 8:4-7; 1 John 5:21).

Jezebel was a special case. Those who followed her knew "the depths of Satan." She had been rebuked and given time to repent by the Spirit of Jesus. Jezebel did not repent. She was therefore condemned to sickness, and her followers to great tribulation unless they repented. Her reprobate spiritual children would be found out and killed, to God's glory. We are not told the outcome of Jesus's warning. Hopefully many repented. Jezebel herself seems to have been incorrigible.

41. **The Beast from the Sea** probably stands for a political entity or a world system, but "he" is presented in the Bible as a person (Rev. 13:1-8) and therefore will be listed as a false prophet. He is given a mouth, "speaking (prophesying falsely) great things and blasphemies." His power and authority come from Satan, the devil. All the world marvel, follow this Beast, and worship him and Satan—all, that is, except the saints (believers, Christians) whose names are written in the book of Life of the Lamb, **Jesus**. But the Beast is permitted to make war against the saints and to overcome them for a limited time. In the end, this Beast is captured and thrown into the lake of fire, along with another false prophet, number 42 below (Rev. 19:19-20).

We do not know exactly who or what this Beast is, or his historical time. Perhaps he is a repeated historical phenomenon. Many eschatologists have come up with many theories.

42. **The Beast from the Earth**, like the Beast from the Sea, number 41 above, may symbolize a world power or system but will be treated here as a person, a false prophet (Rev. 13:11-18). This Beast is actually *called* a false prophet in Scripture (Rev. 19:20). He exercises all the authority of the first Beast and has the added dimension of being able to perform great signs including bringing fire down from heaven,[27] by which signs he deceives those who dwell on earth. He promotes the worship of the first Beast and sets up an image of him that could both speak and kill.

This is the Beast who puts his mark on the right hand or forehead of everyone but the elect—else they cannot buy or sell. And this Beast has a certain number, "the number of a man," 666.

People who worship this Beast/false prophet, or the image he sets up of the first Beast, or who receive the mark of the Beast on their foreheads or hands, are condemned by God to eternal torment (Rev. 14:9-11). Eventually both Beasts are captured and thrown into a lake of fire with brimstone (Rev. 19:19-20).

As in the case of the first Beast, we do not know exactly who or what the Beast from the Earth is, or the time of his influence of earth, or the time of his demise. We will leave this to the eschatologists.

Endnotes and References for Chapter 5

1. Paul sets the number at 23,000 (1 Corinthians 10:8). Calvin suggests that Paul wanted to err on the conservative side and rounded the exact number (if he knew it) down, to the nearest thousand. [John Calvin, *Commentary on the Epistles of Paul the Apostle to The Corinthians*, trans. Rev. John Pringle for the Calvin Translation Society, Edinburgh (repr. 2003, Grand Rapids, Baker Books), 324.]

2. Deuteronomy 4:3; Joshua 22:17; Psalm 106:28–29; Hosea 9:10; Micah 6:5

3. 1 Corinthians 10:8; 2 Peter 2:15; Jude 11; Revelation 2:14

4. Footnote on Revelation 2:14 found in New Geneva Study Bible (n.p.: Foundation for Reformation, 1995).

5. Eating such "spiritually contaminated" food was a great abomination to the Jews and to the early Christians, both Jews and Gentiles (Acts 15:29). Paul was somewhat ambivalent about it, but counseled Christians to abstain from such food for the sake of others' consciences (1 Cor. 8: 10:19-21).

6. Robert Young, *Analytical Concordance* (19th century; repr. Grand Rapids: Associated Authors and Publishers, n.d.), 744.

7. One theory is that Samuel was Saul's guilty conscience, or some kind of psychotic "voice." After all, Saul was mentally ill, "possessed of a distressing spirit" (1 Samuel 16:14–16).

8. Groves or bowers, or a female deity associated with Baal—probably the same as Ashtoreth; cf. Judges 2:13 with 3:7.

9. See Jeremiah 27:12; 28:1. The name Jehoiakim in 27:1 is likely a copyist's error; it is rendered Zedekiah in some ancient manuscripts.

10. John's first and second epistles were probably the last of all the New Testament epistles, written around AD 90–100.

11. Samaria had been the capital of idolatrous Israel eight centuries earlier and had already seen her share of false prophets (Jeremiah 23:13).

12. KJV, NKJV, NIV, RSV, ASV, NASB.

13. Robert Young, *Analytical Concordance* (19th century; repr., Grand Rapids: Associated Publishers and Authors, n.d.), 916.

14. Chandler, in a footnote in Calvin's commentary, suggests that *pharmakeia* means "poisonings" but goes on to describe this as a ritualistic use of "intoxicating draughts and ointments." [John Calvin, *Commentaries on Galatians and Ephesians*, trans. Wm. Pringle (repr., Grand Rapids: Baker Books, *Calvin's Commentaries* vol. XXI, 2003), 165].

15. C. H. Irwin, ed., *Irwin's Bible Commentary* (Philadelphia.: J. C. Winston, 1928), 512.

16. Young, *Analytical Concordance,* 916.

17. "Sorcery" and "witchcraft" in the Old Testament are usually translations of the Hebrew word *kashaph* and its variants. Perhaps this is fanciful, but it is observed that this word is phonetically similar to *hashish*, the strong hallucinogen produced in the Middle East.

18. *New Geneva Study Bible* (Nashville, TN: Thomas Nelson Publishers, 1995), footnote on Titus 1:12, page 1927.

19. Ibid., Introductions to 1 Timothy and to Titus, pages 1906, 1925.

20. Clearly Paul was saying to Timothy that *these* were the "latter times" and not speaking of some future age.

21. *New Geneva Study Bible*, Introductions to 1 Tim and to Titus pages 1906, 1925.

22. Ibid.

23. Ibid.

24. Ibid.

25. Ibid.

26. Ibid.

27. Neither the prophets of Baal, number 10, nor any other false prophet in Scripture except this one, could bring down fire. See Matthew 24:24.

Part III

Special Topics

Chapter 6

Musical Prophecy and Prophets

Introduction

Moreover David and the captains of the army separated for his service some of the sons of Asaph, of Heman, and of Jeduthun, who should prophesy with harps, stringed instruments, and cymbals . . . the sons of Asaph were under the direction of Asaph, who prophesied according to the order of the king . . . [and] . . six, under the direction of their father Jeduthun, who prophesied with a harp to give thanks and to praise the LORD. —1 Chr. 25:1-3

But be filled with the Spirit—let the word of Christ dwell in you richly in all wisdom, teaching and admonishing one another in psalms and hymns and spiritual songs, singing and making melody—with grace—in your hearts to the Lord. —Eph. 5:18-19/Col. 3:16, conflated

And it will happen, when you have come there to the city, that you will meet a group of prophets coming down from the high place with a stringed instrument, a tambourine, a flute, and a harp before them, and they will be prophesying. —1 Sam. 10:5

And [King Hezekiah] stationed the Levites in the house of the LORD with cymbals, with stringed instruments, and with harps, according to the commandment of David, of Gad the King's seer, and of Nathan the prophet; for thus was the commandment of the LORD by His prophets. —2 Chr. 29:25

And Elisha said, . . . "Now bring me a musician." Then it happened, when the musician played, that the hand of the LORD came upon him. And he [Elisha] said, "Thus says the LORD: . . ." —2 Ki. 3:14-16

Peter, in his famous sermon on that Pentecost morning, quoted music lyrics—Psalm 16—and specifically labeled it prophecy. —Acts 2:25-31

* * *

The above Scriptures clearly show that there is such a thing as musical prophecy. Even songs of praise and thanksgiving, when given by God for our use, are prophecy. (See chapter 1, reason number eight in the section "Why God Gives Prophecy.") When music is used in worship, distinctions between praise and other prophecy tend to blur: just observe the intermingling of the terms *prophesied*, *give thanks*, and *praise* in the first Scripture quotation above. All of the Psalms are, or were, set to music. Some are more distinctly Messianic and predictive, such as the one hundred tenth. Others are purely praise, such as the one hundred fiftieth. But both kinds were delivered by musicians who, according to the Bible, were "prophesying." And lest we miss this point, some of these musicians are unequivocally given the titles "prophet" and "seer" in the Bible (1 Chr. 25:5; 2 Chr. 29:30; 35:15; Matt. 13:35/ Psa. 78:2 and title).

Music Compared with Other Forms of Prophecy

True musical prophecy has the same purpose as true spoken or written prophecy: to proclaim or deliver a message from God. However, musical prophecy has some distinguishing characteristics. It is usually uplifting, with relatively few messages of indictment, judgment, punishment, or doom—such as are often found in written and spoken prophecy. As noted previously, Psalms as we now have them—the lyrics of musical prophecy—often blend praise, thanksgiving, predictive, and Messianic prophecy. The predictive passages are typically blessings or promises but are usually more general than the precise prognostications often found in spoken or written prophecies, such as victories or defeats in particular battles, or the fall or rise of particular kings or empires.

Also, musical prophecy requires formal training, rehearsal, and written or memorized messages (psalms). It is craft. Not that the writings of, say, Isaiah aren't carefully crafted, full of poetry and other language arts and skills. But we tend to think of prophets like Elijah and John, the baptizer, prophesying with extemporaneous verbal rebukes of reprobate kings or idolators. Psalms are not spontaneous although some are very pointed.

Another important distinction between musical prophecy and either spoken or written prophecy is that these latter are typically proclaimed by individuals whereas musical prophecy, while it may be humanly authored by an individual, is usually delivered by a group of prophets.

The Bible's Great Stores of Musical Prophecy

The Psalms as we have them in our Bibles are the lyrics of songs. These songs are prophecy, God's word; and many are predictive and/or Messianic (Luke 24:44; Acts 2:25-35; Matt. 13:35). For reasons known to God alone, we have in His holy writ these lyrics; a few obscure musical directions such as "sheminith," "maschil," and "selah;" the names of musical instruments; and some chorus personnel and directions—*but not one note of music itself!* One plausible explanation for this would be that, when the Psalms were written (mostly in the tenth century BC), there were no fixed melodies or musical scores; and that the music was mostly *ad lib.* Another would be that God does not want His people to become enamored with tunes and scores, idolizing the *medium* of prophecy while missing its meaning.

In any case the Book of Psalms is a tremendous repository of prophecy, originally given as music and often, after that music was lost, set to new melodies.

Musical prophecy in the Bible is not limited to the Psalms. The Song of Solomon, also known as Canticles and the Song of Songs, was obviously music, and is considered by many evangelicals to be a prophetic allegory of Christ and His church. One of the canonical (writing) prophets, Habakkuk, included musical directions with his oracle (3:1, 19). This prophet, who has been called the Father of the Protestant Reformation; who so profoundly influenced Paul, Luther, and Calvin; who wrote "The just shall live by his faith" (2:4; cf. Rom. 1:17)—this Habakkuk was a musical prophet! He even specified that his own musical instruments be used in the original presentation of his prophecy (1:19).

Most of the canonical prophets wrote largely in verse. These include Isaiah, Jeremiah, Hosea, Joel, Amos, Obadiah, Micah, Nahum, Zephaniah, Zechariah, and Malachi. At least some of their poetry may have originally been set to music.

In addition, the Bible is replete with short prophetic passages that are, or rather originally were, music. Examples are,

- "The Song of Moses" —Deut. 31:30-32:44
- Mary's "Magnificat" (called in many Bibles "The Song of Mary") —Luke 1:46-55
- The twenty-four elders' "New Song" —Rev. 5:9-10

The Levite Singers

Included in the list of named prophets in chapter 3 are Levites that David and his officers separated, or ordained, for the musical service of God (1 Chr. 25:1-7), both in the new tabernacle containing the ark of the covenant in Jerusalem (1 Chr. 16:4, 37), and in the Mosaic tabernacle at Gibeon (1 Chr. 16:39-42). Indeed, they could not be excluded from any comprehensive list of prophets of the Bible, in view of 1 Chronicles 25. Moreover, the three Levitical "fathers" of music—Asaph, Heman, and Jeduthun—are all titled "seers," without qualification, in Scripture (1 Chr. 25:5; 2 Chr. 29:30; 35:15). Perhaps not incidentally, Heman was the prophet Samuel's grandson.

By analogy, continuance, and some direct Scriptural evidence, the title and office *prophet* is also properly applied to subsequent (post-David) Levite musicians who were properly trained and ordained for the same tabernacle service (later, temple service). Also, the members of certain Levitic *ad hoc* choruses/orchestras that were assembled and consecrated to deliver psalm prophecy on very special occasions are considered prophets, for reasons that will be given when they are discussed.

We may think of a trained Levite choir as being relatively formal and stilted—and unprophetlike? However, this musical ministry did not lack excitement, surprise, drama, and even danger. At least one Levite choir/orchestra led Judah's army into battle, and as they prophesied musically, God caused the enemy army to self-destruct (2 Chr. 20:14-28). Another chorus was directly involved in a righteous but highly dangerous *coup d'etat*, risking their lives as they prophesied (2 Chr. 23:12-19). Several ordained Levite choruses prophesied at major historical events and celebrations. These included the transport of the ark of the covenant of God into Jerusalem, ca. 1000 BC (1 Chr. 15); the completion of the foundation of the postexilic temple, 530 BC (Ezra 3:8-11); and the completion of the rebuilt wall around Jerusalem, ca. 445 BC (Neh. 12:27-43). The greatest excitement and honor of any Levite choir, however, had to be in 958 BC when the glory of God filled the first temple as the musical prophets were playing and singing the Great Refrain,[1]

> *For He is good,*
> *For His mercy endures forever.*

Most of the Levite singers mentioned by name or group in the Bible were not important prophets like Samuel, David, or Isaiah. But then, neither are most of the nonmusical prophets that are mentioned in Scripture, such as the seventy elders of Israel in the wilderness who prophesied just once (Num. 11:16-25). God has His foot soldiers and chorus members as well as His generals and maestros of prophecy. All those who faithfully deliver His revealed word, even if only one time, whether they receive it directly from Him or from another prophet, do prophesy.

It must be noted that not all Israelitish religious music was true prophecy or even praise acceptable to God. Not all Levite musicians were prophets. When Israel had become corrupt, God, through His prophet Amos, said, "Take away from Me the noise of your songs, for I will not hear the melody of your stringed instruments" (5:23). This rebuke was spoken against the Northern Kingdom, which did not have the temple, the ark, nor the ordained Levite psalm prophets. However, many of the Levites associated with temple worship also went astray (Ezek. 44:10; 48:11). Among these were undoubtedly some of the singers.

The Historical Development of Musical Prophecy

Approximate dates, shown in brackets [ ], are BC *for Old Testament and* AD *for New.*

1. Beginnings

[3500] Music itself was originally "fathered" by Jubal, a descendent of Cain (Gen. 4:16-21), who, ironically, murdered the first prophet. Despite this ill-omened beginning, music was adopted and refined by God's chosen people to thank Him, to praise Him, and to prophesy His word both in the Old and New Testaments and continuing today. More than seventy of the named prophets in Scripture, and thousands more who are mentioned but not named, prophesied with music as their principal medium of communication. Others, not normally considered to be musical prophets *per se*, occasionally employed music to prophesy or to accompany prophecy. These include, for examples:

Miriam —Ex. 15:20-21
Deborah —Judg. 5
Elisha —2 Ki. 3:15
Moses —Deut. 31:30-32:44
Isaiah —Is. 5:1
Paul —Acts 16:25

The first musical *prophecy* mentioned in the Bible is attributed to Moses, followed immediately by his older sister Miriam (Ex. 15). The occasion was the Israelites' escape from Egypt by God's miracle at the Red Sea [1440]. Moses "sang this song," and Miriam sang and played the timbrel with a backup group of female dancers and timbrelists.

The next musical prophecy in the Bible involves another woman, the prophetess Deborah [1250]. The words of her singing duet with Barak are recorded in the book of Judges, chapter 5. Again, the occasion was a miraculous victory for Israel, this time over Jabin king of Canaan. Yet another woman, Hannah the mother of Samuel, may have been the third to prophesy musically [1100]. Her prayer, in verse (1 Sam. 2:1-10), may have been sung. It is often compared with Mary's similar song, the Magnificat (Luke 1:46-55).

By the time Samuel the prophet was ready to anoint Saul as the first king of Israel [1050], there were whole companies of musical prophets or music-aided prophets in the land of Israel (1 Sam. 10:5, 10). Flutes, tambourines, harps, and lyres were used as accompaniment. Scripture does not say it, but it seems likely that the prophets sang or chanted words to the music. Samuel himself is not said to have prophesied in music although that should not be ruled out. He clearly had more than a passing acquaintance with these groups of musical prophets and led one of them (1 Sam. 19:20). Samuel was the grandfather of Heman, one of the three fathers of formal music prophecy (1 Chr. 6:33).

Just a few decades later [1000] we see David organizing large numbers of musicians to prophesy at special occasions (1 Chr. 15:16-22) and, regularly, in formal tabernacle worship, especially in connection with the ark of the covenant of God (1 Chr. 6:31-48; chap. 25). Cymbals were added to the musical instruments listed above, harps and strings. Of course the primary instrument of musical prophecy was the human voice, and the Levites in this service were called singers, regardless of whether or not they played a musical instrument. Most of the Psalms (songs) in the Bible were written by David, Asaph, and other prophets at this time. The number of Levite music prophets quickly grew large. At the close of David's reign [970], there were four thousand of them who "praised the LORD with musical instruments" (1 Chr. 23:1-5).

2. The Enhancement of Worship with Musical Prophecy

It is hardly possible to overstate the importance of the changes in both worship and prophecy that God instituted, principally through David, in just a few years at the beginning of the tenth century BC. The centerpiece of these changes was musical prophecy.

From Moses to David, a period of about 440 years [1440-1000], the worship of God by the people of Israel was regulated according to His revelation through Moses. The externals of this worship consisted of animal sacrifices, grain offerings, libations, symbolic memorials and testimonials (lamps, incense, shewbread), cleansings, and intercession—all by priests; plus holy living, vows, tithes, and feasts by the people (Lev.; Heb. 9:1-10). *No* music is ordained in the Mosaic law![2]

But from David onward, for at least six hundred years [1000-400], proper worship services in God's house (tabernacle and temple alike) *necessarily* included music, and with it, prophecy. This permanent addition of "Davidic" worship to "Mosaic" worship is clearly stated in two passages:

> Also Jehoida appointed the oversight of the house of the LORD to the hand of the priests, the Levites, . . . to offer the burnt offerings of the LORD, as it is written in the Law of Moses, with rejoicing and singing, as it was established by David. —2 Chr. 23:18 [830]

> So the service was prepared, and the priests stood in their places, and the Levites in their divisions, according to the king's command. And they slaughtered the Passover offerings; . . . that they might give them to the divisions of the fathers' houses of the lay people, to offer to the LORD, as it is written in the Book of Moses. . . And the singers, the sons of Asaph, were in their places, according to the command of David, Asaph, Heman, and Jeduthun the king's seer. —2 Chr. 35:10-15 [620]

Other passages confirm that Davidic psalm prophecy remained an essential part of proper temple worship even after the return from Babylonian exile.

The most significant change in the service of worship, instituted in about 1000 BC, was not the addition of music. Rather, it was the addition of *audible, articulated prophecy* through the medium of music, specifically psalms. Priests did prophesy before, but not with words. It was only through symbolic actions, like Abel prophesying with animal sacrifices (Heb. 9; 11:4; 12:24). And the nonmusical prophets such as Samuel, Nathan, or Elijah did not prophesy (preach) in the tabernacle or temple as part of formal worship services. Cogent, lingual prophecy first came into the formal worship of God through music! For centuries, it remained the *only* articulated homily, exhortation, or praise in temple worship.

Davidic music prophecy brought into worship increased participation (by Levites appointed to this service) and new dimensions of joy, harmony, and praise.

3. From Solomon to the Captivity [970-586]

Solomon [970-930] continued the tradition of musical prophecy in worship as started by his father David. Solomon was himself a prolific musical prophet although he is better known for his wealth and wisdom. He wrote a thousand and five songs (1 Ki. 4:32). Not all were prophecy—that is, not all are included in Scripture. One of his songs, the Song of Songs, is considered by many Christians to be a prophetic allegory of Christ and His Church. He also wrote the seventy-second Psalm, which is a song of messianic prophecy.

Solomon continued the institution of prophecy choirs and orchestras as part of formal worship (2 Chr. 8:14). In fact, it was during his reign that the glory of God filled the temple when the music prophets sang and played while the priests blew trumpets (2 Chr. 5:11-13).

After Solomon, organized musical prophecy in the Jerusalem temple continued under some, but not all, kings of the Southern Kingdom, Judah. Kings Joash (really, his foster father Jehoida the priest) [836-796], Hezekiah [716-686], and Josiah [640-609], all great reformers, maintained or reestablished Levite choirs and orchestras to prophesy in the temple "according to David" (2 Chr. 23:18; 31:2; 35:15). Attempts at such prophesying in the Northern Kingdom, Israel, are only peripherally mentioned in Scripture, and that in a negative way (Amos 5:23).

During this Divided Kingdom Period, music was also being used outside of the temple by prophets such as Elisha [860] (2 Ki. 3:14-16). Prophets whose writings would become Scripture canon were arranging God's words for musical presentation (Is. 5:1 [740]; Hab. 3:19 [620]).

4. The Exile and Return [586-400]

Following the fall of Jerusalem and the destruction of the temple in 586 BC, some of the captured Levites in exile in Babylonia managed to maintain the art and legacy of musical prophesying as evidenced by the reappearance of this form of prophesying "according to David" after the return of many Jews to Judah/Jerusalem, see below. However, they were sometimes too sad to sing or even practice, and they "hung their harps in willow trees by the rivers of Babylon" (Ps. 137).

The first large company of Jews that returned from exile [537] included over one hundred singers, "sons of Asaph" (Ezra 2:41). They got their first chance to prophesy when the new temple's foundation was completed [536]:

> When the builders laid the foundation of the temple of the LORD, the priests stood in their apparel with trumpets, and the Levites, the sons of Asaph, with cymbals, to praise the LORD, according to the ordinance of David king of Israel. And they sang responsively, praising and giving thanks to the LORD:
>
> *For He is good, for His mercy endures forever toward Israel.*[1] —Ezra 3:10-11

In time—probably after the temple was completed twenty-two years later [514]—they formed choirs that "stood across" from each other, singing and prophesying antiphonally under the direction of Bakbukiah, Mattaniah, Unni, and their brethren (Neh. 12:8-9).

In the next century, to celebrate and dedicate the rebuilt wall around Jerusalem [440], Levite musicians came to Jerusalem from the surrounding villages that they had built for themselves (the city being too unprotected to live in until then). Nehemiah organized these Levites into two large choirs with Davidic instrumental accompaniment. They marched opposite ways upon the new wall and then joined forces in a great choir and orchestra under the direction of Jezrahiah (Neh. 12:27-42). We are not told what they sang, but surely it had to be psalm prophecy, very likely including the Great Refrain.[1] At least two of the Levite singers at that time were direct descendents of Asaph and Jeduthun, two of David's "fathers" of musical prophecy over 500 years earlier (Neh. 11:17).

It is very likely (but not explicitly stated in Scripture) that after the city wall was completed, Nehemiah appointed a regular temple chorus/orchestra according to the ordinance of David. Evidence for this is that the Levite singers, at least the "head" ones, were given lodging in chambers around the temple building, and portions of food, and they were free of other duties (Neh. 12:44-47). Such support had also been given under King Zerubbabel in the previous century (1 Chr. 9:33). Sadly, when Nehemiah left Judah and returned to Babylon, this support (and, probably, formal music prophecy itself) was neglected (Neh. 13:4-13). Nehemiah set affairs right again when he came back to Jerusalem for his second term as governor. We do not know what happened to temple-based, Davidic, music prophecy after this. It is not mentioned in the New Testament although the temple itself had been magnificently restored (John 2:20; Luke 21:5).

5. The New Testament Era [4BC-AD60]

The New Testament contains but a few references to musical prophecy or to music of any kind, but these few are significant. Mary may have actually sung her prophetic "Magnificat" (Luke 1:46-55 [4 BC]). Many Bible commentators and Bible "heading writers" indicate that she did. Angels—a multitude of them—prophesied to some shepherds of Jesus's birth (Luke 2:13-14). Although Scripture does not say so, our school plays and Christmas carols always have them singing.

Jesus and His remaining eleven disciples sang a hymn at the close of the Passover supper they shared (Matt. 26:30) just before His arrest and crucifixion. [30] It may have been Psalm 116. Jesus sang and still sings praise to God His Father in the midst of the assembly (Heb. 2:10-12; cf. Ps. 22:22).

Paul was a singer. He wrote, "I will sing with the spirit, and I will also sing with the understanding" (1 Cor. 14:15). Paul and Silas were apparently prophesying in song in the jail in Philippi: the other prisoners were listening to them, presumably not just to enjoy the tunes (Acts 16:25 [50]). Paul exhorted the Christians in churches in and around Ephesus and Colossae to "teach and admonish" and to "speak" to one another in psalms, hymns, and spiritual songs, singing and making melody with grace in their hearts (Eph. 5:18-19; Col. 3:16).

There is much music in heaven. We have already mentioned Christ singing praise to God in the midst of the assembly. There is other singing in heaven and also instrumental (harp) music (Rev. 14:2). In the book of Revelation, the chorus swells in number from twenty-eight (four living creatures and twenty-four elders, 5:8-10) to 144,000 (the redeemed first fruits to God and to the Lamb, 14:1-3) to all "those who have victory over the beast" (15:2-4).

We might think, at first, that this music is not prophecy, saying to ourselves, "What need is there of prophecy in heaven?" But these songs contain decidedly prophetic passages (see 5:10 and 15:4). The book of Revelation is after all, entirely prophecy (1:3): words from God to people living on earth, then and now. And inasmuch as all prophecy originates in heaven (from God), it is not surprising that musical prophecy is there.

List of Musical Prophets in the Bible: Named and Anonymous, Individuals and Groups (chronological order, alphabetical within group)

Headnotes for List (See also Headnotes for Chapter)

1. This is a list of named and anonymous prophets, both individuals and groups, who prophesied *principally* with music so far as we know, or who produced a major amount of musical prophecy in Scripture. Some prophets who used music only occasionally, such as Elisha and Paul, are not listed here.
2. Musical prophets and groups are listed in chronological order. Within a particular group, any named prophets are listed alphabetically.
3. Groups are numbered with roman, and individuals with arabic, numerals.
4. All the named musical prophets are also listed in chapter 3, generally with more detail there.
5. Only one group (group I) is also listed in chapter 4, part 2 (group 2 there), because it is not clear if their music was prophecy, or if they simply played musical instruments and also prophesied.
6. The criteria for inclusion in this list are,

    - persons known principally as musicians who are also called prophet, prophetess, or seer in the Bible, or who are said to prophesy with music
    - persons whose only known (recorded) prophecy was given musically, e.g., Mary
    - author of a Psalm or any other Scripture that was written to be presented musically
    - Levites in David's original tabernacle chorus/orchestra, according to 1 Chronicles 25, "who should prophesy with harps, strings, and cymbals."
    - Levites in later tabernacle or temple chorus/orchestras, properly trained and ordained "According to the commandment of David, of Gad the king's seer, and of Nathan the prophet; for thus was the commandment of the LORD by His prophets" (2 Chronicles 29:25).
    - other ad hoc Levitic musical groups that logically prophesied in Psalms and became part of a standing, ordained tabernacle or temple chorus/orchestra. This criterion includes the marching musicians who escorted the ark of the covenant of the LORD into its new tabernacle (1 Chronicles 15:16–29) and the two thanksgiving choirs that helped dedicate the rebuilt wall of Jerusalem (Nehemiah 12:31–42).

7. *Not* included in this list are the priests who blew trumpets. Most trumpeting was for mustering, alarming, directing, and rallying the people (see Numbers 10:1–10). There is no clear Scriptural indication that trumpeting was part of musical prophecy, although both were heard on some occasions.

Musical Prophets

1. **Moses** contributed a significant amount of the musical prophecy found in Scripture: Ex. 15:1-18; Deut. 32:1-47; Ps. 90. [ca.1440-1400]

2. **Miriam** was the first prophetess, and her only known prophecy was a song, Ex. 15:20-21. [ca.1440]

3. **Deborah** was a prophetess who judged Israel (Judg. 4:4). [1300's?] She wrote and/or sang, with Barak, a song prophecy of victory and praise (Judg. 5:1-35).

   {Barak is not listed because there is a lack of supporting evidence that he was a prophet although he did sing with Deborah.}

4. **Hannah** [ca. 1100], according to most Bible commentators, actually sang her beautiful prayer of praise-prophecy (1 Sam. 2:1-11), although Scripture only says that she "prayed and said" it. It was composed in verse. The prophecy itself is remarkably similar to Mary's "Magnificat" (Luke 1:46-55). We will side with the majority who say that both Hannah's and Mary's were musically rendered.

   Group I. [1050] A group of prophets, playing or possibly accompanied by others playing four musical instruments, met King-to-be Saul immediately after he was anointed by Samuel (1 Sam. 10:5-10). Saul was caught up into the Spirit and prophesied, but we do not list him as a musical prophet because Scripture is not clear that he was actually singing. Besides, he was such a prosaic character.

   Group II. [1003] An unspecified number of musicians, unnamed except for David, "played music before God . . . with singing," as they escorted the ark of the covenant of the LORD from Kirjath Jearim to the house of Obed-Edom (1 Chr. 13:5-8). This group is included in the list of musical prophesiers because it was led by David, the consummate musical prophet, and because it was the prototype or precursor to both Groups III and IV, the latter of which definitely prophesied with music. Some or all members of this group were very likely in groups III and/or IV.

5. **David** is discussed more fully in chapter 3. He was the foremost of all musical prophets. He wrote many psalms (songs), words of God that came to be prophesied by thousands of others. He introduced music, and prophesying, into the formal worship of God. He organized choir-orchestras (1 Chr.

25). He selected, and possibly invented or developed, musical instruments (Neh. 12:36). He performed (proclaimed), as well as composed, musical prophecy. The first recorded instance of David's music is when he played harp to smooth the distressed spirit of King Saul (1 Sam. 16:14-23); but his participation in Group II may be the first recorded instance of his *prophesying* musically.

Group III. [1003] A marching musical group very similar to Group II, and probably including many of the same personnel, escorted the ark of the covenant of the LORD from the house of Obed-Edom (see Group II) to the new tabernacle prepared for it by David in Jerusalem (1 Chr. 15:16-24). Three of the leaders of this group, and probably most of the rest, were likely members of the permanent tabernacle choir (Group IV), "who should prophesy" (1 Chr. 25:1). Thus, the named members of Group III are all listed below as prophets, numbers 6-23. Priests who only blew trumpets are not listed. Most of the "second rank" (after the four leaders) are listed as gatekeepers first (verse 18), then musicians (verses 20–21).

6. **Asaph** was one of the three principal singers in Group III (v. 17) and a cymbalist (v. 19). He went on to become the chief musical prophet over that portion of the permanent Levite choir that ministered in Jerusalem before the ark of the covenant (1 Chr. 16:4-5, 37; 25:1-7). Asaph was the author-prophet of a significant portion of God's written word (Ps. 50, 73-83). More in chapter 3.

7. **Azaziah** (v. 20) was a harpist in Group III. He is the only "second-rank" musician who was not also a gatekeeper.

{Aziel—Jaaziel} (number 13)

8. **Benaiah** was a string player in Group III (v. 20). He was also a priest who blew the trumpet (v. 24). He became a tabernacle music prophet serving under Asaph before the ark of the LORD in Jerusalem (1 Chr. 16:4-6; 25:1-7).

9. **Chenaniah** (v. 22) was a skillful music-master and instructor of Group III. Thus he was "over" (musically) the all-time greats of musical prophecy: David, Asaph, Heman, and Jeduthun. But he is conspicuously absent from the permanent tabernacle prophesiers, Group IV. A plausible explanation for this is given under his name in chapter 3.

{David (number 5) was also a member of Group III. It got him into "hot water" with his wife. (1 Chr. 15:29)}

10. **Eliab** (v. 20) was a string player in Group III. He went on to a career in musical prophecy serving under Asaph in Jerusalem before the ark (1 Chr. 16:4-5; 25:1-7).

11. **Elipheleh** (v. 20) was a harpist in Group III.

{Ethan—Jeduthun} (number 14)

12. **Heman** was one of the three principal singers in Group III (v. 17). He also played the cymbals (v. 19). Heman went on to become one of the three patriarchs of musical prophecy (1 Chr. 25:1-7), ministering in Gibeon before the Mosaic altar and tabernacle (1 Chr. 16:39-42). More on Heman is given in chapter 3.

13. **Jaaziel**, a.k.a. Aziel (v. 20), was a string player in Group III.

14. **Jeduthun** (a.k.a Ethan) was one of the three principal singers in Group III (v. 17) and played the cymbals (v. 20). He went on to become one of the three chief musical prophets under King David (1 Chr. 25:1-7), ministering along with Heman at the Mosaic altar and tabernacle in Gibeon (1 Chr. 16:39-42). Jeduthun also held the position of choir director or chief musician (titles of Ps. 39, 62, 77). More is given in chapter 3.

15. **Jehiel I** (v. 20) was a string player in Group III. He went on to be a tabernacle music prophet (1 Chr. 25:1-7), serving under Asaph before the ark of the LORD in Jerusalem (1 Chr. 16:4-5).

16. **Jeiel** (v. 20) was a harpist in Group III. Later, he was a musical prophet under Asaph ministering with that segment of the 288 tabernacle singers (1 Chr. 25) assigned to the ark of the covenant of the LORD in its new tabernacle in Jerusalem (1 Chr. 16:4-5). There, he led with both stringed instruments and harps.

{Kenaniah—**Chenaniah**} (number 9)

17. **Maaseiah I** (v. 20) was a string player in Group III.

18. **Mattithiah I** (v. 20) was a harpist in Group III. He went on to be a tabernacle music prophet (1 Chr. 25), ministering under Asaph before the ark of the LORD in Jerusalem (1 Chr. 16:4-5).

19. **Mikneiah** (v. 20) was a harpist in Group III.

20. **Obed-Edom** (v. 20) was a harpist in Group III. After the ark of the covenant of the LORD was installed in its new "house" (tabernacle) in Jerusalem, Obed-Edom stayed there to minister in music under the leadership of Asaph (1 Chr. 16:4-5). It is assumed that these musicians were part of the 288 who were trained and ordained to prophesy in song (1 Chr. 25). Obed-Edom was also a doorkeeper for the ark (v. 24).

21. **Shimiramoth** (v. 20) was a string player in Group III. He was one of those who stayed in Jerusalem to minister before the ark of the LORD, under the direction of Asaph (1 Chr. 16:4-5). This group was evidently part of group IV, 288 musicians who were "separated" and trained to prophesy in song (1 Chr. 25).

22. **Unni I** (v. 20) was a string player in Group III.

23. **Zechariah I** was a string player in Group III (v. 20) and also a priest who blew the trumpet before the ark of God during that procession (v. 24). He stayed in Jerusalem to become a music prophet ministering before the ark, under Asaph's leadership (1 Chr. 16:4-5). These regular tabernacle musicians were appointed and trained to prophesy (1 Chr. 25:1-7).

NOTE: As indicated in some of the write-ups above, the groups of music prophets that ministered at the two tabernacles during David's reign—one in Jerusalem, one in Gibeon (1 Chronicles 16:1–5, 37–42)—are assumed to be part and parcel of the 288 musicians "who should prophesy . . . in the house of the LORD . . . in the songs of the LORD . . ." (1 Chronicles 25:1, 6–7). Thus, separate groups are not listed; they are all Group IV.

Group IV. [1000] A group of 288 or 291 Levites (depending on how the three fathers are counted) was consecrated for the service of musical prophecy in the houses (tents, tabernacles) of God by David and his officers (1 Chr. 25; 6:31-47). Twenty-seven are named in 1 Chronicles 25: three fathers and their twenty-four sons. Each family represented one branch or son of Levi: Gershon, Kohath, and Merari. Each of the sons of Asaph, Heman, and Jeduthun was selected by lot to lead a section of twelve musicians. These may have been twenty-four "independent" ensembles that took turns in tabernacle service; or they may have all prophesied together as one grand chorus/orchestra, at least on certain occasions. We know that initially they were divided into two main branches: one under Asaph, at the new tabernacle in Jerusalem (1 Chr. 16:4-5); the other under Heman and Jeduthun, at the old (Mosaic) tabernacle in Gibeon (1 Chr. 16:39-42).

The twenty-four sons were not selected for their musical abilities. However, they were prophets. Some of the better musicians in this group were named in Group III (q.v.). All 288 of them were "instructed in the songs of the LORD"—probably psalms written by David, Asaph, and others. The sons are listed alphabetically below as musical prophet numbers 24-47. They are identified by their father's initial (*A*-saph, *H*-eman, *J*-eduthun) and by their assigned section number.

		father	section
24.	**Asharelah**	A	7
	{Azarel—Uzziel I} (no. 45)		
25.	**Bukkiah**	H	6
26.	**Eliathah**	H	20
27.	**Gedeliah**	J	2
28.	**Giddalti**	H	22
29.	**Hanani I**	H	18
30.	**Hananiah I**	H	16
31.	**Hashabiah I**	J	12
32.	**Hothir**	H	21
	{Jeremoth—Jerimoth} (no. 33)		
33.	**Jerimoth**	H	15
34.	**Jeshaiah**	J	8
	{Jesharelah—Asharelah} (no. 24)		
	{Jizri—Zeri} (no. 47)		
35.	**Joseph II**	A	1
36.	**Joshbekashah**	H	17
37.	**Mahazioth**	H	23

38.	**Mallothi**	H	19
39.	**Mattaniah I**	H	9
40.	**Mattithiah II**[3]	J	14
41.	**Nethaniah**	A	5
42.	**Romanti-Ezer**	H	24
43.	**Shebuel**	H	13
44.	**Shimei I**	J	10
	{Shubael—Shebuel} (no. 43)		
45.	**Uzziel I**	H	11
46.	**Zaccur**	A	3
47.	**Zeri**	J	4

Group V. [970] There were four thousand (!) Levite musicians in praise service near the end of David's reign (1 Chr. 23:5). This could hardly have been a single chorus/orchestra, and it must have included Group IV as then constituted. There is no basis for calling them all prophets; but on the other hand, many probably were, as they sang and played God's word in psalms of praise. Thus, having no other information, the prophets among them (*up to* four thousand) are designated a musical prophecy group, however they were deployed.

48. **Solomon** [970-930] was a great and prolific prophet (see chapter 3). Much of his written prophecy was, originally, music (Song of Solomon; Ps. 72, 127). He wrote 1,005 songs (1 Ki. 4:32), but other than those just cited, they are not in the Bible and cannot be considered prophecy.

Group VI. [960] The Levite tabernacle singers. This was Group IV in structure, but with all the personnel changes made over three or four decades. They prophesied at the installation of the ark of the covenant of the LORD into the first temple during Solomon's reign (2 Chr. 5:11-14; 7:6). This was a large choir, quite possibly the exact "Davidic" 288 in number (see Group IV). It may have included some of the charter members of Group IV. The new temple superseded and combined the functions of both tabernacles (see

(continued on page 270)

The Great Refrain

There is one particular song, or verse, of musical praise-prophecy that had truly astounding effects when sung by Levite choirs and played by Levite orchestras on certain special occasions. On one of these occasions, the holy, only, God of the Universe came among men in visible, palpable glory as the refrain was sung:

Oh give thanks to the LORD,
For He is good!
For His mercy endures forever.

This "Great Refrain" has had a close association with the ark of the covenant of the LORD, with His temples and tabernacles (houses), and with His indwelling there. There are minor variations in the words of the Great Refrain in the several Scripture passages where it appears, but the last line is always the same: *"For His mercy endures forever."*

The Great Refrain apparently originated with David, in a psalm he composed expressly for the installation of the ark into a tabernacle prepared for it in his new capital, Jerusalem (1 Chronicles 16:8–36). The ark had been captured by the Philistines (1 Samuel 4), became a curse to them (1 Samuel 5), was returned to Israel (1 Samuel 6) and stayed at the town of Kirjathjearim for a long time until David reclaimed it for the tabernacle (1 Samuel 7:1–2; 1 Chronicles 13, 15). This psalm was delivered by David to Asaph and his brethren, to be sung by them with full orchestral accompaniment (1 Chronicles 16:4–7). The Great Refrain itself is verse 34. When the song was sung, *all* the people said "Amen!" and praised God (v. 36).

After this, David left some of the musical prophets under the direction of Asaph to minister regularly before the ark in Jerusalem (1 Chronicles 16:37) and dispatched others, under Heman and Jeduthun, to minister musically at Gibeon, several miles away, at the original Mosaic altar and tabernacle (vv. 39-42; cf 1 Chronicles 21:29). The ministry of this latter group is expressly described in terms of their presenting the Great Refrain: *"To give thanks to the LORD, because His mercy endures forever".*

The Great Refrain is repeated in each of these Psalms: chapter 106, verse 1; 107, verse 1; 118, verses 1 and 29; 136, verses 1 and 26; and, in modified form, 100, verses 4c–5. The last line of the Refrain, *"For His mercy endures forever,"* is repeated five times in Psalm 118 and twenty-six times in Psalm 136.

But its repetition in psalms is not what makes this refrain stand out from other oft-repeated phrases or refrains in Scripture. Rather, it is because, when the Great Refrain was sung and played at the installation of the ark in the first and greatest temple of the LORD, God Himself came down, filling the temple with His glory so visibly and palpably that the very priests had to leave! (2 Chronicles 5:11–14). Now, finally, the ark and the altar were together again in one house—God's house. Now there was one choir and one orchestra joined by 120 priests sounding trumpets. What a sound they must have made! What power! What beauty! No choir, no organ, no orchestra in any cathedral, abbey, or church in Christendom, grand as they may be, ever resounded with music quite like this. For God Himself came to the concert. It was a full house—full of God's glory. What an invocation!

Then King Solomon spoke. He addressed God. He blessed and spoke to the people. He prayed (2 Chronicles 6). God responded again, this time with fire from heaven, and He once more filled the temple with His own glory (2 Chronicles 7:1–2). Then *all* the people took up the Great Refrain, worshipping and praising God with

> *For He is good,*
> *For His mercy endures forever.*

And the Levite singers came back with a reprise,

> *For His mercy endures forever* (2 Chronicles 7:3–6)

Israel never forgot this momentous occasion, nor the music that was such a key part of it.

Once, it was sung by a choir *leading* an army of Judah into battle. The enemy was routed (actually, they self-destructed) *"When they began to sing and to praise . . . saying . . . 'Praise the LORD, For His mercy endures forever'"* (2 Chronicles 20:20–23).

Many years later, after the Northern Kingdom (Israel) had long since been destroyed and the Southern Kingdom (Judah) was in the process of being annihilated by Babylon's army—when the very temple that God had filled with His glory was being destroyed—then the prophet Jeremiah brought this promise of God to His people:

Thus says the LORD: "Again there shall be heard in this place—of which you say, 'It is desolate, without man and without beast'—in the cities of Judah, in the streets of Jerusalem that are desolate, without man and without inhabitant and without beast, the voice of joy and the voice of gladness, the voice of the bridegroom and the voice of the bride, the voice of those who will say:

> *Praise the LORD of hosts,*
> *For the LORD is good,*
> *For His mercy endures forever—*

and of those who will bring the sacrifices of praise into the house of the LORD. For I will cause the captives of the land to return as at the first," says the LORD (Jeremiah 33:10–11).

And was this prophecy fulfilled? Oh yes!—just about fifty years after it was given. For Ezra tells us exactly what a *new* Levite choir and orchestra sang and played, with priests on trumpets again, at the completion of the foundation of the new temple building:

> *For He is good,*
> *For His mercy endures forever toward Israel.*

"Then *all* the people shouted with a great shout, when they praised the LORD," and there was also loud weeping, "And the sound (shouting and weeping) was heard afar off" (Ezra 3:10–13).

We are not told of the singing of the Great Refrain again, not even when the new temple was completed and dedicated about twenty years later (Ezra 6:15–18). Surely they did sing it and play it with all their might. But there was no ark in this temple (it was lost), and God did not fill this house with His own glory, or we would surely have been told of it in His word of Scripture. Nevertheless, *all* of Israel "celebrated the dedication of this house of God with joy" (Ezra 6:16).

What is it about the Great Refrain that made it so special? Certainly the words are very lofty and full of truth and meaning, but are they more so than, for example, the Shema (Deuteronomy 6:4)? Was it the music? Like the ark with which it was so closely identified, the music is lost. We can only imagine what it must have sounded like, to be the words and music of worship that God deigned to honor with His own tangible glory.

Is it all irretrievably lost in the labyrinth of history, then? Just an interesting footnote? NO! For we can still worship, prophesy, and proclaim,

> *Oh give thanks to the Lord Jesus,*
> *For He alone is good among men,*
> *For His mercy and His lovingkindness endure forever.*

We can invite and welcome His Holy Spirit into our bodily temples. And we can sense Him there, palpably, even as those Israelites saw and felt God's presence in the temple as the Great Refrain was sung three millennia ago. Let *all* His people shout with joy. Amen!

note on page 264), so all the singers would have been combined. For reasons already given, the 120 priest trumpeters are not considered musical prophets; but the number of them is another indication that the chorus of singers and instrumentalists was a large one.

This chorus had the signal honor and the unforgettable experience of being, along with the trumpeters, the immediate agency of a rare theophany. God's glory filled the temple as they sang the Great Refrain,[1]

> For He is good,
> For His mercy endures forever.

This refrain was picked up by all the people after Solomon prayed and the theophany was repeated, this time with fire from heaven.

Group VII. [970-940] A regular Davidic (per Group IV) praise-prophecy chorus was maintained by Solomon, probably through most or all of his reign (2 Chr. 8:14). Naturally, there would have been many personnel changes over these three or four decades. This Group (VII) stands for those members who were not in the other Groups (IV, V, and VI) already listed.

HISTORICAL NOTE. Toward the end of Solomon's reign, say, about 940 BC, Israel began a spiritual, moral, and political downslide that continued well into the histories of both kingdoms after their division into Judah and Israel. Formal praise-prophecy, *a`la* Groups IV, VI, and VII, also went into decline. In the northern kingdom of Israel, a totally false religion was established, so we can all but eliminate any possibility of ordained true musical prophecy choirs there. But the temple was in Jerusalem, Judah—where it is reasonable to assume that the priests and Levites, or some of them, continued Mosaic and Davidic worship as best they could in spite of the apostasy of their first two kings, Rehoboam [930–913] and Abijah [913–910]. But no musical prophets or groups are mentioned in Scripture during this time, nor even during the reign of King Asa [910–869], under whom there was a great reformation. Doubtless, musical prophecy was given and heard, but the next recorded instance of it (Group VIII) occurred nearly a century after Solomon.

Group VIII. [860] During the reign of Jehoshaphat, fourth monarch of Judah, about a century after Solomon, a large group of singer prophets (quite possibly a regular Davidic temple choir) took to the field and actually led the Judean army to victory over an alliance of hostile armies (2 Chr. 20:14-28). They approached the enemy "before the army"; and as they began to sing

> *Praise the LORD,*
> *For His mercy endures forever*[1]

God caused the enemy forces to turn on each other and self-destruct. The battalion of music prophets returned to Jerusalem and to the temple rejoicing "with stringed instruments and harps and trumpets."

49. **Jahaziel** was the verbal prophet connected with the miracle of musical battle-victory (q.v. Group VIII). Because he was "a Levite of the sons of Asaph" (2 Chr. 20:14) it seems probable that he was a member of the choir, possibly even its leader, and therefore a musical as well as a verbal prophet.

Group IX. [835] "The singers with musical instruments, and those who led in praise" took part in a very dangerous *coup d'etat* (2 Chr. 23) that was masterminded by Jehoida to restore the rightful heir to Judah's throne (Joash, his seven-year-old foster son), over usurper Queen Athaliah. Athaliah, the daughter of Israel's wicked Ahab and Jezebel, was a blatant idolator, a Baal worshipper, and she had murdered all the other royal heirs, descendents of David. At the moment of confrontation, Athaliah, hearing shouts of rejoicing, came into the temple of the LORD (probably an unfamiliar place to her) where she saw the (supposedly dead) boy king standing, and "All the people . . . rejoicing and blowing trumpets, also the singers with musical instruments, and those who led in praise" (v. 13). These last two categories were probably ordained temple prophet musicians as originally established by David (1 Chr. 25), and apparently had been maintained, at least at some level, through thirteen long years of very wicked monarchs in Judah.

Group X. [835-?] A regular and ongoing choir of Levite temple prophesiers "as it was established by David" was reestablished by Jehoida the priest, the *de facto* king of Judah (guardian and foster father of the boy king Joash) after the successful *coup d'etat* described under Group IX (2 Chr. 23:18). Apparently the temple choir had been in some way reduced or compromised although enough of them (Group IX) remained to participate in the *coup*. The proper number was 288, and all had to be ordained (set aside) and trained in the songs of the LORD (Psalms), to correspond exactly to David's original, Group IV (1 Chr. 25). Group X comprises all the members of this choir, including personnel changes, as long as it continued to proclaim true prophecy.

HISTORICAL NOTE. At some time before King Hezekiah reestablished it in about 715 BC, true musical prophecy in the temple ceased. This lasted for several decades, perhaps half a century, until Hezekiah (see Group XI). Still, there was a faithful remnant of musical prophets, a seed: for Hezekiah started with six "sons" of Asaph, Heman, and Jeduthun.

Group XI. [715] Reformer-King Hezekiah of Judah ordered the priests and other Levites to clean, repair, and sanctify the long-neglected temple (2 Chr. 29:3-19). Included in this clean-up (sanctification) crew were certain descendents of Asaph, Heman, and Jeduthun, the "fathers" of musical prophecy (v. 13; cf. 1 Chr. 6:31-47). Then the priests offered many bulls, rams, lambs, and goats on the altar of sacrifice to make atonement for the sins of Judah and of all Israel. During this entire ceremony a group of Levites sang and played Davidic instruments "according to the command of David, of Gad the king's seer, and of Nathan the prophet; for thus was the commandment of the LORD by His prophets" (2 Chr. 29:25-30). This was nothing less than a revival of musical prophecy, not just pretty music. "King Hezekiah and the leaders commanded the Levites to sing praise to the LORD with *the words of David and of Asaph the seer"*—words of God, prophecy.

This choir was probably led by, or at least included, those Levites named in verse 13 as descendents of great singer-prophets, namely,

50. **Jehiel II**, a descendent of Heman and Samuel

51. **Mattaniah II**, a descendent of Asaph

52. **Shemaiah II**, a descendent of Jeduthun (Ethan)

53. **Shimei II**, a descendent of Heman and Samuel

54. **Uzziel II**, a descendent of Jeduthun (Ethan)

55. **Zechariah III**, a descendent of Asaph

Group XII. [714(?)-680's] A formal Levitic temple choir was reestablished by King Hezekiah after the celebration and rededication of the temple (2 Chr. 31:2). No details are given about this choir, this passage being concerned with their means of support, not their duties or membership. However, judging from Hezekiah's earlier insistence on Levite musicians and the Psalms of David and Asaph (see Group XI), this regular ongoing temple chorus/orchestra was likely patterned after David's original (Group IV), and, therefore, prophesied. Their number may even have been the original 288. Most of Group XI, including those named, were probably involved in this ongoing ministry. It seems unlikely that this choir survived very long into the reign of Manassah [697/686[4]–642], a very wicked man who did his best to undo all his father's reforms.

NOTE. The next and final great reformer king of Judah was Josiah. He ordered certain Levites who "were skillful with instruments of music" to help supervise the physical repair of the temple, putting them specifically over burden bearers and all who did any kind of service work (2 Chr. 34:12-13). This assignment may have been to ensure that the musicians would have proper facilities in the temple. There is no indication that these foremen prophesied during the repair phase.

Group XIII. (2 Chr. 35:15) [622] King Josiah appointed the last group of Davidic musicians known to have prophesied in the original (Solomonic) temple, though not the last of all such groups. Again we may speculate that there were twenty-four sections of twelve men each—288 total—because they were constituted "according to the command of David, Asaph, Heman, and Jeduthun the king's seer", a direct reference to 1 Chr. 25. Of more importance than their number, however, this reference to David et al. means that they *prophesied* the words of God in Psalms. They were initially appointed for the Passover feast in the eighteenth year of Josiah's reign, but they likely continued for some years. After Josiah's death "all the singing men and the singing women" (obviously *not* referring to a Levitic temple choir, which included no women) "speak of Josiah in their lamentations" (2 Chr. 35:25).

56. **Habakkuk** wrote all or part of his biblical book of prophecy as music (Hab. 3:19, ending instruction). [620]

Group XIV. [537] After the captivity and Babylonian exile of the Jews (Judah), the first large group that returned to their homeland with Zerubbabel the king and Jeshua (Joshua) the priest included a number—either 128 or 148—of Levite singers, "sons of Asaph" (Ezra 2:41; Neh. 7:44; 12:1a, 8-9). These were led by:

57. **Bakbukiah I** (Neh. 12:9);

58. **Mattaniah III** (Neh. 12:8); and

59. **Unni I** (Neh. 12:9)—All of whom organized choirs that stood across from one another to sing antiphonally. We know that they prophesied, at least on one occasion, when they celebrated the laying of the foundation of the new temple of God by singing, responsively, with cymbals, and according to the ordinance of David,

> *For He is good,*
> *For His mercy endures forever to Israel*' —Ezra 3:10-11

NOTES: Accompanying the 42,360 Jews who returned to their homeland in 537 BC were 7,337 servants, including 200 (or 245) men and women singers (Ezra 2:65; Neh. 7:67). Because they were not "sons of Asaph" or Levites, and probably not Jews, it seems unlikely that they participated in the psalm-prophecy choirs, so they are not included in this list of musical prophets.

Also, when the new temple was finished in 515 BC, Levites were assigned to their duties "as it is written in the Book of Moses" (Ezra 6:18). Mosaic worship did not include singing or prophecy. There is no mention of the ordinances of David, or of singers. It appears that no "permanent" Levitic praise-prophecy choir was installed at this time. Such singers were still relatively scarce—there was only about half of a full Davidic music force of 288.

60. **Hashabiah II**;

61. **Jeshua;** and

62. **Sherebiah** were ordained Levite music prophets who led "their brothers across from them, to praise and give thanks, group alternating with group, according to the command of David the man of God" (Neh. 12:24). [date uncertain; see Group XV]

Group XV. The tripartite chorus led by the above three music prophets (Neh. 12:24) corresponded to the Davidic original, Group IV, which was also led by three masters of music and was specifically appointed to prophesy (1 Chr. 25:1-7). As an additional indication that these postexilic singers were prophets, David is referenced not as "the king," but as "the man of God," his prophetic title.

The date of this group is uncertain. It could have been "during the reign of Darius the Persian" (Neh. 12: 22)—either Darius II [423–404] or Darius III [336–331], but these seem late. It could have been in the days of Nehemiah and Ezra (verse 26b) [458–430]. However, during their days, other music leaders were named (see musical prophets numbered 63–76). It seems more likely that this particular group was formed in the days of the high priest Joiakim, son of Jeshua (verse 26a)—a generation after the first large influx of emigres. [500?]

HISTORICAL NOTE. [458] Eighty years after the first large group of 42,360 Jews returned from Babylonia and sixty years after the temple was rebuilt, Ezra led another smaller group of about 1,750 back to their homeland (Ezra 7:8; 8:15-20). Originally there were no Levites in the group, so Ezra recruited thirty-eight of them and two hundred of their servants, from a place called Casiphia. Obviously there were few if any singers among them. But Levite singers had come to Judah, trickling in and dispersing themselves in the small villages, as we shall presently see.

Nehemiah came shortly after Ezra, specifically to rebuild the wall around Jerusalem. This project was completed in just fifty-two (!) days (Neh. 6:15), but the city lacked population (Neh. 7:4). Most of the Jews had settled in small towns and villages, which they built for themselves, rather than in the unwalled city of Jerusalem. To repopulate the city, ten percent of the people volunteered or were selected by lot to move in from the countryside (Neh. 11:1-2). Among those who moved into Jerusalem [after 445] were four notable Levitic musicians, namely,

63. **Abda** (Neh. 11:17), a direct descendent of Jeduthun; a.k.a. Obadiah in 1 Chronicles 9:16;

64. **Bakbukiah II**, a direct descendent of Asaph (Neh. 11:17);

65. **Mattaniah IV** (Neh 11:17), a direct descendent of Asaph, and

66. **Uzzi**, a direct descendent of Asaph (Neh. 11:22).

These four are listed as *prophet* musicians, not just because of their genealogies, but also because they were very likely to become members or leaders of the praise-prophecy choruses (groups XVI and XVII) that Nehemiah ordained "according to the command of David and Solomon his son" (i.e., patterned after group IV). In fact, Uzzi is listed as a leader in group XVI (Neh. 12: 42-46).

Group XVI. [445] Two large thanksgiving choirs were appointed by Nehemiah for the dedication of the new wall around Jerusalem (Neh. 12:31). They are listed here as one group because they were parts of the same ceremony and were combined when they got to the temple. They are considered prophets because

- all were Levites (1 Chr. 25:1 ff.)
- they used "the musical instruments of David the man of God" (Neh. 12:36). Two points here: (1) form—the correct instruments; (2) substance—David is referred to in his office of prophet, man of God, instead of king)
- most or all of them very likely became part of a standing Davidic temple choir, Group XVII

The named members of these choirs are:

67. **Azarel II** (Neh. 12:36)

68. Gilalai (12:36)

69. **Hanani II** (12:36)

70. **Jezrahiah**, music director (12:42)

71. **Judah** (12:36)

72. **Maai** (12:36)

73. **Milalai** (12:36)

74. **Nethanel** (12:36)

75. **Shemaiah III** (12:36)

76. **Zechariah III (**12:35), included as a singer-musician, not a priest-trumpeter (Neh. 12: 41, a different person) because he was descended from Asaph and not from Aaron, and because the musicians in verse 36 are called his brethren.

Group XVII. [445-433] A standing temple choir-orchestra was appointed by Nehemiah "according to the command of David and Solomon his son. For in the days of David and Asaph of old there were chiefs of the singers and songs of praise and thanksgiving to God" (Neh. 12:45-46; 7:1; 10:39). This linkage to the choirs and psalms of David, Solomon, and Asaph demonstrates that this, the last temple choir in Scripture, had the same essential prophetic ministry as the original (Group IV) and as others that served in the first temple (Groups VII, X, XII, and XIII). When Nehemiah went back to Babylon after having governed Jerusalem and Judea twelve years, proper temple services were abandoned, and this choir was disbanded or compromised (Neh. 13:10). Then, when Nehemiah returned to Jerusalem for his second term as governor [430-?], he tried to reform things, and with some success (Neh. 13:11-13, 19, 22, 30); but no specific mention is made of the choir.

77. **Mary's** Magnificat (Luke 1:46-55) is believed to have been a song, although Scripture does not expressly say this. If it was a song, Mary is the only New Testament prophetess whose prophecy was principally musical, or who contributed a significant amount of musical prophecy. [4]

78. **Zacharias II** is the only other New Testament prophet whose prophecy (Luke 1:67-79) may have been principally musical, or who contributed a significant

amount of musical prophecy. Like Mary's, Zacharias's prophecy is believed to have been a song although Scripture does not say this. [4]

[AD 30+] Jesus, His disciples, Paul, and others sang on occasion (e.g. Mark 14:26; Acts 16:25), but we do not know what they sang, and they left no written songs that we know of.

NOTE: Heavenly and angelic choirs are not listed.

Endnotes and References for Chapter 6

1. See inset, "The Great Refrain," pages 267-69.

2. True, there were trumpets, but these were used to muster, direct, and alarm the congregation; to invoke God's help in war; and in worship, only to herald or "remind God" of the burnt offerings and sacrifices (Num. 10:1-10; Lev. 25:9; Josh. 6:4-5; Judg. 3:27; 6:34; 7:16-18). These trumpets were not used to make music—or prophesy.

3. Although they were both in Group IV, Mattithiah II was a son of Jeduthun and would have served under his own father [1 Chr. 25:6] whereas Mattathiah I, number 18, served under Asaph (1 Chr. 16:5).

4. Manassah became king when he was twelve years old, and his father was still living although possibly in failing health. They served as coregents for about ten years, during which it seems likely that Hezekiah's reforms remained in place.

Chapter 7

The Biblical History of Prophecy

Introduction

God has been speaking to people by means of His prophets throughout history (Heb. 1:1). The word of God stands forever (Is. 40:8). The spirit of prophecy is eternal; it is focused on Jesus Christ (1 Pet. 1:11; Luke 24:27). These things are constant.

However, the spokespersons, means, abundance, messages, vistas, and effects of prophecy have varied greatly during the forty-one centuries of biblical history. At times, prophets were rare and there was no widespread revelation (1 Sam. 3:1). At other times, prophets and the word of God abounded (Acts 2:16-18). The forms of prophesying have changed—from actions and lives lived, to music, to poetry and other writing, and of course to preaching. (None of these has been the exclusive form at any one period of history, however.) The prophets' relationships to human institutions (the body politic) and to human value systems have seen remarkable changes, from the prophet having near-absolute authority and great respect (Ex. 18:15-16; 1 Sam. 3:19-4:1), to his being ridiculed, rejected, incarcerated, and even executed (1 Ki. 18:4; Mark 6:17-29).

False prophets and prophecy have also changed in numbers, message, style, and reception (although always managing to be popular). Finally, the very essence of prophecy and the office of prophet were clarified, fulfilled, and refocused by Jesus Christ at a certain time in history.

The history of prophecy is in one sense the Bible itself because all Scripture is God's special revelation to us through holy inspired men and women (2 Tim. 3:16; 2 Pet. 1:21). Perhaps this chapter could have been titled "The Bible as a History of Prophecy," and the subject left at that. However, it is both interesting and edifying to arrange in chronological order those men and women, acts, writings, and speeches that can be identified as prophets and prophecies. Significant changes, trends, and developments in prophecy and prophesying appear, which are otherwise hidden in the biblical narrative and sequence of books.

This chapter is a brief historical sketch of prophecy. It is meant to be readable, not rigorous. There is very little extrabiblical material, and most of that is embedded in the resources used for dating and in marginal notes in Bibles. Dates are approximate and are taken from several sources. They are usually shown in brackets, thus [587], BC unless designated AD. The dating system used is explained in an appendix at the end of this chapter.

From Eden to Egypt: The Patriarchal Period

1. First Prophecy (Gen. 3:9-19) [ca. 4100]

The first specific prophecy in history was given directly by God, not through a human prophet. It was given just after the fall of Adam and Eve (mankind) and was addressed to the serpent (the Satan), to Eve (all women), and to Adam (all men). Prototypically of all prophecy, it pointed to Christ, the woman's (and man's) seed.

2. First Prophet (Gen. 4:4) [ca. 4000]

The first human prophet was Abel, second son of Adam and Eve. Unless the Bible student is gifted with extraordinary spiritual insight, he is not likely to realize this fact until he reads, in the New Testament, Christ's own witness that Abel was a prophet (Matt. 23:34-35; cf. Luke 11:50-51). How did Abel prophesy, and what was his message? According to one apostle, Abel spoke and still speaks with shed blood (Heb. 11:4, 12:24)—his own blood and/or that of his acceptable (animal) sacrifice. In this way he prophesied of Christ's sacrifice of His life (blood).

3. Other Patriarchal Prophets

God-callers and God-walkers [3800 and beyond]

In the days of Adam's third known son Seth and of Seth's son Enosh, men "began to call on the name of the Lord (Gen. 4:26)." This "calling on the name" is a phrase used over twenty times in the Bible. It usually suggests worship, although prophesying cannot be ruled out. However, there is no revelation, other than the historical narrative and genealogy, recorded in Scripture between Able and Enoch.

The next known prophet was Enoch (Gen. 5:22-24), of the seventh generation of mankind [3400-3100]. At Enoch's death, about a thousand years had elapsed since Adam was created. Enoch "walked with God," not in heaven, nor into heaven, but here on earth. This phrase may have designated a prophet of those times, like the phrase "man of God" did later. Noah, who prophesied five hundred years later, is also said to have "walked with God" (Gen. 6:9). In any case, Enoch was definitely a prophet, although, as in the case of Abel, we do not know this until we read it in the New Testament. The apostle Jude not only identifies Enoch as a prophet, he quotes some of his prophecy, a prophecy of God's judgment on men of ungodly deeds and words (Jude 14-15). Thus we see that God was sending prophets and warning people of the consequences of sin (ungodliness) even centuries before the wicked days of Noah.

Noah, the Preacher [3000-2200]

Noah is identified as a "preacher of righteousness"—here again, by a New Testament apostle, in this case Peter (2 Pet. 2:5). Just like Adam, Noah—the second progenitor of mankind—along with his sons received a prophecy directly from God, a covenant prophecy (Gen. 9:1-17). [2440] This prophecy is not plainly Messianic, but it does clearly establish the importance God places on the (life) blood of people and beasts—ultimately, the blood of His Son.

We do not have any of preacher Noah's sermons, but his prophecy about his sons does remain (Gen. 9:24-27).

One of the most intriguing passages in all of Scripture concerns Noah and Jesus (1 Pet. 3:18-20). Christ, either preincarnate or after His death on the cross, went and preached to some imprisoned souls (spirits): angels or men that had been disobedient. Perhaps these had rejected Noah's preaching, or perhaps they had been left bereft of God's word when His only prophet was busy building the ark and preparing for the flood.

Abraham, Isaac, Jacob, and Joseph [2040-1840]

The first man to be named a prophet in his own time, in the Old Testament, was Abraham (Gen. 20:7). God Himself gave him that new title, or office. One of Abraham's principal duties as a prophet was intercession (Gen. 18:16-33). Thus, it was established from this early time (if not even earlier) that God's faithful prophets are not just disinterested messengers: They actively pray and plead for the lives of their hearers.

Like Adam and Noah before him, Abraham (Abram) received covenantal prophecy directly from God (Gen. 12:1-3; 15; 17:1-22). At this same time we have the first examples of prophecy coming to man through angels: first to Hagar (Gen. 16:10-12), then to Abraham and an eavesdropping Sarah (Gen. 18:1-15).

Abraham prophesied principally through deeds of obedience, including [ca. 2015] his proffer of his son Isaac's life (Gen. 22:1-19)—clearly prophetic of God the Father offering up His Son. Abraham's son Isaac, grandson Jacob, and great-grandson Joseph were also prophets (q.v. each, chapter 3) but are not given this title in the Bible. Joseph's interpretations of dreams (Gen. 40, 41) and Jacob's last words to his sons (Gen. 49) are among the earliest recorded *verbal* prophecies of men. [1860-1840] These discourses have most of the usual characteristics of prophecy, lacking only that label or the signature phrase "Thus says the LORD."

The Exodus, Wilderness, and Conquest of Canaan

For at least two centuries after Joseph, while the descendents of Jacob/Israel lived in Egypt, they multiplied greatly, from seventy (Gen. 46:27) to a million or

(continued on page 284)

Prophecy Droughts

Prophecy did not flow as a steady stream throughout biblical history. Far from it. Centuries of prophecy silence (no known prophets or recorded revelation from God) occurred while Noah's offspring repopulated the earth—and generally became proud, alienated from God again. Finally this long famine of revelation was broken when God again chose a prophet, Abraham, through whom to reveal His will.

This was the third of seven major droughts of prophecy in biblical history. These were not accidents or oversights. God ordained, and even warned, that such periods would come because of man's unbelief.

> 'Behold, the days are coming', says the Lord GOD,
> 'That I will send a famine on the land,
> Not a famine of bread,
> Nor a thirst for water,
> But of hearing the words of the LORD.' (Amos 8:11)
>
> We do not see our signs;
> There is no longer any prophet;
> Nor is there any among us who knows how long. (Psalm 74:9)
>
> And the word of the LORD was rare in those days; there was no widespread revelation. (1 Samuel 3:1)
>
> See also Ezekiel 7:26; Micah 3:6–7; Isaiah 64:7.

The seven major dearths of revelation are outlined below:

1. No prophet or prophecy at all is mentioned in Scripture from Abel, the first prophet, until Enoch appears about six hundred years later.
2. After Enoch, no prophecy was given until Noah began to preach. Noah was born sixty-nine years after Enoch was taken to heaven, so this drought lasted at least one hundred years, and probably much longer. (Noah was six hundred years old at the time of the flood.)
3. The next prophet after Noah was Abraham (Abram). Noah lived until after Abram's birth, but Noah's last recorded prophecy (Genesis 9) was just after the flood, about three hundred years before Abram was born, and 375 years before God broke His long silence by speaking to Abraham. This was the "tower of Babel" drought.

4. There was a dearth of prophecy during most of Israel's long captivity in Egypt, after Jacob died and Joseph ceased to prophesy. The Bible does not contain any prophecy from Jacob's last words (Genesis 49) until God spoke to Moses in Midian (Exodus 3) about four hundred years later, and Moses and Aaron began to prophesy. Even if Joseph continued to prophesy until his death, this drought lasted 250 years. The Egyptian captivity was truly a spiritual famine.
5. A large amount of prophecy was given through Moses, Aaron, Miriam, and Joshua. But after Joshua, revelation began to wane again. There were few prophets during the Theocracy (Judges) Period, although the high priest was vested with the Urim and the Thummim. No prophet or prophecy at all is mentioned between an anonymous seer (Judges 6:8) and Hannah, Samuel's mother (1 Samuel 2). Dates during these times are uncertain, but based on adding the years of oppression and years of peace surrounding the nine intervening judges, this was a drought of at least 150 years. This famine of God's word is confirmed by 1 Samuel 3:1.
6. Israel and/or Judah were almost never without at least one prophet, and usually had many, during the Kingdom Period, except for a relatively short drought toward the end of it. In the sixty years before Malachi, Ezra, and Nehemiah, no prophet is mentioned, not even a Levite singer; and no prophecy is recorded.
7. The drought of God's word that is the most familiar to Bible students is that between Malachi and the New Testament, which opens with a plethora of prophets (Luke 1–3). This so-called Intertestamental Period was a revelation famine of over four hundred years, the longest since Egypt.

A little further analysis of these droughts reveals two salient facts. First, most of these droughts of prophecy were broken (humanly) by "great" prophets: Noah, Abraham, Moses, Samuel, and, not to belittle the brief prophecy sprinkles of Elizabeth, Mary, Zacharias, Simeon, and Anna, by Jesus and His forerunner John. Perhaps the very fact that these prophets had to break through a long standing and thick darkness accounts in part for their greatness. Put another way, God empowered some of His mightiest prophets for the difficult task of drought breaking.

A second conspicuous fact about these droughts of revelation is that they occurred, or rather ended, on a fairly regular cycle of about 350–700 years. The first drought was broken by Enoch. If he began to prophesy before the age of one hundred, it was about six hundred years after Abel prophesied with his blood. We do not know when in his 950-year lifetime Noah began to preach, only that it was before the flood. If we arbitrarily put it at 250 years before the flood, it would have been seven hundred years after Enoch supposedly began. The next drought breaker, Abraham, was called by God some 625 years later, and Moses broke the drought of Egyptian captivity 625 years after that. Samuel initiated the "golden age" of prophets in Israel/Judah about 350 years after Moses began in Midian and Egypt. Malachi broke a short drought 650 years later, and John/Jesus came 450 years after that. These times, from the end of one drought to the end of the next, were

	600 years
	700 years
	625 years
	625 years
	350 years
	650 years
	450 years
Average:	571 years

Thus we have the fact that prophecy, like certain climatic and other phenomena, is historically cyclical, at least during the four millennia of biblical history. We do not attach any spiritual significance to this; and it would be dangerous to extrapolate to try to find out "where we are" in the prophecy cycle, if indeed it has continued since Jesus came. True, there have been "dark" periods, followed by the reformation and other spiritual renewals, since Jesus was here in the flesh. But since His resurrection "the love of God has been poured out in our hearts by the Holy Spirit who was given to us" (Romans 5:5); and the gift of prophecy has been given by the Holy Spirit to countless Christians (Romans 12:6).

more (Num. 1:45-46, plus women and children); but they fell into a state of unbelief and slavery. There is no prophet or direct revelation from God recorded in Scripture during this long captivity. (See Inset, "Prophecy Droughts," on pages 282-84.)

The second person in biblical history to be called a prophet in his own time was Aaron. [1440] He was actually his younger brother Moses's prophet, or spokesman. Moses was made "as God" to both Aaron and Pharaoh (Ex. 4:16, 7:1).

1. Moses the Archetypical Prophet [1450-1410]

Moses was arguably the greatest of all the prophets of the Bible (Deut. 34:10-12), excepting of course Jesus and, by Jesus's testimony, John the baptizer (Matt. 11:11). Moses once prophesied that Jesus would be "like him" (Deut. 18:15-19).

This likeness was associated, at least in part, with their "face-to-face" relationship with God. Neither Moses nor Jesus had to receive revelation from God in dreams and visions, as other prophets did (Num. 12:6-8). Also, Moses was made "as God" and Jesus *is* God. Moses defined the office of prophet by example and, at least partially, in writing (Deut. 18:18-22). Moses literally prophesied a nation (Israel) into being, prophesied their constitution into existence, and for many years governed that nation—as a prophet. He was the first prophet who was head of state of a major nation.

2. First Musical Prophecy [1450]

Moses was the premier prophet of the Old Testament, the first and foremost in many aspects of the history of prophecy, but a musician? Music would become the principal way of prophesying under David, some 450 years after Moses. However, the earliest examples of musical prophecy were sung just after the Exodus from Egypt, the passing through the Red Sea. "Then Moses and the children of Israel sang this song to the Lord, . . ." (Ex. 15:1) This song is primarily praise—one purpose of prophecy (see chapter 1, "Why God Gives Prophecy," part 4.8). There is a predictive passage in the Song of Moses, too, which finds its ultimate fulfillment in Christ (vv. 14-18). At this same time we also have the Song of Miriam. Not only did she sing this prophecy; musical instruments were used (Ex. 15:20-21). Which brings us to:

3. The First Prophetess [1450]

Miriam is the first prophetess named in Scripture (Ex. 15:20). Although her one recorded prophecy (Ex. 15:20-21) is very brief, she became a sort of standard or model for many prophetesses. Her New Testament namesake, Mary, sang her own prophecy. Miriam prophesied at other times, or claimed to have done so (Num. 12:1-2).

4. Changes of Methodology [1449-]

Several significant changes in the way God gives prophecy occurred during Moses's administration [1450-1410]. First and foremost, God decided that after Moses, He would issue His word to prophets exclusively through dreams and visions (Num. 12:6-8), with only one exception: Jesus. Previous to this, God gave prophecy to man in many ways: through angels that were not visions (Gen. 16:7-12); through His cloud of glory—both at the tabernacle door (Ex. 33:9) and between the wings of the cherubim (Ex. 25:22); on stone tablets (Ex. 34:1, 28); and by direct communication, face-to-face. But from now on it would be only through dreams and visions, with the two exceptions of Moses and Jesus.

A second procedural development that was instituted early in the wilderness experience of Israel was the giving of the Urim and the Thummim (Lights and Perfections). These objects (jewels?) were put on the breastplate of judgment attached to the ephod worn by the high priest when he entered the holy place in the tabernacle, and at other times (Ex. 28:30; Lev. 8:8). The Urim, in particular, gave brief answers from God (such as *yes, no,* or *a tribe name*) to specific questions. Technically, this was an exception to the "dreams and visions only" rule. Thus the high priest was empowered with a limited prophetic function. However, there are very few actual usages of the Urim reported in Scripture. Most of these were for military decisions (Num. 27:21; 1 Sam. 23:9-13; 28:6; 30:7-8). The Urim and the Thummim were still (or again) in use when the Jews returned from Babylonian captivity (Ezra 2:63). They are not mentioned in the New Testament. The high priest, however, still seems to have had some vestige of a prophetic function even in Jesus's day (John 11:51).

A third development in the early years of the wilderness period, strongly related to prophecy, was that God not only established a priesthood, He gave the priesthood (and to some extent the whole tribe of Levi) a teaching ministry (Lev. 10:8-11; Deut. 31:9-13; 33:8-10; Neh. 8:9). To what degree this ministry supported prophecy, or led to prophesying, cannot be ascertained. It seems to be limited to teaching the already-revealed Law of God without elaboration (2 Chr. 17:7-9) although Malachi calls the teaching priest "the messenger of the LORD of hosts" (2:7). Ezra, a priest of the lineage of Aaron, was merely reading the Law of God to the people when they were brought to tears and repentance—a result any prophet would welcome (Ezra 7:1-6/Neh. 8:1-9). Priests also interpreted and applied the Law as judges (Deut. 17:8-11; 2 Chr. 19:8-11). Several of the major prophets were first trained as priests, including Samuel, Ezekiel, and Jeremiah. John, the baptizer, was the son of a priest and possibly trained for it himself. The establishment of the priesthood in the wilderness, at the time of Moses, Aaron, and Miriam, definitely had a major effect on the history of prophecy.

5. Other Wilderness Prophets and Prophecy [1450-1410]

The three siblings—Moses, Aaron, and Miriam—dominated the prophetic stage all during the Exodus from Egypt and the wilderness wanderings of Israel. On one occasion seventy elders prophesied, but they did so only once (Num. 11:24-25). The only other significant prophecy of this period was that of Balaam. Balaam was a false prophet in the service of an idolatrous king, but he was nevertheless compelled by God to prophesy the truth, four times (Num. 23, 24). He later went on to become known as the archetypical false prophet, leading Israel into great sin and misery (Num. 25). This defined his infamous place in the history of prophecy (2 Pet. 2:15; Jude 11; Rev. 2:14).

6. Canaan at Last!—But Prophecy Declines [1410-1100]

Joshua was a great prophet and a great leader—handpicked and trained by God and Moses to succeed Moses and to lead the people of Israel into Canaan and conquer it (Num. 27:15-23; Deut. 31:7-8). Joshua was primarily a prophet of action, adding very little to the verbal and written prophecy of Moses (Josh. 8:30-35).

During the next three and one-half centuries, in which the land of Canaan was settled and populated by the people of Israel, God led them by:

- the heads of families and tribes;
- a priesthood, about which little is written in those times; and
- charismatic judges, only two or three of whom (Deborah and Samuel, and possibly Barak) are identified as prophets.

Only four other prophets, two of them angels (Judg. 2:1-4; 6:11ff), one an anonymous man of God (1 Sam. 2:27), and Hannah the mother of Samuel, are mentioned during this entire period. "And the word of the LORD was rare in those days; there was no widespread revelation . . ." (1 Sam. 3:1)

The Kingdom Period [1100-450]

The centuries when Israel was a political kingdom, counting Samuel's tenure as king-maker, produced by far the largest number of prophets and the most recorded prophecy in the Old Testament. Practically every person known *primarily* as a prophet(ess) lived during these six hundred fifty years. In contrast, most of the people who prophesied during the first three *millennia* of biblical history, from Abel to Samuel, are better known in some other capacity than "prophet": fratricide victim, patriarch, ark builder, father of nations, lawgiver, general, priest, and judge. Samuel, the last judge-leader of Israel, was the first and foremost of all persons known *primarily* as prophets of God (although Moses, at least, should be). Full-time prophets rose up simultaneously with full-time kings in Israel. Both offices continued through the Babylonian captivity and the return to the holy land. The kingdom-era prophets include all the canonical (writing) prophets, almost all the musical prophets and most of the well-known heroic prophets such as Elijah.

Table 1
Chronological List of Prophets of the Kingdom Period
In order of first appearance as prophets

Prophet—Scripture Reference	Approx. Date, BC (First Appearance)
Samuel	1100
Group of prophets—1 Samuel 10:5	
Saul	1050
Group under Samuel—1 Samuel 19:20	
Saul's messengers—1 Samuel 19:20	
Amasai—1 Chronicles 12:18	
Gad	
David	1010
Zadok	
Heman	
Asaph	
Ethan (Jeduthun)	
15 other music prophets—1 Chronicles 15	
Nathan	
24 sons of Heman, Asaph, and Ethan—1 Chronicles 25	
264 other Levite music prophets—1 Chronicles 25	
Solomon	970
Ahijah—1 Kings 11:29	
Shemaiah—1 Kings 12:22	930
Man of God from Judah—1 Kings 13	915
Old prophet—1 Kings 13	
Azariah—2 Chronicles 15:1–9	900
Jehu—1 Kings 16:1–4	890
Hanani—2 Chronicles 16:7	870
Elijah	870
A prophet to Ahab—1 Kings 20:13	
A man of God—1 Kings 20:28	
A man of the sons of the prophets—1 Kings 20:35	
Micaiah—1 Kings 22	853
Jahaziel—2 Chronicles 20:14	
Eliezer—2 Chronicles 20:37	852
Elisha	850

Table 1 (page 2)

Sons of the prophets—2 Kings 2:3, 5, 7	
One of the sons of the prophets—2 Kings 9:1	841
Singers—2 Chronicles 23:13, 18	835
Sent Prophets—2 Chronicles 24:19	
Zechariah (II) son of Jehoida—2 Chronicles 24:20	797
A man of God—2 Chronicles 25:7	
A prophet—2 Chronicles 25:15	
Zechariah (III)—2 Chronicles 26:5	
Jonah—2 Kings 14:25 (First Canon Prophet)	790
Amos	780
Hosea	755
Isaiah	740
Micah	740
Oded—2 Chronicles 28:9	733
Hezekiah	715
Musical prophets, 6 named—2 Chronicles 29:13, 25–30; 31:2	
Nahum	650
"The prophets" or "seers"—2 Kings 21:10; 2 Chronicles 33:18	640
Zephaniah	630
Jeremiah	626
Huldah—2 Kings 22:14	622
Singers—2 Chronicles 35:15	
Urijah—Jeremiah 26:20–23	608
Habakkuk	605
Daniel	604
Ezekiel	593
Obadiah	560
Singers—Ezra 2:41; 3:10–11 (3 named in Nehemiah 12:8–9)	536
Haggai	520
Zechariah VI	520
Ezra	458
Nehemiah	446
Singers, over 20 named—Nehemiah 12	445
Malachi	433
Joel	undatable

Chronological Listing of Kingdom Prophets

The prophets and prophetesses of God, during the kingdom period of Israel/Judah, are arranged in chronological order in table 1. Using this table and our knowledge of the prophets' "various ways" (Hebrews 1:1), some important trends and developments in the history of prophecy are observed in the following section.

1. Overview of Kingdom Prophet Types and Clusters

All of the prophets of the kingdom era (table 1) can be put into one or more of these four categories:

Statesman Prophet
Music Prophet
Hero Prophet
Writer Prophet

The main characteristics of each type will be described below. First, however, it is interesting to observe that these categories are, to a very high degree, separated in historic time. Within the kingdom period of Israel/Judah there are three distinct subperiods, based on the dominant type of prophet. Two prophet categories share the first sub-period, and each of the other two sub-periods has a single dominant category of prophet. This is shown in table 2.

Table 2
Prophet Clusters by Sub-period

Time Period (BC)	Dominant Type of Prophet	Representative Prophets
1100–900	Statesman	Hannah, Samuel, Gad, Nathan, Ahijah, Shemaiah, Azariah
	Musical	David, Asaph, Heman, Ethan, Solomon
900–780	Hero	Hanani, Elijah, Micaiah, Elisha, Eliezer, Zechariah, Jonah
780–430	Writer	The sixteen canonical prophets

Prophets in the first category, statesmen, were political as well as moral and spiritual leaders. They established and upheld the kingdom. They anointed and counseled kings. They were not persecuted, nor was their counsel often disregarded. Each of these prophets had a direct positive impact on national and international affairs and sometimes a direct personal impact (often a rebuke) on their respective kings.

The second category, music prophets, is treated at length in chapter 6, which includes a separate history. For about a century in biblical history, music was the dominant form of prophecy. The statesman prophets who were contemporaries of the music prophets were not as prolific as the latter in terms of recorded prophecy. David, the founder, patron, and himself the foremost of the music prophets, was also a statesman and a hero; but as a prophet he is best known by his psalms.

The hero prophet category emerged—*had to* emerge—after the kingdom split into two parts and both began to decline. Immediately following the reign of Solomon [970-930] came political unrest, rebellion, civil war, and the division of Israel into two kingdoms, Israel and Judah. Moral and spiritual decay had actually begun under Solomon. Idolatry was rampant, and the Northern Kingdom, Israel, set up unauthorized worship centers and an unauthorized priesthood. The role of prophet underwent a corresponding dramatic change. True prophets of God were no longer officially honored or respected as statesmen. Many were persecuted, even executed. Some went underground, literally, into caves (1 Ki. 18:4). [870] The proclamation of God's word through psalm prophecy continued sporadically and only in the Southern Kingdom, Judah, but few new psalms or psalmists appeared. Jahaziel is a transition figure between the music prophets and the hero prophets although he lived well into the period dominated by the latter. A Levite of the sons of Asaph, Jahaziel rallied Judah to overcome their enemies in battle—led by the choir! (2 Chr. 20:14-24) [852]

False prophets abounded and prospered, especially in the courts of kings and queens (1 Ki. 18:19). Yet God did not abandon His people, for from these terrible conditions emerged the great hero prophets like Elijah. They defied the corrupt system and spoke for God, often at the risk of their lives. To get the corrupted people's attention and to validate that their message was from God, these prophets were often given miraculous powers. More wondrous signs and miracles were given during this sub-period of a little more than a century than at any other time in the Old Testament except during the years of Moses.

Another significant milestone in the history of prophecy occurred during this sub-period, and is easily overlooked. God for the first time since Israel became a nation began to send Hebrew prophets to Gentiles—beginning with Elijah (to a widow in Zaraphath of Sidon) and on a major scale with Jonah's mission to Nineveh.

Jonah is the transition figure between the hero-prophet era and the writer-prophet times. Jonah is included in both the hero group and the writer group because the book he wrote,[2] *Jonah*, is about his actions and about miracles, not "The Oracles of God to Jonah." The fact that Jonah presents himself as a coward, not a hero, is easily explained as humility, honesty, and self-deprecation.

In the eighth century BC, the style or form of prophesying again changed quickly and almost completely, as God sent the writer prophets. There were still periodic revivals of musical prophecy, and some of the writers were also heroes and statesmen, but most of the prophets throughout the remainder of the kingdom period of Israel/Judah were primarily writers. They penned approximately one-fourth of the Bible in just nine percent of its history. [780-430] The transition of prophecy to writing, seen chronologically, is astonishing. It is as if writing were suddenly discovered as a channel of prophecy, much as music had been about two centuries earlier. The extemporaneous, verbal, often confrontational prophesyings of, say, Elijah or the martyr Zechariah II, gave way to the careful compositions—no less incisive and, often, no less confrontational—of the pen. And this occurred when the two kingdoms continued to decline and ultimately fall. We can speculate as to the underlying reasons for this change to writing; but we can *know* that it produced an inexhaustible treasure of God's revelation for a hundred generations of mankind. The writer prophets are discussed at greater length in historical order in a separate section, below. Here it is only noted that, of the sixteen canonical prophets, some were also statesmen (as Isaiah, Daniel, Haggai, and Zechariah); some, heroes (as Amos and Jeremiah), and some music prophets (notably Habakkuk).

2. The Surge of Prophets [1100-970]

We now return to the beginning of the Kingdom period of Israel. When Samuel was a boy [ca. 1100], the word of the LORD was rare; there was no widespread revelation (1 Sam. 3:1). Just a few decades later, a whole group of prophets came out to meet king-anointee Saul (1 Sam. 10:10-11). Saul himself prophesied. [1050] The next king, David, was a prolific prophet who surrounded himself with advisor prophets (1 Sam. 22:5; 2 Sam. 7:1-3) and hundreds of musical prophets (1 Chr. 25). [1000]

Clearly, during Samuel's lifetime and immediately thereafter, there was a remarkable increase in the number of prophets in Israel. Local seers were consulted—and paid—for guidance (1 Sam. 9:5-9). There was a group of prophets led by Samuel (1 Sam. 19:20). Near the end of his reign Saul tried unsuccessfully to consult "the prophets"—plural (1 Sam. 28:6). David and his captains appointed 288 Levites to prophesy with music (1 Chr. 25). At the end of David's reign and the beginning of Solomon's, there were four thousand musicians assisting with music prophecy (1 Chr. 23:1, 5). [970]

3. First Prophecy in Formal Worship of God [1000]

Perhaps the most significant development in the history of prophecy under King David—and one of the most significant in all of this history—was the introduction of prophecy into the formal worship of God at the tabernacle, later the temple. Formal worship as instituted under Moses included neither prophesying nor music (Lev.). But both of these elements, prophesying and music, were regularly included, even required, in proper tabernacle/temple worship during and after David's reign (1 Chr. 25) and throughout the monarchy period of Israel/Judah (2 Chr. 23:18 [835]; 2 Chr. 29:25 [715]) and even after the return of the Jews from Babylonian captivity (Neh. 12:45 [450]). *Prophecy came into formal worship through music, not preaching!* More on this subject is given in chapter 6 and under the individual prophets David, Asaph, Heman, Ethan, and others in chapter 3.

4. Opposition to Prophecy Sets In [930-]

Psalm prophecy continued to flourish under King Solomon, reaching a climax at the installation of the ark of the covenant of God into the newly completed first temple [958]. On that occasion, as the prophecy-choir sang the Great Refrain,[3] the glory of God filled His house (2 Chr. 5:13-14). Like his father David, Solomon was a prophet and a patron of music prophets. However, besides these psalm prophets and Solomon himself, the only other prophets even mentioned in Scripture during Solomon's long reign are Nathan, who helped Solomon secure the throne (1 Ki. 1:11ff); Iddo, as a Historian (2 Chr. 9:29); and Ahijah, who was really more involved with Solomon's successor Jeroboam, shortly before Solomon's death (1 Ki. 11:29-40).

Toward the end of Solomon's reign the nation of Israel was corrupted with the tolerated, and even embraced, religions of his foreign wives. Solomon could not bear or submit to the prophecy of Ahijah about his sin, the nation's sin, and the impending civil war and division. {Note that David had sinned, too; but he submitted to the judgments of God that came through Nathan and Gad. David repented (Ps. 51)}. Solomon rebelled against Ahijah's prophecy and actually tried to prevent its fulfillment by seeking to kill Jeroboam (1 Ki. 11:40).

From this point in the history of Israel and Judah, most of the prophets of God were adversaries of their kings and queens. Many were persecuted, beginning with a man of God whose arrest was ordered by Jeroboam (1 Ki. 13:4). Even Ahijah himself, who had anointed Jeroboam, became so alienated from this king that, when Jeroboam desperately wanted to consult God, he resorted to sending his wife to Ahijah—in disguise and with a bribe! (1 Ki. 14:1-3). [910] Only about fifty years later there were state-sponsored mass executions of God's prophets (1 Ki. 18:4); and the great prophet Elijah was a declared enemy of the state (1 Ki. 18:17). [860] It cannot be overstated: *All this was a new and disgraceful thing in Israel!*

We are now accustomed to the idea that biblical prophets were persecuted. It seems to be the norm. Even Jesus talked about it (Luke 11:47-51). Being a prophet is a high-risk occupation. Historically, however, this characterization does not apply during at least five hundred years before Jeroboam I. Moses the prophet was also the head of state. His authority was almost absolute. During the Judges period, the prophetess Deborah was also the national leader; and other prophets were not persecuted, even if they brought hard messages of judgment. The prophet Samuel was Israel's last Judge, the most respected and powerful man in the nation, and a king maker. King David was a prophet and patron of prophets, and he submitted to the word of God brought through other prophets. For half a millennium, there is no record that a true prophet of God was persecuted by the leadership of Israel.

But after Solomon, very few prophets enjoyed official support or honor in Israel or Judah, except for brief periods of time. Haggai and Zechariah, after the Babylonian captivity and return from that exile, were notable exceptions. [520] But later, John the Baptist was imprisoned and beheaded; Jesus, the ultimate prophet, was crucified; and most of the apostle prophets were martyred.

In spite of—or because of—official opposition from their own governments, many true prophets, during the Kingdom Era, received respect and honor from other quarters. As Jesus later put it, "A prophet is not without honor except in his own country and in his own house" (Matt. 13:57). Elisha was not exactly on good terms with his own king, Jehoram (2 Ki. 6:30-31), but he was honored by King Jehoshaphat of Judah (2 Ki. 3:11-13) and by King Ben-Hadad of Syria (2 Ki. 8: 7-8). Daniel was highly respected in a foreign land and by their potentates. So was Jonah even though he despised the very Ninevites who actually heeded his message from God. Jeremiah, imprisoned in his own country, was honored and set at liberty by Nebuchadnezzar (Jer. 39:11-40:4). Micaiah, hated by his own king (Ahab), was severely abused in his own country (Israel), but was respected by King Jehoshaphat of Judah (1 Ki. 22).

5. The Regulation of Prophecy [1050-]

From the very beginning of the Kingdom Period, and continuing for at least two or three centuries, another major development in the history of prophecy emerged. Prophecy began to be institutionalized and regulated. Schools or seminaries for prophets sprang up. Prophets were formally trained. *Prophet* became a college major, a career, a job title, even a family trade.

If Moses's seventy elders (Num. 11:16-25) be excepted (and they were, after all, "temporaries"), the first organized group of prophets in Scripture surfaces when Samuel told Saul that a "group of prophets" would meet him (1 Sam. 10:5). [1050] Later, Samuel presided over this or another group of prophets (1 Sam. 19:20). At the beginning of Samuel's ministry, "the word of the LORD was rare" (1 Sam. 3:1)—hardly indicating that there were organized groups of prophets. Thus, we can surmise that Samuel was the founder-leader of the first school(s) of prophets.

We have already noted the explosion and regulation of musical prophecy, especially under King David. [1000] More on this subject is given in the historical section of chapter 6, Musical Prophecy. This form of prophesying, more than others, required training—not only in vocal and instrumental music, but also in the words of prophecy: psalms, usually written by other prophets. Musical prophesying was a family trade; only Levites were allowed to practice it in formal worship. Prominent music prophets are called sons of Asaph or similar family appellations, centuries after the time of Asaph, one of David's leading Levite singing prophets (Ezra 2:41). [537]

Musical prophecy, and training for it, continued for at least a century and a half in Jerusalem, but we have no mention of organized groups or schools of writing or preaching prophets until the days of Elijah's public ministry. [870-850] At Elijah's death (or ascension) there were at least two major compounds or schools of prophets, one at Bethel and the other at Jericho. The latter one had at least fifty residents (2 Ki. 2:3, 5, 7). Elijah may have founded these institutions, and/or they may have been largely the survivors of Jezebel's massacre.

Elisha, called directly from farming and privately mentored as Elijah's servant (1 Ki. 19:19-21), was actively involved at the campi of "sons of the prophets" at Bethel and Jericho and also at Gilgal and perhaps other places (2 Ki. 2:15; 4:38-41; 6:1-7; 9:1). He lived at one of these. Elisha's connection to these schools is uncertain—dean, or just visiting lecturer—but it was certainly a position of authority and respect.

The phrase "sons of the prophets" that occurs often in 2 Kings almost surely means students or disciples, not biological progeny. In this same way musical prophets are often called "sons of Asaph." Over fifty years after the time of Elisha, Amos used the term "son of a prophet" to indicate one who was trained, schooled, or perhaps born into prophesying (Amos 7:14).

It must be acknowledged that only two individual prophets, both anonymous, are known to have matriculated in any of these schools (1 Ki. 20:35; 2 Ki. 9:1). Many of the writing prophets begin their books with credentials: their family, hometown, call from God, etc.; but none mentions an "alma mater" except Daniel, who was forced to attend the godless University of Babylon (Dan. 1:4). Amos, as we have seen, emphatically denied being a prophet by birth, trade, or education. Jeremiah, Ezekiel, and perhaps others were trained to be priests, not prophets.

Nevertheless the schools did exist and prophets were trained. *Prophet* was an office, and prophecy skills were developed.

6. Resurgence of False Prophets and Soothsayers [930-]

False prophets were not a new phenomenon in the Kingdom Period. Long before, Egyptian diviners opposed Moses and Aaron (Ex. 7-9). Then there was Balaam, in the wilderness, at Peor. The land of Canaan was full of soothsayers, interpreters of omens, etc., just before Israel occupied it (Deut. 18:9-12). We may suppose that every false religion, god, or idol has its prophets. However, from the time they left Egypt, Israel *did* make an effort to keep them out of her culture, except for the affair of Peor (Num. 25; Rev. 2:14), up to the Kingdom Period, even to the latter part of Solomon's reign. Certainly neither Samuel nor David countenanced or encountered any false prophet. Saul, near the end of his life, did consult a witch (because God would no longer speak to him through His prophets), but he had made divining illegal and put mediums and spiritists out of the land (1 Sam. 28:3ff).

However, the proliferation and regulation of godly prophets in the Kingdom Period was paralleled by a rise of imitators and competitors variously known as false prophets, prophets of false gods and idols, and soothsayers. Many of these were court prophets in Israel as well as Judah. (Not all court prophets were ungodly—witness Nathan, Gad, Asaph, and others.)

Although we are not expressly informed of it by Scripture, there were likely to have been prophets of the false gods Ashteroth, Chemosh, and Milcom that were openly worshipped in Israel during Solomon's later years (1 Ki. 11:33), and of the two golden calves set up by Jeroboam I (1 Ki. 12:25-33). There is no question, however, of the existence of many false prophets in Israel some sixty years later [865], when King Ahab gathered them together at Mount Carmel (1 Ki. 18:19-22). The prophets of Baal and Asherah who were there numbered eight hundred and fifty. Elijah executed these, at least the four hundred and fifty prophets of Baal (1 Ki. 18:40). But another and perhaps more sinister brood of false prophets took over Ahab's court, four hundred strong! (1 Ki. 22:6). These are not said to be prophets of Baal. Perhaps they pretended to be God's prophets, but they were in fact liars and soothsayers, telling the king only what he wanted to hear—to his ultimate demise (1 Ki. 22:1-23, 37). [853]

Ahab's son Ahaziah reverted to, or continued, Baal worship (1 Ki. 22:51-53; 2 Ki. 1:2). Although Ahaziah's brother and successor Jehoram did make moderate reforms, Elijah still considered him an idolater at heart, and referred him to the false prophets (2 Ki. 3:1-3, 13). The prophets of Baal did make a comeback, but they were definitively exterminated by King Jehu (2 Ki. 10:18-28). [841]

Nevertheless, false prophets continued to plague the Northern Kingdom for the remainder of her existence, more than a century. Toward the end, God rebuked the false prophets of Israel and the people who listened to them through His real prophets Isaiah (9:15-16; 28:7) and Micah (2:6-11; 3:5-7). [740]

The Southern Kingdom, Judah, was at first relatively free of false prophets, at least state-sponsored ones. Several of Judah's kings "did what was right in the sight of the LORD," and Mosaic-Davidic temple worship was generally maintained; but the idolatry that had crept in during Solomon's later years was not eliminated—it sometimes flourished (1 Ki. 14:22-24 [930]; 2 Ki 16:1-4 [735]). King Manassah was himself a false prophet, a practitioner of soothsaying and witchcraft (2 Ki. 21: 1-9 [690]). God's prophet Zephaniah condemned the Baal worship, star worship (astrology?), and Milcom worship that was going on in Jerusalem and all Judah in the latter part of the seventh century (Zeph. 1:4-5). Undoubtedly these "gods" had their prophets, but we are thankfully spared their names and specific crimes, other than idol worship.

But the greatest blight in Judah/Jerusalem during the last few decades of their existence [626-586], before being destroyed and carried captive to Babylon, was a plethora of prophets claiming to be of God, but lying and soothsaying. These vermin insisted that God would never let His beloved Jerusalem fall to Babylonian infidels, and they constantly predicted "Peace, peace." God condemned these imposters at great length through Jeremiah (23:9-40; ch. 27-29) and Ezekiel (13) and to a lesser extent through other prophets. We do not know what became of the liars when their "peace" prophecies proved false. However, Jewish false prophets also misled the exiles in Babylon, telling them they wouldn't be there long. This prompted a sharp letter of rebuke from Jeremiah (29). He singled out three by name: Ahab, Zedekiah, and Shemaiah.

False prophets again plagued the Jews who returned from Babylon. [535] The early Jewish re-settlers were harassed and frustrated in their attempts to rebuild the temple by a bunch of "hired Counselors" (Ezra 4:4-5). Almost a century later, Nehemiah was opposed by "the prophetess Noadiah and the rest of the prophets who would have made me afraid" (Neh. 6:14).

7. The Writing Prophets in Historical Order [780-430]

As shown in table 1 and as previously discussed, the canonical (writing) prophets all lived during the Kingdom Period of Israel/Judah. Furthermore, they were all clustered in the last three and one-half centuries of that period. Almost all of the prophets of that time, except musical prophets, were writers.

The arrangement of the books of the writing prophets in the protestant Bible (Isaiah through Malachi) is not to be mistaken as historical order—not even approximately, except for the last three. "In general, . . . the order of the prophetic books is a compromise of overlapping considerations of length, date, and authorship."[4] Arranging these prophets in chronological order, as best we can, and looking at their ministries in the context of the flow of history, gives us some insights that may not be obvious when they are considered only in canonical order. Each of these writing prophets is also portrayed more fully in chapter 3; this section is concerned primarily with their places in history.

The set of seventeen books at the end of our Old Testament canon is commonly called The Prophets. These books are named for the prophets who wrote them (we will not enter disputes about authorship), except Lamentations, written by Jeremiah. These sixteen men comprise less than ten percent of the total named prophets of the Bible (chapter 3), so they are distinguished in this book by calling them *writing* prophets rather than *the* prophets. Technically Moses, Samuel, David, Solomon, Ezra, and possibly others were also Old Testament prophets who wrote much of God's Word, prophecy; but they wrote primarily histories and wisdom/poetical books that are not expressly labeled as prophecy or visions and oracles from God. Other prophets also wrote, but their writings are not expressly in Scripture, although they may have been source material; nor are they otherwise extant. These include Gad, Nathan, Ahijah, Iddo, Shemaiah, Jehu, and Hozai (1 Chr. 29:29; 2 Chr. 9:29; 12:15; 20:34; 33:19).

Jonah [ca. 780-]

Jonah was the first canonical prophet (in order of *his* first appearance, not necessarily the first-written book of the "prophets"). Jonah's prophecy cited in one of the history books (2 Ki. 14:25) must be dated before the borders of Israel were restored by Jeroboam II. This puts Jonah prophesying, but not *in* the book of Jonah, before Amos, who wrote after these borders had been secured (Amos 6:14). Jonah and Amos were contemporaries but may have not known each other except by reputation. Jonah was from Gath Hepher in northern Israel (2 Ki. 14:25), and Amos was from Tekoa in rural Judah (Amos 1:1). The book of Amos could well have been written before the book of Jonah; but Jonah preceded Amos as a prophet.

God used Jonah to prophecy to Israel, as we have seen in 2 Kings; and also to Nineveh, in the book Jonah. Nineveh was the capital of the most powerful nation on Earth, Assyria. This book contains only one sentence of what we commonly call prophecy (3:4). Jonah is mostly a narrative about an episode in the prophet's life. Literarily, it is more like the accounts of Elisha and Elisha in the books of Kings, than the visions and oracles in the other writing prophets' books. The book of Jonah is a bridge or transition of style, just as Jonah himself was a transition figure from heroic to writing prophets. He was both.

It is both historically and theologically significant that Jonah was God's first foreign missionary: the first Israelite prophet to be sent on a major mission to a Gentile nation. Others had witnessed to individual Gentiles, such as Elisha to Naaman (2 Ki. 5). Jonah's mission to Nineveh itself prophesies of God's ultimate plan to reveal Himself through Jesus Christ and His followers to all nations and peoples (Acts 1:8).

Amos [ca. 770]

The next writing prophet was Amos. God called him from obscurity—a lowly sheep breeder and farmer from a small place in Judah (1:1; 7:12-15)—to prophesy in the Northern Kingdom, Israel. It was sometime in the first half of the eighth century BC. Elisha had recently died, probably in the 790s, after being the principal prophet for over fifty-five years. Jonah was probably still living. Under Jeroboam II [793–753] Israel was enjoying a period of relative peace and prosperity, but "did not depart from the sins of Jeroboam (I)" (2 Ki. 14:23-24). Amos prophesied against the sins of Israel, Judah, and the surrounding nations. He called for Israel's repentance (5:4-15) but correctly prophesied of her destruction (8:1-9:10)—*the first prophet to do this.*

Hosea [ca. 760-710]

Next came Hosea, who prophesied over a very long time, from sometime during Jeroboam II's reign [793–753] until sometime during Hezekiah's reign [715–686] (Hos. 1:1). During his ministry, the Northern Kingdom, Israel, fell to Assyria and ceased to exist as a nation. Hosea prophesied almost exclusively to the Northern Kingdom. Once he even calls Judah righteous by comparison (11:12) although other references to Judah are not so complimentary (5:10; 6:4). Hosea earnestly pleads with Israel to repent and follow God again even *after* she was destroyed as a nation! (13:9-11). God did not see His chosen people as a political kingdom only, but as a family.

Isaiah and Micah [ca. 740-690]

Contemporaries with Hosea, but continuing for some years after him, were Micah and Isaiah. They were the first writing prophets to clearly set forth the coming Messiah, prophecies literally fulfilled by Jesus of Nazareth (Mic. 5:2-5; Is 42:1-4; 52:13-53:12). Both are often quoted at Christmas time (Mic. 5:2; Is. 7:14).

The times of Isaiah and Micah were tumultuous, to say the least, in both Israel and Judah. Israel was destroyed by Assyria (2 Ki. 17 [722]), and Judah narrowly escaped the same fate (Is. 36-37 [701]). Unlike Hosea, both of these prophets conveyed God's words of concern, warning, and promise toward Judah and Jerusalem, more than toward Israel. Both were Judeans. Isaiah was a highly educated, polished man, and a Jerusalem "insider," at least during Hezekiah's reign, while Micah was an "outsider" from a small country village, Moresheth (1:1). Although King Hezekiah frequently turned to Isaiah in national and personal crises (2 Ki. 19:1-4; 20:1-11), it was Micah's prophesying that is credited with turning Hezekiah back to God and sparing Judah at that time (Jer. 26:17-19).

Isaiah was the more politically active of the two. His written book of prophecy deals with, in addition to Israel and Judah: Babylon, Assyria, Plilistia, Moab, Damascus (Syria), Ethiopia, Egypt, Edom, Arabia, and Tyre—more nations than any other prophet addressed by name (13-23). He directly addressed and counseled king Ahaz (7:1-9) as well as Hezekiah. The book Isaiah contains a historical passage (36-39) that replicates 2 Kings 18:13–20:19. Isaiah was an important historian (2 Chr. 26:22; 32:32) as well as a history-making prophet.

Isaiah was the *first* prophet to foretell the captivity of Jews by Babylon (39: 6-7). He was also the *first* to foretell the return from exile, even specifying the name of the Persian king who would facilitate it, Cyrus (44:24-45:13). And Isaiah was the *first* to prophesy of the "New heavens and the new earth," today still to come (65:17; 66:22).

Nahum [between 660 and 612]

It was a long time—forty years or more—before the next prophet of *any* type appeared. His name was Nahum, another writer. Nahum's "burden" was entirely against Nineveh, the capital of Assyria (1:1). Nahum foretold the fall of Nineveh in 612 BC at the hands of Babylonia. It is certainly worth noting that two of the writing prophets' books, Jonah and Nahum, deal exclusively with Nineveh, the capital of a cruel, warlike nation, an enemy of Israel and Judah. Early in the eighth century BC, God spared Nineveh after her people repented under the preaching of Jonah. But now in the latter part of the seventh century, it was different. God called Nahum to bring a scathing indictment and judgment against Nineveh. Perhaps this was because Nineveh (Assyria), after being spared by God earlier, destroyed Israel and severely reduced Judah. Perhaps it was also to warn Judah against submitting to or allying with Assyria, a nation that would soon itself be destroyed.

Zephaniah [between 640 and 612]

Zephaniah prophesied during the reign of King Josiah in Judah [640–609 BC] and before the fall of Assyria in 612 BC (Zeph. 1:1; 2:13). He was a contemporary of Nahum, and also of Jeremiah, who continued to prophesy for at least twenty years after Zephaniah. Zephaniah's prophecy concentrates principally on Judah and Jerusalem: their sin, impending punishment, and the eventual restoration of a faithful remnant. He also pronounced God's judgments on Philistia, Moab, Ammon, Ethiopia, and Assyria (ch. 2). Zephaniah may have been one of the prophets summoned by King Josiah (2 Ki. 23:1-2) to hear the reading of the rediscovered Book of the Law (possibly Deuteronomy), but it was Huldah the prophetess, not Zephaniah or Jeremiah, who was first consulted about this discovery (2 Ki. 22:14). Still, Zephaniah may have had a large influence on this affair and on the king himself, for his book condemns exactly the same religious sins (1:4-6) to which Josiah put a stop, after hearing God's Law (2 Ki. 23:3-25).

Jeremiah [626-586 and beyond]

Jeremiah dates his God-given messages from the thirteenth year of King Josiah's reign [626] until King Zedekiah's eleventh year [586], the year Jerusalem was sacked and the temple destroyed by the Babylonians (1:1-3). However, he continued to act and to prophesy for some time after this. The historical narrative in the book of Jeremiah continues after 586 BC, through Gedeliah's governorship, Ishmael's brief takeover, and Johanan's leadership including a forbidden flight into Egypt (ch. 40-43). Jeremiah's last prophecy was in Egypt and about Egypt (43:8-13).

Through Jeremiah, God clearly reaffirmed His sentencing of the apostate nation Judah to certain defeat and destruction at the hands of Babylonia. Good King Josiah's reforms (2 Ki. 23:1-25) had only delayed the execution of this judgment. But the people of Judah refused to believe it. Jeremiah's message was exceedingly unpopular and was opposed by many false prophets who cried up peace and prosperity. Jeremiah's life was threatened for speaking God's truth in the temple courtyard (Jer. 26). His written prophecies were burned by King Jehoiakim, but he rewrote them with fresh inspiration and additions from God (36). Jeremiah was imprisoned on charges of treason, and he almost died in a dungeon (37-38). He was rescued from the dungeon, but remained incarcerated in the court of the prison until the day Jerusalem was taken by the Babylonians (38:28).

Jeremiah was liberated from prison by orders of King Nebuchadnezzar of Babylon (39:11-14), but was being taken in chains with other captives to Babylon when the captain of the guard, one Nebuzaradan, gave him complete freedom. Jeremiah was given three choices: to go on to Babylon as a free man; to stay with "the poorest of the land" under a provisional governor, Gedeliah; or to go anywhere he wished (40:1-6). He chose to stay with the poor survivors in Judah.

Jeremiah prophesied of salvation and restoration after the exile (30-31). He famously predicted that the duration of the exile would be seventy years (25:11; 29:10; cf. Dan. 9:2).

Habakkuk [ca. 610-590]

"The burden which the prophet Habakkuk saw" (1:1) came near the turn from the seventh to the sixth century BC, during the last years of Judah/Jerusalem but before her destruction in 586 BC. The Chaldeans (Babylonians) were the new world power (1:6-7), having supplanted Assyria which fell in about 612 BC. Habakkuk wrote before 586 BC because he gave musical directions for the last portion of his book, indicating that the temple still stood in Jerusalem and he expected the Levite musicians to present his prophecy (3:19).

Unlike his contemporary, Jeremiah, Habakkuk was not politically active—at least, his name does not appear in any historical context. These were appalling times when nothing seemed to go according to accepted principles and wisdom. Habakkuk struggled with the same kinds of theological problems as did Job. Among the writing prophets, Habakkuk is unique in its literary format: a dialogue with God, a musical prayer, and a psalm or hymn.

Daniel and Ezekiel [605-537]

Daniel and Ezekiel were God's prophets in exile in Babylonia. The first deportation took place in 605 BC and included Daniel. A larger group, including Ezekiel, was deported when Jerusalem was captured (but not yet destroyed) in 597 BC. Both prophets apparently spent the rest of their lives in Chaldea—Daniel, at least, until Persian rule [after 539].

Daniel was a Jewish noble, taken captive while yet a youth, "In the third year of the reign of Jehoiakim king of Judah" (1:1). His prophesying began soon thereafter, when he interpreted Nebuchadnezzar's dream while he was in mandatory training for the king's service (2). God endowed Daniel with extraordinary wisdom and righteousness, and he became a very important government official in Babylon. Daniel's career as a prophet spanned a very long time. His last dated vision (10) came in the third year of Cyrus, king of Persia (10:1)—about sixty-seven years after his first one. This was the same year [537] that the first large party of Jews returned to Jerusalem from Babylonia. Daniel was an important man *in* history, and his unique prophecies are very important *to* history. For he alone foretold, in considerable detail and with unerring accuracy, the progression of world events and empires, from his time right up to that of Jesus!

Ezekiel, a priest by birth and training, lived among the Jewish exiles in Babylonia. The prophecies in the book of Ezekiel are precisely dated (1:1; 8:1; 20:1; 24:1; 29:17); they span about twenty-two years. [593-571] Although Ezekiel and Daniel operated in different spheres in and around Babylon and may not have collaborated or even met, Ezekiel knew of Daniel and had the highest respect for him (14:14, 20; 28:3). Ezekiel does not mention his contemporary in Jerusalem, Jeremiah, although some of their prophecies are very similar, particularly with regard to the false prophets that plagued them both. Daniel knew Jeremiah through the latter's writings, already published (Dan. 9:2).

God gave Ezekiel detailed visions of events actually taking place several hundred miles away in Jerusalem (8), including the final siege and the fall of that city in 586 BC. Ezekiel's visions changed dramatically, from judgment and doom to hope and restoration, after Jerusalem and the temple were destroyed (33:21). God gave Ezekiel detailed visions of a new, united state of Israel; a new Jerusalem; and a new temple (36-48). These continue to mystify (and divide) students of the Bible as to whether they are allegorical, fulfilled, or unfulfilled prophecy.

Obadiah [between 605 and 537]

Obadiah probably prophesied during the years of Babylonian exile, although other times, from the ninth century to the fourth, have been argued. Textual evidence for the exile period includes (1) that Judah, Israel, and Jerusalem are described in the book as having undergone calamity, destruction, distress, and captivity (12-13, 20); while (2) their future deliverance and repossession of the land of Canaan is predicted (17-21).

Obadiah's vision "concerning Edom" has in view that nation's complicity and callous delight in Judah's downfall (10-14). Edom is twice reminded that Judah is "your brother" (10, 12), referring to the fact that the two nations were derived from twin brothers, Jacob {Israel} and Esau {Edom} (Gen. 25:21-30; ch. 36). For committing fratricide, both actively and passively, Edom is told, "As you have done, it shall be done to you" (Ob. 15); and "No survivor shall remain of the house of Esau" (18). The fulfillment of the first part of this prophecy began quickly. "During the sixth century BC, the Negeb" (southern Judah) "was occupied by the Edomites, who were pushed out of their former territory by Arab tribes. Thus began Idumea, the Greek name for the new 'Edom'".[5] The other part of Obadiah's prophecy, quoted above, was not as quickly fulfilled. For Herod the Great, named "King of the Jews" by Rome (he who tried to kill the child Jesus) [4] was not a Jew—he was an Idumean.[6]

Although Obadiah's book is a condemnation of Edom, it was written for the Jews as a promise of their restoration and God's rule (21).

Haggai and Zechariah [written 520-518]

Soon after King Cyrus of Persia decreed that the Jews could return to their land and rebuild the temple in Jerusalem (Ezra 1:2-4) [538], 42,360 of them emigrated (Ezra 2:64). The temple foundation was laid, but the project foundered. God then raised up two prophets, Haggai and Zechariah, to spearhead the completion of the temple (Ezra 5:1; 6:14). It was finished exactly seventy years after the original temple was destroyed. [516]

Haggai and Zechariah are especially interesting writing prophets. First, they worked as a team. Second, they were not persecuted by the government. In this sense they were "throwbacks" to the statesmen prophets of old. Third, they must have prophesied verbally much more than their written books contain because they were constantly on the job over a period of four years or more, exhorting the workers and possibly even pitching in with physical labor (Ezra 5:1-2). It is clear that the new temple would not have been built without them, and it is inconceivable that they provided only written prophetic exhortations.

The messages in Haggai were rendered entirely in "the second year of King Darius" (Hag. 1:1; 2:1, 10). [520] They are directly aimed at restarting the temple project. Zechariah's recorded visions started just two months after Haggai's (Zech. 1:1) and continued for at least two years (Zech. 7:1). The book of Zechariah is much more extensive and figurative than Haggai. Zechariah's prophecies gave hope and encouragement to the temple builders through apocalyptic glimpses of a glorious future, including a coming Messiah, or Branch (3:8). He also gave direct encouragement to the workers (4:9-10).

Malachi [ca. 450]

The last writing prophet in the Old Testament canon, as well as in Old Testament history, was Malachi. He was a contemporary of Ezra and Nehemiah, who also wrote prophecy, but are not usually counted as writing prophets. These three, together with a number of singing prophets, followed a period of more than sixty years when there was no new revelation from God. They broke the sixth and shortest drought of prophecy, and immediately after them began the famous intertestamental drought (see "Prophecy Droughts" inset, pages 282-84).

Malachi's burden of prophecy was directed "to Israel" (1:1), that reconstituted nation, smaller but no longer divided, and now about one hundred years old. Through Malachi, God dealt with specific problems of that time such as failure to tithe, corrupt priests, contempt for holy things, and divorce. And He promised a coming Messenger (3:1-3) {in the denouement, John the baptizer} to prepare the way for the "day of the LORD"—Jesus (4:5-6).

Joel [n.d.]

There is one more writing prophet in the Old Testament canon, Joel. Joel cannot be historically placed with any degree of confidence.

Writing Prophet Summary

The writing prophets, so-called, all came during a period of about three and one-half centuries within the Kingdom Period of Israel/Judah. Their times included the last two hundred years of the divided kingdom, the Babylonian captivity, and the first century of the restored kingdom of Israel. God gave these writing prophets to warn His people of impending disaster, because of their idolatry and other sins; and to call them to repentance, revival, and security in Him. Nevertheless they would not heed these warnings and calls, except for sporadic respites. Both nations fell. During and after their captivity in Babylon, God sent other writing prophets with messages of hope and encouragement, including the promise of a righteous Messiah, or Branch. Through these writing prophets, He also continued to correct and rebuke His chastised people, now free of idolatry but not of sin.

The New Testament Era

1. The Old in the New

Malachi, Ezra, and Nehemiah received and wrote the last revelation from God for over four hundred years. During this intertestamental prophecy drought, much happened in human history including the fulfillment of many of Daniel's accurate predictions; but nothing happened in the history of prophecy itself.

As soon as the New Testament begins—rather, in the opening pages of the portion of Scripture we call the New Testament—we are met with new prophecy and new prophets, namely, Elizabeth, Mary the mother of Jesus, Zacharias, Simeon, Anna, and John the baptizer. Although these prophets appear in the pages of the New Testament (Luke 1:41-45; 46-55; 67-ff; 2:25-32, 36; 3:2-ff), they really belong to the Old Covenant, for Jesus Christ had not yet changed all things, including prophecy. In these prophets, we see strong associations with "older" Old Testament prophets, especially Mary with Hannah and John with Elijah (q.v. all, chapter 3). Commenting on the origins and style of the first two chapters of Luke, where we meet all these prophets, Machen[7] remarks that

> it has often been observed that the characteristic Greek sentence of the prologue, Luke 1:1–4, is immediately followed by the most strongly Hebraistic passage in the New Testament (Luke 1:5–2:52);

and that

> the first two chapters of Luke are in spirit really a bit of the Old Testament continued to the very threshold of the New.

2. The New World[8]

Although these pre-Christian New Testament prophets were of the same cloth as their Old Testament counterparts, the world they lived in was vastly different. The golden age of Greece—philosophers first, then conquerors—had come and gone, leaving behind, among other things, a world language. Israel, as we left her in Nehemiah and Malachi, was a tiny but independent kingdom under the benevolent protection of Persia. She subsequently fell under the control of Egypt (Ptolemy) and then Syria. One of Syria's rulers, Antiochus IV (called Epiphanes), tried to stamp out Jewish religion. He desecrated the temple. The Jews revolted and, after much bloodshed, gained a measure of freedom, only to be taken over by the new world power, Rome.

Now Israel was bigger but hardly a sovereign nation. She was rather more a region called Palestine or Judea, which included states named Judea, Idumea, Galilee, and Perea. All Palestine was subjugated under Syria, a province of the mighty Roman empire. Yes, Israel had a king, Herod, called the Great. This so-called King of the Jews was actually an Idumean (New Edomite) who gained his crown by political intrigue and kept it only by his loyalty and subservience to Rome. Jewish patriots or "zealots" hated Roman rule, and rebellion was usually in the air. Another source of unrest was that the Parthian Empire to the east challenged Rome over the control of Palestine (Judea). In spite of these threats, internal and external, Herod, backed by Rome, expanded his kingdom and built many great works including an enlarged, more beautiful temple for the Jews, whom he wished to placate.

Judaism had fragmented (or resolved?) into several religious sects. The Sadducees were the priestly party, centered on the temple ministry, aristocratic, politically conservative, and with little interest in prophecy—at least, in eschatology. The Pharisees were more pious but, too often, overly legalistic. They supported the temple ministry because it was Scriptural, but they emphasized local synagogue worship and education in the Law as they understood it. Theirs was the most energetic and vital sect, and the only one to survive the fall of Jerusalem in AD 70 and to preserve Judaism. The Essenes were monastic, disciplined, lived in "communes" with shared property and meals; mostly men, celibate, and strongly Messianic.

The prevailing culture in the empire was not Roman but Hellenistic (Greek). Many Jews, especially those living outside Judea, were Hellenists. Herod promoted Hellenism. Greek was widely spoken throughout the Roman Empire. In Judea, Aramaic was more commonly spoken and written, and Hebrew was also preserved as a living language.

Most Jews were not members of a sect, nor were they any more Hellenistic than they had to be to get by. They were hardworking folk caught in a crossfire of cultural, religious, and political unrest.

3. John [AD late 20's]

John, the baptizer, is a key prophetic link between the old and new testaments. His special ministry, unique in all history, was clearly foretold by both Isaiah (40: 3-5; cf. Luke 3:4-6) and Malachi (3:1; cf. Mark 1:1-3). In his style of life and manner of prophesying, John was a throwback to Elijah the great hero prophet, just as Malachi had predicted (4:5) and as Jesus confirmed (Matt. 11:14; 17:10-13).

Some have speculated that John was an Essene, or was strongly influenced by this sect. Jesus simply called him a prophet, yes, "And more than a prophet . . . Among those born of women there has not risen one greater than John the Baptist" (Matt. 11:9, 11). Like every hero prophet, John was persecuted. He was arrested, imprisoned, and finally beheaded (Matt. 14:3-12)—all because he named the sin of Herod Antipas, the tetrarch of Galilee and Perea, with his brother's wife Herodias: adultery.

4. Other New Testament Prophets [AD 1-100]

Before we come to Jesus, Who changed prophecy forever, and Who should fittingly close this history of biblical prophecy, let us look at the other prophets of the New Testament, if for no other reason than to establish the continuity of this office through the apostolic period.

Save for John the baptizer, Jesus, and the pre-Christian prophets Zacharias and Anna, no person is named a prophet, prophetess, seer, or prophesier in any of the four Gospels—no, none other was named prophet until after the ascension of Jesus into heaven and the giving of His Holy Spirit to men on Pentecost Day and at other times. We know that many others did prophesy during Jesus's lifetime on earth:

at the very least, the twelve disciples sent out to preach (prophesy) the kingdom of God (Luke 9:1-12), and the seventy sent out later with a similar message from Jesus-God (Luke 10:1, 9) . However, none was called "prophet" or a similar title.

Twelve people are specifically identified as prophets in the book of Acts, *after* Jesus's resurrection and ascension. Agabus came from Jerusalem (with some other unnamed and unnumbered prophets) to minister in the church at Antioch in Syria (11:27-28). Agabus reappears years later in Caesarea to bring a warning from God to Paul and his party, who were journeying toward Jerusalem (21:10-11). Back in Antioch, after Agabus left, there were certain other prophets and teachers: Barnabas, Simeon (Niger), Lucius, Manaen, and Saul/Paul (13:1). Judas (Barsabas) and Silas were prophets in the church at Jerusalem who came down to Antioch with a decree from the Jerusalem Council concerning the circumcision of Gentile Christians, and prophesied there (15:22, 32). Lastly, the four virgin daughters of Philip the Evangelist were prophetesses (21:8-9).

These are all who are expressly named as prophets or prophesiers in the New Testament (apostolic) era after Jesus's death and resurrection. But there were many more. At the very least, all of the apostles who were there on the day of Pentecost [AD 30] just after Jesus's ascension must be included because they prophesied that morning in various actual foreign languages {not unintelligible tongues} (Acts 2: 1-4). Two of them also wrote gospel books as did Mark and Luke; and two or three wrote God's word in epistles. Stephen must also be included among the prophets (Acts 7). The gift of prophecy was given to certain Christians in the churches that sprang up (1 Cor. 12:4, 7, 10; 14:29). There could have been hundreds of such prophesiers. The Book of Revelation, given through John, is similar to the Old Testament books called "the prophets"—direct visions from God; and it closes the entire Bible with a book of sheer prophecy by anyone's definition. [AD 95]

Wherever and whenever there are prophets of God, it seems that there are also false prophets. Jesus knew that false prophets would try to pervert the truth and destroy the church, so He warned His disciples in advance (Matt. 7:15; 24:11, 24-25). Then, after these false prophets began to appear, the apostles John, Peter, and Jude all wrote to the churches about it (1 John 4:1; 2 Pet. 2; Jude 8-19). False prophets named in the New Testament include Simon the sorcerer, who made a false profession of faith when Philip preached in Samaria (Acts 8:9-ff) [AD 34]; and a Jewish sorcerer named Bar-Jesus or Elymas, who gave Paul and Barnabas trouble on their first mission trip (Acts 13:6) [AD 46 or 47]. Finally, the Revelation speaks of a false prophet who would be able to work wonders and deceive many, for the sake of a beast-god (Rev. 16:13; 19:20).

5. Jesus

Introduction

The previous section shows that the office and title of prophet, specific instances of prophesying, and false prophets did continue in the New Testament era, even after John the baptizer, to the very end of the Apostolic Era and the New Testament canon. But none of this even begins to tell what really happened to prophecy then. There were three major developments in prophecy, all brought about by Jesus: developments that reshaped, refocused, and reinvented prophecy. They are,

1. Jesus, God Himself in the flesh, undertook and executed the office of prophet—perfectly.
2. Jesus fulfilled all previous prophecy concerning His first coming, His suffering and death, and His glorification including His resurrection and ascension to heaven.
3. Jesus's Holy Spirit gave the gift of prophecy to countless Christians for the building up of His church.

Jesus, the Perfect Prophet

It is very important to understand and acknowledge that Jesus was not *just* a prophet, as some thought in His own days on earth, and as some still think. A prophet is not a Redeemer, not a Savior, not the Son of God unless he is Jesus. The Lord Jesus Christ was and is much, much more than a prophet. But He was a prophet. Jesus accepted and executed the office of a prophet. He did everything that a prophet can do, and Jesus did it perfectly.

During His life on earth, Jesus was widely regarded by other people as a prophet. Once He asked His disciples, "Who do men say that I, the Son of Man, am?" They answered, "Some say John the Baptist, some Elijah, and others Jeremiah, or one of the prophets" (Matt. 16:13-14). Right after Jesus miraculously fed a crowd of five thousand, some of the men who saw it said, "This is truly the Prophet who is to come into the world" (John 6:14) When Jesus raised a widow's son from the dead, a gathered crowd glorified God, saying, "A great prophet has risen up among us" (Luke 7:16). A Samaritan woman said to Jesus, "Sir, I perceive that you are a prophet" (John 4:19). At the Feast of Tabernacles, after Jesus promised the Holy Spirit, part of the crowd said, "Truly this is the Prophet." {Others said, "This is the Christ."} (John 7:40-41). A man who was born blind, to whom Jesus gave sight, said under hard questioning, "He is a prophet" (John 9:17). When Jesus entered Jerusalem in triumph on what we now call Palm Sunday, the citizens of that city asked, "Who is this?"; and the multitude who cheered Him on answered, "This is Jesus, the prophet from Nazareth in Galilee" (Matt. 21:10-11). Just after Jesus's crucifixion and resurrection, two of His disciples who were walking to Emmaus told the "stranger" who fell in with them about "Jesus of Nazareth, who was a Prophet mighty in deed and word before God and all the people" (Luke 24:19).

There can be no doubt, then, that *many people in Jesus's own day thought He was a prophet,* even the Prophet whom Moses had promised in Deut. 18:15. But that was their opinion. Far more important than these testimonies is the fact that *Jesus*

Himself adopted the role, accepted the title, and executed the office of a prophet. Near the beginning of His public ministry, in Galilee, Jesus read from Isaiah 61:1-2:

> The Spirit of the LORD is upon Me, . . . to preach . . . to heal . . . to proclaim . . . to set at liberty . . . to proclaim the acceptable . .

and told the people in attendance, "Today this Scripture is fulfilled in your hearing" (Luke 4:16-21). Most of the infinitives in this Isaiah passage have to do with prophesying. On the same occasion Jesus, referring to Himself, said, "No prophet is accepted in his own country" (Luke 4:24). Another time He said, in the same vein, "A prophet is not without honor except in his own country and in his own house" (Matt. 13:57), again referring to Himself. As He started His final journey to Jerusalem, where He would be crucified, Jesus said, "I must journey today, tomorrow, and the day following; for it cannot be that a prophet should perish outside Jerusalem" (Luke 13:33). The Gospels are full of Jesus's preaching and His attesting miracles, in the manner of the prophets of old. Perhaps His discourse that most satisfies all definitions of prophecy is Matthew 24 with all its eschatology.

Jesus was the "Prophet like me" whom Moses had promised to Israel over fourteen centuries before (Acts 3:17-26; cf. Deut. 18:15). God spoke to both of them face-to-face, not through dreams and visions as He did with other prophets (Num. 12:6-8). But Jesus was superior to Moses. He not only communicated to man what He heard directly from His Father (John 8:26-28); Jesus could prophesy on His own authority, as God (John 10:30). Only the Perfect Prophet could do this.

Many prophets performed signs and wonders—miracles—to authenticate their call, mission, and message as being from God, and sometimes also to illustrate or demonstrate their message. Moses, Elijah, and Elisha were God's instruments of most of the miracles in the Old Testament. Jesus outdid them all. He opened blind eyes and deaf ears, made the lame walk, cleansed lepers, cast out demons, cured many other diseases, and raised the dead. Besides these healing miracles, Jesus walked on water, stilled a storm, caused fish to be caught, withered a fig tree, turned water into wine, and fed multitudes.

Most of Jesus's miracles were not "original"—other prophets had performed similar ones. And most of His miracles were not meant to show that Jesus was God's Son, come to save men by His perfect life, death, and resurrection. Instead, they had more to do with Jesus's identity as a prophet, and His message. Two or three examples should suffice. When Jesus raised the dead son of a widow in Nain (Luke 7:11-15), it was very near Shunem, where Elisha the prophet had also raised a widow's dead son (2 Ki. 4:8-37). The people got the point: "They glorified God, saying, 'A great prophet has risen up among us'" (Luke 7:16). Again, when Jesus healed a paralytic (Mark 2:3-12), it was to teach a lesson about forgiveness. And when He withered the fig tree (Matt. 21:18-22), it was to frame a message about faith.

Unlike some other prophets, Jesus would not do any miracle that would kill or hurt people (Luke 9:51-56). Nor would He use supernatural power to rescue or glorify Himself (Luke 4:1-12).

In miracles, then, Jesus is again seen as a prophet, but a Supreme and Perfect Prophet.

All prophets are communicators. That is their task—to communicate God's word to people. In the Christian church, the gift of prophecy is better than the gift of tongues (1 Cor. 14:1-18). Prophets must find effective ways to communicate the message God has given them. Moses, a poor speaker, communicated through his brother Aaron. Ezekiel used visual aids and demonstrations. Others were eloquent speakers, powerful writers, compelling musicians. *Jesus was the best communicator of all the prophets.* When He opened His mouth to speak, people instinctively listened—whether a Samaritan woman (John 4:1-26), His disciples (Matt. 5-7; John 6:68), or a large crowd. "And so it was, when Jesus had ended these sayings, that the people were astonished at His teaching, for He taught them as one having authority, and not as the scribes" (Matt. 7:28-29). Jesus's parables, alone, communicate truth better than most writing prophets' entire books (Matt. 13:34-35). One of the best tributes to Jesus' communication ability, because it came from such an unexpected source, was when the officers who were sent to arrest Jesus returned without Him because, "No man ever spoke like this man" (John 7:46). Jesus also communicated, as we have seen, with miracles and demonstrations. Much of His teaching and prophecy has been written for us, by men inspired with His Spirit. Jesus was not only the best communicator of all prophets; He alone among them backed up His words from God with a perfect life of obedience, self-denial, sinlessness, and servitude.

Jesus as a prophet did not invent a new medium or language. He did not perform a new kind of miracle. He did not overwhelm, coerce, or "pull His rank" to get His message across. When Jesus took and executed the office of a prophet He stayed within its traditional parameters. Yet He enhanced it forever, by executing the office perfectly.

Jesus, the Fulfiller of Prophecy

The second major development in the history of prophecy that occurred in the New Testament Era is that most prophecy was fulfilled in Jesus Christ's sufferings, and, following His death, His glorification (1 Pet. 1:10-12; Luke 24:25-26). Jesus was the main subject of Old Testament prophecy. "You search the Scriptures . . . which testify of Me," said Jesus (John 5:39). Again, "And beginning with Moses and all the prophets, He expounded to them in all the Scriptures the things concerning Himself" (Luke 24:27). Another time Jesus said, "Do not think that I come to destroy the Law or the Prophets. I did not come to destroy but to fulfill" (Matt. 5:17). The Gospel of Matthew is replete with phrases like "That it might be fulfilled, which was spoken by the prophet . . ."; and, "For it is written, . . ."—all pertaining to Jesus and His ministry. After Jesus had risen from death, Peter said, "Yes, and all the prophets, from Samuel and those who follow, as many as have spoken, have also foretold these days" (Acts 3:24).

When Jesus came, lived, died, and rose again, much already-given prophecy was changed from the future tense and from being shrouded in a good deal of mystery, to the present, fulfilled tense—and made plain. Jesus said, "I tell you that many prophets and kings have desired to see what you see, and have not seen it, and to hear what you hear, and have not heard it" (Luke 10:24). Peter wrote, "Of this salvation the prophets have inquired and searched carefully, who prophesied of the grace that would come to you, searching what, or what manner of time, the Spirit of Christ Who was in them was indicating when He testified beforehand the sufferings of Christ and the glories that would follow. To them it was revealed that, not to themselves, but to us they were ministering the things which now have been reported to you through those who have preached the gospel to you by the Holy Spirit sent from heaven—things which angels desire to look into" (1 Pet. 1:10-12). At about the same time—early AD 60's—Paul likewise wrote, ". . .by revelation He made known to me the mystery . . . which in other ages was not made known to the sons of men, as it had now been revealed by the Spirit to His holy apostles and prophets . . . To me . . . this grace was given, that I should preach among the Gentiles the unsearchable riches of Christ, and to make all see what is the fellowship of the mystery, which from the beginning of the ages has been hidden in God Who created all things through Jesus Christ; to the intent that now the manifest wisdom of God might be made known by the church to the principalities and powers in the heavenly places, according to the eternal purpose which He accomplished in Christ Jesus our Lord" (Eph. 3:3-11).

Prophecy has not changed from its original focus, Jesus Christ, especially His humiliation and glorification; but now, since He came and has fulfilled, prophecy concerns what Jesus has already done for us, and Who He was and is, in plain and simple terms.

The Spiritual Gift of Prophecy

The third major development in the history of prophecy, that took place in the New Testament Era, was that the Holy Spirit poured out the gift of prophecy to many individuals in His church. Prophecy has always been the gift of God. However, in the Old Testament it was either given quite temporarily, as in the cases of the seventy elders (Num. 11:24-25) and of Saul (1 Sam. 10:11-13); or it was given as an ongoing capability and office to only a very few—less than one hundred fifty individuals identified in the four thousand years before Christ. But ever since Jesus Christ rose from the dead, ascended into heaven, "And gave gifts to men" (Eph. 4:7-8), an untold multitude has prophesied. "He Himself gave some to be . . . prophets, . . . for the equipping of the saints for the work of ministry, for the edifying of the body of Christ, . . " (Eph. 4:11-12). He gave both the gift and the ministry of prophecy. Some New Testament churches had more than one person who could prophesy (1 Cor. 14:29). Women prophesied (1 Cor. 11:5). The gift of prophecy was a preferred gift, one to be sought after (1 Cor. 14:1, 39). Local churches in apostolic times may or may not have had full-time preachers, but they did recognize and listen to those in their midst who had the gift of prophecy.

This outpouring of the gift of prophecy was foretold by the prophet Joel, whom Peter quoted in his Pentecost morning sermon:

> And it shall come to pass in the last days, says God, that I will pour out My Spirit on all flesh; your sons and your daughters shall prophesy, your young men shall see visions, your old men shall dream dreams. I will pour out My Spirit in those days, and they shall prophesy.—Acts 2:16-18, cf. Joel 2:28-29

This outpouring started on Pentecost Day, AD 30, and continued at least throughout the apostolic era. For example, many Christians in the church at Corinth prophesied, twenty-five years after that Pentecost (1 Cor. 11:4-5; 14:29-32). As Joel foretold, both men and women participated.

It would be exciting as well as challenging to try to follow this development in the history of the church, down to modern times. One thinks of "pentecostal" outbreaks and Quaker meetings, as well as "ordinary" gifted preachers and seminary courses in homiletics. But this is a *biblical* history of prophecy and ends here, at the close of the apostolic era in the New Testament.

Chapter 7 Appendix

Dating System

The dates given in chapter 7 and elsewhere in this book are not claimed to be precise, and may even be inconsistent here and there. Even with this broad disclaimer, however, the long-suffering reader who happens to be knowledgeable in such things deserves an explanation of our dating methods and sources.

Most modern scholars agree, within a decade or so, on the dates of King David's reign (e.g., references 9, 10, 11, 12, 13, 14.) We will adopt 1010–970 BC for David's reign, following Wood[10] and the New Geneva Study Bible.[9] All dates before David can then be derived or interpolated from Scripture sources only. Solomon's fourth year would have been 966 BC. Thus, 1 Kings 6:1 sets the date of the Exodus from Egypt at 1446 BC, which we will round to 1450 BC to avoid the appearance of single-digit precision.

This first time-step backward from David/Solomon is not without a problem. Paul says that the time period from the conquest of Canaan until the prophet Samuel (the Judges period) was about four hundred and fifty years (Acts 13:20). He could have gotten this number from the book of Judges by adding the stated times of oppression, peace, and judgeships, as if they were consecutive, from the first oppression (3:8) until the death of Samson (16:31), a total of 410 years; plus forty years to cover the periods between Joshua's death (2:7–10) and the first oppression, and between Samson and Samuel. If we add to this Pauline 450 years for the Judges Period, the wilderness years (40); the conquest of Canaan (say, fifteen years); Samuel's career before Saul (say, twenty years); and Saul's and David's reigns (eighty years), we will have over six hundred years from the Exodus to the fourth year of Solomon—much more than 1 Kings 6:1 plainly says. But most scholars now believe that some of the times given in Judges were overlapping, and that the total period from Joshua to Saul was close to 350 years,[15] which agrees well with 1 Kings 6:1.

The next major time bloc, proceeding backward in time, was that of the Hebrews' sojourn in Egypt. Both Genesis 15:13 and Acts 7:6 put this at 400 years. Exodus 12:40 says it was 430 years. The difference may be whether Joseph's or Jacob's descent to Egypt is taken as the beginning of this sojourn. For our purposes, we will say that Joseph came to Egypt 430 years before the Exodus from Egypt, when he was about twenty years old (Genesis 37:2), in the year 1880 BC; and that Jacob came down in 1867 and died seventeen years later (Genesis 47:28) in 1850 BC, four hundred years before the Exodus.

All previous dates, back to the beginning of history, are obtained from the patriarch's ages given in Genesis 5, 11, 25:7, 35:28, 47:28, and 50:22. These are charted on figure 5. This biblical dating puts the creation of Adam in the year 4100 BC. We make no apology for our Archbishop Ussher-like dating, and are a little disappointed "the beginning" did not come out at his famous 4004 BC.

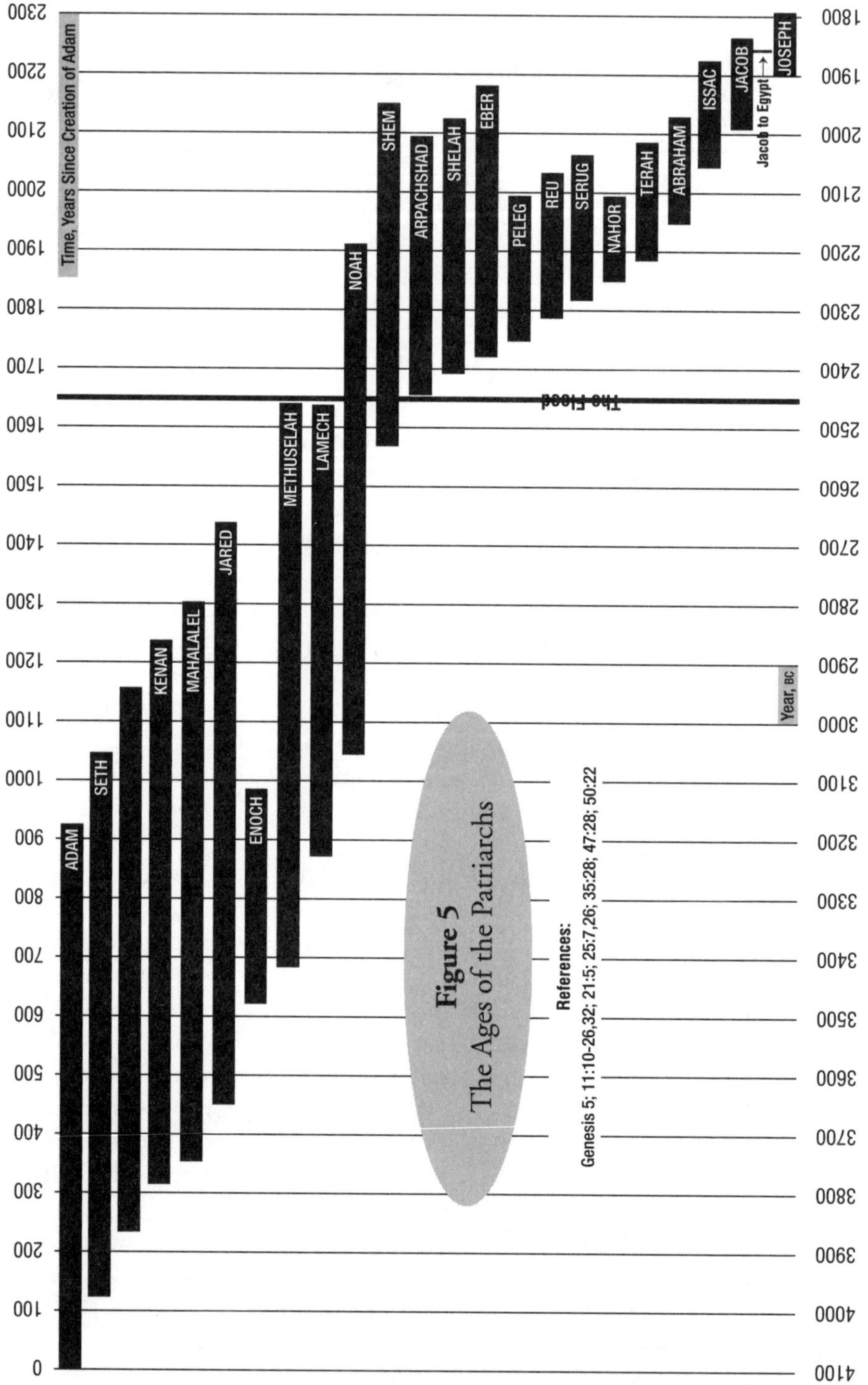

The Ages of the Patriarchs

Having anchored our dating system thus far on the reign of David being 1010–970 BC according to several authorities including the New Geneva Study Bible (NGSB)[4], we will stay with the same reference in proceeding forward in the Old Testament. Dates pertaining to prophets are derived from kings' reigns as given in the NGSB,[9] reproduced here as table 3. Thus, if the Bible says that a prophet's visions came during the reigns of K1 and K2, or that he prophesied to K3, these kings' dates are applied to his prophecies, with reasonable interpolations where needed. For postexilic Old Testament dates, notes in the NGSB[4] are generally used.

New Testament dates are generally taken from Eerdman's Handbook,[16] particularly from the time charts on pages 466–467 and page 549. In this system, Jesus's birth year is given as 4 BC, and His death and resurrection took place in AD 30.

Table 3

The Kings of Israel and Judah

The United Kingdom
Saul 1050–1010 BC
David 1010–970 BC
Solomon 970–930 BC

The Divided Kingdom

Judah		BC	Israel	
		950		
Rehoboam	930–913		Jeroboam I	930–909
		925		
Abijah	913–910		Nadab	909–908
		900	Baasha	908–886
			Elah	886–885
Asa	910–869		Zimri	885
		875	Tibni	885–880
			Omri	885–874
Jehoshaphat	872–848		Ahab	874–853
		850	Ahaziah	853–852
			Joram	852–841
			Jehu	841–814
Jehoram	848–841			
		825		
Ahaziah	841			
Athaliah	841–835			
		800	Jehoahaz	814–798
			Jehoash	798–782
Joash	835–796			
Amaziah	796–767			
		775	Jeroboam II	793–753
			Zechariah	753
Azariah	792–740			
		750	Shallum	752
			Menahem	752–742
Jotham	750–735			
			Pekahiah	742–740
		725	Pekah	752–732
			Hoshea	732–722
Ahaz	735–715			
		700		
Hezekiah	715–686			
		675		
Manasseh	697–642			
		650		
Amon	642–640			
		625		
Josiah	640–609			
Jehoahaz	609			
Jehoiakim	609–598	600		
Jehoiachin	598–597			
Zedekiah	597–586	586		

Endnotes and References for Chapter 7

1. In the days of Seth and Enosh, men began to call upon the name of God (Genesis 4:26). But we do not know if they prophesied, and we have no recorded prophecy from that period.

2. Authorship of this book is discussed in chapter 3, "Jonah."

3. See inset "The Great Refrain," pages 267-69.

4. *New Geneva Study Bible* (Thomas Nelson and Sons, 1995), "Introduction to the Prophets," 1018.

5. G. E. Wright and F. V. Filson, ed., *The Westminster Historical Atlas to the Bible* (Philadelphia: Westminster Press, 1956), 69.

6. Charles F. Pheiffer, *Old Testament History* (Grand Rapids, MI: Baker Book House Company, 1973), 587.

7. J. Gresham Machen, *The New Testament* (Edinburg: Banner of Truth, 1976), 209.

8. Most of the material in this section is derived or paraphrased from reference 5, pages 71-84.

9. Reference 4, page 473.

10. Leon J. Wood, *A Survey of Israel's History* (Grand Rapids, MI: Academic Books, 1970 and 1986), 217.

11. Charles F. Pheiffer and Howard F. Vos, *The Wycliffe Historical Geography of Bible Lands* (Chicago: Moody Press, 1967), 231.

12. Reference 6, page 607.

13. Reference 5, page 15.

14. Bernard Grun, *The Timetables of History* (New York: Simon and Schuster, 1975 and 1979).

15. Reference 4, "Introduction to The Book of Judges," 331.

16. David Alexander and Pat Alexander, ed., *Eerdmans' Handbook to the Bible* (Grand Rapids: Eerdmans, 1973).

INDEX

With one exception ("Holy Spirit") proper nouns are not listed. Topics/words that appear very frequently are not listed. These include *prophet, prophecy, prophesy, word (of God), write (in all its forms), and music.*